THE ARMCHAIR
QUARTERBACK

THE ARMCHAIR QUARTERBACK

Edited by John Thorn
with David Reuther
Illustrations by Bob Carroll

CHARLES SCRIBNER'S SONS
New York

For Jed and Isaac
and Kate and Jacob

796.33264

A

Permissions appear on page 308.

Library of Congress Cataloging in Publication Data

Main entry under title:

The Armchair Quaterback.

1.Football — Addresses, essays, lectures. 2. Football stories.   I. Thorn, John, 1947-   . II. Reuther,
David L., 1946–
GV951.A74   1982   796.332'64   82-5957
ISBN 0-684-17657-2   AACR2

CONTENTS

Introduction

The common wisdom is that baseball, with its pastoral beauty, its stately symmetry, its deliberate pace, is The Writer's Game, appealing to the mind, while football, a contest of grappling masses, calculated collisions, and darting rhythms, aims at the viscera, appeasing The Brute Within.

I say that is horsefeathers, and the book in your hands bears me witness. In the last decade or so, a football literature has sprung up that is the equal of this splendid game. *The Armchair Quarterback* spans the entire life of professional football, from the flying wedge to the nickel back; of its fifty-one offerings, however, thirty-two were written after 1970. Quietly, the golden age of pro football writing has come upon us.

What is generally known as The Golden Age of Sport (and Sportswriting) dawned more noisily, shouting over the roar of the 1920s with heroic figures on the field and in the press box. But in the eyes of the raccoon-coat crowd, play-for-pay football sullied the reputations of college heroes, and thus the romanticized style of the 1920s never quite fit the pros.

The pros show to better effect in a less sentimental light, and this has been late in arriving. In 1964, when Jack Newcombe compiled *The Fireside Book of Football*, the spiritual ancestor of this book, he allotted relatively few pages to the professional game but acknowledged that "a football anthology of the future might include far more examples of sound reporting on the skills and techniques seen in the pro leagues and 'ewer expressions of 'youthful joys and follies.'" That remark has proven foresighted, thanks in large measure to the increased sophistication of the television audience through the wonders of videotape. (For a dissenting view of the electronic age see the lovely piece by Heywood Hale Broun.) The boom in technical writing has brought with it the attendant evil of writers and announcers who make X's and O's seem more complex than $E = mc^2$, but John Madden, Tom Landry, Wayne Lockwood, and Mark Ribowsky shun the hocus-pocus and expand our understanding of the game.

There has been a boom in pro football fiction as well, of which this book contains three prime examples, by Frederick Exley, Pete Gent, and Dan Jenkins; their novels are five-o-clock shadows compared to the rosy cheeks of "Stover at Lawrenceville" or *Frank Merriwell at Yale*. Examples of first-rate verse on the subject are not yet plentiful (nor are they likely to be), but in James Dickey and Ogden Nash the game has attracted two all-pros.

The Armchair Quarterback also includes flavorful memoirs by coaches, players, and a player-impersonator. These range chronologically from Benny Friedman and Johnny Blood to Steve Wright and Jack Tatum, aided by a gaggle of non-galloping ghosts. And there are spot reports by distinguished newsmen and commentary by such dyspeptic, amused, or tormented souls as Murray Kempton, Larry Merchant, and Hunter Thompson.

In bringing these writers together under one roof, my guideline has been simply to select the best writing on professional football that, when collected, would afford a panoramic view of the game. I imposed upon myself the further restriction that no writer could be represented more than once, a yoke against which I strained mightily — and violated technically, though not in intent, by choosing two player memoirs from Myron Cope's book *The Game That Was*. If I could have, I would have reprinted Cope's book in its entirety, and more by Roy Blount, Jr., and Gary Smith, and Paul Zimmerman, and . . . I could go on. For those readers to whom the writers gathered here are unfamiliar, let *The Armchair Quarterback* serve as a consumer guide to future reading; there's more where this came from.

I wish to thank Maron Waxman, this editor's editor, who had faith in the book; Joe Horrigan and Bob Carroll, colleagues in the Professional Football Researchers Association who helped me a good deal and whose own work is on display here; Megan Schembre, whose efforts were indispensable in seeing this anthology through to publication; David Reuther, my collaborator and friend; and Sharon, my wife and cheerleader.

JOHN THORN
Saugerties, New York

THE ARMCHAIR
QUARTERBACK

What better way to kick off than this? It's 1950, pro football's golden age is about to begin, and so is the domination of the NFL by the Cleveland Browns. Scourges of the All-America Conference in its four years of life, Paul Brown's men are headed toward a title-game confrontation with the Los Angeles Rams, who themselves were born as a Cleveland franchise in the American Football League of 1936. This match of exotic pedigrees will produce the greatest pro football game ever played. And the story is told by Dave Anderson of *The New York Times*, one of the finest sports columnists abroad in the land today.

DAVE ANDERSON

Long Live the Revolution!

He hasn't changed that much. Paul Brown is still standing on the sideline on Sunday afternoon, still peering out from under his snap-brim hat, still sending in the next play. As the sixty-six-year-old coach of the Cincinnati Bengals of the National Football League, he is the essence of the establishment. But once he was the rebel of professional football. In the years just after World War II, coaching in a rebel league, he created a monster that was so brutally efficient it destroyed the element of competition and virtually the league itself. But his team, the Cleveland Browns, along with two other teams from the All-America Conference, were absorbed by the NFL for the 1950 season. The San Francisco 49ers won three games that year; the Baltimore Colts won one; but the Browns—named after their coach—emerged as the NFL champions. The rebel emerged as the ruler.

The image of the rebel in pro football today involves Larry Csonka, Paul Warfield, and Jim Kiick signing contracts to jump from the Miami Dolphins to the new World Football League in 1975 for $3.3 million. Or it's the memory of Joe Namath's provocative life-style while guiding the New York Jets of the American Football League to a Super Bowl III victory.

But in his time and in his way, Paul Brown was just as much a rebel. Perhaps significantly, he was also involved in establishing the credibility of another league—or at least the credibility of the team that had dominated that league. In the beginning he was a rebel primarily because of his philosophy of organization. Until he formed the Browns, pro football franchises had been operated casually. The coaches and players disbanded when the season ended and regrouped at training camp. Scouting consisted mostly of studying the college football magazines. Paul Brown changed all that. He popularized the organizational approach to pro football.

Many of the techniques that are accepted procedure today were unknown until Paul Brown introduced them: year-round coaching staffs, notebooks and classrooms, film scouting, grading players from film study, lodging the team at a hotel before home games, specific pass patterns, face bars on helmets, intelligence tests for players to determine learning potential, switching college offensive players to defense, using messenger guards to bring in the next play from the sideline. He also exercised complete control over the Browns' organization.

"Complete control," he said when he returned to football with the newly formed Bengals in 1968, six years after he had been dismissed by Arthur Modell, the Browns' owner, who had intruded on his control. "There is no other way for a team to operate and be a winner."

In the Bengal organization, says a club official, "There is only one vote and Paul has it." And there was only one vote in the Browns' organization when he ran it. His one vote was enough for his four AAC teams to win forty-seven games against only four losses and three ties, plus one playoff and four championship victories. In the 1948 season the Browns were undefeated in fifteen games, including a 49–7 rout of the Buffalo Bills in the championship game. Over a ten-year span through 1955 that included the Browns' first six years in the NFL, his teams won a divisional title each season, four AAC titles and three NFL titles. But when the Browns joined the NFL in 1950, skeptics snickered.

Nearly two decades later, Joe Namath had skeptics, too. He was the quarterback of the Jets, who were about to be sacrificed to the Baltimore Colts, the NFL champions, in the Super Bowl game. At a Touchdown Club dinner in Miami during the week, Namath took a sip of scotch out of a napkin-wrapped old-fashioned glass and stood up to address an audience that included many Colt followers. During his short speech, he said, "And we're going to win Sunday, I guarantee you." The skeptics snickered. But the Jets fulfilled his prophecy, 16–7.

At another Touchdown Club dinner, in Washington in the early months of 1950, another guarantee was made. Otto Graham, the Browns' quarterback, was on the dais with O. T. Kessing, who had been the AAC commissioner. When he got up to speak, Kessing sounded grateful for the invitation.

"It's unusual," Kessing said, "for the head of a defunct league to be invited to such an affair."

"The AAC isn't defunct," Graham insisted a few minutes later. "We simply absorbed the NFL."

Most of the audience laughed derisively, but George Preston Marshall bristled. The president of the Washington Redskins, who had once owned a prosperous laundry, had mentioned earlier that the Browns wouldn't dominate the NFL as they had the AAC. Now, noticing Marshall's displeasure, Graham turned toward him.

"Mr. Marshall," the quarterback said, smiling, "maybe you better buy back a piece of that laundry business if we play the Redskins."

"You probably won't even have a job next winter," the Redskin owner snapped angrily. "Maybe you'd like to drive one of my laundry trucks."

Graham laughed. His guarantee hadn't been quite as explicit as Namath's, but he was clearly confident.

Yet, so was the NFL establishment. When the 1950 schedule was announced, the challenge to the Browns was obvious. In their season opener, the Browns would oppose the Philadelphia Eagles, the NFL champions the preceding two seasons. And the game would be in Philadelphia, providing the Eagles with a hometown edge. Not that the NFL types were concerned.

"Our weakest teams," George Preston Marshall often said, "could toy with the Browns."

Earle (Greasy) Neale, the coach of the Eagles, minimized the Browns' football skills. "To me," Neale sneered, "the Browns are a basketball team. All they can do is throw."

True, the Browns had dominated the AAC with their passing attack. Graham's favorite targets were his ends, Dante Lavelli and Mac Speedie, and he also threw often to Dub Jones, a running back who occasionally lined up as a flankerback. But the Browns did more than throw. With 238-pound Marion Motley as their fullback, they ran. And if their offense stalled, they salvaged field goals, with Lou (The Toe) Groza as their placekicker. They also played strong defense, with Len Ford as a feared pass rusher and Bill Willis at middle guard.

But as the Browns-Eagles opener approached, the NFL mystique prevailed. Oddsmakers established the Eagles as a 3-point betting favorite, even though the two-time NFL champions were without their most devastating runner, Steve Van Buren, limping on a broken big toe.

When the Browns won the opener easily, 35–10, they astonished NFL partisans. Graham threw for three touchdowns on plays of 59 yards to Jones, 26 yards to Lavelli, and 13 yards to Speedie. He also scored a touchdown himself, on a one-yard quarterback sneak. He completed 21 of 38 passes for 346 yards as the Browns accumulated 487 yards of total offense.

In the Eagles' locker room, Greasy Neale was asked about the "basketball" team. "They've got a lot of guns, don't they?" Greasy Neale said. "And they use them."

But the most perceptive words were uttered by Pete Pihos, an Eagle pass receiver who had been on their two championship teams. Pihos had showered and dressed, and now, outside the locker room, he walked over to where his wife was waiting.

"What in the world happened?" asked his wife, echoing the reaction of millions.

"Honey," said Pete Pihos with a shrug, "we met a team from the big league."

Not that the Browns breezed through all the NFL teams. Two weeks later they lost to the New York Giants, 6–0, and three weeks after that they lost to the Giants again, 17–13. But these were the only games the Browns lost during the 1950 season. Their 10–2 won-lost record included two victories over the Washington Redskins, 20–14 and 45–21, keeping George Preston Marshall quiet. But the Giants also lost only two games, forcing a playoff for the Eastern Conference title. The Browns won, 8–3, on two field goals by Groza and a safety, qualifying them for the NFL championship game in Cleveland against the Los Angeles Rams, the Western Conference winner. The match-up involved many elements beyond the basic football game.

■ The Browns still symbolized the AAC, while the Rams hoped to uphold the NFL's honor.

■ In an unusual rivalry, two Cleveland teams were actually involved. The Rams had once played alongside Lake Erie, even winning the 1945 NFL title. But despite the championship, the Rams claimed to have lost $50,000 that year, and Dan Reeves, the Rams' owner, became the first major-league sports entrepreneur to transfer to the lucrative West Coast market. Twelve years later, the baseball Dodgers and Giants would move to Los Angeles and San Francisco—but the Rams had been the pioneers. Now in 1950 they were returning to the city they had abandoned to the Browns and the AAC.

■ The contrast in coaches was obvious. Paul Brown was a career coach, an icy disciplinarian. Joe Stydahar of the Rams, once a feared six-foot, four-inch, 250-pound tackle for the Chicago Bears, was a bourbon drinker and a tobacco chewer.

■ The Browns were composed primarily of virtual unknowns who had been on service teams coached or scouted by Paul Brown during World War II, while the Rams flaunted such famous college All-America players as quarterback Bob Waterfield from the University of California at Los Angeles, pass receiver Elroy (Crazy Legs) Hirsch from Wisconsin, and running back Glenn Davis, the Heisman Trophy winner from Army, his service hitch finally over.

As a youngster growing up in Waukegan, Illinois, Otto Graham had not appeared likely to develop into a six-foot, one-inch, 195-pound quarterback. He played the piano, the violin, the cornet, and the French horn. He also played basketball better than he played football.

He went to Northwestern as a basketball player, but the football coach, Lynn (Pappy) Waldorf, saw him throwing passes in an intramural game and suggested he join the varsity. He was a tailback in the single-wing offense when Paul Brown, then coaching Ohio State, first noticed him. After his graduation in 1944, he entered a Naval pilot training program. He was also drafted by the Detroit Lions of the NFL, but during the 1944 season he played for a Naval preflight team attached to the University of North Carolina. He later was transferred to the Glenview, Illinois, Naval Air Station, where Paul Brown visited him.

"When the War is over," Brown said, "I'm going to coach the Cleveland team in a new pro football league. I want you to be my T-formation quarterback."

Otto GRAHAM

THEY NICKNAMED THE GREAT CLEVELAND BROWN PASSER "AUTOMATIC OTTO," BOTH AS A TRIBUTE TO HIS MANY SMOOTH PERFORMANCES AND AS A SLY DIG AT CLEVELAND'S PRACTICE OF CALLING PLAYS FROM THE SIDELINE YEARS BEFORE IT BECAME FASHIONABLE TO DO SO. GRAHAM'S CRITICS CALLED HIM A "ROBOT."

BUT THEY COULDN'T ARGUE WITH SUCCESS. DURING HIS TEN YEARS (1946-1955), THE BROWNS WON FOUR STRAIGHT ALL-AMERICA FOOTBALL CONFERENCE TITLES AND FOLLOWED WITH THREE WORLD CHAMPIONSHIPS AND SIX DIVISION CROWNS ONCE THEY JOINED THE NFL. GRAHAM'S PINPOINT PASSING, SLICK BALL-HANDLING, AND STEADY LEADERSHIP KEPT CLEVELAND AT THE TOP OF THE STANDINGS —"OTTO-MATICALLY."

Except for a few plays installed by Ray Bray, a guard for the Chicago Bears, on the Naval team in North Carolina the previous season, Graham had never been exposed to the intricacies of the T formation, then a relatively new offense.

"I'm not a T quarterback," Graham said.

"Don't worry about that," Brown said. "You've got the ability and we'll teach you the rest."

"But the Detroit Lions have drafted me."

"That's the NFL, we're a new league, the All-America Conference. We're hoping the War will be over soon so we can play in the 1946 season. If you sign, we'll pay you $250 a month as a bonus until the team is ready to play."

"You've got a deal," Graham said.

At the time he visited Graham, Paul Brown was coaching the Great Lakes Naval team. Before that he had been the head coach at Ohio State for three years, and before that, as a high-school coach in Massillon, Ohio, he had an 80–8–2 record over nine seasons.

Brown wasn't selecting players at random or on newspaper headlines. He was building the Browns with players he knew from personal observation. Dante Lavelli, for example, had arrived at Ohio State as a running back but was switched by Brown to end.

"He saw something in my stride," Lavelli once recalled. "I think my steps weren't short and choppy enough to suit his idea of how a back should run."

Lavelli had only one varsity season in 1942 before entering the Army, where he was a sergeant in a rifle platoon during the European campaign. After his discharge, he returned to Ohio State, but not to play football. Paul Brown remembered him and signed him. Paul Brown also remembered another end, Mac Speedie, from the Fort Warren team that opposed his Great Lakes squad. "They have two things in common," Brown once said. "They can catch anything they can touch and after they catch it, they can run like halfbacks."

Lavelli was a six-foot, 192-pounder. Speedie was six feet, three inches, and 205 pounds. Ray Flaherty, the coach of the New York Yankees and the Chicago Hornets of the AAC, described them as "those two track stars," but the Browns' pass receivers, each selected to the All-AAC team in 1948, had different styles. "Lavelli has the strongest hands I've ever seen," Brown once said. "Nobody can take the ball away from him once he gets his hands on it. Speedie is more instinctive and more deceptive."

Speedie's speed was remarkable. When he was eight years old, he was a cripple. Because of a bone problem since babyhood, his left leg was two inches shorter than his right leg. He was ordered to wear a steel brace on his left leg from his hip to his ankle. Each week for four years he visited an orthopedist, who adjusted a screw on the brace to stretch the leg to its proper length. When the brace was removed, he quickly developed into a star running back and basketball center in Salt Lake City, Utah, then emerged at the University of Utah as a world-class hurdler.

"I don't suppose I ever would have been ambitious enough to excel at athletics if I hadn't been a cripple as a kid," Speedie once said. "I spent so much time eating my heart out because I couldn't play normally that when they took the brace off and I found I had legs that matched, it was like turning a frisky colt out to pasture after a year in a box stall."

Paul Brown remembered Lou Groza, too. Groza had played on the freshman team at Ohio State in 1942 but then entered the Army, which shipped him to the Pacific.

"I was on Okinawa and in the Philippines," recalls Groza, "but wherever I was, I used to rig up something that looked like goal posts and practice kicking."

Paul Brown was perceptive in signing virtual unknowns. He was also lucky. He had remembered Graham, Lavelli, Speedie, and Groza but he had forgotten Bill Willis, who had played at Ohio State for him. Willis was an All-American in 1944, Brown's first year as the Great Lakes coach. During the 1945 season, Willis disappeared into an assistant coach's role at Kentucky State, but when he heard that Brown was organizing an AAC team, he asked his former coach for a tryout.

"Is it all right?" Willis wondered.

"It's all right," Brown assured him.

Brown knew what Bill Willis meant. Bill Willis was black. Many years earlier there had been black players in the NFL, but none had competed in recent years. Late in 1945, the baseball Brooklyn Dodgers had signed Jackie Robinson, who was playing on their Montreal farm team in the International League when the Browns opened their 1946 training camp. In the NFL the Rams, now in Los Angeles, were preparing to sign Kenny Washington and Woody Strode, two black players. Willis joined the Browns and impressed the coaches with his agility as a middle guard.

"He's offside," the Browns' center kept insisting whenever Willis sped past him. "He's got to be offside."

Bill Willis wasn't offside. He simply moved faster than the center after the ball was snapped. Middle guard, although the forerunner of the middle linebacker, was a different position with different requirements. The middle guard was considered to be a defensive lineman. Unlike a middle linebacker, he had no pass-defense responsibility. Although a muscular six feet, two inches and 210 pounds, Willis was small by comparison with today's middle linebackers. But in the Browns' programs, he was listed as 225.

"That was a psychological thing," Willis once said. "Paul Brown didn't want the other team to know I was only 210."

Not long after Brown signed Willis, the coach remembered another virtual unknown, another black player. Marion Motley had been a fullback at nearby Canton McKinley High School when Paul Brown was the Massillon coach. Later he had been a fullback when Brown coached the Great Lakes team. When he heard about the Browns, Motley wrote for a tryout.

"Paul wrote back," Motley often has said, "that he thought he had enough backs."

But after the Browns had been in training camp, Motley got a phone call one night.

"I was told," he recalls, "that if I still wanted to try out, to come to their training camp at Bowling Green. But I think I know why they called me. They had signed Bill Willis and I believe they thought they needed a black roommate for him. I don't think they really felt I'd make the team."

Marion Motley not only made the team, he *made* the team. He provided the Browns with a devastating runner to complement their passing. He was also a brutal pass blocker, and was inserted as a linebacker in the goal-line defense.

"He was a great, great linebacker," says Blanton Collier, an assistant coach with the Browns then, later the successor to Paul Brown as head coach in 1963. "Marion Motley was the greatest all-around football player I ever saw. He had no equal as a blocker. And he could run with anybody for 30 yards."

Motley's speed created the draw play, in which the quarterback fades back as if to pass, but hands off to the fullback.

"Most of the people who talk about how great Marion was are thinking of when he came into the NFL with the Browns in 1950 when he was thirty and had two bad knees," says Lou Saban, the Browns' defensive captain during their AAC reign, now the Buffalo Bills' coach. "But he was just a shadow of himself then. They should've seen him in 1946 and 1947, he was really something then."

Even with two bad knees, Motley led the NFL in rushing in 1950 with 810 yards. In one game that season, he galloped for 188 yards in only eleven carries—a 17.1 average that still stands as a one-game NFL record for ten or more carries.

Graham, Speedie, Lavelli, Motley, Groza, and Willis formed the nucleus of the Browns' teams that dominated the AAC. By the time Cleveland joined the NFL, the team had added other talented performers. Dub Jones, an obscure running back with the Miami Seahawks and the Brooklyn Dodgers, was obtained in a 1948 trade. Len Ford, the first towering defensive end at six feet, five inches and 260 pounds, was acquired when the Los Angeles Dons disbanded in the AAC collapse. Meanwhile, Brown was recognized as the dominant genius who sent offensive plays to his quarterback by shuttling guards on every play.

Clearly, the Browns were ready. But the Rams arrived in Cleveland for the championship game with the most explosive offensive team in NFL history. They had set twenty-two records for season offense, scoring 64 touchdowns and 466 points and gaining 5,420 yards total offense in the course of compiling a 9–3 won-lost record.

Those people in Cleveland who remembered the Rams knew it was not an accident. They knew the Rams' quarterback. Bob Waterfield had directed the Cleveland Rams to their 1945 title, the last NFL championship team with a rookie at quarterback. Waterfield was chosen as the NFL's most valuable player that season, a rare honor for a rookie. And by 1950 he had emerged as the symbol of the Los Angeles Rams, not only as their passer, placekicker, and occasional defensive back, but also as the husband of Jane Russell, the glamourous movie star.

He had a quietly firm personality. "Old Stone Face," his wife called him. His team-mates spoke of his "inner strength," and they didn't argue with him in the huddle. Once, after Elroy Hirsch had requested a pass that was intercepted, Waterfield glared at him.

"If you don't know what you're talking about," Waterfield said sharply, "keep your damn mouth shut."

During the 1950 season Waterfield had shared the quarterback position with Norm Van Brocklin, then in his second season. Van Brocklin had the more impressive statistics, completing 127 of 233 passes for 2,061 yards and 18 touchdowns. Waterfield had completed 122 of 213 passes for 1,540 yards and 11 touchdowns. But in the Western Conference playoff with the Chicago Bears the week before the championship game, Van Brocklin suffered broken ribs. Although weakened by intestinal flu, Waterfield threw three touchdown passes to Hirsch and kicked a 43-yard field goal in the 24–14 victory.

Besides Hirsch, Waterfield had another spectacular pass receiver in Tom Fears, who led the NFL that season with 84 receptions, then a record. And behind Davis and little Vitamin Smith, swift runners, the Rams had four big backs — Dick Hoerner, Deacon Dan Towler, Tank Younger, and Ralph Pasquariello.

Despite the Rams' formidable offense, oddsmakers had established the Browns as a three-point betting favorite — the reverse of their role against the Eagles in the season opener. Moments after the game began, however, Waterfield whipped a pass to Glenn Davis near midfield for an 82-yard touchdown play. In vast Municipal Stadium, only 29,751 customers had shown up, ready to endure intermittent snow flurries, 25-degree cold, and a 30-mile-an-hour wind whipping in off Lake Erie. The Rams' score after just twenty-seven seconds astonished the Browns loyalists among them. But the Browns and their coach remained calm.

"Don't worry about it," Paul Brown told his players. "Just stick to our game plan."

Quickly moving 70 yards in only six plays, the Browns produced the tying touch-down when Graham collaborated with Jones on a 31-yard pass play. But the Rams retaliated with an 80-yard drive in only eight plays, with Hoerner smashing three yards for the touchdown and a 14–7 lead. Early in the second quarter, Graham found Lavelli for a 35-yard touchdown play. But on the extra point, with Lou Groza poised for the kick and Tommy James crouched as his holder, a gust of wind blew the ball away from James' outstretched hands. James lunged and caught the ball, but with the Rams rushing him, there wasn't enough time for him to spot it. Groza stood by helplessly as James tried to throw the ball to a teammate in the end zone. But the pass misfired, and suddenly the Browns, spoiled for five years by Groza's automatic extra points, trailed, 14–13.

Not that the Browns were discouraged. They realized that the Rams weren't perfect, either. For one thing Waterfield had missed a 16-yard field goal. Shortly after the second half began, Graham and Lavelli generated another touchdown on a 39-yard play. But the Rams rallied for two quick touchdowns to go ahead 28–20. Hoerner completed an eleven-play drive by scoring from the 1. And on the ensuing kickoff, Larry Brink of the Rams scooped up Motley's fumble on the 7 and trotted into the end zone. In the span of only twenty-one seconds, the Rams had taken an 8-point lead with about five minutes remaining in the third quarter.

Early in the final quarter, Graham whipped a 14-yard touchdown pass to Rex Bumgardner, one of his running backs. That narrowed the Rams' lead to 28–27, the difference being the wind-blown snap on the extra point.

With about three minutes remaining, the Browns seemed to be on their way to scoring again, either a touchdown or a field goal. But pressured out of the passing pocket by the Rams' rush, Graham ran and fumbled on the Rams' 25-yard line. Milan Lazetich recovered for the Rams, who were jumping up and down in anticipation of the NFL title. In front of the Browns' bench, Graham's head was down. He avoided his teammates' eyes.

"That's all right," Paul Brown assured him. "We're going to get the ball back. We're still going to win. We've got time."

There would be enough time only if the Browns' defensive unit prevented the Rams from getting a first down. And the Browns did just that. Waterfield had to punt, and Cliff Lewis returned it 18 yards to the Browns' 32-yard line.

Up on the scoreboard clock, one minute and forty-eight seconds remained. This time, Otto Graham knew there would be no second chance.

Pressured out of the pocket on first down, Graham ran, as he had when he fumbled. But this time he ran 14 yards for another first down, and he didn't fumble. Graham didn't have to select the plays, since Brown was sending them into the game with his messenger guards. But the play selection was obvious. Sideline passes. If the pass was completed, the receiver immediately stepped out of bounds, stopping the clock.

In quick succession, Graham hit Bumgardner at the Rams' 39, Dub Jones at the 22, Bumgardner again at the 11. Sure field-goal range.

But with the ball on the left hashmark, Graham realized that Groza would be attempting the winning field goal from a difficult angle. Brown sent in a running play on which Bumgardner would carry the ball in front of the goal posts. But when Graham called it in the huddle, Bumgardner had a suggestion. "Why take the chance of fumbling a handoff?" he said. "You can run a sneak without as much risk."

Graham agreed, without knowing why Bumgardner had preferred not to carry the ball on such a vital play.

"My hands were wet and cold from falling in a snowbank after catching the pass on the previous play," Bumgardner confessed later. "I was afraid I might fumble. I knew Otto wouldn't."

Otto didn't. He even gained one yard, moving the ball to the 10. Then he turned and waved for Groza.

This time the wind didn't destroy the snap. Tommy James placed it perfectly, and

Lou Groza kicked it perfectly for the 16-yard field goal that put the Browns ahead, 30–28. But there were still twenty seconds remaining—time enough for a miracle play. Jerry Williams returned the kickoff to the Rams' 47. Strangely, though, when the Ram offense took the field, Bob Waterfield remained on the sidelines. With time for one play, Joe Stydahar wanted Norm Van Brocklin's stronger arm. Predictably, the young quarterback faded back and threw a long pass. Warren Lahr, one of the Browns' defensive backs, intercepted it at the five-yard line. The Browns had won, 30–28.

"This was the greatest football game I ever saw," NFL Commissioner Bert Bell said, "and the Browns are the most intensely coached team I ever saw."

Strategically, the Browns had proved that the forward pass was the most potent weapon in pro football. Otto Graham had completed 22 of 32 passes for 298 yards and four touchdowns in freezing, windy weather. Waterfield had been intercepted four times, but he had completed 18 of 31 for 312 yards and one touchdown. Between them, the Browns and the Rams had shown the other NFL teams that there was a new way to play the game. More than that, Paul Brown had shown the other NFL teams that there was a new way to coach the game. And the skeptics had been silenced, because the Cleveland Browns, from the All-America Conference, were now the National Football League champions.

The rebel had emerged as the ruler.

Wagering on pro football, though legal only in the state of Nevada, has become a national pastime unto itself, the regular habit of one fan in four. Action on the Super Bowl frees up more loose change than the gross national products of several countries. Do you who bet on two-legged athletes, then, violate morality as well as the law? On the contrary: Winston Churchill believed "football pools, and all that, constitute the sustaining background of the life of a man upon whose faithful daily toil and exertion all the progress of society depends." High rollers and low, take a bow.

PETE AXTHELM

Going for Broke

Kevin O. started as a small bookmaker on Staten Island. Late in the 1966 football season, he was growing into the biggest bookmaker on Staten Island. This happened largely because of his knowledge of the American Football League. Every week, Kevin tilted his lines on the AFL, begging people to bet certain games. The people bet, and Kevin won. In the AFL championship game, he loved Kansas City over Buffalo. The Chiefs won 31–7. The night after that game, Kevin gave his wife a mink coat.

On January 15, 1967, Kansas City played Green Bay in the first Super Bowl. Kevin loaded his profits for the season on his beloved Chiefs. The Packers won 35–10. That night he went straight for the closet. He took out his wife's coat, wrapped it in a box and, in a fury, turned to wave it at her. "Who do you think you are?" he screamed. "Who ever heard of a girl from Staten Island wearing a mink?"

When Kevin resold the mink at a small loss, he started a tradition as integral to the Super Bowl as Roman numerals. This is a game that affects gamblers' lives like nothing else in sports. Every solid bettor knows that the really good bets occur on obscure early season events, before the linemakers have factored everything into their equations. Yet every January, otherwise reasonable players find themselves plunging deeply into the Super Bowl. "To guess what any guy is going to bet on the Super Bowl," says one leading bookmaker, "take his normal regular-season wager and add a zero. For guys who go to the game or get wrapped up in it in saloons, add two zeros." This has something to do with the two-week hiatus between conference title games and the big one. Also pride. You can only brag for so long about spotting Cincinnati as a live underdog against Pittsburgh in September.

The Super Bowl is the big one for bettors and bookies alike. No betting event has created as much lore since Arnold Rothstein fixed the 1919 World Series. So I offer for posterity this review of Super Bowl wagering.

SB III: The Game that Created the Greek: Jimmy Snyder was a successful Las Vegas oddsmaker and PR man before the 1969 game between the Baltimore Colts and the New York Jets. Then Dave Anderson of *The New York Times* asked him to make a line on the game. "Colts by 17," said the Greek. The last guy who made as much money in one phrase said, "Buy Dome Petroleum."

The irony is that most people think the Greek was wrong. When the Jets won, everyone had a good laugh. Saloons across America reverberated with ridicule of the Greek. History should note two facts: First, the Greek was right. The public bet the game up to 19½. If you followed the Greek, you would have figured a 17-point margin, bet the Jets plus the 19½—and won. Second, and more important for the Snyder family trust, it didn't matter whether anyone followed the Greek's advice. The point was that people talked about him. Endlessly. The next year, there were banners at the Super Bowl making fun of him. This hurt him so deeply that he signed fourteen advertising endorsements and a network contract.

SB IV: Which Dawson Did You Bet?: Len Dawson was the quarterback for the Chiefs when they met Minnesota in New Orleans. Donald "Dice" Dawson was a Detroit gambler. A few days before the Super Bowl, it was revealed that the two men were casual acquaintances. If SB IV had been a regular-season game, it would have been off the board. But Russia could invade California and a Super Bowl would not come off the board.

Bettors were left to wonder about Dawson. He was exonerated, but some folks figured that the brouhaha would interfere with his concentration. Minnesota was favored by 13½. As it turned out, Dawson could have enjoyed a craps game with his namesake during timeouts, as the Chiefs won 23–7.

SB V: Craig Morton Begins His Personal Attack on My Wallet: The Dallas Cowboys were vastly superior to the Baltimore Colts in Miami this day. Well, if not vastly, certainly more than the three-point spread. But Morton's ineptitude, combined with Duane Thomas's fumble at the goal line, handed the game to the Colts 16–13. For the losers, there was only the wisdom of silent Duane. "Is this the ultimate game?" he was asked.

"If it's the ultimate," he asked in return, "why are they playing it again next year?"

SB VI: The Decline and Fall of the Pink Dinosaur: The man called the Dinosaur was $500,000 in debt to the Mafia as Miami lined up to play Dallas in New Orleans. "They say it's $800,000," he confided. "But when you're this far gone,

SUPER BOWL	FAVORITE: SPREAD	FINAL SCORE	DATE: LOCATION
I	Green Bay: 14	Green Bay 35 Kansas City 10	January 15, 1967: Los Angeles
II	Green Bay: 13	Green Bay 33 Oakland 14	January 14, 1968: Miami
III	Baltimore: 19½	New York Jets 16 Baltimore 7	January 12, 1969: Miami
IV	Minnesota: 13½	Kansas City 23 Minnesota 7	January 11, 1970: New Orleans
V	Dallas: 3	Baltimore 16 Dallas 13	January 17, 1971: Miami
VI	Dallas: 6	Dallas 24 Miami 3	January 16, 1972: New Orleans
VII	Washington: 1½	Miami 14 Washington 7	January 14, 1973: Los Angeles
VIII	Miami: 6½	Miami 24 Minnesota 7	January 13, 1974: Houston
IX	Minnesota: 3	Pittsburgh 16 Minnesota 6	January 12, 1975: New Orleans
X	Pittsburgh: 6½	Pittsburgh 21 Dallas 17	January 18, 1976: Miami
XI	Oakland: 4½	Oakland 32 Minnesota 14	January 9, 1977: Pasadena
XII	Dallas: 6½	Dallas 27 Denver 10	January 15, 1978: New Orleans
XIII	Pittsburgh: 4½	Pittsburgh 35 Dallas 31	January 21, 1979: New Orleans
XIV	Pittsburgh: 11½	Pittsburgh 31 Los Angeles 19	January 20, 1980: Pasadena

how can they expect you to keep track of the interest?" Whatever the figure, the Dinosaur hoped to wipe it out with one big play. On the Dolphins. "The Super Bowl is a conservative, cautious game," he said. "It hinges on mistakes. And I'm betting on a guy like Csonka who hasn't fumbled all year."

The Dinosaur bet $500,000. Csonka fumbled on his second carry. The Cowboys won 24–3.

A week later, the Dinosaur took his final shot. He got a tip that a jockey would "hit" a horse with a battery at Liberty Bell Park. This would make the filly spurt to the wire in front, and the Dinosaur would begin his comeback. Moments before the race, a jockey's agent met the Dinosaur. "I like that filly," the agent said. "I just hope they don't fool around with a battery. My jock used one on her last spring and she tried to jump the inside fence."

The Dinosaur felt like he was watching Csonka fumble all over again. The filly was two lengths in front at the eighth pole, and the Dinosaur was clutching $30,000 worth of exacta tickets on her. Then the jock applied the battery to her neck. "It all went careening over the rail and down the frozen infield," recalled the Dinosaur. "The filly, the jockey, my bankroll and my Super Bowl memories." The filly broke her shoulder. The jockey broke his arm. The Dinosaur attempted to kidnap his bookie and hold him for ransom. He watched the next six Super Bowls from the recreation room at La Tuna Federal Penitentiary.

SB X: The Prevent Bowl: Every coach that uses a prevent defense should be incarcerated in a small room at La Tuna and forced to watch films of this game. The Pittsburgh Steelers, favored by 6½, were far superior to the Dallas Cowboys. The Steelers took a commanding 21–10 lead. Then coach Chuck Noll gathered the wagons in a circle. Roger Staubach led the Cowboys downfield unopposed. In the closing moments, Percy Howard raced toward the end zone. Percy Howard, who had never caught a pass in his pro career. Percy Howard, who would never catch another one. But against the mighty Steelers, Percy Howard grabbed a 34-yard touchdown pass from Staubach. The final was 21–17. The Steelers won the game. Dallas won the bet. This created a disconcerting situation for a writer who had bet his winter vacation on the Steelers. There is no worse feeling than interviewing guys pouring champagne over one another in triumph — when they have failed to cover.

SB XII: The Last Teaser Show: The teaser is the worst sucker bet in the world. You get three teams and you add 10 points to your spread and it looks very inviting. Which is precisely the idea.

Al the Tease is the richest bookie I know. This may have something to do with the fact that he specializes in teasers. He even offers bargains. You can tease one game and leave it "open," filling in the next two games later. In 1977, this was beautiful. In pro basketball, Portland never lost at home. So you could tease them when they were 10-point favorites and get them at pick-'em. Then you could use them the next time and add that on to the three-team tease. Terrific.

I stocked up a lot of Portland games, threw in a few others, and ended up with thousands of dollars worth of open teases to use on the team I loved in the Super Bowl. Denver. The Broncos were 6½-point underdogs and, with my teasers, I was getting 16½. Gamblers go through lifetimes without getting 16½ points on a tough defensive team that might win the whole game.

The Broncos did not win. Morton saw to that. He was their quarterback now instead of the leader of Dallas. But whenever Craig saw guys with stars on their helmets, he reacted instinctively and began throwing interceptions. Still, the Broncos were losing by only 10 in the fourth period. Then Cowboy fullback Robert Newhouse threw an option pass for a TD. Armed with my 16½-point teaser advantage, I bowed by 27–10. Some blamed the fact that a fullback who never passes had thrown the clinching touchdown. I knew better. It was all part of Al the Tease's master plan.

SB XIII: The Year Nobody Lost: Pittsburgh opened 3½ over Dallas. Astute gamblers figured the spread would go higher. Those who liked the Steelers bet early and laid the 3½. For once, the bettors were right. By game time, the number had climbed to 4½. Dallas bettors hopped aboard.

The Steelers rolled to a 35–17 lead. Then Noll ordered his reliable prevent defense, and the Cowboys rallied to make it 35–31 at the end. This meant that if you bet Pittsburgh minus 3½, you won. If you bet Dallas plus 4½, you also won. Only the bookies lost that glorious game. When I applauded this fact in a *Newsweek* column, one of the biggest bookies in New York wrote an angry letter to the editor. "Why can't Axthelm have a heart? Bookies are people, too."

I try to remind myself of this fact every time I get ready to bet another Super Bowl. But sympathy for a bookmaker seems as out of place as a mink on Staten Island.

George Sauer, Jr., loved the game but hated The Game. What the NFL had become for him by 1970 was what America had become for Dave Meggysey, Rick Sortun, and Chip Oliver, who also left football at the height of their competitive abilities. But unlike them, the star receiver of Super Bowl III still longed to play. Here the god descends from Olympus to frolic once more in the midst of mere mortals. (For a look at pro football's first ringer, see Don Smith's piece later in the book.)

IRA BERKOW

George Sauer Incognito

February, 1974

George Sauer, Jr., never wanted this story told for fear it might crumble the ego of a certain Joe from Oberlin, O.

However, the bald details must now be exposed since George Sauer, Jr., after lying low in the past few years, is in the news again in controversial fashion.

Sauer has announced that he plans to play for the Boston team of the embryonic World Football League. This causes a disruption among football aficionados for two reasons. One, Sauer is apparently still under contract to the New York Jets, a team he quit while still an All-Pro receiver four years ago, after the 1970 season.

The second reason for an emotional shuffle is that Sauer quit because he said football had become "dehumanizing" and "fascistic."

As for his Jet contract, only time and the law will tell. Regarding the second point, Sauer looks forward to playing for a respected and liked former teammate, Boston coach Babe Parilli. Also, the WFL, Sauer imagines, may be as pleasantly unpretentious and uncomputerized as the American Football League was when he first entered—and as the National Football League is not.

Mainly, though, Sauer at age twenty-nine has never quite relieved himself of the itch to catch a pass.

This fellow named Joe can tell you that. So can a fellow named Cass Jackson.

Jackson is the head coach of the Oberlin College football team. Sauer, on a volunteer basis, was the assistant coach in charge of the offensive line. Now hear Jackson on Sauer, and Joe:

"I knew George still liked to play because when we both lived around San Francisco we'd toss the ball around in a park for three, four hours and then we'd stop and chat, and soon George would be up and running again, running pass patterns. He was like a kid. He almost wore my arm out.

"Sometimes we'd talk about the pros, and about all he'd say — and he mostly said it with his eyes — was, 'I wish it had been different, but it was fun while it lasted.'

"George stayed in shape. When he came to Oberlin to help me out, he was jogging five, six miles a day. And he watched his diet. Sometimes he'd have just a couple of glasses of orange juice for supper. And he kept his head in shape by reading Camus or James Joyce.

"Since I knew he still loved football I thought when he came to the Oberlin campus I'd take him out to play in the local sandlot pick-up game. It was funny. You had to see this to believe it.

"The local hotshots, all of us black, play every Sunday evening in summer. This is serious stuff, although we have fun. A lot of us were high school or college heroes. And I even played defensive back in the Canadian League.

"We play just below Oberlin hill, with trees on either side of the field. It's a beautiful setting, with the sun going down. And maybe a hundred people come out to watch — wives, girl friends, buddies, little kids.

"The week before I had brought an Oberlin philosophy teacher, who is white. It was embarrassing, he was so bad. He had been chosen on the team opposing mine, and after the game one of the guys whispered that I shouldn't bring back any more white dudes like that.

"During the next week, George arrives. I suggest he play on Sunday. He says okay. I bring him out to the field and guys are giving me dirty looks. George doesn't look like much of a player. He's wearing a sweatshirt and black shorts and he's tossing the ball real loose. And he's wearing his glasses the way he does down on his nose.

"Nobody realizes this is George Sauer. I keep quiet just to see what happens.

"There are about twenty players. Sides are chosen and George isn't picked. But one of the guys on the other team tells me if I want my friend to play he's got to be on my side. I say, well, okay.

"I throw the first pass of the game to George. It's an 80-yard touchdown. Nobody can believe what they've just seen, especially Joe, who is a star defensive player.

"He figures there was a slip-up somewhere. He says, 'I got this new cat.' The next play we run, George puts this fantastic move on Joe. George gets behind him, fakes toward the goal post. Joe lowers his head and starts chugging. George spins around and breaks to the sideline. I put the ball right on the money. Meanwhile, Joe is on the other side of the field. The crowd goes berserk.

"Now guys are on Joe. 'Hey, man, this cat's burnin' you up. Two TD's.' I figure now it's time, I got to fill 'em all in. 'This is George Sauer,' I say.

"The guys say, 'Whooo?' I say, 'George Sauer.' And again, 'Whoooo?' Someone says, 'Namath's receiver?' I say, 'Yeah.' And Joe pipes up, 'I got him.'

"So George scores four more touchdowns. We win 60–0. It became the biggest story of the season in the black neighborhood in Oberlin. Joe's a great athlete and he can laugh about it, too. He can even laugh at his new nickname. Everyone now calls Joe, 'I Got Him.'"

In the late 1960s, inspired by the tape-recorded reminiscences of old-time baseball players in Lawrence Ritter's landmark work *The Glory of Their Times*, Myron Cope traveled around the country interviewing the pioneers of pro football. The result was a wonderfully evocative book called *The Game That Was*—"not a history in the classic sense," Cope wrote in his preface, but "merely a story. It is a story of a game that was, and of an America that we shall never see again." Read on, of the hobo halfback who took his name from a movie marquee.

JOHNNY BLOOD
with Myron Cope

A High Resistance to Culture

Known as the Vagabond Halfback, Johnny Blood was a lanky, fatalistic itinerant whose Irish twinkle and adventuresome outlook not only brought him proposals of marriage but a sense of certainty that life was his apple. Although from time to time his misadventures nonplussed his coaches, they usually understood that Blood's transgressions sprang from a blithe spirit. St. Louis police, sirens screaming, chased him down and arrested him for stealing a taxicab, but he had not meant to keep it. Minutes earlier, he had had a chorus girl on his arm and no transportation. "The cab was standing there with the motor running, but I couldn't find the driver," he explained. "So I borrowed it." Long on gallantry, Blood hesitated no more than a few moments before forking up his last seventy-five dollars to bail out the chorus girl, and then settled down to a night's rest behind bars.

He ranked among the swiftest men in pro football and possessed an uncanny knack for scoring a touchdown when one was most needed. He would snatch a touchdown pass while covered by as many as three defenders. His fifteen-year NFL career, 1925–39, included seven stops: Milwaukee, Duluth, and next, John O'Hara's Pottsville, Pa., where the local firehouse, which served beer twenty-four hours a day, enabled Blood and his teammates to beat Prohibition; Green Bay was the fourth stop, then Pittsburgh as a player-coach.

His real name was John Victor McNally, his beginnings, classic Midwest. In New Richmond, Wisconsin, the rather elegant white frame house where he grew up still stands on a tree-shaded corner lot, suggesting a time when the smells a boy knew were those of fresh bread and muffins baking, and when the sounds of an evening were those of voices around the parlor upright. The McNallys were people of means. Yet at a time when a large segment of the public looked upon pro football as a tramp's occupation, their son made it his calling. He did not marry till the age of forty-five, and later, after a divorce, remarried at sixty-two. With his second wife, he now leads a quiet, contemplative life in St. Paul, Minnesota, having sown a good deal more wild oats than most of us have had the pleasure or stamina to sow.

I couldn't say, particularly, that I was the black sheep in my family, though some people were inclined to view some of my episodes with less than applause. Well, by way of explanation, there *is* a difference between pro football now and pro football then. I'm referring to, say, the early 1930s, during the Depression. In 1931 I was all-pro right halfback. I had scored thirteen touchdowns, which at that time was a league record, and I was in the all-pro backfield along with Red Grange, Ernie Nevers, and Dutch Clark. I had played for Green Bay three years and we had won three championships. But when it came time to go back to Green Bay for the '32 season, I had no money to get across the state from my home in New Richmond. I had only a dollar or two in my pocket.

So I decided to ride free on the train. They called it the Soo Line, but its real name was the Minneapolis, St. Paul & Sault Sainte Marie Railroad, and in order to get to Green Bay you would have to change trains at Amherst Junction to the Green Bay & Western. I got on the Soo Line and rode the blinds down to a place called Stevens Point, where there was a stop. I got off and inquired about connections at Amherst Junction and was told that the Green Bay & Western would get into Amherst Junction a couple of minutes before the Soo Line but if you wired ahead they would hold the train. They did this for passengers. So I wired ahead and then got back on the blinds again and rode to Amherst Junction. There I got off the Soo and ran down a cut and grabbed on to the blinds of the Green Bay & Western. After the trainmen waited around for a few minutes for the passenger who had wired ahead, they gave up and started the train.

Well, about ten miles from Green Bay, the door of a freight car opened and one of the crew looked out and saw me and said, "John, what are you doing out there?" Everybody on the Green Bay & Western knew the Packer football players. The guy said, "Come on in and wash up." So I got me a bowl of water, and while I was washing up, he looked at me and said, "Say, where did you get on?" I said, "Amherst Junction." And he started laughing. He said, "Oh, so you're the guy who wired ahead! Well, you're the first hobo I ever heard of holding a train for." And this, in essence, shows you the difference between pro football in 1932 and pro football today.

By the way, when I told Ollie Kuechle, a Milwaukee sportswriter, how I got to camp, he said, "We're going to call you the Hobo Halfback." I didn't say anything. That was his business if he wanted to call me the Hobo Halfback. But Curly Lambeau, our coach, didn't like it. He thought we were on the big time and going to win another championship. He didn't like the term. So Ollie said, "Well, okay. We'll call him the Vagabond Halfback." For years after, I was known as the Vagabond Halfback, and maybe all this is a partial answer to your question as to whether my relatives regarded me as the black sheep.

I'm a schizophrenic personality. I was born under the sign of Sagittarius, which is half stud and half philosopher. The stud, of course, is the body of a horse, and I was always full of *run*. Running all the time when I was a kid. In the sign of Sagittarius the body of the horse joins with the chest of a man, who is aiming a bow and arrow. This is a man who's looking for a target and is going to hit it, which I take represents the philosopher in him. So with that combination of philosopher and stud, I always felt I was going two ways. My life illustrates it. Let me put it this way. I had an aunt, a big, husky doll, and one day she asked me, "John, what are you really interested in?"

"Well," I said, "I guess I'm really interested in the theory of morals and the theory of money."

She started to laugh. I said, "What are you laughing at, Aunt?" And she said, "Well, isn't that funny! You'll never have any of either!"

I come from a group of Irish people. The names of my eight great-grandparents were McNally, Barrett, Reilly, McCormick, Murphy, McGraw, McGannon, and McGough. Our outfit came over and settled in Wisconsin because it was just opening up around 1850, and from that group, some of them succeeded quite well and some did not. They all stayed out of jail and all got decent funerals, and some of them did quite well, that's correct. My father was a McNally and my mother was a Murphy. Father became the general manager of a successful flour mill, and my mother's two brothers became publishers of the Minneapolis *Tribune*. But I claim my poor relatives as well as my rich ones.

I got out of high school at fourteen and a half, really. It wasn't that I was precocious but that I was *pushed* along by my mother, who had been a schoolteacher. I had no signs of athletic ability, because I was too small. Even later, when I matured, I matured late. My parents had tried to make me master the violin and be a debater and recite poems. They wanted to make a cultured individual out of me, but I had a high resistance. In the seventh or eighth grade I once put on a very poor public performance with the violin, playing "Turkey in the Straw," which was a very humiliating experience for me. I haven't gotten over it yet.

Well, as I say, I was a runner. I used to run away from home. I'd catch freights. The fact is, I can remember my father giving me several memorable drummings with a shillelagh, which I recall with no malice at all. I was still in knee pants when I graduated from high school and a little young to go to college, so I studied bookkeeping and typewriting, and the following year, 1919, my parents sent me to River Falls State Normal, about twenty miles away. They went to California and left me with a checkbook, which turned out to be a mistake. Because of that, I eventually decided to join the Navy to avoid a confrontation with my parents.

The Navy, however, turned me down because my eyesight wasn't up to standards, although I subsequently made a living in football with my eyesight, and in World War II, when they weren't quite so choosy, the Army took me and I served as a cryptographer in China. Anyhow, I left River Falls State Normal and went to work in a packing plant at New Richmond and then went up to Dakota to put in the crops. I slept in a wagon. I can remember that on the longest day of the year, June 21, 1919, after I got up and finished getting the bugs off me, I fed the horses before the sun came up and then spent the entire day, till sundown, alone on a section of half-broken land, which I was cultivating—"disking," they called it. So I figured out that this was too tough a way to make a living. That was my terminal experience on the farm.

From there I went to St. John's University in Minnesota, which was where Eugene McCarthy later went to school. At the time, there were about six hundred students in the university, but that's what they called it—a university. It was a Benedictine institution, but I was an antitheological misfit. However, I played my first football game there, in the intramural league. I played for a team called the Cat's Pajamas. That was an expression current at the time—it meant something like "a superior guy." Anyway, I was an immediate success with the Cat's Pajamas. By that time I was sixteen and a half. I was tall but frightfully skinny, but the summer up in Dakota had toughened me up. We won the intramural league, and later I started competing for the college team.

After three years there, I had a little confidence in myself and felt ready for a bigger sphere. I went down to Notre Dame and went out for the freshman squad. The Four Horsemen were playing for Notre Dame that season, and as it turned out, the only contribution I made to Notre Dame football was that I wrote Harry Stuhldreher's poetry assignments. You see, they wanted to make a tackle out of me. I was six feet tall, but I weighed only 160 pounds and felt that my function was to avoid contact rather than to make it. So I did not stay long on the football squad, and the following St. Patrick's Day I took a little trip and had an unexplained absence from school. When the officials began investigating my absence, they discovered that in addition to my dormitory room, I kept another room in town. They took exception to the nature of my existence and suspended me. So I got a motorcycle and took a big trip. About thirty years later, when I decided to resume my education, I went back to Notre Dame to inquire about my credits, if any. They showed me my record. Inscribed upon it was no mention of any accomplishments but only the words, "Gone, never to return."

After the motorcycle trip, I went to work on a Minneapolis newspaper as a stereotyper, but it didn't take me long to see that a stereotyper's work was not for me. Meanwhile, I heard that there was a way of making a little money in the fall playing football. There were four teams in a semi-pro league in Minneapolis, and one of these teams was called the East 26th Street Liberties. They had a small practice field alongside the railroad track with one light, which was in the center of the field. That was the lighting by which they practiced. Well, I and another stereotyper decided to try out. As we went out to the field, riding my motorcycle, we went by a theater where the marquee advertised a picture titled *Blood and Sand*. Being that both of us still felt we might have some college eligibility left, and knowing that semi-pro football would ruin our amateur standing, I realized we had to have fake names if we played semi-pro ball. So when the East 26th Street Liberties asked us what our names were, it popped into my head right there. I said, "My name is Blood and this guy's name is Sand."

We won the league championship that fall, and then were paid for the entire season. We got ten dollars for our effort. We spent it that night.

The following year, 1925, I got an offer to play for a team in Ironwood, Michigan, for seventy-five dollars a game. I played three games there, then jumped the team for an offer from the Milwaukee Badgers of the National Football League. I remember we played in Steubenville, Ohio—that was really quite a fun city—and it was there that I became convinced that I might have a future in pro ball. Steubenville had a guy named Sol Butler, who had been a broad jumper in the Olympics. I caught a pass and ran away from Sol Butler, and that was the first time I really thought I was a ballplayer. Nobody believed in the future of pro ball at that point, but I believed I was a pro ballplayer.

You see, I had been drifting along in the sense that I was looking for my life-style, as they say nowadays. I wanted a life in which I could do something I enjoyed and still have leisure to do other things that I enjoyed. Football was an escape, certainly, but an escape into something that I enjoyed. In the off-season I would ship out to the Orient as an ordinary seaman and enjoy the beauty of the Pacific islands. Or I would winter on Catalina Island off the coast of Los Angeles. Understand, I was not afraid of work. I had sufficient energy that work did not bother me at all. I was a hard worker. To me, freedom did not mean being able to do only the nondifficult but, rather, to do what I chose to do. One winter in Catalina, I worked three shifts. I worked in the brickyard all day, making bricks. I worked the next eight hours in a gambling hall as a bouncer. And the next eight hours, I "honeymooned" with a redhead.

The football season was a great time of year. During the seasons I played for Green Bay, the ballplayers stayed at the Astor Hotel. They'd sit around the hotel and gossip, or they'd go to libraries—well, maybe one out of a hundred pro ball players would go to a library. We played golf, we went hunting, we drank—the ordinary activities of young men when they're at leisure. We had no difficulty passing the day. The fall weather in Green Bay was beautiful, and just to do *nothing* was marvelous. Just watching the autumn turn golden was a pleasure.

The ordinary ballplayer made seventy-five to a hundred dollars a week, but it was tax-free and it was a dollar worth twice as much as the dollar is worth today. There weren't too many people getting that kind of money at our age. And right across the street from the hotel was the YWCA, where you could get a good dinner for seventy-five cents. That's where we usually ate. The boys from the South watched their money, because things were tough down South and they were trained that way. But as for myself, I can say that in spite of my interest in monetary theory, I always remembered that "they who harvested the golden grain, and they who flung it to the winds like rain, alike to the same aureate earth are borne." It takes a guy who's really loose with money to think about it freely.

Curly Lambeau used to say that I trained harder than anybody on the club. That is, I spent more energy on the training field than the average guy, and I believe that to be true or I would not repeat it. But in 1933 Lambeau fired me. We were in New York that year to play the Giants, and we were having a medium season, with about three or four games to go. It was a Friday night, about eight o'clock, and I got a call at the hotel from some millionaire's wife — the wife of some millionaire from the Fox River Valley around Green Bay. She wanted me to meet her at the Stork Club.

I said, "Oh, no. I couldn't do that. The game's only day after tomorrow." So I got ready to go to bed, and here two goddamned nurses rapped on the door. So my room-mate and I ordered up a few drinks. Well, we got pretty loaded. Next morning, I went out to practice in not the best of condition. Alcohol, you see, hangs on to me. I don't sober up real fast. It's a family characteristic — I have plenty of recuperative power, but alcohol doesn't fall out of me. It hangs on to me.

So I went out to practice and got ready to punt, and the first ball I kicked, I fell flat on my ass. Lambeau sent me back to the hotel. He came up afterward and said, "I've got to let you go." I didn't argue with him. I never argued. Well, the team played New York without me and lost the game, but the fact was that I was fired. I went over to Paterson, New Jersey, and played a couple games with a Paterson semi-pro team, and finally the Packers were playing Chicago in their last game of the season, and Lambeau got in touch with me to come back. He got to thinking about next year, I suppose, and that I'd be a free agent if I was still fired. About June the next year, 1934, he sold me to Pittsburgh.

Art Rooney, the Pittsburgh owner, had taken a fancy to me. He liked Irishmen. But after I got to Pittsburgh he no doubt was a little disappointed in me. He pressed me to go to confession, to make a better Roman Catholic of me. Let's just say that I came under the heading, but spell it with an *i*, an *n*, and an apostrophe. I *was* a roamin' Catholic.

Anyway, after a season in Pittsburgh I decided the next summer that I wanted to get back with Green Bay. I knew that the Packers were training up in northern Wisconsin and that they had scheduled an exhibition game with the Chippewa Falls Marines and two more with the La Crosse Loggers. So I got on with both of those semi-pro teams and played three games against Green Bay and did all right. I talked to Art Rooney and told him I had a chance to go back with the Packers, and he said okay, go ahead. But it was from that point on that I started having real trouble with Lambeau.

He began to push me around. This was because I had gotten quite a reputation around Green Bay. Lambeau was football in that town. He became jealous of me. He would sit me on the bench. The game would be practically lost and the fans would be hollering, "Put him in! Put Blood in!" So then, when we were just about dead, he'd say to me, "Get in!" I'd have to come up with a big play, and that's how I got the reputation of being a clutch player. Lambeau wouldn't play me unless he had to play me!

After two years of that, I went back to Pittsburgh as a player and head coach, and later, in the early 1950s, I was head coach at St. John's for three years. We won about 75 percent of our games. I'm neither awfully proud of my coaching record nor am I ashamed of it. But I would not say that my temperament was designed for coaching. A coach can't be concerned with the poor ballplayer. If the player can't make it, he's got to be out right away. It's a very tough aspect of coaching, and in this aspect I was weak. Also, some guys get fat on coaching—they get healthy and strong—but other guys get ulcers. At St. John's, I got ulcers. All those guys in black suits who had been there all their lives, they'd say, "We know all about this coaching. We have the best boys. We know our boys are the best boys. *Why* are they the best boys? They're at St. John's, *that's* why they're the best boys." So I got ulcers, which is not necessarily inconsistent with my temperament. A lot of clowns have ulcers.

I gave up coaching in 1953 and since then have spent the years meditating. I inherited enough money to take it a little easier. I wrote a book called *Spend Yourself Rich*, which deals with my theory that riches consist of consuming products. Actually, I wrote the book a long time ago, in 1940, and then got it out to rework it twenty years later. The first time, I had written it in a madhouse. Yes, in a madhouse. See, I had some friends who once said, "John, you've been on a big song and dance. Maybe you'd better slow down." At Winnebago there was a hospital run by the State of Wisconsin, so I went there and stayed ninety days and dashed off this tome. Twenty years later I went back to the manuscript to see if there was anything wrong with it, and I decided there wasn't anything wrong with it. The book is now out of print. Well, actually, it was never published. But hell, it didn't do me any harm to get it off my chest. I'd been carrying a typewriter in the back of my car for years, not knowing why.

The first black quarterbacks in the NFL were George Taliaferro and the aptly named Willie Thrower, both of whose careers were even shorter, if happier, than that of Joe Gilliam. In the years since 1976, when Roy Blount, Jr., wrote this piece for *Esquire*, the gifted Jefferson Street Joe continued to have personal problems, attempted a comeback with a minor-league outfit, but did not return to the NFL. It was left to other men—notably James Harris and Doug Williams— to still at last the offensive question, "Can a black play quarterback in the NFL?"

ROY BLOUNT, JR.

The Short, Happy Life of Joe Gilliam

Billy Dee Williams in the recent black baseball movie *The Bingo Long Traveling All-Stars & Motor Kings* reminds me of Joe Gilliam: skinny, springy, with a lot of frustrated zest in him. But that movie was too trivial and soft to show the way frustrated zest marks you. Joe Gilliam's looks are more bothersome than Billy Dee Williams'. Gilliam is a gaunt twenty-five-year-old.

I remember Joe Gilliam on the Pittsburgh team bus, early in the '73 season when he was on the Steeler taxi squad, not getting to wear a uniform on game days. Running back Rocky Bleier said to him, "Down there in Tennessee, what would you say to 'em in the huddle, Joe?"

"On the five-yard line?" cried Gilliam. "On the five-yard line?" He jumped up. "I'd say to 'em: 'All right, dig it! Double-clutch right on two!'" Then he did a little dance step: one-two, one-two. "'*Git* it!'"

"Aw, *Tennessee*," said tackle Dwight White. "Do sumpin' *here*."

"I'm goin' to. I'm goin' to," Gilliam said. "If they'll gimme a *suit!*"

"Hey," said White, "you be here for fifteen years, they have a ceremony, and they say, 'For long and dedicated service, we are . . . gonna give you . . . your *suit!*"

A year later Gilliam not only had his suit, he was the hottest thing in the league: Jefferson Street Joe Willie Gillie, the man who put the arm back into football, the first dominating black pro quarterback. Now he's out of work and under a cloud. For insufficiently dedicated service.

For Gilliam to be out of football makes about as much sense as it did for young director Orson Welles to be kept out of movie making. Less sense, because athletes have fewer years to work in. Welles, incidentally, didn't learn discipline while out of action.

By the time this column appears, Gilliam *might* be doing what he should be doing: quarterbacking a National Football League team, jumping around in the pocket like Jiminy Cricket and hitting people's hands with off-balance forty-yard passes. But that is unlikely. The New Orleans Saints say they won't consider inviting him back to their camp until next year, and every other N.F.L. team passed him up this summer before the Saints bought him for one hundred dollars from the Steelers. Gilliam's father has told people that Joe will probably sit out this season in Nashville, where he can "get his feet on the ground."

At this writing, anyway, Gilliam is in limbo and not speaking to the press. Doubtless he would prefer no more publicity, following those newspaper stories about his arrest for possessing drugs, possessing a pistol, and recklessly fleeing police. But what he has been through during the past three years needs looking at from a nonofficial point of view.

He was wonderful to watch, from any point of view, during the six exhibition and six regular-season games in '74 when he was winning, reveling in, and losing the Steeler starting-quarterback job. Often he seemed to be throwing off the wrong foot or with both of them in the air — Blanton Collier, the old Cleveland Brown coach who took an interest in Gilliam when he was in college, "told me off-balance was a matter of opinion," Gilliam said. But once the ball left his hand, people were reminded of classical dropback heroes like Norm Van Brocklin. Usually he held the ball unclassically down low before he threw, instead of up by his ear. But they used to say Cassius Clay held his hands too low, too. Gilliam's delivery was so quick — no matter how slow Steeler film analysts ran footage of him throwing, his arm was still a blur — he could hold his hands where he pleased.

And wouldn't he hang the ball up there. He would throw eight or nine incompletions and keep on throwing, and hit the next eight or nine in a row. During the exhibition season one opposing coach called him "fantastic" and another said he might have given "the finest performance I've ever seen by a quarterback." In leading the Steelers over the Colts in their regular-season opener he hit 9 of 11 for 151 yards in the second quarter alone. In a terrific, rowdy 35–35 overtime tie with Denver the next week, he completed 31 of 50 passes for 348 yards. Most contemporary pro quarterbacks' personalities are masked by armor, caution, zone defenses, and real or simulated sangfroid. Gilliam, when a big play clicked, would beam and bounce around with both hands in the air. Once he openly waved off a play sent in by head coach Chuck Noll. Another time he doubled up laughing when one of his offensive linemen flattened a rusher.

He threw too much, though. He kept on throwing even into the teeth of complicated defenses rigged up with his proclivities in mind. He had a couple of bad games. To win it all in the N.F.L. these days, it appears, you have to play a carefully controlled offense founded on the run. (And count on your defense to kick the shit out of the other guys.) The Steelers were about to come to a head as a team and didn't want to take any chances. Noll went back to the quarterback whom Gilliam had supplanted, Terry Bradshaw, and after a couple of bad games of his own, Bradshaw worked his own great, though less flamboyant, talents into Noll's system so well that the Steelers went on to win two straight Super Bowls. Gilliam was once again an understudy. Then a black sheep. Then an outcast.

You can't say the Steelers didn't want a black quarterback, unless a black quarterback is defined as one who can't stand to get bogged down in all that grinding-it-out mess. They gave Gilliam a good shot. Everybody in football seems to feel that Gilliam's being out of it is his fault, that he blew it, that he let himself down. "He let *us* down," says a Steeler who is black. The Steelers couldn't even get a good player in return for Gilliam when they gave up on him. "That's the real tragedy of the thing," says Steeler vice-president Art Rooney, Jr. "He could have been making a hundred thousand dollars a year here, counting pension and playoff money. He lost all that." And his market value.

But wait a minute. On another team, one that was building, Gilliam could have had a much better chance to use and develop his gifts. Why is it necessarily right to take a lot of money in return for not doing what you most want to do in life? What if actually getting out there on the field and playing quarterback regularly was so important to Gilliam that he'd rather leave the world champion Steelers and join a team that he could hope to start for?

Well, in pro football, unlike in America, you can't just up and quit one company and go to work for another. It would have taken Gilliam all the way through the '77 season to finish his long-term contract (which, like all pro-football contracts, bound him to the team, but not the team to him) and play out his option year. The only way for Gilliam to get another chance like he had in '74, short of serious injury to the robust young Bradshaw, was for him to force a trade.

That is what many people assume Gilliam was trying to do last year, however consciously or unconsciously: force the Steelers to trade him. That is like trying to be so obnoxious to your landlord that he will let you out of your lease. Joe had been known to be late to team meetings before — a serious sin in pro football. Last season he was late to a lot of them, missed whole practices, was out way, way after curfew one night on the road, and seemed to be detached from things. "He would drift off somewhere," says Art Rooney, Jr. Joe Greene asked team captain Andy Russell to talk to Gilliam, ask him why he was the only one who seemed to get caught in tunnels on his way to practice.

"I guess I've just got buzzard's luck," Gilliam told Russell. "But I can't get down on myself."

Everybody else could get down on him, though. Russell, who loves to blitz and made a name for himself that way, largely eschews blitzing so as to conform with the new disciplined Steeler defense. Other Steelers who might well be starting for other teams are accepting loyal-backup roles. Why couldn't Gilliam be a good citizen?

If you're on the bench and grumbling, you've usually got plenty of fellow sufferers. But what if you're on an essentially harmonious team that's winning a lot of money and corporate glory and greatly wants you for quarterback insurance, and you have a desperate desire to *play?* You are supposed to keep that desire burning, of course, but what if you want to take it off to some other team where you can use it — against, quite possibly, the team you're on now? Then nobody's on your side. It must be hard to be surrounded by a tightly knit team that's not on your side.

Your wife and kids' interests, financial ones at least, are against yours, too. And your parents' — well, Gilliam's father is a highly respected but self-deprecatory defensive coach at Tennessee State College, where the colorful head coach, John Merritt, gets the acclaim.

"My daddy used to be the coach at Kentucky State," Gilliam said once, "and there was a big beer bust and the president of the school got rid of the whole team, except for one guy who wasn't at the beer bust. My daddy had to use the freshman team. Then they fired my daddy.

"My sophomore year at Tennessee State, I was the quarterback, and we were going to play against Kentucky State. My daddy got up and talked to us before the game, told us how much it meant to him. Tears running down my daddy's face. They ruined his football team and then they fired him. Well, we went out and beat 'em eighty-three to *nothin'.*

"Fire *my* daddy."

I have met Joe's parents and they are very nice people, and I'm sure they've stuck with Joe through his difficulties. But they can hardly have rallied behind him in his contrariness, certainly not as aggressively as Joe stuck up for his father against Kentucky State. "His father has more Wasp-type attitudes than you'd think a black man would have," says Art Rooney, Jr. "Very puritanical and middle-class."

So when he stopped getting along by going along, Joe was pretty much alone. His nadir as a Steeler, as a quarterback, was the last game of the '75 season, against the Rams, a game the Steelers coasted through and lost, having already won their division title. Gilliam was scheduled to play the second half. "During half time everyone was looking for Joe to go over the defenses," a Steeler says, "and nobody could find him. Finally we found him in the furthest toilet stall." When he took the field, Gilliam was not sharp. And one of the Steeler offensive linemen had heard that Gilliam had said he was no good. The Ram that offensive lineman was supposed to block shot straight in and creamed Gilliam twice. Joe had to leave the game. He was the only Steeler who didn't play in the Super Bowl.

The Steelers were trying to trade him by then, but no one wanted a "problem" quarterback. Certainly not — racism can't be discounted — a black one. Finally, when he slept through one practice and was late for another during the Steelers' early rookies-and-quarterbacks camp this year, he was put on waivers. If more than one team had claimed him, the Steelers would have taken him back off waivers and tried to make a deal, but only the Saints spoke up.

The Saints' starting quarterback, Archie Manning, had had a bad year followed by arm surgery. It was a good team for Gilliam to make it on. Then, a couple of weeks before he was to report, he and a friend were arrested in Nashville after a high-speed chase, Gilliam driving. Police found marijuana and a firearm in the car and recovered some cocaine that had been thrown out the window.

So that was hanging over his head when he reported early, July 4, to the Saints' camp. On the sixth he borrowed another player's car and disappeared from camp for four days. When he returned he apologized to the team, accepted a $1,000 fine, and then in Saturday scrimmage he completed sixteen of the nineteen passes he threw, and two of the other three were dropped. Joe Willie *Gillie!*

But Monday he had the flu and when he returned to practice Wednesday he wasn't impressive and on Thursday he *missed breakfast.* "We don't have an overabundance of rules and regulations, but the ones we have will be followed to the letter," said Saint head coach Hank Stram. "If I don't enforce them, I'm doing a bad job as a coach." All meals in the Saints' camp are mandatory. Gilliam was cut loose.

He got a better deal in court. All the charges will be wiped away if he does sixty days of public-service work in the next nine months. He passed a lie-detector test saying the coke wasn't his. If every NFL player who's had pot on him had to go to jail, it would look more ragged than the WFL out there. And a lot of players carry guns in their cars. I remember a former Steeler who weighed some two hundred eighty pounds reflecting with relish on how the person who'd just stolen his car was going to react when he started looking at what was inside it. "First he's going to find my gun, and say, 'Uh-oh,'" he chuckled, "and then he's going to see the size of my *clothes.*"

But if Gilliam was trying to get traded, why didn't he straighten up for the Saints? Well, becoming a pariah isn't the most stabilizing exercise in the world. "Some who have known Gilliam speculate that his emotions had finally reached a breaking point," says *Jet.* That makes sense, and it doesn't seem disgraceful.

People—players as well as management—also mention drugs. This factor seems to have been figured into his official profile already, or I wouldn't mention it. "We felt he was enjoying some funny stuff," says Art Rooney, Jr. "And we don't think this was an all-American boy who got into this only after something was taken away from him. Our understanding was that he had experience with something like that before."

Well. That would not have made him unique in pro football, certainly. And there are plenty of players who win approval for their performances on speed. And the Steelers were long famous for their *drinking* quarterbacks. And I was just reading in the New York *Daily News* that people are working stoned in *banks.* "Drugs" seem a dubious devil theory to me.

Now I don't deny that the Steelers and Saints have grounds for exasperation. Clearly Gilliam is going to have to act more middle-class, or something, if he is going to be allowed to wear another NFL suit. But people might consider that during the last two years he took the only course his need to play allowed him to take, maybe a more admirable course — I'm talking human spirit, now, not prudence or teamsmanship — than sitting there stifling his instincts, being punctual, and keeping his nose clean.

Duane Thomas was such a beautiful runner, but once he got wiggy the game stiffed him. He did get very wiggy, of course, but things like being rude to sportswriters and going after hecklers in the stands are not what you could call entirely unreasonable, and things like refusing to take a three-point stance strike me as comparable to an inspired two-finger-typing sportswriter's refusing to learn the touch system. There would be less in the way of disruptive dissidence in sports if all dissidence weren't automatically considered disruptive. And I'll be damned if I don't think pro football would be more interesting on Sunday if rules required all key players to miss at least one practice every week.

"I had such *desires*," says baseball's troubled, splendid Richie Allen, "and then they wanted me to go to *meetings*." At one point Allen was so upset by his clashes with standard off-the-field procedure that when a kid came up to him for an autograph he cried, "Get away! I can't stand it!"

"You can't let them [the powers that be] kill the little boy in you," says Reggie Jackson, who has managed to flout the system to some extent and yet stay on top of things. Jackson's sport, baseball, is somewhat more tolerant than football, but each sport perpetuates the childhood of players, complains about their childishness, and crushes them when they try to take any aspect of the game more threatening than balls and bats into their own hands.

Football's image of Joe Gilliam now, presumably, is: trouble. My image is of what he was like when he was doing what he loved to do, turning pro football into something more than grim head-knocking, romping around out there like a young dog with a stick in his mouth. Talk about enjoying funny stuff! Football is supposed to be something fans can get off on, isn't it! If pro football knows what is good for it, it will bring Joe back. Off-balance is a matter of opinion.

Here's Harry Wismer in 1960. The American Football League is new, and so are his New York Titans. These are happy days, filled with the spirit of entrepreneurship and adventure. But too soon, Harry's chronic joie de vivre went the way of his cash: with no one coming out to see his team cavort in the decrepit Polo Grounds, the payroll checks bounced in November 1962, and the league was forced to pick up the tab. Wismer was down for the count, and the foundling Titans were left on the doorstep of Sonny Werblin and friends, who renamed them the Jets. But let's not forget Harry Wismer, without whom there would have been no TV contract and thus no league, as the World Football League was to discover in 1975.

ROBERT H. BOYLE

Horatio Harry

Arrayed against the walls of the living room in the Park Avenue apartment of Harry Wismer, the sports announcer who is president of the New York Titans pro football team, are inscribed photographs of General Omar Bradley, Vice-President Richard Nixon, President Dwight Eisenhower, Senator George Smathers, former President Harry Truman, Senator Styles Bridges, Thomas E. Dewey, Moose Krause (the Notre Dame athletic director), George Halas (owner of the Chicago Bears), and J. Edgar Hoover. When a visitor remarks upon the display, Wismer beams. "I've got more inside," he says.

"Those pictures," says a friend, "are Harry's badge of success. Some people work for dollars, Harry works for pictures." Whether at lunch in the Waldorf or in South Bend for a game, Wismer is with tycoons. "Harry," says a college publicity man, "is a radio version of Sugár Ray Robinson. He always has big shots he has to get into the press box."

When not palling around with the power elite, Wismer mingles with the masses. He regards himself as a one man people-to-people program. "I love humanity," he says. He has gotten the wine stewards at El Morocco in New York and the Pump Room in Chicago to become pen pals. "Why shouldn't they write to one another?" he asks. "They're in the two best rooms in the country."

When Wismer runs into an old friend, he is something to behold. "Congratulations!" he exclaims, hurtling his stocky frame forward, his right hand at the ready for a crunching handshake. "I always say congratulations," Wismer explains. "It makes people feel good. 'Congratulations!' And they say 'How do you know?' And I say, 'I keep pace.'"

In a crowd Wismer reacts differently: he spreads rumors. His latest is, "So they shot Castro!" Says Wismer, "You get a lot of emotional reaction from people."

With the press Wismer is all business. He doles out scoops alternately to A.P. and U.P.I. "It wouldn't be good sense to take sides," he says. After he calls U.P.I. he dashes to his office to watch the story move on his private teletype. "Harry's got an integrity that a lot of people don't give him credit for," says Mims Thompson, U.P.I. first vice-president. "He's given me dozens of tips on stories and not a bum one yet."

Wismer likes to keep his face as well as his name before the public. His picture on the Titan ad in commuter trains is so large there is barely room for the schedule. When the Los Angeles Chargers requested Titan pictures for the press, they received not photographs of players but a dozen portraits of Wismer.

"If you knew Harry for a month or two, you'd hate him," says a friend. "After a year, you'd begin to reverse yourself. If Harry would only let his accomplishments speak for themselves instead of letting himself speak for his accomplishments, he'd be much better off. There are so many compensating qualities to the man. When a Redskin player got a fractured skull, Harry paid him a year's salary out of his own pocket." Says another friend, "Harry's the greatest contact man in the United States. He's always maneuvering. If he had someone to curb him, he'd be a very great man."

Only physical force could curb Wismer — he is immune to criticism, insult, the cold cut, or the hot rebuke. Once while broadcasting a pro playoff he announced breathlessly, "He's on the 30, the 35, the 40, the 45, the 50, the 55!" Another time he described a field-goal attempt: "He kicks! And it's a beautiful kick! End over end! Terrific! And it's no good!" Wismer has been criticized for broadcasting that celebrities were at a game when, in truth, they were thousands of miles away. "I do that a lot," says Wismer. "I plug my friends." I say, 'Dean Acheson is here. President Eisenhower just walked in. There goes Dick Nixon.'"

Wismer's zest has been with him since birth. He was born in Port Huron, Michigan, forty-seven years ago. His father, now retired, was manager of a clothing store, and the family lived in modest circumstances. His mother had five children, one of whom, a girl, died of diphtheria a few weeks before Harry was born. His mother had also come down with the disease, and Wismer says, "I think I was born to keep driving. My mother often said that she was so determined to have me born that it helped her live, and I think some of the strength and determination might have crossed over. Like *What Makes Sammy Run!* — only I've never stopped running. I used to read extensively when I was a kid. Those Horatio Alger and Merriwell books. They used to send a chill up and down me! I read every book about this man's success, that man's success. I'd wipe the dishes for my mother, and I'd say, 'Don't worry. Someday you won't have to worry about all those bills. I'll take care of everything.'"

A good athlete, Wismer won a scholarship to a Wisconsin prep school and went to the University of Florida on a football scholarship. He stayed a year, then left for Michigan State, taking the coach, Charley Bachman, with him. Wismer had learned through a friend that the State coaching job was open.

A leg injury put Wismer on the sidelines, and when Bill Stern and the late Graham McNamara came out to broadcast a Michigan State game, he served as a spotter. "If those two guys can do it, this is the business for me," Wismer told Bachman after the game. He began broadcasting on the college station, and he took Frank Bachman in tow again. "I want to run you for College All-Star Coach," he said. "Be great publicity for the school. We ought to go down to Detroit and meet all those industrialists and get some backing." In Detroit, Wismer met G. A. Richards, owner of the Lions and station WJR. "He took a liking to me, and I became his protégé," Wismer recalls. "He would go all out for Bachman if the Lions got first crack at Michigan State players."

Wismer put Lion players to work making up petitions for Bachman by copying names from the phone book. Bachman finished second in the voting, but when the winner became ill, he got the All-Star coaching job. Wismer himself got a job as the Lions' public address announcer. He was so enthusiastic that Richards put him on WJR five nights a week at eleven dollars a broadcast as "Lions Cub Reporter." He hitchhiked 160 miles a day back and forth from Michigan State to Detroit to keep the job. A year later he quit school.

He successfully ran Gus Dorais for 1937 All-Star coach; he substituted Dorais' name for the names of former office seekers on petitions stored in the county building and began doing the Lions' games on radio. The next year Wismer decided to run Harry Kipke, who had been fired from Michigan, as All-Star coach. Kipke told Wismer to check with Harry Bennett, Henry Ford's chief lieutenant. Wismer did, and Bennett, who was planning to make Kipke a regent at Michigan, agreed that Kipke should try for the All-Star job.

"When Bennett spoke, people jumped," Wismer says. "We had petitions made out and sent to every Ford plant in the world. We were getting millions of votes! It was like a presidential election! But Arch Ward, sports editor of the *Chicago Tribune*, the paper sponsoring the vote, was running Bo McMillan, and Kipke couldn't catch up. I even offered Ward a Lincoln car to get Kipke in. I was young and foolish — but he wouldn't take it, of course. On the last day I wired in two and a half million votes, and we were still second. But Kipke was elected regent of the university."

In 1941 Wismer married Betty Bryant, the favorite niece of Henry Ford. They have two children, a son, Henry, named after Ford, and daughter, Wendy. Wismer and his wife are now divorced, and she is married to Charles Potter, former Senator from Michigan. When he was an intimate of the Ford family, Wismer lunched at noon with old Henry and again at one with Bennett. "I would have lunch to meet people," he says.

"The more people I could meet the better it was. In many ways, it's true — it's not what you know but who you know. If you're lucky enough to have any brains and coordinate them with who you know, you've got a chance of getting someplace."

In 1942 Wismer went to Washington, D.C., to broadcast the Washington Redskin games. "I had found that government was having more to do with the running of business," he says, "and I felt it would be wise for me to know the people who had so much to say."

Wismer prospered. Today he is worth almost $2 million. He bought a 25 percent interest in the Redskins from their owner, George Marshall, the laundry executive. As a stockholder, Wismer began to make his complaints known to Marshall. "I told him," Wismer says, "that it was very obvious that Negroes were playing an important part in pro football, and that we should draft Negroes. He was adamant against it. He said, 'I was born in West Virginia' — or some damn place — 'and I will never play a Negro on the Redskins.'" The breach widened, and Wismer now has his stock up for sale. "They always call Marshall 'The Laundryman,'" says Wismer. "Hell, the only laundry he knows about is the shirt he's wearing."

At present Wismer is rocketing back and forth across the country broadcasting Notre Dame games and pushing both the Titans and the new American Football League, even if it means knocking the rival National Football League. "We don't have any ex-bookmakers or dog track operators in our league!" he tells one and all. AFL attendance has been low, but each team gets $200,000 or more a year for television rights. "The whole difference in this league is the sale of television, and your old buddy here sold it," Wismer says, modestly. "The American Football League is the league of the future."

To protect that future Wismer will go to any lengths. When he heard that Lamar Hunt and Bud Adams, the young Texas millionaires who founded the league, were going to meet secretly with an NFL representative, he had them tailed by a private eye. "They were going to meet with Halas at the Chicago Athletic Club," he says. "I know the rooms, everything. Certainly I know they met with Halas. I had to make sure these boys would stand up. They did. After all, we weren't lifelong friends. We're going all the way, and I've got to make sure the people with me are going all the way. I've gambled everything. I'm not getting a dime. I don't have an H. L. Hunt, a Boots Adams, or a Conrad Hilton to back *me* up."

Wismer's day begins at 6:30 in the morning and lasts till midnight. He is constantly on the go. His personal phone bill averages $1,200 a month. In the evening he often roams his home turf, the East Forties and Fifties of Manhattan, boosting his Titans. One night last week, for example, he ranged from the Quo Vadis to a Lexington Avenue bar distributing passes and Titan pens. His foray into Le Pavillon was typical.

"Congratulations!" he cried to Henri Soulé, the proprietor. When Henri looked blank, Wismer added, "You're doing the greatest job in the country!"

Wismer gave passes to André, the bartender, and to the girl behind the cashier's counter. He moved into the dining room, where he greeted Corrine Griffith, the silent screen star who is George Marshall's ex-wife. Then he spied an old friend. "Hi, Richard!" he called.

"Harry!" exclaimed the Vice-President of the United States.

"Pat!" said Wismer. "Fred!" said Wismer to the Secretary of the Interior. "Bill!" said Wismer to the Attorney General.

Back at the bar, Wismer exulted. "I'm not afraid of anyone," he said, "and I know how to operate. What the hell, how many guys would go in and say what I said to Nixon? What the hell, he's an American citizen! If he doesn't like it, he can get lost."

Wismer left Le Pavillon joyous. "Those people genuinely like me! See that little girl?" He stopped, closed his eyes and clasped his hands together in imitation of the cashier. "She's praying for me!"

Yes, Virginia, once upon a time there was an all-Indian team in the NFL and, no, they did not come from Cleveland. The curious tale of Jim Thorpe and his Airedale-advertising band is taken from a "media guide" created by three members of the Professional Football Researchers Association. This organization, open to anyone interested in the history of the game, was founded in 1979 by Bob Carroll, whose drawings as well as his prose grace this volume.

BOB BRAUNWART, BOB CARROLL, JOE HORRIGAN

The Oorang Indians

"Let me tell you about my big publicity stunt," wrote Walter Lingo, owner and operator of the Oorang Kennels in a 1923 edition of *Oorang Comments*, his monthly magazine devoted to singing the praises of himself and his Airedales. "You know Jim Thorpe, don't you, the Sac and Fox Indian, the world's greatest athlete, who won the all-around championship at the Olympic Games in Sweden in 1912? Well, Thorpe is in our organization."

Lingo went on to explain that he had placed Thorpe in charge of an all-Indian football team that toured the country's leading cities for the express purpose of advertising Oorang Airedales. As far as Lingo was concerned, that was the only thing that really mattered—how good Thorpe and company made his dogs look. Football was a game he never really cared for very much.

Ironically, Lingo's "stunt" produced the most colorful collection of athletes ever to step onto an NFL gridiron. In American sports lore, there never was, and surely never will be again, anything like the Oorangs, the first, the last, and the only all-Indian team ever to play in a major professional sport league.

Although Thorpe was given three full pages in *Oorang Comments*, very little was said about the performance of his team. It was just as well; they weren't very good, despite the presence of two future Hall of Famers and several other former All-Americans in their lineup. In the two years that they operated, they managed only four NFL victories. In fewer than half their league games could they score even a single touchdown. They lost games by horrendous scores: 41–0, 57–0, and 62–0! And yet, inevitably they will be remembered long after more successful teams are forgotten.

To understand why they existed and why they played as they did, one must begin with Walter Lingo.

Never was a man so in love with a breed of dogs as was Walter Lingo with Airedales. In his magazine he explained: "About sixty years ago, the common man of Great Britain found it necessary to create a dog different from any in existence. The bird dog became lost in the bush when at stand, the hound was too noisy, and the retrievers lacked stamina. Therefore these folks secretly experimented by a series of cross-breeding old types, including the otter hound, the old English sheep dog, the black and tan terrier, and the bulldog. From this melting pot resulted the Airedale, so named because he was first produced by the people along the dale of the Aire river between England and Scotland. The new dog combined the good qualities of his ancestors without their faults. It was a super dog."

Not only were Airedales the Ultimate Dogs, but Lingo had the Ultimate Airedale in King Oorang, a dog he had produced by bringing in and breeding great Airedales from all over the world. King Oorang was "the greatest utility dog in the history of the world," according to *Field and Stream*. With the king as his kingpin, Lingo operated the famous Oorang Kennels out of the little town of LaRue in very rural Ohio.

The kennels were anything but a neighborhood dog pound. They were the "Airedale" of pet stores, a mail-order puppy factory that spread over acres of Lingo's land and employed countless trainers, night watchmen, kennelmen, cratemakers, hunters, and a whole kennelful of clerks who did nothing but keep records on the temperament, instincts, and "pluck" of the hundreds of Airedales being bred there. A prominent dog show writer of the period allowed that, after he had covered thousands of kennels all over the world, "nothing has been seen or imagined such as Walter Lingo's mail-order dog business."

Although America had gone slightly gaga over movie star Rin-Tin-Tin and German shepherds were the big item in dogdom, Lingo was certain that he could make the whole country Airedale-conscious with just a little more advertising. He was already spending $2,000 a month for ads in a dozen or more leading magazines, but what he really needed was to lure thousands of people at a time into watching the Airedales perform.

Enter Jim Thorpe.

Next to Airedales — although not a close "next" — Walter Lingo loved Indians. He had grown up hearing Indian tales — LaRue was the site of an old Wyandotte village — and somehow he had convinced himself that a supernatural bond existed between Airedales and Indians. "I knew that my dogs could learn something from them that they could not acquire from the best white hunters."

The most famous Indian in the world was Jim Thorpe, the greatest athlete of his, and perhaps any other, time. Thorpe had endeared himself to Lingo by telling a nice dog story. When a local farmer accused Lingo of raising a pack of sheepkillers, Thorpe remembered that he once knew an Oorang Airedale that had saved a six-year-old girl from being trampled by a bull. The girl's name was Mabel, he recalled.

In 1921, Lingo invited Thorpe and his buddy Pete Calac to LaRue for a little hunting. In between dog stories — Lingo had one for any occasion — they decided on a novel way both to advertise Airedales and to employ Jim Thorpe, who, if the truth be known, was a little down on his luck just then. Lingo would purchase a franchise in the young National Football League, and Thorpe would run the team, which was to be composed exclusively of Indians. With the asking price for an NFL franchise at $100 and the asking price for a superior Oorang male at $150, Lingo's investment was actually quite modest. Of course, by the time Lingo's kennels joined the league at the June meeting of pro moguls, there was on the books a requirement of posting $1,000 as a guarantee against playing collegians with eligibility remaining, but such things were quite "negotiable" in the NFL's early years. And, with a potential drawing card like an all-Indian team, no one needed to concern himself too closely with trivia.

Lingo wanted the team to play out of little LaRue, but that was hard to justify as the little town had no football field. Admittedly, the team would perform almost exclusively on the road, where they could draw the biggest crowds and best advertise the dogs, but everyone agreed that it would be nice to keep the Indians at home once or twice to show off for the home folks.

Fifteen miles away was Marion, a comparative metropolis of 30,000, which had a suitable field. Additionally, Marion had just been "put on the map" as the home town of the just then extremely popular President Warren G. Harding. Marion was booming. Riding the crest of Harding's popularity, it was industrializing, had plans for a 150-room hotel, and even had scheduled Al Jolson into the Chautauqua Auditorium. As a result of all these circumstances, the Indians will forever go down in the record books as representing Marion, Ohio.

Thorpe set about putting together his team. Indians came from all over to try out, many from Jim's old school, Carlisle. Most of them had not played in quite a while and were older than Thorpe, whose age ranged from thirty-four to fifty depending on what account you wanted to believe. Lingo said he was thirty-eight, and by Jim's own admission, "I was getting up toward forty and I couldn't breathe so good."

Some writers have suggested that Thorpe filled out his roster with several palefaces; they've even gone so far as to say that on a rainy day some of the red skins ran faster than the redskins. There seems to be little basis for the charge. Although many of the Indians were not pure-blooded — Thorpe himself was three-eighths Irish — every identifiable team member has proved to have at least some Indian blood.

JIM THORPE

THE KING OF SWEDEN CALLED THORPE "THE GREATEST
ATHLETE IN THE WORLD" WHEN THE BIG SAC AND FOX
INDIAN EARNED HIS GOLD MEDALS AT THE 1912
OLYMPICS. CERTAINLY HE WAS THE GREATEST
FOOTBALL PLAYER IN THE WORLD WHEN HE JOINED
THE PRO CANTON BULLDOGS IN 1915. HE WAS THE
BEST, OR NEARLY THE BEST, RUNNER, PASSER, KICKER,
AND DEFENDER IN THE GAME, WELL WORTH THE THEN-
ASTONISHING $250 PER GAME HE WAS PAID.

AFTER LEADING CANTON TO SEVERAL NATIONAL PRO TITLES,
HE WAS NAMED THE NFL'S FIRST PRESIDENT IN 1920.

With such players as Sanooke, Red Fang, Downwind, War Eagle, Lone Wolf, Running Deer, and Eagle Feather representing the Cherokees, Chippewas, Winnebagos, Mohawks, and Mohicans, the Oorang Indians hit the warpath against the NFL.

Unfortunately, the warpath hit back. Had Sitting Bull's braves applied themselves in battle with the same tenacity that Thorpe's team applied to its games, General Custer might be alive today. After the horrible 62–0 massacre at Akron, one newspaper headlined "JIM THORPE'S INDIANS LOAF."

That was part of it.

The team found it difficult to take their football seriously because the team owner was far more interested in the pregame and halftime activities than he was in the game itself. They gave exhibitions with Airedales at work trailing and treeing a live bear. One of the players, 195-pound Nikolas Lassa, called "Long-Time-Sleep" by his teammates because he was so hard to wake up in the morning, even wrestled the bear. There were fancy shooting exhibitions by Indian marksmen with Airedales retrieving the targets. There were Indian dances, fancy tomahawk work, knife and lariat throwing, all done by Indians. "The climax," explained Lingo, "was an exhibition of what the United States' loyal Indian scouts did during the war against Germany, with Oorang Airedale Red Cross dogs giving first aid in an armed encounter between scouts and huns in no man's land. Many of the Indians and dogs were veterans of the war — the Oorangs up front."

After such a workout, Thorpe's players must have looked upon the game as purely a secondary matter.

Another reason for the team's lack of success, according to Ed Healey, the Chicago Bears' Hall of Fame tackle, was that Thorpe was not a good coach, especially where discipline was concerned. However, Healey insisted the players were tough. "I have a vivid recollection of how they used the 'points.' By that I mean the elbows, knees, and feet in their blocking and tackling. They'd give you those bones and it hurt. They were tough S.O.B.'s, but good guys off the field."

Perhaps too good. Most of the stories told about the team focus on their off-the-field antics.

There was the time in Chicago when the bartender wanted to close up and the Indians tossed him into a telephone booth, turned it upside down, and drank until dawn. Then they went out and got slaughtered by the Chicago Bears.

There was the time in St. Louis when they left a bar late, only to find their trolley headed in the wrong direction. Using muscles they didn't always exert on the football field, they lifted the vehicle off its tracks and turned it around to face in the right direction.

And there were the many times they put Nikolas Lassa up against touring carnival strongmen. After his experience with the bear, Long-Time-Sleep had little trouble staying the required distance to win the ten or twenty dollars that would allow the whole team to party all night.

Leon Boutwell, a Chippewa quarterback, explained: "White people had this misconception about Indians. They thought they were all wild men, even though almost all of us had been to college and were generally more civilized than they were. Well, it was a dandy excuse to raise hell and get away with it when the mood struck us. Since we were Indians we could get away with things the whites couldn't. Don't think we didn't take advantage of it."

On occasion—whether hung over or not—the Indians could rouse themselves for a super play: Thorpe punted 75 yards in the air at Milwaukee and Joe Guyon ran an interception back 96 at Chicago. But the most spectacular play involving the team was made against them. It happened in 1923 in Chicago when Bear end and coach George Halas picked up a Thorpe fumble and mushed down a muddy gridiron for 98 yards and a touchdown, a record that stood until 1972.

Through it all, Walter Lingo got what he'd paid for: a showcase for his dogs and for his Indians. Without a doubt, the colorful costumes and the colorful stories helped bring out the fans. And then there was Thorpe's still magic name (although Lingo kept billing him by his Indian name, "Bright Path"). Old Jim seldom played more than a half and often sat out the whole game. But every once in a while he could call up the old greatness and lead his team to an at least respectable performance. One news story put it this way: " . . . they looked like a real football team when Indian Jim was in. . . . Rarely has the presence of one player made so great a difference as when Thorpe went in. It seemed as if the team improved fully 50 percent. Their defense stiffened and they started carrying the ball down the field. Thorpe took it many times himself and showed he can forward pass."

After two years, Lingo gave up his team. The novelty was beginning to wear thin. Crowds in 1923—especially on the second trip to a city—were smaller than the year before, and that was no way to sell Airedales. The publicity stunt had run its course.

The Indians scattered. Some went back to the reservation; reportedly Lassa gave up drinking, raised a family, stopped wrestling bears, and became a respected member of his community. Others went right on playing football for other teams. Thorpe played for six more years, Guyon for five, and Calac for four.

Walter Lingo's kennels continued to prosper at LaRue (they were still going strong when he died in the mid-1960s), but fifteen miles away everything seemed to go sour for Marion all at once. The Indians were gone and so was Harding, dead after being disgraced by Teapot Dome. Both the team and the President had looked better on paper than in performance, although time has been kinder to the memory of the football team.

Although "the records tell you differently," wrote John Short in the Marion *Star*, Harding's old paper, "the passing years have given them a powerful image." But they will be remembered, not for their record, but because "they came and gave the game incredible color at a time when it needed color badly."

Memory seduces. It dims the lights, softens the hard edges, and imparts a glow to distant wonders. Will the video generation, its noses rubbed in reality by repeated instant replays, be impervious to the charms of candlelight? Heywood Hale Broun, a television journalist and writer of distinction, waxes warm and eloquent on the subject.

HEYWOOD HALE BROUN

Farewell the Gods of Instant Legend

In the dim yesterday, when athletes traveled on trains, the back platform of the observation car was the framework in which many Americans saw their sports heroes for the only time in their lives.

When the train stopped at a crossroads town to drop mail or pick up water, the whole population would be waiting for the magic moment when the great man, up to then a smudgy newspaper picture, appeared in the round, in the flesh, in that nearness which was just short of the bliss suggested by the old line "Shake the hand that shook the hand of John L. Sullivan."

When my father was a baseball writer traveling through spring training with the New York Giants it used to amuse Ring Lardner to take him onto the back platform and introduce him to the circle of sport worshipers as Jess Willard, a man my father resembled only in weight. The fake Willard would say a few modest words, clasp his hands in the traditional fighter's gesture and withdraw, leaving a knot of excited Floridians discussing their unexpected celebrity bonus.

There are probably still old folks down there who remember seeing Willard when they were kids, a Willard whom even today they remember as appearing shockingly out of shape for a fighter, but a jolly good fellow for all of that.

This is, in a sense, a perfect example of an old-time sports memory. It is vivid, exciting, highly personal, and wildly inaccurate. Of course, lots of other people saw the actual Jess Willard but if you were to ask for a description they would strain the reality through so many layers of subsequent experience that they might well come up with a picture of my father.

So great was the hunger in those old days for a look, a touch, a close view of the gods of games that when it happened, excitement and near hysteria vibrated the eye and ear and turned the memory into the broad and golden outline of instant legend.

When George Halas announced that he had signed Red Grange to play with the Chicago Bears, the lines began to form next morning outside the Spalding store where tickets were announced as available, and stretched four abreast, around and around the block. Later that year people paid twelve and a half Coolidge dollars per ticket to see him play a Florida exhibition.

If now, fifty-odd years later, you asked those ticket buyers to tell you about the Grange they saw, they would take out a memory as loved and polished as old ivory and give you a description of something no human being could ever have accomplished. They would describe to you the flight of a bird in a football suit and they would tell you that nobody they see nowadays on the television has ever come close.

Television has, of course, given us a closer and more accurate view of what goes on. By the use of instant replays, it permits us to see exactly what happened in the detached atmosphere of hindsight so that we are infinitely more knowledgeable, and our memories are a great deal more accurate. What it has taken from us in exchange for this is the moment of mad immediacy when adrenalin has blinded us to the true picture and given us a myth disguised as an observation.

My own first memories of professional football go back to a man I remember as being approximately three feet high, Davey O'Brien, quarterback of the Philadelphia Eagles. In my mind's eye — and the mind is that of a frenzied college freshman now somewhat tattered through being stored in the head of a middle-aged man — O'Brien is a tiny creature who has to reach up to take the ball from the center and who then fades desperately back like someone from one of Charles Schulz's Peanuts teams lost in a nightmare of ill-intentioned monsters. Somehow the little O'Brien escapes the huge linemen and passes the ball 100 yards through the air and we are all cheering and crying and dealing to each other almost as much punishment as the players are managing on the field.

Some factual researches have revealed to me that O'Brien, though small for a football player, actually weighed 160 pounds at the time, and is a person whom I, at 163 pounds, am not entitled to regard as spectacularly undersized. My factual researches have no impact on the vivid picture I project on my personal screen when I summon up that impossibly sunny Sunday in the Middle Jurassic Age, however.

Neither is it true—or rather can it be true that the head of Bill Hewitt, who never wore a helmet, actually changed shape like a squeezed melon as he dove in for a tackle? It seems medically unlikely, but that is the way I remember it.

"There were giants walking the earth in those days!" cry all we middle-aged and more than middle-aged rememberers of the sports figures of our childhoods and youths, and there are no tapes or films or objective views of a small glass square to say us nay.

It is, of course, the refuge of all of us to feel, when youth is far enough behind us, that it was the world's last age of innocence. The medieval adventurers who went on the First Crusade used to shake their heads over the sad lot who marched off to the Second, as my father thought my 1930s idols, Carl Hubbell, Tuffy Leemans, and Davey O'Brien, to be pale shadows of such demi-gods as Christy Mathewson or Charley Brickley, who drop-kicked five field goals against Yale—a feat mysterious to me because I never saw anybody drop-kick anything against anybody.

The young of my son's generation and those who came after are, and will be, so impressively informed that one wonders if they will have the chance to make or hold those larger-than-life images which are such stuff as dreams are made on.

Split screens, isolated cameras, and slow-motion replays will give a heretofore impossible dimension to watching. As the astronauts know far more about the moon than is contained in all the poets' speculations, so tomorrow's fans will see more than did the wisest of coaches and scouts twenty years ago. Also, in the new trend to absorb sports heroes into the worlds of commerce and entertainment, there is inherent a more extensive acquaintance with Olympus than was possible to those who waited in the depot for the glimpse of Jess Willard waving from the observation car.

Of course, the facts and photos brought back from the moon have the immediacy and excitement that goes with authenticity, but the poetry and fantasy tend to fade and the pale-faced moon from which we hoped to plunk bright honors is no longer a ghostly galleon tossed upon cloudy seas.

There will still, naturally, be the special excitement of being actually on the scene, but even the following day's delayed tape will show what really happened, thus fixing and clarifying the memory. It is a remarkable prospect and as the techniques are refined, it may be possible to check through, at will, an electronic box of great moments which can be mixed according to the whim of the viewer.

It is going to be remarkable and I am sorry that I am not going to be around for much of it. I have a consolation, however. I have a recollection, uncontradicted by any earthbound film, of Davey O'Brien, no taller than my knee, throwing a football the length of the field on the fly.

What's this piece about—Brown, or Caruso, or Cannon? It's about greatness, just what the title says, and that's a thing all three had in common. I'll leave comparisons of Caruso and Pavarotti for others to make, but concerning the two Jimmys, it is gospel that as Brown was in a class by himself, so was Cannon. A protégé of Damon Runyon, he spun out essays in a hard-boiled, epigrammatic style that long ago ceased to be fashionable, despite a brief flourish when practitioners of The New Journalism sought to adopt a dismayed Cannon as their paterfamilias. Fashions come and fashions go, that is their nature; and maybe nobody asked me, but . . . Cannon's description of Jim Brown waiting for his blockers is a model of great writing, and it always will be.

JIMMY CANNON

Greatness

Watching Jimmy Brown play football yesterday took me back to my boyhood in the old neighborhood. It had nothing to do with Cleveland beating the Giants, 35–24, and yet this is what it was all about. The memory of greatness lasts forever.

It hasn't happened often since. When it does I hear that glorious voice singing in a language I couldn't understand. But I realized how special it was without knowing why. Joe the Barber had a three-chair shop on Spring Street off Varick, and yesterday I could smell the witch hazel again and hear the plume of steam rise tittering from the boiler where the hot towels were stacked.

My old man shaved himself with a straight razor until the day he died. But he went to Joe's every Saturday for a low trim. I'd go along and listen to the talk about horses and fights and the doorway crap games. On this day Joe said come in the backroom. We walked through the ropes of beads which were the curtain. Joe put a record on one of those hand-cranked phonographs that had a tulip horn.

"Wait'll you hear this guy sing," Joe said. "He's the champion of the world."

I figured it would be John McCormack. We were Irish. Who else could it be? I wasn't an opera man, then or now. But I knew Joe the Barber was right. This wasn't just singing. It was something more. I found out then why Joe shut up the store and stood on line all day for gallery seats when Caruso played the Met. It was like watching Jack Dempsey fight.

Jim BROWN-

NEARLY TWO DECADES AFTER HE LEFT PRO FOOTBALL TO PURSUE A MOVIE CAREER, BROWN IS STILL REGARDED BY MOST EXPERTS AS THE GREATEST RUNNER IN NFL HISTORY.

PLAYING A SHORTER SCHEDULE THAN TODAY'S STARS, HE RACKED UP THOUSAND-YARD SEASONS IN SEVEN OF HIS NINE YEARS. HIS 12,312 YARDS AND 106 TOUCHDOWNS ARE THE TOP CAREER TOTALS FOR ANY RUNNER.

The Browns haven't been beaten yet and in their first five games the bookkeepers got Jimmy Brown carrying an average of 157 yards a game. Yesterday he used his legs to travel 123 and grabbed four passes for 86 more. But the numbers can't define it. Ask the Giants and they'll tell you that Brown is killing you even when he is just standing around and someone else is running with the ball. He doesn't block either.

"He puts pressure on you with or without the ball," said Allie Sherman. . . .

Other guys ran on the Giants this season. The Steelers busted them open. No one's supposed to do that to their defensive unit. Age may be turning them the other way. But it was how Brown put it to them that shook them. It was like being in a dark room with a guy after you with a ball and bat. They had no chance.

In modern football you don't key on a man and ignore the other guys. They tell themselves that. But it's different with Jimmy Brown. Brown isn't moving the ball, he's pretending he might. As a decoy he pulls some of the other people off the runner. You better wait. The hesitation hurts and, in that way, Brown's mixed up in every play the Browns call.

That improved Ernie Green, and he had a hell of a Sunday. He's an accomplished back but he was going with the best of it. They were setting their ambushes for Brown. They couldn't come with a rush at Frank Ryan either. They gave him more time to pass and Ryan threw sixteen times and hit his people with twelve of them. There's no way you can cheat with Jimmy Brown.

The new coach, Blanton Collier, has a lot to do with it. The old one, Paul Brown, made Jimmy Brown's excited skills subservient to his domineering will. But Collier turned Jimmy loose. Now he uses his impulses to find his way if the defense anticipates his intentions.

"They beat Jimmy like a dog and whipped him like a pup," a guy shouted in the Cleveland dressing room. "But he showed them." They worked him over, and there was blood crusted on his muddy white uniform. But he praised Sam Huff for the hard tackles. Once in the first quarter Brown pushed five of them ahead of him for four yards when he reached a hole that was sealed by their slamming bodies. The third time he scored wasn't as spectacular as the second touchdown when he ran 72 yards with that bent-knee shrugging gait after catching a screen pass.

But they were at him and he shouldn't have gone the 32 yards. He angled along, stepping lightly, as if he were afraid his big positive feet would bruise the grass. Patiently, Brown waited for the blockers, like a guy under an awning hoping a shower will pass. He stalled until he got his shot, and then went across field, turning it on with a sudden clap of speed.

"You got to honor him," Sherman said, speaking for everyone who ever played football against Jimmy Brown.

It's been forty years since I heard Enrico Caruso sing in Joe the Barber's place. Since then I've seen many of the best in numerous fields. None in any line ever did what they were paid to do better than the singer and the football player. Each, in his own thrilling way, is the greatest of his kind. They never come two at a time.

Is Tom Landry a cold fish? Could be; as a mover of men, he's no Lombardi. But his mark on the modern game is indelible, and his team sure does win a lot. In recent years pro football has been awash in "dynasties": not on the order of the Ming—football people tend to telescope things—but say a championship or two. The Packers, the Dolphins, the Steelers come to mind; throw in a mention for the Raiders and Colts. Yet none of these teams—in fact, none since Cleveland under that other alleged mackerel, Paul Brown—can equal the sustained brilliance of the Dallas Cowboys.

GARY CARTWRIGHT

Tom Landry: God, Family, and Football

It is Saturday afternoon, early November. A chilled old-time wind chases the fire and baked bronze of dying leaves, and Tom Landry sits in his office on the eleventh floor of a suburban tower in North Dallas, looking down with the sort of detachment that Baron Frankenstein must have experienced as he watched the villagers fight fear with sticks and hayforks.

The Monster is loose again!

The extent of his capering again will be apparent in the agate type of the Sunday sports pages. Ohio U. defeats Cincinnati 60–48. Virginia holds off Tulane 63–47. Yale tears up Princeton 42–17. *Yale!* The blunderbuss of the dime novel, the twenty-three pound turtleneck sweater in grandpa's attic, scoring with basketball propensity. Even Landry's old school, the University of Texas, is lacing TCU (47–21) with unparalleled freedom of expression.

Records fall like leaves, then blow away under the gusts of new records. Someone named Mike Richardson (forget that name) wipes Kyle Rote and Doak Walker from the SMU record book. Michigan's Ron Johnson is a jet-age ghost, cremating the memory of Grange and Harmon in his fantail. In a radio interview former Los Angeles Rams' center Art Hunter refers to O. J. Simpson as "the best of Jimmy Brown and Gale Sayers rolled into one." And Texas's Chris Gilbert, the little tailback who has broken all the Southwest Conference rushing records and threatens more of the same to every career rushing record in the history of college football, will have difficulty making it as a first team All-America.

What was once a game of patience, prudence, and pogroms enacted more or less in the geographical center of a seven-diamond defense now looks as though it were invented by the French. Even the college teams who are not, strictly speaking, relying on the "pro-type" offense, are gaining three or four hundred yards a game. "Ten yards and a cloud of dust": that's how Texas Tech coach J. T. King describes the University of Texas attack.

The Monster is everywhere, legends tumbling on his vibrations.

"I still feel that the defense will stand up to the test," Tom Landry is saying on this particular Saturday afternoon. Landry is seemingly oblivious to the riots that are at this moment taking place on the campuses across the land: Landry is talking of the National Football League, specifically of the game in the Cotton Bowl Sunday between his Cowboys and the New York Giants, a game that will go a long way in settling the winner of the Capitol Division. There are those in football, Giants' president Wellington Mara among them, who feel that Tom Landry has perfected, maybe even invented, football's modern defense. Landry credits the invention to Steve Owen, the genius of the Giants from 1931–53, though it was Landry who defined the relationship of the linebacker to the width of the playing field, thus establishing what Mara calls "the inside-out theory of defensive football"—protecting the middle while trusting the flanks to hot pursuit.

Landry was one of the first to recognize tendencies and traits in his opposition, and one of the first to devise "keys" which would unlock the secrets of the mysterious huddle. Many coaches eventually reached that conclusion, but *Landry did it as a player*. And when it was perfected—and when the Giants were the most feared defense in football—Landry started experimenting with offensive weapons which could conceivably destroy his life's work. It was a restless imitation of art and life: from the missile came the antimissile came the anti-antimissile. . . .

But listen to Landry on this Saturday afternoon:

" . . . The defense will stand up. But sometimes you wonder (he says this with some irony in his normal monotone; his oyster eyes twinkle; his Ice Age smile, collected through centuries of slow but constant seepage, is alert to history's carnage). . . .

"You see what's happening to college football. The two-platoon rule opened it up to the multiple offense, and the multiple offense created an impossible situation in terms of how a college team can defense it. The key to *defense* is execution; in order to execute well enough to contain a multiple offense a team must play together four or five years . . . at least that long . . . which is impossible for the colleges. As long as colleges play a multiple offense . . . a T-formation offense, with quarterbacks in the pass pocket . . . as long as that happens, the colleges will never be able to defense it: they will never have enough experience to cope with the many problems. The colleges must either return to one-platoon football or resign themselves to big scores."

Somewhere in the corners of your mind you hear Baron Frankenstein speak, identifying his work, preaching caution, almost amused at the misunderstanding. Lay aside your hayforks, melt down your silver bullets: your icons are powerless, your dogs less than useless. The Monster is not the creation but the creator. It is the *Landry Monster*, that gangling apparition of spreads and slots and double-or-triple wings and men-in-motion and abrupt shifts, coordinated to wreck anticipation, delight the fans, and make supermen from human tissue.

They used to laugh at it. Such great-but-stylized coaches as Buddy Parker used to warn Landry that the multiple offense would never work, that it would strangle on its own complications; and for a time in the early 1960s it seemed as though they were right. But Landry *had it in his mind* when he resigned as defensive coach of the Giants to take the head job with the newly formed Dallas Cowboys in 1960.

His conviction never wavered. "It was, and still is, the only way to attack the basic 4–3 defense," Landry says. On the other hand: "If you have the time and patience to coordinate your defense . . . the experience to handle all the complicated sets . . . defense will prevail."

In his ninth season with the Cowboys, Tom Landry is the dean of NFL head coaches. He had five straight losing seasons before his team broke even in 1965. Since then the Cowboys have dominated the Eastern Conference, barely losing to Green Bay in two NFL Championship games. Landry's is the first expansion team in modern sports history to achieve championship status, and his ideas on multiple offense have filtered down to the most primitive level of football. If the Dallas Cowboys appear awesome on your television screen, they are nowhere near as awesome as Landry intends.

Like brilliant men in every field, Tom Landry is self-made. Or, as Landry chooses to put it, he is the product of destiny and divine counterplay.

"It is hard to put your finger on why you make the decisions that you make," says Landry. "I'm a great believer in my own convictions, but I pray a great deal that I'll make the right decision. I have no doubt that there is something other than man himself that leads man."

That something, of course, is the Christian God. There was a time eight or nine years ago, in the scruffy, early years of the Cowboys, when some of the older players referred to their coach as *Pope Landry I*. Less pious in recent years, Landry expresses his deepest beliefs in the stereotype of selected banquet speeches, and in answers to direct questions. "If Landry has ever saved any souls," says one current player, "he did it without anyone knowing."

In the early years many players found Landry confusing and noncommunicative. "He would never pat you on the behind and tell you 'good job,' " complained one former defensive back. "If you intercepted a pass, Landry looked at you like *that's what you're supposed to do!"* But that is Landry's style—taciturn without being shy, confident without being boastful; he exudes rather than expounds his philosophy. Except for the practice field or meeting room, Landry permits himself almost no personal contact. There is one minor exception: he sometimes lifts weights with the players in the off-season. Landry is as trim and maybe as strong as any man on his team. With Tom Landry, the priority is God, family, and football.

"I grew up in a Christian home," says Landry, "but I wasn't truly converted to Christ until 1958. I lived a moral life but I wasn't a true Christian. Most people go through life always looking. . . always seeking. I found out that a Christian commitment is the only real purpose in life."

Landry says that he did not have "a religious experience" in 1958 so much as he "matured into it."

"You could never get Tom to talk about his background," recalls Father Benedict Dudley, the Giants' chaplain.

Says Cowboy president Tex Schramm, "Tom isn't the easiest man in the world to communicate with. You have to hit him with a two-by-four to get his attention: but once you get it, you get his whole attention. Tom has a rare perspective. For instance, he is known as a progressive coach, but in a lot of ways he's very conservative. He holds strong with tradition, yet he is an innovator. If you remember, he used to alternate quarterbacks (before Don Meredith reached maturity). He recognized this wasn't the ultimate answer, yet there we were in 1962 leading the league in offense. And with *nothing!"*

Sportswriters who have known Landry for a few years find him strikingly honest, easy to interview. I remember a party in 1963 after team owner Clint Murchison, Jr., destroyed Landry's original five-year contract and signed him to a new eleven-year contract, an unprecedented vote of confidence.

Everyone was whooping it up but Landry, who was sitting alone in one corner, serene as a Ming vase. "Why aren't you living it up?" someone asked him. "This is your party."

"No," said Landry. "This isn't my party. This is the team's party."

Later that night his wife, Alicia, told me: "No one will ever have to fire Tommy. He would quit if he didn't win. The new contract is a vote of confidence in the *football* team, not in *Tommy!"*

Tom Landry takes his aspirations seriously—and one at a time. Aside from beating the Green Bay Packers in a championship game, Landry's idea of personal fulfillment is to have a positive influence on as many young men as possible. This is his passion and it traces back to his own boyhood which was, in a contemporary sense, unique.

Landry was born in 1924, a half block from the First Methodist Church of Mission, Texas. Mission is a small town with a large Mexican-American population in the lush citrus valley between the Gulf of Mexico and the Rio Grande. Tom's father ran a garage; he served as Fire Chief and superintendent of Sunday school at the church down the street. Tom played every sport in season, made mostly A's in his school subjects, and had an exemplary Sunday-school attendance record.

"Mission was a great place for a boy to grow up," he recalls. "I learned something playing in the sandlots . . . something that today's youngsters aren't able to experience. Here is where you learn to cry and to fight . . . to overcome all situations according to your own abilities and initiative . . . without some (adult) supervisor always looking over your shoulder."

With characteristic clarity Landry remembers that his final high school team (1) played the Notre Dame box formation; (2) went undefeated in twelve games; (3) allowed only one touchdown—on a pass interference penalty. Landry was a good college player at the University of Texas, a standout passer until he broke the thumb on his passing hand, at which time he was forced to surrender his starting position to another passer of some ability, Bobby Layne. Converted to fullback in the week between the thumb injury and the game against North Carolina (the Choo-Choo Justice team), Landry ran for more than one hundred yards that Saturday afternoon. Though he had less speed than your average pulling guard, Landry played six seasons at cornerback with the Giants (1950–55), the last four as a player-coach. By the late 1950s he was such a valued assistant coach with the Giants that head coach Jim Lee Howell referred to him publicly as "the best coach in football."

The Giants in those glory days were pretty much the product of two assistant coaches—Landry on defense, Vince Lombardi on offense. "Jim Lee Howell gave them a lot of leeway," admits Wellington Mara. "He kept the power of veto, but he recognized their abilities. I recall back about 1956, everyone was defending the end sweep by dropping off the ends (who became linebackers) and forcing the play inside. Landry wanted to defense it inside-out, stop them up the middle with the idea that the pursuit would take care of the outside. Quite simply, Tom was talking about today's 4–3 defense—where the four (defensive) men (up front) are charged with the responsibility of keeping the five (offensive) linemen from getting a clean shot at the middle linebacker. Jim Lee accepted Tom's idea; the rest is history."

In 1959 Lombardi heard the call, moving to Green Bay. *His* success is football cliché. Not long after, Landry tentatively accepted a position as head coach of the new Houston Oilers of the AFL, but destiny was squeezing curious patterns. In the middle of the 1959 season, while the Giants were posting a 10–2 record and winning another Eastern Conference championship, Mara called Landry, advising him that the new NFL franchise in Dallas had expressed interest in him. If Mara knew at the time that Jim Lee Howell would announce his retirement at the end of that season ("Those ten victories," said Howell, "don't make up for the two defeats"), Mara did not mention it to Landry; but the opportunity to remain in the NFL (not to mention the opportunity of challenging Lombardi) prevailed. So Landry took the Dallas job.

Much of the fascination in Landry's rise is that he came up through the ranks: from player, to player-coach, to coach. Only Don Shula of the Colts has approached Landry's success both as a player and a coach, making the transition while still retaining respect and command.

The message is one of pace and temperament. "The day Landry became a non-playing coach," recalls Giants' publicity man Don Smith, "it was as though he had been *coach* for twenty years. You pull a shade, you go to sleep, the next morning you wake up with a lifetime of wisdom under your pillow. There is no sense of time passing. Even today when I run into Tom I get the feeling—there has been *no passage of time.*"

"Landry is a born student of the game," says Em Tunnell, the great defensive back who played with (and later for) Landry. Tunnell had been with the Giants two seasons when Landry came as part of the peace package negotiated when the old All-America Conference folded before the 1950 season. The Giants and the New York Bulldogs each picked five players from the newly defunct New York Yankees. On the recommendation of Gus Mauch, the Yankees' trainer, the Giants selected three of the four members of the Yankees' secondary—Otto Schnellbacher, Harmon Rowe, and Landry. By 1951, the Giants had the best defensive backfield in football.

"Landry was sort of weird," Tunnell recalls, "but we were a unit back there (in the secondary), getting closer and closer. I remember when we shut out the great Browns' team in 1950, didn't even let 'em get close enough to try a field goal. After the game me and Schnellbacher and Rowe would go out for beer, but Tom would disappear. He was always off with his family. You never knew what was going through his mind. He never said nothing. He just always knew what was going on. We didn't have words like 'keying' in those days, but Tom made up his own keys and taught 'em to the rest of us."

Landry remembers it well: "By training I was an industrial engineer." (He was on his way to a career in engineering when the Yankees signed him as a punter and defensive back in 1949; he also played running back with the Yankees.) "I had to know what was going on. It was my nature. I couldn't be satisfied trusting my instincts the way Em did. I didn't have the speed or quickness. I had to train myself, and everyone around me, to key various opponents and recognize tendencies."

Where Vince Lombardi was a gurgling volcano, blistering everyone in his path, Landry was placid as a mountain lake. These contrasting personalities had no small effect on the Giants.

"Lombardi was a much warmer person," says Mara. "He went from warm to red hot. You could hear him laughing or shouting for five blocks. You couldn't hear Tom from the next chair. Lombardi was more of a teacher. It was as though Landry lectured to the upper 40 percent of the class and Lombardi lectured to the lower 10 percent."

Again, that was Landry's style. Intellectual but nonaggressive. At the same time Landry's physical presence went unquestioned; it was a lineal strength that ran through the team, a central nervous system. He had been one of them through all kinds of hell.

When the Giants lost both of their quarterbacks in a game with Pittsburgh in 1953,

Landry came over from defense and ran the team for most of the last half. Though Landry had never worked at quarterback, he was obviously the only man on the team who might be expected to play the position cold.

"I was lucky," Landry recalls. "Pittsburgh was the only field in the league where you could draw plays in the dirt."

The Giants lost 24–14. The following week against Washington, New York again lost 24–21. Landry played fifty-nine minutes of this game, directing both the offense and defense.

That mystical and saintly presence which sustained the Giants (in ways that it took them years to realize) has never abandoned Tom Landry.

"He tells you what's going to happen," says Cowboy halfback Dan Reeves, "and on Sunday it happens."

Says Don Meredith: "Landry used to be ultra-frustrating. I thought I knew a *little* about football. But Landry would be up at the blackboard saying, 'Okay, we'll do this . . . then they'll do that . . . then we'll . . .' You'd interrupt him and say, 'Coach, what if they *don't* do that?' . . . Landry would just look at you and say, *'They will.'*"

But this is a Saturday afternoon, early November 1968. Landry is absorbed by new peril, not old glory. Until two weeks ago his team was undefeated, rolling Packer-like to another conference championship, true to the vow he made in training camp: *this time*, Landry vowed, the Cowboys would be more than a match for the Packers in the championship game. But it is beginning to look as though Landry is wrong. For one thing, the Packers show scant inclination to win their own division: coach Lombardi is now *Mr.* Lombardi, elder statesman to pro football. Then two weeks ago in the Cotton Bowl the erstwhile headless horsemen of Green Bay rode through Dallas as though it were Sleepy Hollow. It was no contest.

"They were the Packers of old," Landry is lamenting. "They tested us in areas (of defense) that we thought we had under control. You never know how good you are . . . or how far you've come . . . until Green Bay tests you. It's always been a measure of my defensive team how well we've been able to do against Green Bay, and up until now we have never matched them with experience and execution. When we do, we will have arrived."

Anticipating that the Packers are somehow still the team his Cowboys must beat, Landry made one key change—he moved Mel Renfro, his talented free safety, to left-side cornerback. Meanwhile, the Cowboys must win their own division. If they beat their only challenger, the Giants, on Sunday, they will have a three-game lead with five games to play. Since New York in its last two games lost to lowly Atlanta and was shut out by Baltimore, victory seems simple, if not assured.

But now it is Sunday, a dark, cold, windy afternoon. Meredith's first pass is crippled by a thirty-m.p.h. headwind and falls into New York hands. Dallas gets it back on a fumble recovery, but Meredith can't get it going and after an exchange of punts Fran

Tarkenton takes New York in for a 7–0 lead. Bruce Maher intercepts a second Meredith pass and runs it 89 yards to the Dallas 6. Tarkenton throws and New York has a 14–0 lead.

On the sideline Landry watches his pass rushers play Chinese chess with Tarkenton: "Tarkenton's uniform won't be sent to the cleaners this week," moans a Dallas sportswriter. Landry's face is tight as a coffin when he tells Meredith: "They're outhitting us. They're outplaying us every way. We've got to get tough."

Now Meredith is brilliant. He first hits Bobby Hayes, then Lance Rentzel, with touchdown passes. The Cowboys struggle to a 14–14 tie by halftime. The second half opens with Tarkenton throwing a 60-yard touchdown pass to Homer Jones.

"Get tough!" one of Landry's assistants yells from the sideline. The Cowboys are on the march. Meredith scrambles for six yards and a first down, then he comes limping to the sidelines: Meredith is back in the game after three plays, but his knee cartilage is torn and won't be sound for the remainder of the 1968 season. It's more pain for Meredith, Landry knows. Fullback Don Perkins bolts for seven yards. The Vikings have just defeated the Packers, announces the public-address system. Dallas halfback Les Shy drops a touchdown pass at the goal line. The Cowboys continue to march. On a great second effort, halfback Craig Baynham, who has replaced Shy, pounds over from the New York 1. The game is again tied 21–21.

In the final quarter Dallas goes against the wind, New York with it. Tarkenton throws 35 yards to Homer Jones, then Pete Gogolak kicks a field goal, pushing New York in front 24–21.

"All the way, Lance-*baby!*" an asistant coach shouts from the sideline, but Lance Rentzel signals for a fair catch and fumbles in a gust of wind. Gogolak kicks another field goal. New York has a six-point lead. Landry has never seemed more composed. He glances at the clock. A little more than two minutes remain.

First and ten. Dallas has the ball on its 45. Things look normal, which is to say they look good. The *toughness* to pull a game out, the sacrifice of a self-extracted wisdom tooth, that has been Landry's lesson to his team. Now Meredith rolls right, now Lance Rentzel is open near the Giants' 20, now the pass hangs on the wind, and now Spider Lockhart is making the sweet interception.

Landry is four feet out on the playing field, shouting, "Dammit, why did you . . ." but he never says who, he never says what. It is dark now in Dallas. The lights are on: dew collects on the pale green grass. It seems much later than it is and Meredith jogs back to the sideline, his face broad with wonder, twisted with regret. The whole thing must seem too stupid for words: while the Cowboys were losing two of their last three games, Meredith went from *third* to *first* on the league passing chart. Too stupid for words . . . too painful. Landry wears that same expression you have seen so often on the lead film preceding all NFL telecasts, that classic eyes-closed-to-earth muffled sob, that God-imploring anxiety caught on film as Landry realized that an illegal-motion penalty had sealed Dallas's defeat in the 1966 championship game in this same stadium, in this same paralyzing dark cold, in this same and endless quest for something attainable in an unattainable sort of a stupid way.

"You don't think it didn't hurt to walk off that field?" Landry asked writers at his press conference the following Wednesday. "There's no criticism *you* could make that could hurt like that."

In Landry's mind it was simple. He had taught them offense, he had taught them defense. He had taught them how to come from behind; he had provided the leadership that gives a man confidence in the system, if not in himself. In some cases . . . in Meredith's case, for example . . . Landry had in fact saved a soul. For what? For what came *next*.

What comes next, Landry is quick to explain, is toughness. He will have to remind them of toughness. Chances are good that they have already reminded themselves, but he will call it to their attention with some very hard work.

"You don't build character without somebody slapping you around," Landry tells his press conference. "We got to the point where we thought we could take it easy and win. Why even my wife was talking of an undefeated season. That's a sure sign of death. . . . I'll tell you this, we'll be a different team *next* week."

Nearly booed to oblivion as a young quarterback, New York's Charlie Conerly became ever more popular with each new gray hair. In his thirty-seventh year, the transformation from roast of the town to toast of the town complete, Charlie handed the reins to Y. A. Tittle, who had been driven from San Francisco by the boo birds and Red Hickey's shotgun. Conerly's return to Clarksdale, Mississippi, however, deprived New York of one of its most elegant and engaging columnists, namely his wife, Perian. This piece is an excerpt from her book *Backseat Quarterback*.

PERIAN CONERLY

To Boo or Not to Boo

Stormy weather? . . . No reminiscence would be complete without some mention of The Lean Years—when the Polo Grounds was festooned with *Back to the farm, Conerly* signs; when catcalls rang out because Charlie often found it necessary to "eat the ball"; and when newspaper accounts of Giant games were frequently unfriendly.

I am told that human nature kindly endows us with the tendency to suppress unpleasant memories and recall more vividly the happier experiences. Nevertheless, in answer to a question about how the foregoing unpleasantries affected our lives, I could not, in good conscience, admit to anything so dramatic as a poignant family scene, fraught with emotion, in which either Charlie or I was visibly desolated by the press notices or the signs or the boos. Not even for the sake of a good story.

I am sure the expressions of disapproval left their scars, but Charlie is a master at hiding his feelings . . . even from me. Describing him as a stoic would not be far from the truth. He never complains. He never offers an alibi. He rarely allows disappointment to affect him. (Exceptions: an unsatisfactory game of cards or golf.) He accepts undeserved criticism and valid censure with equal calm—and without expressing malice toward his detractors in either case. The ravings of his severest critics after a poor performance could never compare with the reproach he gave himself.

As for me, I am a most un-stoical creature. I *do* complain. I alibi. I can always manage to find someone or something to share the blame for anything. Therefore, I too am able to exhibit a calm exterior in the face of adversity. I live in a little world where I am Queen, and the unseemly subjects who berate My King are several kinds of idiot. I must admit that I was taken aback when exposed for the first time to a thunderous chorus of boos directed at Charlie. I had been reared in accordance with my parents' practice that "If you can't say something nice about somebody, don't say anything at all." And of course in college, fans blame the *coach* for everything. I really believe the worst part of it all is feeling the eyes of the other wives as they look sympathetically down the row to see my reaction to the uncomplimentary vocalizing. But I just used to sit there, staring straight ahead, playing Queen.

I think it actually became fashionable to boo Charlie in the early fifties. In one game he completed the first nine passes he threw. When the tenth fell incomplete, the stands booed lustily!

Miles of copy have been written about the fact that the protection given Charlie by his line some years left something to be desired—and that his receivers in those days were not always terribly sure-fingered. I have had players apologize to *me* after a game in which Charlie absorbed a particularly stout drubbing.

"I'm just not big enough," an offensive guard told me once. "I weigh 220 and some of those guys across from me weigh 260. I just can't keep them off of Charlie. What makes it worse, he never complains. Just once I wish he'd give me a little hell in the huddle. It wouldn't make me try any harder, cause I'm trying as hard as I can right now, but I think I'd feel better."

Occasionally shouts of abuse are directed at the wives, but I never reply in kind because that would gratify the insulters. Boo birds are practiced in their art. They have a repertoire of standard replies with which I could never compete and are anxious for the opportunity to play comedian for their fellows. Generally when people sitting near us realize we are players' wives, they tactfully tone down any uncomplimentary remarks that come to mind.

However, after one game during which the Stadium air had been rent with cries of "Get Conerly outa there. We want Heinrich!" a very excited woman was waiting for us at the end of the wives' row. As we approached, she began to shake her fist and shout, "Your husbands stank today, the bums! Especially that bum Conerly!" And on and on.

I ignored her tirade, pretending I was somewhere else (waltzing in the palace ballroom, perhaps). But the fair complexion of the wife walking with me always belies her fiery temper. Whenever she becomes unduly excited a spot of brilliant red appears on each cheek. (We often tease her with, "What's the matter now, Barbara? You've got your clown rouge on.")

Barbara sprang into action. "Let me tell you one thing . . . " she began, her nose almost touching that of the vehement dissident.

The woman was startled, but not silenced. "Eat the ball! Eat the ball! That's all that dumb coward Conerly knows how to do . . . "

Barbara's cheeks turned the color of strawberry soda. "It's obvious that you don't know anything about football or you'd know it takes guts to eat the ball and be plowed under two or three big linemen. Dumb, you say? I'll have you know it takes quick thinking and skill to deliberately throw the ball away when your receivers are covered—just close enough to your own man so the official can't call it intentional grounding, but far enough from the defender covering him to prevent an interception. And if Charlie had had a line in front of him today, he wouldn't have had to do either . . ."

"You must be Mrs. Conerly," the woman jeered.

"No, I am Mrs. *Heinrich!*" Barb replied grandly. Whirling, she took me by the arm and flounced up the steps as only Barbara Heinrich can flounce.

Meanwhile, down on the field . . . "I guess all pro players have 'rabbit ears,'" Charlie observes, "but I imagine quarterbacks have the most sensitive hearing of all. At the Polo Grounds, in order to reach the playing field, we had to pass within a few feet of a section of bleacherites who evidently spent most of their spare time between Sundays thinking up new insults. I think it was a kind of game with them to see who could come up with the cleverest abuse. The fastest running I did on any Sunday was sprinting past that section. I'd always put on my helmet too—to help drown out the static. I don't think the remarks affected my performance one way or the other. But it gets to some fellows. Maybe we should have put up some of those signs they have in zoos: 'Please don't annoy the animals'! Sometimes they would actually lean down and take a swipe at us as we ran by. I'm glad no one ever succeeded in hitting me. I couldn't have ignored that."

As a matter of fact, Charlie did slap a "fan" once. I got the word first from one of the players who preceded him to the apartment after the game. "Well, Charlie hit a kid today," he said, smiling. "I was standing right there and I don't blame him a bit."

I was frantic. A series of imaginary headlines flashed through my mind. POOR SPORT CONERLY ATTACKS CHILD. FATHER INSTITUTES MILLION DOLLAR SUIT. My fears were calmed somewhat as the story unfolded. On the way to the dressing room after a Giant loss, Charlie had been accosted by an unruly teenager, who was as tall as he and much stockier. The big youth cursed Charlie, who ignored him and tried to pass. He blocked his path and began to shove Charlie, calling him every vile name he could think of.

"Take your hands off me . . ." Charlie began. His warning was interrupted as the teenager drew back and threw a punch which glanced off Charlie's shoulder. Charlie slapped him in the face, hard, and ambled off the field.

"I guess I should have turned the other shoulder," he told me later. "I can take the talk, but when somebody starts shoving me around . . ."

Ironically, though the incident followed a Giant defeat, newspaper accounts described the game as "one of Charlie's finest performances." Perhaps the frustrated youngster had bet his week's allowance—from the Parole Board—on the Giants. Or his hard-earned wages—after selling hubcaps.

With the exception of an occasional "Ya bum ya!" directed at Charlie by a dissatisfied customer who recognized him on the street, such expressions of discontent were generally confined to game day. However, one extracurricular demonstration stands out in my memory. Back in 1952 or 1953 the Giants and their wives were invited by the management of Madison Square Garden to attend a Ranger game. Since many of us had never seen ice hockey played, over half the team accepted. We were enjoying the thrilling sport immensely, but our pleasure was short-lived. During an intermission (or third-time) the announcer boomed: "As the guests of the Garden, sitting in section so-and-so, we have the members of the New York Football Giants and their wives. Please stand."

As we rose, the rafters rang with the most deafening booing I have ever heard. I was taken so by surprise that the smile froze on my face, and not until Charlie tugged on my arm did I realize that I was the only one of our group still standing. We decided that only poor sports would leave before the game was over. Besides, we were afraid of another unpleasant demonstration should we stand up again, now that our position had been exposed. So we sat uncomfortably throughout the game, the object of insulting clichés shouted by wiseacres from a safe distance whenever there was a lull in the proceedings.

We lingered until the Garden was nearly empty in order to make our exit as inconspicuous as possible. As we began to shuffle out, a lone dissident far above us on the top row began to bombard Charlie with unflattering epithets. We ignored him. The affronts continued. What the little fellow lacked in stature, he made up in volume.

"Let me handle this, Charlie," offered Arnie Weinmeister, a soft-spoken but fearsome tackle of gigantic proportions. Arnie shouted, "Hey up there!" at the same time taking three or four giant steps toward the vocalizer.

The jeer-leader did not wait to see that Arnie had no intention of real pursuit, but turned and scurried out the nearest exit with an astounding burst of speed.

"We ought to catch that fellow and sign him up as a halfback. He's faster than anybody on the team," cracked Bill Austin.

Jim Duncan smiled. "Yeah, but who could catch him?"

The sting of such incidents was mitigated by a constant trickle of encouraging letters from loyal fans.

Though the scrapbook contains at least one write-up describing every Giant game since 1948, the "bad" games are noticeably less well represented than the good. This inequity stems not from any attempt at whitewashing, but from a dearth of clippings which allude to the unhappier contests. On any ordinary day Charlie often buys and reads all seven New York daily papers; but after an unfortunate game, he resists the temptation.

"I don't mind being knocked when I deserve it, and there are plenty of times I do," he explains. "But *I* know when I play poorly, and reading some reporter's description of it isn't going to help me improve. I'd probably just get mad at some nice guy who is only doing his job. They have to write what they see — but I don't have to read it."

When one of these bad reviews falls into my hands, I am likely to mutter darkly:

"One would think you were the only man on the field today . . ."

To which he replies philosophically, "And reading some of the flattering write-ups of games we won, you might think the same thing. The quarterback receives more than his rightful share of the credit when things go well, so he should be prepared to accept a lion's share of the blame when they don't."

After years of careful consideration (and practical experience) I have arrived at certain conclusions concerning the practice of booing at professional football games. Likely the custom has its roots in ancient Rome, where spectators attending various exhibitions of manly skill and courage commonly expressed disapproval of a gladiator's unsatisfactory performance by turning "thumbs down." Happily, today's losers live to play another day. Therefore, since booing neither influences a coach's decision nor spurs a player to greater effectiveness, it serves no practical purpose other than calling attention to the booer — which is probably the whole idea, after all.

Leaning heavily on an overactive imagination and a vague memory of a course in freshman psychology, I have relegated the booers to several categories. Boos come from:

1. The fellow in the company of friends who know little about football and consider him something of an expert. To prove that he does indeed have a full grasp of the subject he sprinkles his enlightened explanations of the proceedings with rousing cat-calls emitted at the slightest provocation.

2. His friends.

3. The same fellow in the company of his girl friend.

4. His girl friend.

5. The extrovert who has come to the game alone and wishes to strike up a conversation with his neighbors.

6. His neighbors.

7. The introvert who is browbeaten all week by a domineering employer and, unable to strike back at his boss, transfers his wrath to the players on the field, thereby gaining an outlet for his pent-up emotions. (Psychiatrists might do well to recommend this type of therapy to patients suffering from insecurity and inferiority complexes.)

8. The man sitting on his left.

9. The introvert who is browbeaten by his wife.

10. The man sitting on his right.

11. A category already hinted at in numbers 2, 4, 6, 8, and 10 results in Dr. Conerly's maxim: People sitting next to people who boo, boo too. It seems to be a form of mass hysteria participated in by impressionable people caught up in the spirit of the occasion — a mild form of mob violence.

12. The fellow who has come to the game only to get away from the kids for a few hours. He really doesn't know what is happening and therefore is bored. An occasional good boo helps immeasurably to relieve the monotony.

13. The small man who tried out for the team in high school and was told by the coach, "Son, come back when you grow six inches and gain thirty pounds." He has had

no trouble adding the pounds these last ten years, but unfortunately got no taller. He delights in venting his frustration on the king-size players, all of whom represent the star tackle who stole his girl in high school.

14. The big fellow who was told by his high school coach, "Son, come back when you have lost thirty pounds." Folks still call him "Tubby."

How does Charlie feel about being the object of spectator disapproval? Mr. C. contends that the ticket purchased by the malcontent entitles him to express any opinion he might hold — however loudly.

How do I react? I locate the knavish songbird, place him in one of the foregoing categories, and mentally summon the Royal Executioner.

Jack Cusack was a Canton lad of sixteen in 1906 when his town's Bulldogs lost a celebrated 12–6 decision to the archenemy Massillon Tigers. It soon came to light that Canton's coach and captain, Blondy Wallace, had conspired with several of his players to throw the game, thereby costing his team's supporters a bundle in lost bets. The disgust over this episode was enough to put pro football into mothballs until 1912, when Canton reorganized, not as the Bulldogs, a name still too redolent of scandal, but as simply the Professionals. Cusack became their manager. Here is his story of how the Canton eleven, bolstered by a Jim Thorpe still in his prime, came to revive their historic rivalry with Massillon.

JACK CUSACK

Jim Thorpe and the Canton Bulldogs

Late in 1914, I was faced with a personal career decision. After seven years in the gas company office I was now, at twenty-three, the chief clerk, the only employee entrusted with the combination of the money vault, my principal duty being to take charge of the daily cash receipts and make the bank deposits. A year before, I had been told by Ralph Gallagher, the general superintendent (and later president of the Standard Oil of New Jersey), that I would have to give up football or resign from the company, and I promptly resigned. Mr. Gallagher, however, relented and gave me a year's extension, and now my time of grace was up.

"Well," said Mr. Gallagher, "what shall it be—football or the company?"

"Football," I replied—for I felt that the professional setup had a bright financial future, which proved true for me as well as for some of the others who followed after me.

The year 1915 brought the beginning of the big-time era in professional football, and happily it brought Massillon back into play. A group of Massillon businessmen, headed by Jack Whalen and Jack Donahue, invited me to a meeting to discuss details, and they were now willing to agree with the principles I held out for the year before. Their decision to field a team brought back the old rivalry that all of us needed so badly and furnished the drawing power that meant good gates. With the return of Massillon, another pleasant thing occurred — the sportswriters, having all but forgotten the 1906 scandal, began referring to the old rivals again as the Canton Bulldogs and the Massillon Tigers. We were back in business once more at the old stand.

I knew that in order to compete properly with Massillon we had to secure for Canton the best available talent, so I contacted every All-American I could locate, either by mail or personally, but found the response somewhat reluctant. The colleges and most sportswriters around the country were opposed to professional football, as were many of the coaches and graduate players, and many of those I contacted refused to play. Some of those who did agree to consider playing jobs insisted on the use of assumed names, particularly the coaches, who wanted to protect their jobs. The various clubs booked the strongest teams possible from around the nation but only four were outstanding in 1915 — Canton, Massillon, Youngstown, and Columbus. Peggy Parratt withdrew from Akron at this time but did place a fine team in Cleveland the following year.

The Canton Bulldogs opened the 1915 season with Wheeling, West Virginia, and racked up a 75–0 victory, and on October 18 we defeated the Columbus Panhandles, 7–0. Meanwhile, I succeeded in strengthening the Bulldogs with some of the star players of that era, one of the best recruits being Bill Gardner, a great tackle or end from Carlisle, the government's famous Indian school in Pennsylvania. Another was Hube Wagner, an All-American end and former captain at Pitt who had been picked second All-American by sportswriters 26 times during his college career. I also signed Greasy Neale, then coach at West Virginia Wesleyan, an outstanding end and halfback with considerable All-American mention. I also acquired John Kelleson, a fine tackle, assistant coach to Neale.

On October 25 we lost, 3–9, to the Detroit Heralds in a hardfought game on their home grounds. This was our first defeat by the Heralds, with whom we had contested during the two previous seasons. On November 1 we defeated the Cincinnati Colts, 41–12; the Colts had a better team than the score indicates because their players were largely former college stars. And on November 8 we took a 38–0 victory over the Altoona Indians, composed mainly of Carlisle stars and self-styled "champions of Pennsylvania."

Then, just in time for Canton's first game with the newly revived Massillon Tigers, I hit the jackpot by signing the famous Jim Thorpe, the Sac and Fox Indian from Oklahoma who was rated then (and still is today) as the greatest footballer and all-around athlete that the world of sports has ever seen!

He had first won world acclaim as the one-man track team who swept the 1912 Olympics for the United States at Stockholm, Sweden; he had been the backbone of the Carlisle football team during his school years there, a powerfully built halfback who was unequaled anywhere as a line smasher, kicker, and runner; and he was destined to become, at a later time, a top-rated baseball outfielder with the New York Giants, the Boston Braves, and the Cincinnati Reds.

In 1915, when I conceived the idea of hiring this already living legend of sportdom, Jim had lost his amateur standing (and his Stockholm medals) because he had played a little semi-pro baseball for $25 a week, and at the moment he was doing backfield coaching at the University of Indiana. I sent Bill Gardner, his old Carlisle teammate, over to Indiana to see him, and shortly thereafter I had Thorpe under contract to play for the Canton Bulldogs for $250 a game. The signing also marked the start of a warm friendship between us that lasted until Jim died of a heart attack, in 1953.

Some of my business "advisers" frankly predicted that I was leading the Bulldogs into bankruptcy by paying Jim the enormous sum of $250 a game, but the deal paid off even beyond my greatest expectations. Jim was an attraction as well as a player, and whereas our paid attendance averaged around 1,200 before we took him on, we filled the Massillon and Canton parks for the next two games—6,000 for the first and 8,000 for the second. All the fans wanted to see the big Indian in action.

The first game was played at Massillon and Canton was defeated, 0–16. Here were the starting lineups:

CANTON 0		MASSILLON 16
AXTEL, Kenyon	LE	ROCKNE, Notre Dame
EDWARDS, Notre Dame	LT	JONES, Notre Dame
POWELL, Ohio State	LG	COLE, Unknown
SCHULTZ, Sandlot	C	LEE, Unknown
SCHLOTT, Sandlot	RG	PORTMANN, W. Reserve
WALDSMITH, Akron U.	RT	CAMPBELL, Unknown
GARDNER, Carlisle	RE	FINNEGAN, Notre Dame
HAMILTON, Notre Dame	QB	DORAIS, Notre Dame
WAGNER, U. Pitt	LH	BRIGGS, Ohio State
JULIAN, Mich. Aggies	RH	FLEMING, W&J
PETERS, Carlisle	FB	HANLEY, W. Reserve

Touchdown—Hanley.

Goal from TD—Fleming.

Field goals from dropkick—Dorais, 3.

Substitutions, Canton—Drumm for Schlott; Raymond for Waldsmith; Waldsmith for Schultz; Speck for Powell; Wagner for Gardner; Gardner for Axtel; Thorpe for Wagner; Wagner for Julian; Julian for Peters; Peters for Julian; Julian for Thorpe; Neale for Wagner; Julian for Peters; Thorpe for Julian.

Substitutions, Massillon—Kagy for Finnegan; Collins for Hogan; Bowie for Kagy; Kagy for Fleming; Fleming for Kagy; Kagy for Bowie.

Referee—Connors.   Umpire—Durfee.   Head Linesman—Bast.

Most of the Massillon lineup played under assumed names which still remain unknown to me, but if you will take a look at the Massillon roster in the preceding box you will find at least one player who was using his correct name. The Rockne listed there is the famous Knute, who already was putting Notre Dame on the map and who was destined to go down in football history as that university's greatest great among its players and coaches. Rockne, as left end, and his Notre Dame teammate, Quarterback Dorais, made a tricky and famous combination on passes.

In order for the reader of this narrative to have the full import of the first 1915 Canton-Massillon game, I quote from the writeup of Warren Cross, a highly respected sports scribe for *The Canton Repository*, who recently retired after half a century of reporting:

> Only the slippery surface of the field kept the Indian [Thorpe], ideal in build and a finished football man, from scoring at least one touchdown. In the second period he broke through the Massillon defense and headed for the goal, with only Dorais in his path. In attempting to get by the Massillon luminary he lost his footing and slipped, going out of bounds on the 8-yard line. On another occasion, after skirting Massillon's left end, he slipped with almost a clear field in front of him. He was the only Canton man feared by the Massillon defense. He showed the 6,000 yelling fans the reason for this fear.
>
> Fisher [Greasy Neale], the unknown halfback from the East, and Carp Julian were the only other Canton men able to accomplish anything. For Massillon, in addition to Dorais, there stood out Fullback Hanley and Ed Kagy, Captain. The first scoring came in the first quarter when Dorais of Massillon dropped the ball over from the 28-yard line. Just before the close of the period, Thorpe trotted onto the field, heralded by cheers from 6,000 throats. He took left half.
>
> Early in the second quarter, a pass from Dorais to Kagy took the ball to the Canton two-yard line. Canton held for three downs. On the fourth attempt, Hanley plunged through. Fleming booted the goal. Score: Massillon 10, Canton 0.
>
> After the next kickoff and the exchange of punts that followed, Canton made its best showing. Gardner intercepted a pass on Canton's 41-yard line. Thorpe grabbed a short pass over the line for nine yards and then shot outside of Massillon's left tackle for the longest run of the game. He covered 40 yards before he slipped and went out of bounds on the 8-yard line. Massillon's line held, Canton making only four yards in three attempts. On the fourth down Julian shot a pass over center, the ball was batted down by a Massillon forward and into the arms of Guard Drumm. He pushed through and over the goal line, but the touchdown was not allowed. Umpire Durfee ruling that a Canton man had touched the ball before it was batted down

by the Massillon lineman. Protest was unavailing, although it appeared to be a legal touchdown for Canton. Not until late in the third quarter could Massillon score again. Then Dorais scored a dropkick from the 42-yard line. An intercepted pass by Massillon paved the way for the last scoring, another Dorais dropkick from the 45-yard line.

After a lapse of nine years barren of the intense rivalry that has always been the outstanding feature of the athletic relations between the two cities, the same old Massillon Jinx still holds its mystic power over Canton. Massillon and the Jinx conquered, 16 to 0.

In preparation for our second game with Massillon, to be played at Canton on November 29, I further bolstered the Bulldogs with the addition of Robert Butler, Walter Camp's All-American tackle from the University of Wisconsin; Abel, another Camp All-American tackle from Colgate; and Charlie Smith, a fine tackle from the Michigan Aggies, and to my knowledge the first Negro to play professional football.* Jim Thorpe was now serving as the Canton captain.

And here were the lineups for that second game:

<table>
<tr><td colspan="4" align="center">CANTON 6</td><td colspan="2" align="center">MASSILLON 0</td></tr>
<tr><td>GARDNER, Carlisle</td><td>............</td><td>LE</td><td>.......</td><td>ROCKNE, Notre Dame</td></tr>
<tr><td>ABEL, Colgate</td><td>...............</td><td>LT</td><td>.......</td><td>JONES, Unknown</td></tr>
<tr><td>EDWARDS, Notre Dame</td><td>........</td><td>LG</td><td>.......</td><td>COLE, Unknown</td></tr>
<tr><td>WALDSMITH, Akron U.</td><td>.........</td><td>C</td><td>.....</td><td>HAES, Unknown</td></tr>
<tr><td>DAVIS, Indiana U.</td><td>............</td><td>RG</td><td>.......</td><td>PORTMANN, W. Reserve</td></tr>
<tr><td>BUTLER, Wisconsin</td><td>............</td><td>RT</td><td>.......</td><td>DAY, Unknown</td></tr>
<tr><td>WAGNER, U. Pitt</td><td>.............</td><td>RE</td><td>.......</td><td>KAGY, W. Reserve</td></tr>
<tr><td>LAMBERT, Wabash</td><td>............</td><td>QB</td><td>.......</td><td>DORAIS, Notre Dame</td></tr>
<tr><td>THORPE, Carlisle</td><td>..............</td><td>LH</td><td>.......</td><td>KELLEHER, Notre Dame</td></tr>
<tr><td>NEALE, W. Va. Wesleyan</td><td>......</td><td>RH</td><td>.......</td><td>FLEMING, W&J</td></tr>
<tr><td>JULIAN, Mich. Aggies</td><td>.........</td><td>FB</td><td>.......</td><td>HANLEY, W. Reserve</td></tr>
</table>

Canton scoring—Dropkick by Thorpe; placekick by Thorpe.

Substitutions, Canton—Smith for Abel; Speck for Edwards; White for Lambert; Schultz for Waldsmith.

Substitutions, Massillon—Cherry for Kagy; Sacksteder for Kelleher; Briggs for Sacksteder.

Referee—Conners of Bates.   Umpire—Cosgrove of Cornell.   Head Linesman—Jones of Ohio State.   Timers—MacGregor of Canton and Bast of Massillon.

*Researcher Milt Roberts has revealed that the first black pro was Charles W. Follis of the 1904 Shelby, Ohio team. The first black in the NFL was Rock Island's Bobby Marshall.—ED.

Our Canton park would hold as many as 8,000 people, but on this November afternoon we had an overflow crowd of spectators. Not wanting to lose any gate admissions, we sold standing room in the end zones and, in agreement with Massillon, adopted ground rules providing that any player crossing the goal line into the crowd must be in possession of the ball when he emerged from the crowd—and as things turned out, this proved to be a lucky break for Canton.

The contest was a hard-fought, nerve-knotting game with both teams about equally matched on line play. We were able to make but two first downs on line play, while Massillon was held to one. We made several forward pass attempts without completing one, while Massillon completed four. Jim Thorpe succeeded in making a dropkick from the 18-yard line and later followed up with a placement kick from the 45, giving Canton a 6–0 advantage. Massillon was held scoreless in the first three quarters, but in the final quarter the visitors opened their stock of passes and the situation began to look bad for Canton.

At this juncture I saw that something was wrong with Abel, our new tackle. Our opponents were making far too much yardage through his position, and when Captain Thorpe made no move to replace him I took it upon myself to do so—in keeping with an agreement I had with Thorpe that it would be my right to substitute from the bench if I felt it to be necessary. (I might mention, too, that Jim was sometimes hesitant to substitute, especially as to replacing a player with All-American qualifications.) I found that Abel was ill with a heavy cold, and I replaced him with Charlie Smith, the Negro from Michigan Aggies.

Then, with only a few minutes left to play, the fireworks really started. Briggs, right end for Massillon, caught a forward pass on our 15-yard line and raced across our goal line right into the midst of the "Standing Room Only" customers. Briggs fumbled—or at least he was said to have and the ball popped out of the crowd right into the hands of Charlie Smith, the Canton substitute who had been following in hot pursuit. Referee Conners, mindful of the ground rules made before the game, ruled the play a touchback, but Briggs had something to say about that.

"I didn't fumble!" protested the Massillon end. "That ball was kicked out of my hands by a policeman—a uniformed policeman!"

That was ridiculous on the face of it. Briggs was either lying or seeing things that didn't happen to be there—for most everybody knew that Canton had no uniformed policemen in those days. But Briggs was unable to accept this solid fact.

"It *was* a policeman!" he insisted. "I saw the brass buttons on his coat."

Both teams had a lot going on this end-zone play. The 1915 championship of the so-called Ohio League was at stake, along with "championship of the world," as the sportswriters called it. If Referee Conners' decision were allowed to stand, Canton had the title wrapped up by 6–0, while if Briggs' touchdown had been completed the score would have been 6–6, giving Massillon the undisputed championship.

The spectators, brightly aware of all this, could stand the strain and tension no longer. With only three minutes left to play, the fans—of both Massillon and Canton persuasion—broke down the fences surrounding the playing area and swarmed across the field by the thousands, the Massillon fans protesting the referee's decision, the Canton citizens defending it. The officials strove manfully to clear the field and resume play but found the task impossible and called the game.

It wasn't all over yet, however. The Massillon team and its loyal supporters demanded that the game officials settle the matter conclusively by making a statement on the referee's decision, and at last they agreed to do so—on the condition that the statement be sealed and given to Manager Langford of the Courtland Hotel, to be opened and read by him at thirty minutes after midnight. This arrangement was made in order to give the officials plenty of time to get out of town and escape any wrath that might descend upon them from either side. Tension remained high throughout the evening, and the hotel lobby was filled with a bedlam of argument until Manager Langford read the statement at 12:30 A.M. It backed Referee Conners' touchback decision, saying that it was proper under the ground rules, and the Canton Bulldogs and Massillon tied for the championship.

The "Mystery of the Phantom Policeman" who had caused Briggs of Massillon so much unhappiness was solved about ten years later, long after I had left professional football and had gone to live in Oklahoma. While on a visit back to Canton I had occasion to ride a streetcar, on which I was greeted by an old friend, the brass-buttoned conductor. We began reminiscing about the old football days, and the conductor told me what had happened during that crucial final-quarter play back in 1915. Briggs, when he plunged across the goal line into the end zone spectators, fell at the feet of the conductor, who promptly kicked the ball from Briggs' hands into the arms of Canton's Charlie Smith.

"Why on earth did you do a thing like that?" I asked.

"Well," he said, "it was like this—I had thirty dollars bet on that game and, at my salary, I couldn't afford to lose that much money."

And that's how the Canton Bulldogs tied for the 1915 championship—on Jim Thorpe's two field kicks, with assists from a streetcar conductor and a lucky catch by Charlie Smith.

In a mid-November meeting of these two teams, the Bears drove down to the Washington 6-yard line; trailing 7–3, they had time enough for only one more play. Sid Luckman rifled a pass in the end zone to Bill Osmanski, who couldn't hold it. The infuriated Bears claimed that defensive back Frank Filchock had interfered with the receiver but to no avail. Afterward Redskins owner George Marshall, whose mortifying propensity for shooting from the lip was on display in the first piece in this volume, said to newsmen: "The Bears are front runners, quitters. They're not a second-half team, just a bunch of crybabies." Whoops. Three weeks later the front-running crybabies, despite a lead of 28–0, did not quit at halftime; in the next thirty minutes they scored 45 more.

ARTHUR DALEY

Bears 73, Redskins 0: December 8, 1940

The weather was perfect. So were the Bears. In the most fearsome display of power ever seen on any gridiron, the monsters of the Midway won the Ed Thorp Memorial Trophy, symbolic of the world football championship, before 36,034 stunned and deriding fans in Griffith Stadium this balmy afternoon.

It being a Sunday, the Washington Humane Society had the day off. So the Bears had nothing to combat in the playoff except the Redskins, who were pretty feeble opposition indeed. Hence it was that the Chicago Bears scalped the Capital Indians, 73–0, the highest score in the history of the National Football League.

This was simply dreadful. The only question before the house was whether the Bears could score more points when they were on the offensive or when Washington was on the offensive.

Before fifty-six seconds had passed the Bears had a tally. Then, when the second half began, they cut that time down, registering another marker in fifty-four seconds.

There never was anything quite like this. Three weeks ago the Redskins edged out the Bears, 7–3. Today it was something else again. Chicago was a perfect football team that played football of such exquisite class that Washington could not have won with a brick wall and line of howitzers instead of backs. The Bears would have battered down everything.

By the second half the Redskins showed a marked improvement. Their defense against points after touchdown had reached such perfection that four out of seven were missed. Washington had the misfortune to have to face a team that could have beaten the other nine elevens in the league just as badly.

This was football at its very best. The Bears had the timing for their quick opening plays down to the hundredth of a second. They riddled the Redskins at will with the overwhelming power of their ground game, rocked them with their infrequent passes, and smothered them with their defensive power. The blocking was fiendishly accurate and it almost was a physical impossibility for them to make a mistake.

The Bears registered three touchdowns in the first period, one in the second, four in the third, and three in the last. Halas used every eligible man on his squad, thirty-three of them, and fifteen had a share of the scoring.

Halas used Sid Luckman, an Old Blue from Columbia, as his first-half quarterback, and no field general ever called plays more artistically or engineered a touchdown parade in more letter-perfect fashion. But the Lion sat out the second half and still the mastodons from the Midwest rolled.

Ray Flaherty's young men were physically in the game, but that was all. After Bill Osmanski had romped 68 yards for the first touchdown, the 'Skins reached the Bear 26, only to have Bob Masterson's 32-yard field-goal effort fail. That was a blow from which George Preston Marshall's lads never recovered. Had they scored, it might have been different.

The first touchdown was a 75-yard zip to a score. George McAfee picked up seven yards and then Osmanski, cutting inside Washington's right tackle, went 68 yards more. George Wilson erased two men with the same block to clear the way for the counter.

Then the Bears rolled 80 yards in seventeen plays, the payoff being Luckman's quarterback sneak from the six-inch line. A moment later Joe Maniaci, the old Fordham Flash, streaked 42 yards for another counter. Jack Manders, Bob Snyder, and Phil Martinovich added the extra points and it was 21–0.

Redskin fans who had watched their heroes win their first seven games of the league season could not believe their eyes. Yet even they were to become convinced that they were watching one of the greatest football teams of all time in action.

The Bears reached the 16 in the second quarter and fumbled. Washington made a gesture by going 63 yards to the 18 on ten successive passes, only to lose the ball on downs. Ray Nolting boomed through with one of the eight Bear pass interceptions and the victors were off to the races. Luckman flipped a 30-yarder to Ken Kavanaugh in the end zone for another counter. Snyder converted.

The third quarter saw the Redskins give up the ghost. Hampton Pool, an end, intercepted Sammy Baugh's lateral flick to Jimmy Johnston on the 16 for a marker. Then the Capital crew tried a fourth-down pass from their 33. It was batted down. So the Bears took over. Nolting gained 10 yards. But he was just warming up. On the next play he burst through the middle, feinted Baugh into the middle of the Potomac on the 8 and went across standing up.

McAfee intercepted a Roy Zimmerman pass for 35 yards of gorgeous broken-field running for a touchdown and Joe Stydahar split the bars with a placement. The Redskins made an effort to score, reaching the 16, only to lose the ball on downs. Later, Zimmerman's pass was intercepted by Bulldog Turner on the 30. He scored, thanks to a block by Pool, and it was 54–0.

The league champions rumbled 74 yards for their next touchdown in the fourth quarter, Harry Clark going 42 yards on a double reverse for the tally. On this he feinted Frank Filchock into Chesapeake Bay.

The hapless Redskins' Filchock fumbled in the shadow of his goal posts. Jack Torrance, the reformed shot-put world-record holder, fell on the ball on the 2. So Famiglietti burst across on a quick opener. The last touchdown resulted from a 52-yard drive that was culminated by a one-yard dance by Clark through the middle.

There was no Redskin hero outside of Flaherty, who had to sit on the bench and absorb it all, too much of a beating for so fine a gentleman and coach. The Bears had thirty-three heroes. Luckman, Nolting, McAfee, Osmanski, and Maniaci in the backfield were outstanding. So were Lee Artoe, Stydahar, Danny Fortmann, Turner, and Plasman in the line.

The day was gorgeous. The crowd was representative, with high government officials scattered throughout the stands. Everything was under the control of the Magnificent Marshall, except the Bears.

At the end the Redskin band played "Should Auld Acquaintance Be Forgot." If said acquaintance is the Chicago Bears, it should be forgot immediately. At the moment the Bears are the greatest football team of all time.

As the totality of a man's life is said to flash before his eyes in the moment of dying, so is the quarterback's vision a kaleidoscope of linked images as he fades back, flirting with annihilation. One of America's most honored poets, James Dickey is a former college athlete of note who knows whereof he speaks. This poem is taken from his 1970 collection entitled *The Eye-Beaters, Blood, Victory, Madness, Buckhead and Mercy*.

JAMES DICKEY

In the Pocket

Going backward
All of me and some
Of my friends are forming a shell   my arm is looking
Everywhere and some are breaking
In   breaking down
And out   breaking
Across, and one is going deep   deeper
Than my arm.   Where is Number One hooking
Into the violent green alive
With linebackers?   I cannot find him he cannot beat
His man   I fall back more
Into the pocket   it is raging and breaking
Number Two has disappeared into the chalk
Of the sideline   Number Three is cutting with half
A step of grace   my friends are crumbling
Around me the wrong color
Is looming   hands are coming
Up and over between
My arm and Number Three: throw it hit him in the middle
Of his enemies   hit move scramble
Before death and the ground
Come up   LEAP STAND KILL DIE STRIKE
Now.

Before the days of domed stadia and neutral-site Super Bowls, bad weather was no stranger to the NFL championship game — the frozen field of 1934, the arctic temperatures of 1945 and 1967, the mud of 1949 and 1964. But only one such game was ever played in a continuous, driving snow, and that was the Blizzard Bowl described below. The ankle-deep snow took away the pass and the end run as well as the yard markers, giving the hardy souls in attendance a time-machine look at what pro football was like before 1900. After three scoreless periods, those few cognoscenti who kept up with rule changes shuddered at the realization that if neither team could score, the new sudden-death provision would be in effect, and they might never get home.

LOUIS EFFRAT

Eagles 7, Cardinals 0: December 19, 1948

Perhaps the National Football League playoff between the Philadelphia Eagles and the Chicago Cardinals should not have been held today at Shibe Park. A driving snowstorm providing a four-inch fall that completely covered the gridiron eliminated any pretense of a true football test. Postponement would have been in order and fair to all concerned, including players and spectators.

However, don't say that in the presence of any faithful Philadelphia followers. Wet, cold, and uncomfortable though they might have been, they were happy because, on this snow-bound afternoon in the City of Brotherly Love, a sixteen-year-old dream came true. The Eagles won their first league — Commissioner Bert Bell insists it's the "world" — championship by beating the defending Cardinals, 7–0.

There will be some who will say that Greasy Neale's charges registered an upset over the Chicagoans, who were favored to win by 3½ points. But the victors never agreed that they should have been cast in the role of underdogs. All along they rated themselves at least the equals of the Cardinals, this despite the record that showed five straight triumphs over the Eagles by Jimmy Conzelman's men. Two of these were in exhibitions and one was the 28–21 conquest in the playoff at Chicago last year.

Because they believed in themselves, the Eagles never gave the Cardinals a real opportunity to show to advantage. Not once did the visitors advance deeper into Philadelphia territory than the 30-yard line. This they reached late in the first period and Pat Harder's attempt for a 37-yard field goal missed. The Cards got to the 39 in the second and to the 31 in the third. In the fourth they got nowhere, handling the ball for only six plays in the final fifteen minutes.

Charley Trippi, Elmer Angsman, and Harder, with Ray Mallouf quarterbacking the plays, were unable to make serious inroads and at no time succeeded in making a gain longer than eleven yards. It was different on the other side.

Steve Van Buren, the league's leading individual ground-gainer and the hero of today's contest, rarely was stopped and once he exploded for 26 yards. Bosh Pritchard, who did most of the wide running, hit for 16 on another play and Tommy Thompson ran and field-generated his club flawlessly. Statistics will convince all that the Eagles outplayed the Cardinals by a wide margin. It was 16–5 in first downs and 225 yards to 96 in running. The passing on both sides was negligible, of course, because of the wretched weather.

Despite the one-sidedness of the action, which saw the Eagles dominate the battle virtually all the way — Cliff Patton tried but missed three field goals, failing from 15, 34, and 44 — the home team needed to solve two problems before it was able to achieve the victory.

First, the Eagles needed a "break" and, if and when it did materialize, they needed to make the most of it. Held scoreless through three periods, the men of Neale waited patiently. It finally came in the closing minute of the third quarter when Mallouf, trying to hand off to Trippi on his own 19, fumbled. Frank Kilroy, the big guard from Temple, playing his seventh year in the professional loop, was on the spot to recover for Philadelphia on the 17.

Time remained for only one play in this period and Pritchard, taking a handoff from Thompson after the latter had faked a pitchout to Van Buren, ripped through for six yards. Then the teams changed sides to start the last fifteen minutes. Based on the earlier action, there was little reason to believe that the Eagles would go all the way without the aid of skis or snowshoes. They had been sloshing and slipping in the snow all afternoon.

Anyway, it was second down on the Chicago 11 when play was resumed and Joe Muha, who had done some excellent punting for the Eagles, gained three to the 8. On a quarterback sneak, Thompson went for a first down on the 5. It was then that Van Buren, former Louisiana State ace, turned the trick. Taking the handoff from Thompson, Van Buren crashed outside his own right tackle and reached the end zone.

Right then and there the Cardinals were beaten. The 28,864 fans who braved the elements to witness this playoff knew it. The Eagles knew it and the Cardinals knew it. However, Patton came in to placekick the extra point, his sixty-first in a row this year and his sixty-seventh straight since last year.

The game's lone touchdown was fashioned in 0:53 of the fourth quarter. The remaining fourteen minutes and seven seconds saw the Eagles maintaining possession most of the time. In fact, when the clock ran out, Philadelphia was on Chicago's 2-yard line.

Starting a half hour late, this contest presented a difficult problem for the spectators and the experts. There were no line markers anywhere and this resulted in much guesswork. Commissioner Bell ruled that there would be no measurements, with referee Ronald Gibbs being the sole judge of first downs and touchdowns. Three alternate officials, in addition to the regular five, operated along the sidelines and in the end zone.

Of course, anything spectacular was out of the question. The nearest approach to an eye opener came the first time the Eagles gained possession. They had kicked off to Chicago, which failed to advance and Mallouf punted to the Philadelphia 35. There Thompson fired a long pass to Jack Ferrante who, though covered by two defenders, caught the ball on the Cardinal 20. His face in the snow when he fell, Ferrante was the first to untrack himself and, while the two Chicagoans sprawled in the snow, he picked himself up and mushed into the end zone.

"Touchdown!" the fans yelled.

"Offside," said linesman Charley Berry. The Eagles forfeited five yards, not to mention the 65 and 6 points they thought they had earned. Thereafter, it was a matter of sloshing around in the white snow until Kilroy recovered Mallouf's fumble and Van Buren made the game-winning tally.

The running of Van Buren, who carried 26 times and gained 98 yards, and the sweeping of Pritchard, along with the beautiful faking and ballhandling of Thompson, heretofore noted because of his passing, highlighted the encounter, as Philadelphia became the first Eastern team to annex the title since Washington did it in 1942.

Frederick Exley's *A Fan's Notes*, a first novel published in 1968, quickly became a cult classic of the campus. It is no more "about" pro football than *A Remembrance of Things Past* is about a biscuit. As this excerpt from Chapter Two opens, Exley is recoiling from life's disappointments by confining himself to his aunt's couch. He might have stayed there, too, if it hadn't been for Steve Owen and Frank Gifford.

FREDERICK EXLEY

"I Know Steve Owen. I Know Frank Gifford, Too."

For months I hadn't been able to read anything except advertisements. Sustaining my literary fantasy had required such fierce concentration that my energies were not in long enough supply for even cursory reading, but now, in boredom, I forced myself to read. Even then I did not at first understand what was happening to New York Giants coach Steve Owen. The newspapers kept using the euphemisms "retiring" and "resigning," and it was only after I had gone to the columnists that I began to piece together the truth. When I did so, I was outraged. Owen always had maintained that defenses win football games. Professional football was increasingly deferring to the forward pass as the ultimate and only weapon, and apparently Owen was being asked to step aside by men whose vision of the game proclaimed it unalterably given over to offensive techniques. These "men" were, of course, shadowy, never identified; but one had only to understand the childishly petulant character of the New York sportswriter (he takes every New York defeat as if he had been out there having his own face rubbed in the dirt) to know who the men were. Owen had been losing for a number of years now, and the writers had been on him. Victorious, there was something nauseatingly reprehensible in their doleful, sentimental invitations to the public to come to the Polo Grounds on Sunday to witness Owen's swan song as head coach.

I never would have left the davenport that murderously damp Sunday in 1953 had I not read that Frank Gifford was starting for the Giants at halfback. When I read that, my mind — as isolated minds are wont to do, offered the least stimulation — began to fabricate for itself a rather provocative little drama. I began to imagine how wonderful it would be if Gifford single-handedly devastated the Detroit Lions as a farewell present for Owen. I had had encounters with both of these men at different times in my life. In a way both had given me something, Gifford a lesson in how to live with one's scars, and Owen no less than perhaps my first identity as a human being. And so that bleak, cold Sunday, I rose — to the astonishment of my aunt, I might add — from the davenport, bundled up as warmly as I could, took the commuting train to Grand Central, sought directions to the Polo Grounds, and got on the subway to the Bronx.

I met Steve Owen in the late thirties or early forties, when I was somewhere between the ages of eight and eleven. I suspect it was closer to the time I was eight, for I remember very little of what was said, remembering more the character of the meeting — that it was not an easy one. My father introduced me to him, or rather my father, when the atmosphere was most strained and the conversation had lagged, shoved me in front of Owen and said, "This is my son, Fred."

"Are you tough?" Owen said.

"Pardon, sir?"

"*Are you tough?*"

"I don't know, sir."

Owen looked at my father. "Is he tough, Mr. Exley?"

Though more than anything I wanted my father to say that I was, I was not surprised at this answer.

"It's too soon to tell."

Owen was surprised, though. He had great blondish-red eyebrows, which above his large rimless glasses gave him an astonished expression. Now he looked baffled. As the meeting had not been a comfortable one to begin with, he said in a tone that signaled the end of the conversation, "*I'm sure he's tough, Mr. Exley.*" Turning abruptly on his heels, he walked across the lobby to the elevator of his hotel, where this meeting took place.

This was a few years after my father had quit playing football, when he was managing the Watertown [New York] semiprofessional team, the Red and Black. A team that took on all challengers and invariably defeated them, they were so good that — stupefying as it seems — the ostensible reason for our journey to New York had been to discuss with Owen the possibility of the Red and Black's playing in exhibition against the Giants. I say "stupefying" now; but that is retrospectively fake sophistication: I thought we could beat the Giants then, and I use the "we" with the glibness of one who was committed unalterably to the team's fortunes—the water boy. On the wall in the bar of the Watertown Elks' Club hangs a picture of that team; seated on the ground before the smiling, casual, and disinterested players is an anguishingly solemn boy— the solemnity attesting to the esteem in which I held my station. I still can remember with what pride I trotted, heavy water bucket and dry towels in hand, onto the field to minister to the combatants' needs. Conversely, I recall the shame I experienced one day when, the team's having fallen behind, the captain decided to adopt a spartan posture and deprive his charges of water, and he had ordered me back from the field, waving me off when I was almost upon the huddle. My ministrations denied in full view of the crowd, I had had to turn and trot, redfaced, back to the bench. Yes, I believed we could beat the Giants then. Long before Owen so adroitly put my father down, though, I had come to see that the idea of such a contest was not a good one.

The trip began on a depressing note. The night before we were to leave, my father got loaded and ran into a parked car, smashing in the front fenders of our Model A Ford roadster. It was one time—in retrospect—that my father's drinking seemed excusable. Such a journey in those days was one of near-epic proportions, made only at intervals of many years and at alarming sacrifices to the family budget; I have no doubt that that night my father was tremulous with apprehension, caught up in the spirit of *bon voyage,* and that he drank accordingly. Be that as it may, because he was drunk he left the scene of the accident; and the next day, fearing that the police might be searching for a damaged car, my mother wouldn't let him take the Ford from the garage. For many hours it was uncertain whether we should make the trip at all; but at the last moment, more, I think, because I had been promised the trip than for any other reason, it was decided we should go on the train.

We rode the whole night sitting up in the day coach, without speaking. My father was hung over, deeply ashamed, and there was a horrifying air of furtiveness hanging over us, as if we were fleeing some unspeakable crime. As a result, the trip—which might have been a fantastic adventure—never rose above this unhappy note. In New York we shared a room at the YMCA (I can remember believing that only the impossibly rich ever stayed in hotels), and the visit was a series of small, debilitating defeats; bland, soggy food eaten silently in barnlike automats; a room that varied arbitrarily between extreme heat and cold; a hundred and one missed subway connections; the Fordham-Pittsburgh game's having been sold out; the astonishment I underwent at no one's knowing my father; and finally, the fact that our meeting with Owen, which I had been led to believe was prearranged, was nothing more than wishful thinking on my father's part.

I don't know how many times we went to Owen's hotel, but each time we were told that he was "out." Each time we returned to the YMCA a little more tired, a little more defeated, and with each trip the Giants' players whose names I knew, Ken Strong and Ward Cuff and Tuffy Leemans and Mel Hein, began to loom as large and forbidding as the skyscrapers. At one point I knew, though I daren't say so to my father, that the idea of such a game was preposterous. Moreover, for the first time in my life I began to understand the awesome vanity and gnawing need required to take on New York City with a view to imposing one's personality on the place. This was a knowledge that came to haunt me in later years.

It was not until my father, his voice weary, suggested that we make one final trip to the hotel that I saw that he, too, was disheartened. All the way there I prayed that Owen still would be "out." I had come to see that the meeting was undesired by him, and I feared the consequences of our imposition. The moment we walked into the lobby, however, the desk clerk (who had, I'm sure, come to feel sorry for us) began furiously stabbing the air in the direction of a gruff-looking, bespectacled, and stout man rolling, seamanlike, in the direction of the elevator—a fury that only could have signaled that it was Owen. My father moved quickly across the lobby, stopped him, and began the conversation that ended with Owen's *I'm sure he's tough, Mr. Exley.* As I say, I don't remember a good deal of the conversation prior to my being introduced; I do remember that Owen, too, thought the idea of such a contest ridiculous. Worse than that, my father already had been told as much by mail, and I think that his having made the trip in the face of such a refusal struck Owen as rather nervy, accounting for the uneasiness of the meeting. On Owen's leaving, I did not dare look at my father. It wasn't so much that I had ever lived in fear of him as that I had never before seen any man put him down, and I was not prepared to test his reaction to a humiliation that I unwittingly had caused. Moreover, my father's shadow was so imposing that I scarcely had ever, until that moment, had any identity of my own. At the same time I had yearned to emulate and become my father, I also had longed for his destruction. Steve Owen not only gave me identity; he proved to me my father was vulnerable.

On the subway going up to the Polo Grounds, I was remembering that meeting and contemplating the heavy uneasiness of it all anew when suddenly, feeling myself inordinately cramped, I looked up out of my reverie to discover that the car was jammed and that I somehow had got smack among the members of a single family—an astonishing family, a family so incredible that for the first time in my life I considered the possibility of Norman Rockwell's not being lunatic. They were a father, a mother, a girl about fifteen, and a boy one or two years younger than she. All were dressed in expensive-looking camel's hair coats; each carried an item that designated him as a fan—the father two soft and brilliantly plaid wool blankets, the mother a picnic basket, the girl a half-gallon thermos, and the boy a pair of field glasses, strung casually about his neck—each apparently doing his bit to make the day a grand success. What astonished me, though, was the almost hilarious similarity of their physical appearance: each had brilliant auburn hair; each had even, startlingly white teeth, smilingly exposed beneath attractive snub noses; and each of their faces was liberally sprinkled with great, outsized freckles. The total face they presented was one of overwhelming and wholesome handsomeness. My first impulse was to laugh. Had I not felt an extreme discomfort caused by the relish they took in each other's being—their looks seemed to smother each other in love—and the crowdedness that had caused me to find myself wedged among them, separating them, I might have laughed. I felt not unlike a man who eats too fast, drinks too much, occasionally neglects his teeth and fingernails, is given to a pensive scratching of his vital parts, lets rip with a not infrequent fart, and wakes up one morning to find himself smack in the middle of a *Saturday Evening Post* cover, carving the goddam Thanksgiving turkey for a family he never has seen before. What was worse, they were aware of my discomfort; between basking in each other's loveliness they would smile apologetically at me, as though in crowding about me they were aware of having aroused me from my reverie and were sorry for it. Distressed, I felt I ought to say something—"I'm sorry I'm alive" or something—so I said the first thing that came to my mind. It was a lie occasioned by my reverie, one that must have sounded very stupid indeed.

"I know Steve Owen," I said.

"Really!" they all chimed in high and goodnatured unison. For some reason I got the impression that they had not the foggiest notion of what I had said. We all fell immediately to beaming at each other and nodding deferentially—a posture that exasperated me to the point where I thought I must absolutely say something else. Hoping that I could strike some chord in them that would relieve the self-consciousness we all were so evidently feeling, I spoke again.

"I know Frank Gifford, too."

"Really!" came their unabashed reply. Their tone seemed so calculated to humor me that I was almost certain they were larking with me. Staring at them, I couldn't be sure; and we all fell back to smiling idiotically and nodding at each other. We did this all the way to the Bronx where, disembarking, I lost contact with them—for the moment at least—and felt much relieved.

It seems amazing to me now that while at USC, where Gifford and I were contemporaries, I never saw him play football; that I had to come 3,000 miles from the low, white, smog-enshrouded sun that hung perpetually over the Los Angeles Coliseum to the cold, damp, and dismal Polo Grounds to see him perform for the first time; and that I might never have had the urge that long-ago Sunday had I not once on campus had a strange, unnerving confrontation with him. The confrontation was caused by a girl, though at the time of the encounter I did not understand *what* girl. I had transferred from Hobart College, a small, undistinguished liberal arts college in Geneva, New York, where I was a predental student, to USC, a large, undistinguished university in Los Angeles, where I became an English major. The transition was not unnatural. I went out there because I had been rejected by a girl, my first love, whom I loved beyond the redeeming force of anything save time. Accepting the theory of distance as time, I put as much of it between the girl and myself as I could. Once there, though, the prospect of spending my days gouging at people's teeth and whiffing the intense, acidic odor of decay—a profession I had chosen with no stronger motive than keeping that very girl in swimming suits and tennis shorts; she had (and this, sadly, is the precise extent of my memory of her) the most breath-taking legs I ever had seen—seemed hideous, and I quite naturally became an English major with a view to reading The Books, The Novels, and The Poems, those pat reassurances that other men had experienced rejection and pain and loss. Moreover, I accepted the myth of California the Benevolent and believed that beneath her warm skies I would find surcease from my pain in the person of some lithe, fresh-skinned, and incredibly lovely blonde coed. Bearing my rejection like a disease, and like a man with frightfully repugnant and contagious leprosy, I was unable to attract anything as healthy as the girl I had in mind.

Whenever I think of the man I was in those days, cutting across the neat-cropped grass of the campus, burdened down by the weight of the books in which I sought the consolation of other men's grief, and burdened further by the large weight of my own bitterness, the whole vision seems a nightmare. There were girls all about me, so near and yet so out of reach, a pastel nightmare of honey-blond, pink-lipped, golden-legged, lemon-sweatered girls. And always in this horror, this gaggle of femininity, there comes the vision of another girl, now only a little less featureless than all the rest. I saw her first on one stunning spring day when the smog had momentarily lifted, and all the world seemed hard bright blue and green. She came across the campus straight at me, and though I had her in the range of my vision for perhaps a hundred feet, I only was able, for the fury of my heart, to give her five or six frantic glances. She had the kind of comeliness—soft, shoulder-length chestnut hair; a sharp beauty mark right at her sensual mouth; and a figure that was like a swift, unexpected blow to the diaphragm— that to linger on makes the beholder feel obscene. I wanted to look. I couldn't look. I had to look. I could give her only the most gaspingly quick glances. Then she was by me. Waiting as long as I dared, I turned, and she was gone.

From that day forward I moved about the campus in a kind of vertigo, with my right eye watching the sidewalk come up to meet my anxious feet, and my left eye clacking in a wild orbit, all over and around its socket, trying to take in the entire campus in frantic split seconds, terrified that I might miss her. On the same day that I found out who she was I saw her again. I was standing in front of Founders' Hall talking with T., a gleaming-toothed, hand-pumping fraternity man with whom I had, my first semester out there, shared a room. We had since gone our separate ways; but whenever we met we always passed the time, being bound together by the contempt with which we viewed each other's world and by the sorrow we felt at really rather liking each other, a condition T. found more difficult to forgive in himself than I did.

"That?" he asked in profound astonishment to my query about the girl. "That?" he repeated dumbly, as if this time—for I was much given to teasing T.—I had really gone too far. "That," he proclaimed with menacing impatience, "just happens to be Frank Gifford's girl!"

I never will forget the contempt he showered on me for asking what to him, and I suppose to the rest of fraternity row, was not only a rhetorical but a dazzlingly asinine question. Nor will I forget that he never did give me the girl's name; the information that she was Gifford's girl was, he assumed, quite enough to prevent the likes of me from pursuing the matter further. My first impulse was to laugh and twit his chin with my finger. But the truth was I was getting a little weary of T. His monumental sense of the rightness of things was beginning to grate on me; shrugging, I decided to end it forever. It required the best piece of acting I've ever been called upon to do; but I carried it off, I think, perfectly.

Letting my mouth droop open and fixing on my face a look of serene vacuousness, I said, "Who's Frank Gifford?"

My first thought was that T. was going to strike me. His hands tensed into fists, his face went the color of fire, and he thrust his head defiantly toward me. He didn't strike, though. Either his sense of the propriety of things overcame him, or he guessed, quite accurately, that I would have knocked him on his ass. All he said, between furiously clenched teeth, was: *"Oh, really, Exley, this has gone too far."* Turning hysterically away from me, he thundered off. It had indeed gone too far, and I laughed all the way to the saloon I frequented on Jefferson Boulevard, sadly glad to have seen the last of T.

Frank Gifford was an All-America at USC, and I know of no way of describing this phenomenon short of equating it with being the Pope in the Vatican. Our local *L' Osservatore Romano, The Daily Trojan,* was a fairly well-written college newspaper except on the subject of football, when the tone of the writing rose to an hysterical screech. It reported daily on Gifford's health, one time even imposing upon us the news that he was suffering an upset stomach, leading an irreverent acquaintance of mine to wonder aloud whether the athletic department had heard about "milk of magnesia, for Christ's sake." We were, it seems to me in retrospect, treated daily to breathless items such as the variations in his weight, his method of conditioning, the knowledge that he neither smoked nor drank, the humbleness of his beginnings, and once we were even told the number of fan letters he received daily from pimply high school girls in the Los Angeles area. The USC publicity man, perhaps influenced by the proximity of Hollywood press agents, seemed overly fond of releasing a head-and-shoulder print showing him the apparently proud possessor of long, black, perfectly ambrosial locks that came down to caress an alabaster, colossally beauteous face, one that would have aroused envy in Tony Curtis. Gifford was, in effect, overwhelmingly present in the consciousness of the campus, even though my crowd—the literati—never once to my knowledge mentioned him. We never mentioned him because his being permitted to exist at the very university where we were apprenticing ourselves for Nobel Prizes would have detracted from our environment and been an admission that we might be better off at an academe more sympathetic with our hopes. Still, the act of not mentioning him made him somehow more present than if, like the pathetic nincompoops on fraternity row, we spent all our idle hours singing his praises. Our silence made him, in our family, a kind of retarded child about whom we had tacitly and selfishly agreed not to speak. It seems the only thing of Gifford's we were spared—and it is at this point we leave his equation with the Bishop of Rome—was his opinion of the spiritual state of the USC campus. But I am being unkind now; something occurred between Gifford and me which led me to conclude that he was not an immodest man.

Unlike most athletes who could be seen swaggering about the campus with *Property of USC* (did they never see the ironic, touching servility of this?) stamped indelibly every place but on their foreheads, Gifford made himself extremely scarce, so scarce that I only saw him once for but a few brief moments, so scarce that prior to this encounter I had begun to wonder if he wasn't some myth created by the administration to appease the highly vocal and moronic alumni who were clamoring incessantly for USC's Return to Greatness in, as the sportswriters say, "the football wars." Sitting at the counter of one of the campus hamburger joints, I was having a cup of chicken noodle soup and a cheeseburger when it occurred to me that he was one of a party of three men seated a few stools away from me. I knew without looking because the other two men were directing all their remarks to him: "Hey Frank, how about that?" "Hey, Frank, cha' ever hear the one about. . . ." It was the kind of given-name familiarity one likes to have with the biggest man on the block. My eyes on my soup, I listened to this sycophancy, smiling rather bitterly, for what seemed an eternity; when I finally did look up, it was he—ambrosial locks and all. He was dressed in blue denims and a terry-cloth sweater, and though I saw no evidence of *USC* stamped anyplace, still I had an overwhelming desire to insult him in some way. How this would be accomplished with any subtlety I had no idea; I certainly didn't want to fight with him. I did, however, want to shout, "Listen, you son of a bitch, life isn't all a goddam football game! You won't always get the girl! Life is rejection and pain and loss"—all those things I so cherishingly cuddled in my self-pitying bosom. I didn't, of course, say any such thing; almost immediately he was up and standing right next to me, waiting to pay the cashier. Unable to let the moment go by, I snapped my head up to face him. When he looked at me, I smiled—a hard, mocking, so-you're-the-big-shit? smile. What I expected him to do, I can't imagine—say, "What's your trouble, buddy?" or what—but what he did do was the least of my expectations. He only looked quizzically at me for a moment, as though he were having difficulty placing me; then he smiled a most ingratiating smile, gave me a most amiable hello, and walked out the door, followed by his buddies who were saying in unison, "Hey Frank, what'll we do now?"

My first feeling was one of utter rage. I wanted to jump up and throw my water glass through the plate-glass window. Then almost immediately a kind of sullenness set in, then shame. Unless I had read that smile and that salutation incorrectly, there was a note of genuine apology and modesty in them. Even in the close world of the university, Gifford must have come to realize that he was having a fantastic success, and that success somewhat embarrassed him. Perhaps he took me for some student acquaintance he had had long before that success, and took my hateful smile as a reproach for his having failed to speak to me on other occasions, his smile being the apology for that neglect. Perhaps he only was saying he was sorry I was a miserable son of a bitch, but that he hardly was going to fight me for it. These speculations, as I found out drinking beer late into that evening, could have gone on forever. I drank eight, nine, ten, drifting between speculations on the nature of that smile and bitter, sexually colored memories of the girl with the breath-taking legs back East, when it suddenly occurred to me that she and not the girl with the chestnut hair was the cause of all my anger, and that I was for perhaps a very long time going to have to live with that anger. Gifford gave me that. With that smile, whatever he meant by it, a smile that he doubtless wouldn't remember, he impressed upon me, in the rigidity of my embarrassment, that it is unmanly to burden others with one's grief. Even though it is man's particularly unhappy aptitude to see to it that his fate is shared.

Leaving the subway and walking toward the Polo Grounds, I was remembering that smile and thinking again how nice it would be if Gifford had a fine day for Owen, when I began to notice that the redheaded family, who were moving with the crowd some paces ahead of me, were laughing and giggling self-consciously, a laughter that evidently was connected with me in some way. Every few paces, having momentarily regained their composure, they would drop their heads together in a covert way, whisper as they walked, then turn again in unison, stare back at me, and begin giggling anew. It was a laughter that soon had me self-consciously fingering my necktie and looking furtively down at my fly, as though I expected to discover that the overcoat that covered it somehow had disappeared miraculously. We almost were at the entrance to the field when, to my surprise, the father stopped suddenly, turned, walked back to me, and said that he was holding an extra ticket to the game. It was, he said, the result of his maid's having been taken ill, and that he—no, not precisely he, but the children—would deem it an honor if I—"knowing Owen and all"—sat with them. Not in the least interested in doing so, I was so relieved to discover that their laughter had been inspired by something apart from myself—the self-consciousness they felt at inviting me—that I instantaneously and gratefully accepted, thanked him profusely, and was almost immediately sorry. It occurred to me that the children might query me on my relationship with Owen—perhaps even Gifford—and what the hell could I say? My "relationship" with both of these men was so fleeting, so insubstantial, that I unquestionably would have had to invent and thereby not only undergo the strain of having to talk off the top of my head but, by talking, risk exposure as a fraud.

My fears, however, proved groundless. These people, it soon became evident, had no interest in me whatever, they were so bound up in their pride of each other. My discomfort was caused not by any interest they took in me but by their total indifference to me. Directing me by the arm, father seated me not with the children who, he had claimed, desired my presence but on the aisle—obviously, I thought, the maid's seat (accessible to the hot dogs)—and sat himself next to me, separating me from his wife and children who had so harmoniously moved to their respective seats that I was sure that the family held season tickets. Everyone in place, all heads cranked round to me and displayed a perfect miracle of gleaming incisors.

It only had begun. The game no sooner was under way when father, in an egre-giously cultivated, theatrically virile voice, began—to my profound horror—com-menting on each and every play. "That is a delayed buck, a play that requires superb blocking and marvelous timing," or "That, children, is a screen pass, a fantastically perilous play to attempt, and one, I might add, that you won't see *Mr.* Conerly attempt but once or twice a season"—to all of which the mother, the daughter, and the son invariably and in perfect unison exclaimed, "Really!" A tribute to father's brilliance that, to my further and almost numbing horror, I, too, soon discovered I was expected to pay—pay, I would expect, for the unutterable enchantment of sitting with them. Each time that I heard the *Really!* I would become aware of a great shock of auburn hair leaning past father's shoulder, and I would look up to be confronted by a brilliant conglomeration of snub noses, orange freckles, and sparkling teeth, all formed into a face of beseechment, an invitation to join in this tribute to Genius. I delayed accepting the invitation as long as I could; when the looks went from beseechment to mild reproachment, I surrendered and began chiming in with *Really!* At first I came in too quickly or too late, and we seemed to be echoing each other: *Really! Really!* Though this rhythmical ineptness chafed me greatly, it brought from the family only the most understanding and kindly looks. By the end of the first quarter I had my timing down perfectly and settled down to what was the most uncomfortable afternoon of my life.

This was a superb Detroit team. It was the Detroit of a young Bobby Layne and an incomparable Doak Walker, of a monstrously bull-like Leon Hart and a 300-pound Les Bingaman, a team that was expected to move past the Giants with ease and into the championship of the Western Division. Had they done so—which at first they appeared to be doing, picking up two touchdowns before the crowd scarcely was set-tled—I might have been rather amused at the constraints placed on me by the character of my hosts. But at one thrilling moment, a moment almost palpable in its intensity, and unquestionably motivated by the knowledge of Owen's parting, the Giants recovered, engaged this magnificent football team, and began to play as if they meant to win. Other than the terrible fury of it, I don't remember the details of the game, save that Gifford played superbly; and that at one precise moment, watching him exe-cute one of his plays, I was suddenly and overwhelmingly struck with the urge to cheer, to jump up and down and pummel people on the back.

But then, there was father. What can I say of him? To anything resembling a good play, he would single out the player responsible and say, "Fine show, Gifford!" or "Wonderful stuff there, Price!" and we would chime in with "Good show!" and "Fine stuff!" Then, in a preposterous parody of cultured equanimity, we would be permitted to clap our gloved right hands against our left wrists, like opera-goers, making about as much noise as an argument between mutes. It was very depressing. I hadn't cheered for anything or anybody in three years—since my rejection by the leggy girl—and even had mistakenly come to believe that my new-found restraint was a kind of maturity. Oh, I had had my enthusiasms, but they were dark, the adoration of the griefs and morbidities men commit to paper in the name of literature, the homage I had paid the whole sickly aristocracy of letters. But a man can dwell too long with grief, and now, quite suddenly, quite wonderfully, I wanted to cheer again, to break forth from darkness into light, to stand up in that sparsely filled (it was a typically ungrateful New York that had come to bid Owen farewell), murderously damp, bitingly cold stadium, and scream my head off.

But then, here again was father—not only father but the terrible diffidence I felt in the presence of that family, in the overwhelming and shameless pride they took in each other's being and good form. The game moved for me at a snail's pace. Frequently I rose on tiptoe, ready to burst forth, at the last moment restraining myself. As the fury of the game reached an almost audible character, the crowd about me reacted proportionately by going stark raving mad while I stood still, saying *Really!* and filling up two handkerchiefs with a phlegm induced by the afternoon's increasing dampness. What upset me more than anything about father was that he had no loyalty other than to The Game itself, praising players, whether Giants or Lions, indiscriminately. On the more famous players he bestowed a *Mister*, saying "Oh, fine stuff, *Mr.* Layne!" or, "Wonderful show, *Mr.* Walker!"—coming down hard on the *Mister* the way those creeps affected by The Theater say *Sir* Laurence Olivier or *Miss* Helen Hayes. We continued our *fine show's* and *good stuff's* till I thought my heart would break.

Finally I did, of course, snap. Late in the final period, with the Giants losing by less than a touchdown, Conerly connected with a short pass to Gifford, and I thought the latter was going into the end zone. Unable to help myself, the long afternoon's repressed and joyous tears welling up in my eyes, I went berserk.

Jumping up and down and pummeling father furiously on the back, I screamed, "Oh, Jesus, Frank! Oh, Frank, *baby! Go! For Steve! For Steve! For Steve!"*

Gifford did not go all the way. He went to the one-foot line. Because it was not enough yardage for a first down, it became fourth and inches to go for a touchdown and a victory, the next few seconds proving the most agonizingly apprehensive of my life. It was an agony not allayed by my hosts. When I looked up through tear-bedewed eyes, father was straightening his camel's-hair topcoat, and the face of his loved ones had been transfigured. I had violated their high canons of good taste, their faces had moved from a vision of charming wholesomeness to one of intransigent hostility; it was now eminently clear to them that their invitation to me had been a dreadful mistake.

In an attempt to apologize, I smiled weakly and said, "I'm sorry—I thought *Mr.* Gifford was going all the way," coming down particularly hard on the *Mister*. But this was even more disastrous: Gifford was new to the Giants then, and father had not as yet bestowed that title on him. The total face they presented to me made me want to cut my jugular. Then, I thought, *what the hell*, and because I absolutely refused to let them spoil the moment for me, I said something that had the exact effect I intended: putting them in a state of numbing senselessness.

I said, my voice distinctly irritable, "Aw, c'mon, you *goofies. Cheer. This is for Steve Owen! For Steve Owen!"*

The Giants did not score, and as a result did not win the game. Gifford carried on the last play, as I never doubted that he would. Wasn't this game being played out just as, in my loneliness, I had imagined it would be? Les Bingaman put his 300 pounds in Gifford's way, stopping him so close to the goal that the officials were for many moments undetermined; and the Lions, having finally taken over the ball, were a good way up the field, playing ball control and running out the clock, before my mind accepted the evidence of my eyes. When it did so, I began to cough, coughing great globs into my hands. I was coughing only a very few moments before it occurred to me that I also was weeping. It was a fact that occurred to father simultaneously. For the first time since I had spoken so harshly to him, he rallied, my tears being in unsurpassably bad taste, and said, "Look here, it's *only* a game."

Trying to speak softly so the children wouldn't hear, I said, "F—you!"

But they heard. By now I had turned and started up the steep concrete steps; all the way up them I could hear mother and the children, still in perfect unison, screeching *Father!* and father, in the most preposterously modulated hysteria, screeching *Officer!* I had to laugh then, laugh so hard that I almost doubled up on the concrete steps. My irritation had nothing to do with these dead people, and not really—I know now—with anything to do with the outcome of the game. I had begun to be haunted again by that which had haunted me on my first trip to the city—the inability of a man to impose his dreams, his ego, upon the city, and for many long months had been experiencing a rage induced by New York's stony refusal to esteem me. It was foolish and childish of me to impose that rage on these people, though not as foolish, I expect, as father's thinking he could protect his children from life's bitterness by calling for a policeman.

Frank Gifford went on to realize a fame in New York that only a visionary would have dared hope for: he became unavoidable, part of the city's hard mentality. I never would envy or begrudge him that fame. I did, in fact, become perhaps his most enthusiastic fan. No doubt he came to represent to me the realization of life's large promises. But that is another part of this story. It was Owen who over the years kept bringing me back to life's hard fact of famelessness. After that day at the Polo Grounds I heard of Owen from time to time, that he was a line coach for one NFL team or another, that he was coaching somewhere in Canada—perhaps at Winnipeg or Saskatchewan. Wherever, it must have seemed to him the sunless, the glacial side of the moon. Owen unquestionably came to see the irony of his fate. His offensively obsessed detractors had been rendered petulant by his attitude that "football is a game played down in the dirt, and always will be," and within three years after his leaving, his successors, having inherited his ideas (the Umbrella pass defense for one), took the Giants to a world championship with little other than a defense. It was one of the greatest defenses (Robustelli, Patton, Huff, Svare, Livingston, *et al.*) that the game has ever seen, but, for all of that, a championship won by men who played the game where Owen had tenaciously and fatally maintained it was played—*in the dirt*.

Benny Friedman's daring brand of quarterbacking revolutionized the pro game. He passed on first down, he passed from inside his own 40-yard line, he passed from punt formation. Before he entered the NFL in 1927, no one had thrown as many as ten touchdown passes in a season. Benny's totals in his first four years: 13, 11, 19, and 14. A tutor of quarterbacks from Harry Newman to Joe Namath, Friedman may be the best player *not* in the Hall of Fame. This interview is taken from Bob Curran's 1969 book *Pro Football's Rag Days*.

BENNY FRIEDMAN
with Bob Curran

The Pass Master

When the talk among football people turns to forward passing, the name "Benny Friedman" is quickly brought up. It should be, because Benny Friedman did as much to popularize the forward pass as any man who has played the game.

At Michigan, where he and Benny Oosterbaan comprised one of the best combinations of all time, Friedman was an All-American selection twice. As a professional playing under the handicaps he tells about here, he helped open the game at a time when it was seeking ways to attract fans.

During his collegiate days and professional career, Friedman never had an intercepted pass returned for a touchdown. A keen student of football, he had strong theories on passing that he now teaches at his quarterback camps for youngsters.

When I visited Benny in his sumptuous apartment in New York City I read many of the letters written to him by boys who learned quarterbacking and passing at his camp. They testify that his theories are as valid today as they were in the days of the fat ball, mundane pass patterns, and journeymen receivers.

Here is how Benny remembers his days in the pros:

I graduated from Michigan in 1927 and at that time, of course, pro football was in its embryonic stages. Every ball club wanted to have one star, so to speak, one guy to publicize. I was asked to play with a couple of different ball clubs and one of my friends in Cleveland, which was my home town, got after me to play for Cleveland. Of course, that seemed all right. There was a chap in Cleveland by the name of Grant who had a large restaurant supply business, and he and another friend of mine by the name of Sammy Deutsch, who was in the jewelry business, recruited me for what was then called the Cleveland Bulldogs. The Cleveland Bulldogs had been the Kansas City Blues. They had just moved to Cleveland to become the Bulldogs in the National Football League.

I was the only chap east of the Mississippi on that ball club. The rest of them came from Nebraska, Oklahoma, Texas, and the like.

I first met the boys out at Excelsior Springs, Missouri. It's one of those health spas where they have sulphur water for people with bad kidneys and what not. It sure was hot there. The coach was a chap by the name of Leroy Andrews. I might tell you one funny story about our Cleveland Bulldogs. We played then in a place in Cleveland called Luna Park—a big amusement area that had a little stadium. They had a big wooden fence around it and had painted on the fence, "Home of the Cleveland Bulldogs." We were right on the edge of Little Italy, the Italian section, and one day one of these old Italians walked in and said he wanted to buy one. We had quite a tough time trying to explain to him that we didn't have any bulldogs for sale.

We played the Giants, the Bears, the Cardinals, the Providence Steamrollers, the Frankford Yellow Jackets, etc. I want to say that pro football at that time was a far cry from today. The home team got its own officials, so that sometimes our games were a bit weird. When we first played the Chicago Bears, for example, they had an old character as the referee, and every time we had the ball and time was out he'd start talking to me about Fielding Yost, my old coach at Michigan.

He wasn't calling anything that was happening and we were getting the hell beat out of us physically. Finally, I stopped him and I said, "Mr. Durfee, I'm not interested in Fielding Yost today but I am interested in what's going on in this game and apparently you're not." I said, "Why don't you stop talking about Fielding Yost and pay attention to what's going on."

When we went up to play the Providence Steamrollers—they used to pay off the newspaper people at that time for the publicity they gave them by using them as officials in the games—you can imagine the kind of officiating we had.

We said to the Bears after we played them that first time that we would play them again if we got impartial officials. There wasn't any league office that assigned them, you know. When we played them the second time we had a little fellow named Tommy Hughitt from Buffalo act as the referee. I'll never forget the third play of the game. I took the ball and went through the middle of the line and picked up a dozen yards. I was tackled and, as the whistle blew, boom, this big fullback came flying into me while I was on the ground. Little Tommy grabbed this big character by the shoulder and threw him out of the game. Then he penalized the Bears 15 yards for piling on.

After that they knew who was boss and we beat the hell out of them.

I might say, by way of comparison, last year there was a great to-do made because Green Bay played twenty-three games during the course of the year, including their exhibition games. Well, back in 1927 I played in twenty-three games with my team, only there was a little difference. They had forty-two men on their squad at Green Bay, plus their taxi squad. We had seventeen men on ours and played twenty-three games.

You couldn't get hurt and we, of course, didn't get hurt. And we had to go sixty minutes. I remember playing in Frankford on Saturday because in Pennsylvania, with their Blue Laws, you couldn't play on Sunday. We then played in Cleveland on Sunday. I would say we were rugged. On defense I would play either safety or halfback.

One of the teams we played against that year was the Duluth Eskimos and that team had, like all of the ball clubs had, one individual star. The star of the Duluth team was Ernie Nevers, the great fullback from Stanford, and Ernie, to me, was a very unusual individual. I used to think of him more as a crusader with a flaming sword. I never saw anyone who epitomized the idea of a will to win more so than Ernie. He was a tremendous football player, tremendous leader, both on offense and defense. And you always knew you were in a battle when you played against one of his teams.

The Eskimos were scrimping along and the guy who owned their ball club was an awfully cheap character and Ernie used to come in and borrow tape. He had bad ankles and bad knees and he used to have to use a lot of tape, which we loaned him.

That first year I made about $22,000. We barnstormed on the coast after the season ended. We played up in Frisco for two games, then down in Los Angeles for three. And the deal was that I was to get $750 a game and the other boys $50. I might say this in retrospect—I was the highest paid ballplayer in football but I was the cheapest one.

It's a paradox, but I say that because they never had to worry about me because I was never hurt. I never had to be taken out of the ball game for injury and was always ready to start the next one, even though, of course, I was banged up a bit. Take a boy like Sid Luckman, who was a great quarterback. He had his nose broken eight times. I never had mine broken. No face masks either in those days. And I had no bad knees— no nothing.

Football is, I believe—and I teach the youngsters this in my quarterback camps— nothing but habits at work, and if you learn the right habits there's no question about what you're going to do. I think there's a good deal missing today in the way of a lot of people thinking the equipment is going to do it. It's not the equipment—it's the coaching that will solve the injury problem.

The next year we moved up to Detroit and I went into the brokerage business up there. That summer twenty friends of mine decided that they'd like to have pro football in Detroit. Believe it or not, they bankrolled the team with $10,000. Each man put up $500, so we moved the team up from Cleveland. In those days all you had to do was put up $2,500 with the league. The league was Joe Carr, who was the president. And that was all.

Very often the people who put up the $2,500 check would tell Joe Carr, "Don't put

Benny Friedman

BILLED AS "THE WORLD'S GREATEST FORWARD PASSER," FRIEDMAN WAS CERTAINLY WITHOUT PEER IN PRO FOOTBALL DURING HIS CAREER. BEFORE SO-SO SUPPORT AND COACHING DUTIES SLOWED HIM DOWN, HE TORE THE NFL APART. FROM 1927 THROUGH 1930, HE AVERAGED BETTER THAN ONE TD PASS PER GAME AND TALLIED MORE THAN 150 POINTS WITH HIS RUNNING AND KICKING.

it in the bank." Anyway my friends bankrolled the team and we became the Detroit Wolverines. You see, in those days there was a lot of franchise moving. Teams moved around so much you could forget where they started. The present Detroit Lions were really the Portsmouth, Ohio, team; the Philadelphia Eagles, of course, were the Frankford Yellow Jackets; and the present Washington Redskins were the Boston Redskins. A lot of teams went out of existence, like Staten Island and the Duluth team. The Chicago Cardinals, of course, moved around and you didn't know from year to year who was going to be there, other than the Bears, Green Bay, and the Giants.

We did fairly well in Detroit. At the end of the year each backer got back $350 of his $500. We played out at the University of Detroit Stadium and drew all right. After that year Tim Mara, who was a wonderful, wonderful individual, wanted me to come to New York, and Leroy Andrews, who was still coaching and managing the ball club, made the deal with him. So we joined up with the Giants. I was paid $10,000 a year with the Giants.

That first year here in New York you knew there had to be a lot of promotion along the way. When I was with Cleveland, Ed Bang, who was the sports editor of the *Cleveland News*, was our publicity man, and he and I used to travel a day or two ahead of time to the city we were going to play in. Ed would buy two bottles of whiskey and we'd walk into a newspaper office. He'd hand one bottle to the sports editor and the other to the sports columnist, he'd introduce me, and then we'd kibitz. That was the way we got our publicity. It wasn't like it is today at all. It was real barnstorming. When I got to New York in 1929 I spoke in every high school in the city of New York trying to promote professional football. I did not have to do this, but I was asked to do it.

The youngsters in the high schools in New York had what they call a G.O. organization and we made an arrangement whereby the kids could come to the Polo Grounds with their G.O. ticket and 50 cents and could get admission to the game. And by the time we played the Green Bay Packers on Thanksgiving Day we had 12,000 of them come in. That $6,000 was enough to pay for the Green Bay guarantee.

Then we had other outfits. There was a Young Man's Philanthropic League — a group of young Jewish business and professional people who had a club that sponsored some charities. They were always fans of anything that was athletic. They would take a big batch of tickets at half price and sell them for full price, using the other half to help support their charity. There was a lot of this sort of thing needed to promote football.

I might further say that in 1928, the year before I came with the Giants, Tim Mara lost $54,000. In 1929, the first year I was with him, he made $8,500. In 1930 he made $23,000 and in 1931 he made $35,000.

I think one of the highlights along the charity trail was when we played the Notre Dame alumni for Major Jimmy Walker's unemployment fund in the depths of the depression. Somebody got this idea — which was a good one — and he corralled a bunch of Notre Dame seniors and some alumni and they agreed to play us.

There were a couple of funny things that came out of it. Just before the game Rockne walked into our dressing room with a cane—he wasn't well at the time. I was getting my ankles taped. (I was coaching the ball club too at the time.) I looked up at him—he was one of my idols—and said, "Hi, Coach," and he said, "Hello, Benny."

I said, "How do you feel?"

He replied, "So, so, and you?"

I said, "Fine."

He said, "That's too bad."

I asked, "What can I do for you?"

He started giving me a story about some of these old men that he had, and he told me that one of these guys had taken a big step off a Pullman and got a charleyhorse. He said, "I think we ought to have free substitution."

I said, "Okay, Coach, anything else?"

He said, "Yes, I think we ought to cut the quarters down to ten minutes—from fifteen."

I said, "Oh, Lord, we can't do that. There are 45,000 people out there who have paid five bucks apiece to see this game. I'll tell you what we'll do—we'll cut it down to twelve minutes and a half and if it gets bad we'll cut it down some more in the second half." I then said, "Anything else?"

He said, "Yes, for Pete's sake, take it easy."

Now we go out and we play this ball game and we beat them I think around 21–0.

Adam Walsh, the captain of the Four Horsemen team, was center for the Notre Dame alumni that day. He was also line coach at Yale, where I was the backfield coach during the week. When the game ended, he grabbed me by the shoulders and put his light blue eyes right against my face, and they were blazing. Then he said, "Who gave you the signals for our defenses?"

I laughed and said, "Adam, you should know better than to play percentages against me."

He didn't say anything for a minute. Then he laughed and he told me about one particular play. It seems Hunk Anderson was playing left guard next to Rip Miller, who was left tackle. In those days we used the six-man line on defense, and the left guard, when he thought a pass was coming, would take sort of a chuck step and then drop back to cover. On this play Hunk said to Rip in a stage whisper, "I'm dropping back."

Well, I guess they thought I would think they were kidding. Anyway, I decided to try this hipper-dipper play I liked. I'd take the ball from center and raise my arm back as if I was going to pass. Then the fullback and blocking back would come over to the weak side and I'd follow them through the hole at left guard. I used that fake pass and went right through Anderson's spot for 24 yards and a touchdown.

Adam told me later in the game he heard Hunk tell Rip he was going to drop back again. Rip looked across the line and there was Les Caywood, a tackle for us who shaped oil field drills in the off-season. He was like concrete. The end next to him was just a wee bit smaller. Rip looked at Hunk and said, "If you think I'm going to stay here alone you're crazy!"

A few days later I dropped into Tim Mara's office. We'd agreed to go down to City Hall together with the financial report. Now I'd agreed to play for nothing. But the other boys got paid. And the Notre Dame fellows had expenses. When I came into the office Tim showed me the expenses. Boy, they were many and varied! The last item on the list was "Miscellaneous — $5,000." And I said to Tim, "I don't remember Miscellaneous. Where did he play?"

We had $116,000 left. I said to Tim, "We have made no arrangement with them as to how we'd pay them. So why don't we keep the $16,000. We can use it. And we'll give them an even $100,000. You know what's going to happen to that money, Tim." Remember this was in the heyday of Tammany — Tin Box Farley and all those characters. "Come on, Tim," I urged. "Let's keep $16,000."

"Oh, no," said Tim, "we can't do that."

So we went down to City Hall and we made the presentation to Jimmy Walker while some other officials looked on. That check went right by my nose and you can believe I wanted to stop it.

The next year I came into Tim's office and there was that canceled voucher in a frame on the wall. And Tim was looking at it. Before he could say hello, I said, "I know what you're thinking."

He said, "I'm thinking of how much I could use $16,000 right now. You, my friend, are looking at a dumb Irishman!"

I have been told that I revolutionized the game some when I came in. At the time everyone was conservative about passing. In fact, the whole offense was conservative. When you were inside your own 30-yard line, you kicked on third down. And you never passed this side of your own 40.

When I came into the pros, I decided I would pass wherever and whenever I wanted to. I had a lot of confidence because in my time at the University of Michigan I had never had an interception taken back for a touchdown. The credit for that goes to my great coach Fielding Yost, who once told me, "Don't ever throw a Nevers-to-Layden pass."

What he meant was this: In the Notre Dame-Stanford game of 1925, Ernie Nevers had torn the Notre Dame line apart. But on two occasions he had thrown flat passes that were intercepted and taken back for touchdowns by Elmer Layden. Nevers had thrown the ball into the flat and had taken no precaution about having a man to cover in case the ball was intercepted.

When I finished throwing the ball, I was always on balance and ready to cover. And I was accurate. One time two coaches from Princeton came to Michigan and asked Fielding Yost how I could be consistently accurate. Mr. Yost said that he couldn't answer but that they were welcome to watch me. They did and after a week they told me what they had found. They said that before I let the ball go, my feet were planted in the line along which the ball would travel. Simple enough but I don't see any passer today who does it.

But back to my early pro days. As I said, we were conservative. Of course, we had other handicaps. The ball was very fat. Not good for passing but good for dropkicking. When they streamlined the ball to make it easier to pass, the sharp point practically did away with dropkicking.

Then there was the rule that you had to be five yards behind the line of scrimmage when you threw the ball. This eliminated the jump pass and almost any kind of a quick pass.

Also we had a shortage of good receivers. In fact, I can think of only one great one in the pros—Don Hutson. And I had a great one at Michigan—Benny Oosterbaan. But for the most part the receivers were quite ordinary. Today, of course, you have a whole slew of skilled receivers who can run many pass patterns to perfection and then grab the ball if they can get a hand on it.

In our day we knew little about pass patterns. I remember one of our ends, Lyle Munn, who was a good all-around end but who had no moves to speak about. Our other two receivers weren't much better.

Still, I was determined to use the forward pass as I had at Michigan. After one day against the Bears everyone in the league knew I meant what I said. We were ahead 6–0 and there was about seven minutes to play and we were on our own 3-yard line.

We went into punt formation and I sent our fullback into the line for one yard. Then we tried the same play and he picked up a yard and a half. Now with third and seven the Bears were expecting a punt. Instead I called for a pass. You know in those days we called all the plays from the line of scrimmage. We had no huddle.

This was supposed to be a pass to my right end, a fellow named Sedbrook. But when I looked down field, there was no Sedbrook. I ran around a little and then I saw Lyle Munn about 30 yards away. I let fly and Munn caught the ball. We were out of the hole and we had killed time.

When we lined up, I walked over to Sedbrook and said, "Where were you on that play?"

He said, "Why, I was blocking the tackle as I always do on punts."

Well, we won the ball game anyway and that play was the key play.

My weight then was about what it is now—180 pounds. And I stood about five-foot-ten and a half." And remember we had to play both ways all the time then. The Giants had what was for those days a big squad—nineteen players—but the regulars were still expected to go all the way.

This meant that I was exposed to some brutality that today's quarterbacks don't know. Like the time Bronko Nagurski broke through on me. I was playing safety as usual and Bronko broke through a hole so fast he was on me before our halfbacks could close in on him.

Now when Nagurski came at you all you could see was the whites of his eyes and his white shoelaces. I had and still have a theory that when two men meet each other the low man wins. So I aimed at his shoelaces. I got him, too, although he dragged me for five more yards before he went down.

Then there was a time Ken Strong almost burst on me like that when he was with the Staten Island Stapletons. I say "almost" because I went up to meet him. I put my head down and stuck my helmet into his groin. I heard him grunt and he went down.

I have the feeling that if more of today's backs did what we did in those days—be the pitcher, not the catcher—they would have fewer injuries.

People talk about players from small colleges today as if this were a new phenomenon. It isn't. We had a lot of boys from small teams in our time. Kansas Wesleyan, Emporia State, Phillips College. These boys weren't flashy but they were solid players. They could block and tackle and they put out all the time. I used to feel for them in one way. They were farm boys and they were used to getting up at five o'clock in the morning. When they got to New York they'd still get up at five and, of course, there was nothing for them to do at that hour.

One of this bunch was a real character—the only Bohemian I ever met in pro football. His name was Joe Westoupal and he came from West Point, Nebraska. He was a lean fellow—about 200 pounds—and tough as whipcord. He played center for us and every once in a while he'd develop a mental block.

As I said, we called all the signals from the line of scrimmage. The first series of numbers would tell the team what play we were going to run. The second series would tell them the number on which the ball would be passed. You could say this was all analogous to the automatics they use today.

At least once every game there'd come a play when, on the given signal, ten men would spring into action. The eleventh man, Joe Westoupal, would remain holding the ball. I'd come over and say, "Okay, Joe, throw the ball back on the signal." He'd shake his head. Then I'd say, "Joe, we can't run the ball until you throw it back. Now be a good guy." After a few seconds, he'd nod and then we'd be all right for a while. But we never knew when he'd have his next mental block and there'd be no ball to play with.

The gap between pro ball and college ball was developing then and I can remember some rude awakenings some college stars got when they came into the pros. One of the most memorable cases was a fellow named John Law from Notre Dame—a 165-pound guard. Some people figured if he could make it at that weight at Notre Dame, with their tough brand of football, he could make it in the pros.

When I was with the Brooklyn Dodgers after I left the Giants we played against Law's team—I can't remember who it was—in an exhibition game. We had a fellow playing tackle named Swede Ranquist, who looked like a sailor off a Scandinavian freighter. He weighed 230 pounds and chewed snuff and was a very rough customer. On the first play Swede hit John Law, and that was the end of the Notre Dame star for the day. Later I heard he was the coach at Sing Sing.

I also remember one of the first games Chris Cagle played for the Giants. You know Chris had been a big star at West Point and it was expected he'd be big with us. When he got into his first game, I wanted to use him so that we could loosen up the other team—the Green Bay Packers. Often when another back was going to run with the ball, I'd step over to the fullback slot. That meant the threat of a pass was there and this would keep the defense honest.

On the first play Chris carried, he ran smack into a big end named Tom Nash. When he got up, his forehead was bleeding. He left the game and went over to the sidelines, where the trainer put a gauze bandage on the cut. When Chris came back into the game, I decided to try to break him loose again right away. So on the first play I threw him a short pass that he took over his right shoulder. Then he started upfield with that stride of his. He had a stride like a 440-yard runner.

Playing for Green Bay that day was a guard named Mike Michalske, whom I rate as the best lineman I ever played against. Mike was out of Penn State and the Giants had him. But for some reason they let him go and Green Bay grabbed him. He's now in the Hall of Fame.

Anyway, Mike came flying through the air and he hit Cagle right below the knees. Well, it was like that trick where you pull a tablecloth off a table without disturbing the dishes. Cagle went up and then down. As he lay on the ground the gauze bandage, which had become separated in the crash, came slowly floating down by itself. I'll never forget that scene.

After the 1931 season I went in to see Tim Mara about a proposition. All of these years I had played without a contract and I had no complaints. Now I wanted Tim to give me a piece of the ball club.

My timing was off. If I had asked him in the years when the team was like a plaything to him, I probably would have got what I wanted. But at the time I asked him it was his sole asset. He said, "No, I'm keeping it all for my sons."

That was that. I thought I deserved a piece of the club because I felt I had played a big part in moving it from the red ink to the black ink. And when Tim turned me down I felt I should move along, that I couldn't stay with him.

At that time a fellow named Bill Dwyer from Brooklyn approached me. He had a club called the Brooklyn Dodgers and he wanted me to play quarterback and coach them for the same money I was making with the Giants. I agreed, and in the season of 1932 I went over to Brooklyn.

I was never happy in Brooklyn. Bill, one of the biggest bootleggers in the United States, was a good guy. But he was surrounded by some strange characters.

After the first season, he sold out to Shipwreck Kelly, the former Kentucky player, and Chris Cagle. They brought Colonel John McEwen in to coach. It was a cloak-and-dagger operation and after the 1933 season I called it quits. Mayor LaGuardia had asked me to coach City College of New York and I thought that this was as good a time as any to step down.

I had some good years left, but of course I didn't know pro football was going to progress as much as it did. If I had, I might have stayed in. I would like to have coached later and I know I could have contributed something. I still think I can. I still say there isn't a passer in either league who throws the ball right.

And I think the coaching could stand some improvement. Just giving a guy a title "Coach" doesn't make him one. The offenses I see are all so stereotyped and each team looks like a mirror of the next team.

Looking back, I have few regrets. I made some good money playing pro ball. But I'll say this and back it up. Considering the time I put in, I was a bargain.

For five years, 1964 through 1968, Pete Gent was a flanker for the Dallas Cowboys, which experience is reflected in this excerpt from his first novel, *North Dallas Forty*. Although no slouch as a football player, he is an even better writer: this depiction of contract "negotiation"—the game as it is played off the field—is bitterly real.

PETE GENT

"This Is Nothing Personal"

It was 7:15 P.M. as I drove back north on the expressway. . . . I passed the North Dallas Towers. The tenth floor was brightly lit. They would be watching the New York films, designing the game plan for Sunday.

The light was on in Clinton Foote's office. The general manager was working late too. I was reminded of one particular meeting in that office. Late one March I had been notified (a form letter addressed "Dear Player") that my option had been picked up. I had answered by form letter and was quickly summoned by phone to the North Dallas Towers. Clinton's was a corner office that smelled of fresh paint. One wall was covered by a full-color superstat of a fifty-yard-line ticket from Super Bowl I. The furniture was stainless steel and there was a complete selection of last year's game programs on the glass coffee table.

Clinton was on the phone when his secretary ushered me inside. He waved me to take a seat and continued his conversation.

"No. No. Absolutely not." His foot tapped loudly under the desk. Clinton worked long hours and often relied on Dexamyls from the trainers to keep going. The way his foot was working was a sure sign that time pills were going off somewhere. "No. Absolutely not, you can't have it." He hung up and picked a piece of paper off the desk. It was my letter to him. "Before we go any further, why did you send me this smartassed letter?"

The letter had been mimeographed and addressed "Dear General Manager."

"You sent me one. You could have just picked up the phone."

"I got more than one contract to negotiate and more important things to do than concern myself with your delicate sensitivities." He wadded up the letter and tossed it away.

"Sorry, it seemed like a good idea at the time. I apologize." I hadn't expected him to get quite so mad. It had seemed funny while I was doing it. I didn't need to be putting obstacles in my own path.

Negotiating with Clinton Foote was extremely difficult for three reasons. First, Clinton owned a small part of the club and had an override on profits. Thus, a percentage of any money Clinton saved in overhead (i.e., player's salaries) came back into his own pocket. Second, Clinton tried never to let a player know the whole truth about his status with the club. It kept the players off balance and easier to control. A player didn't need to know any more than was necessary to play on Sunday. Third, Clinton Foote was one smart son of a bitch.

Contract negotiations were honorless, distasteful, and totally frightening experiences. There were no fixed rules and behavior varied radically, depending on the individuals involved.

"Well, Phil," he had been gazing at a yellow note pad. He set it down and looked directly into my eyes. The man who extracted millions from the television networks was about to extort a measly few thousand from a fool. "How much do you want?"

I shifted uneasily in my seat. My head was crammed with facts: number of catches, number of touchdowns, yards per reception, and so on. My head was also crammed with considerations: I was the starting flanker, I was younger than Gill — he was healthier but that could change — and more. The contest would be between my head, jammed full of assumptions, facts, and fear, and Clinton Foote's note pad, a neat outline of undisputable truth.

"Well, Clinton, I . . ." My voice cracked. I cleared my throat and started again. "I was the starter last season and we won the division and I caught thirty passes, so . . ."

"Only two of those passes were for touchdowns." (I had known he was going to say that.) His eyes were on the pad.

"That's right," I came right back, "but, twenty of those thirty were key third downs and . . ."

"I see you've been studying your own statistics." Disgust edged his voice. Nothing is more despicable than an athlete who keeps his own score. He glanced at me and then dropped his eyes to the pad. He wrote something. I could hear his foot still tapping. It seemed slightly louder. My stomach churned nervously.

"Well . . ." Clinton always spoke in a firm, measured voice. Every word was carefully selected and clearly and loudly pronounced. "How much do you want?" He boomed it out.

I wanted $20,000. The Player's Association survey listed the average starting flanker's salary at $25,000. I would start there, knock off $5,000 for my unpopularity and Clinton's tightfistedness, and arrive at $20,000. It seemed fair to me. Billy Gill was getting $24,500 and I had already beaten him out before I got my knee fixed.

"Twenty-five thousand."

Clinton laughed in my face. "I'm sure we'd all like twenty-five thousand, but it's out of the question."

I had expected to be refused but there was a note of disrespect I hadn't anticipated. It left me shaken and feeling foolish.

"What do you mean?" I was scrambling and trying to reorganize.

"Just what I said. You're not worth it." He ran his finger down the margin of the yellow pad. The finger stopped and a smile turned the corners of his mouth.

There was something I didn't know. I dove back into my head: Griffith Lee, a spade from Grambling, was the only other possible threat to my starting job, but with Delma Huddle at split end and Freeman Washington starting at tight end, they wouldn't give another black a shot unless he was awful good. Griffith Lee wasn't that good. I was safe there. Where was my weakness?

"You paid that kid from New Mexico thirty-five thousand and he didn't even make the team." I knew that was a bad argument. In the early years of the club, Clinton had ordered the players not to discuss their salaries with anybody, including other players. The rule lost much of its effectiveness with the increased press coverage that came with winning, but a vestige of it still hung on in Clinton's mind. He shot me an angry glance.

"What other players earn is not the concern here." His foot started tapping louder. Christ, it would be just my luck if the damn trainers had given him a fifteen-milligram Benzedrine. I discarded my argument about Billy Gill making $24,500. "Besides, that's one reason why we can't pay you twenty-five thousand. I only have so much budget allotted for salaries. Mistakes like that have to be made up somewhere."

I didn't know how to argue with that kind of logic. It was based on the spirit of competition and free enterprise. Teammates have to fight each other for their piece of the pie. My confidence vanished. I sat dumbfounded and scared.

"Well, Clinton . . . how much then?" When he started whittling he wouldn't stop at any $20,000.

The general manager and director of player personnel took a long, slow look at his yellow note pad. His eyes ran up and down the page. He made a great show of figuring. Finally, he straightened up and cleared his throat.

"Thirteen thousand for one year."

My heart stopped.

"Thirteen thousand! Christ, you paid me eleven thousand to sit on the bench. You mean, you're only going to give me two thousand more for starting on a championship team?"

"It's all you're worth. Besides, when you add in playoff and championship money, it comes to quite a bit."

"But, Clinton, the average starter's salary is over twenty-five thousand."

"Don't believe everything you read. And even if it was true, and it's not, the players who are making that much signed for a lot more as rookies than you did."

"You mean what you pay me now depends on how I signed out of college."

"Of course, I've got a budget to balance. It wouldn't be fair to your teammates if I gave you a bigger raise just because you didn't have the foresight to sign for more money as a rookie."

My rookie negotiations had been carried out over the phone. I was an eighteenth-round draft choice and signed for $11,000, after receiving Clinton's personal promise that Dallas was signing only three other rookie receivers. Nineteen flankers showed for rookie camp but Clinton was quick to point out that only three were white.

"Goddammit, Clinton, I'm worth more than thirteen thousand. I'm the starter."

"That remains to be seen." His eyes were back on the note pad. What did he mean? I had beaten Gill out. They couldn't possible by thinking of Griffith Lee. That would mean three blacks catching passes. "B.A. is considering Gill the starter until we see how your leg responds."

My intestines fell out on the floor. I was the starter. I had started all the games. They couldn't bench me in the off season. Could they? My face collapsed. I could maintain no pretenses.

"My knee is fine. Ask the doc." My voice was small. "I won't play for that. Trade me."

"I doubt if we could get much for you . . . coming off surgery and all."

"All right." I had begun to control the panic. "What if I don't sign and come to camp and if my leg is fit then we'll talk contract." I knew I could beat out Gill. They wouldn't move Lee to flanker. I was a sure bet by league season.

"Doesn't matter. You're still only worth thirteen thousand." He took a long look at his yellow pad. "I could give you a little more if you signed for three years."

"No cut?"

"I don't give no-cut contracts." That was a lie. At least nine men, including Maxwell and Billy Gill, had no-cut contracts.

"How much money?"

Clinton took another long look at the note pad. He looked at me and frowned. "I shouldn't do it. Conrad'll be on my ass, but I'll give you sixteen thousand for three years."

"That's not enough Clinton, and you know it. It's nine thousand dollars under the average."

He shrugged. "Take it or leave it and hurry up, I've got other appointments." He looked at his watch and started tidying up his desk.

"I'm not signing. Gill can have the flanker spot. I won't come to camp."

"Then you'll be fined one hundred dollars a day until you do. You're still under option to us. I could make you play for 90 percent of what you got last year, but instead

I've made a fair offer. And don't go out of here thinking you'll get an agent to do your talking. I won't deal with one." He picked up the yellow note pad and tapped it against the desk. "I've already discussed your contract with B.A. and he thinks it's fair. You just overrate yourself."

"I won't sign." I got up and started out. Clinton stopped me at the door.

"Phil," he called, smiling and sliding the yellow note pad into the desk drawer, "this is nothing personal, you know."

"I guess not," I answered, "if you can separate what you do in your job from what you are as a person. I can't." I slammed the door.

Clinton never called me back.

The day before camp opened Bill Needham, the team business manager, phoned me.

"I have to know if you need a plane ticket to training camp," he said.

"I'm not coming."

"Hold on a minute."

A moment later B.A. came on the line.

"Phil, this is B.A. I don't care about your contract squabbles with Clinton. That's between you and him. I make it a point to never get involved. If you can get more money, more power to you. But I expect you in camp tomorrow, or I'll fine you a hundred dollars a day for every day you miss. If I was in your position, I would have come out early."

I arrived in camp the next day. That night I signed a three-year contract calling for $15,000 base salary per year plus a $1,000 incentive clause if I started. I took it all very personally.

Can a pro team beat a top college eleven? The question seems preposterous today, yet it inflamed the public and the press for many a year. In 1932, when Grange wrote this article for the *Saturday Evening Post*, his position on the issue was distinctly in the minority. Pro football had as much credibility then as pro wrestling has now, with most people believing the pros played not to win but merely to put on a good show. Grange's historical stature and quaint choice of detail are what make this period piece entertaining today; those of elevated literary sensibilities may consider themselves forewarned and move on to the next offering.

RED GRANGE
with George Dunscomb

The College Game Is Easier

"Red, you've played both college and professional football; do you believe a great college team, such as Notre Dame or Northwestern or Southern California, could beat one of the good teams in the National Pro League?"

That's a question people ask me frequently. My reply is that I believe the college eleven would have little, if any, chance of winning. I add that the professionals' margin of victory should be more than one touchdown. So saying, I bare my reddish locks to the storms of criticism which will fall on my head.

That belief in pro superiority isn't prompted by commercial loyalty to the business which still yields an excellent living for me. It is grounded on the experience of three years of comparative skylarking on college gridirons and six bruising years in professional football.

I believe that in blocking the collegians have the edge on the pros; that in ball carrying it is about a toss-up; that in tackling and general defense the professionals are far superior; that in headwork and in cool sureness, in utilizing every ounce of immense brawn, the professionals have a marked advantage.

The college players have two things in their favor which can't be laughed off. One is their pregame emotional frenzy which publicity, campus tension, the bands and fire-eating alumni create.

In my own university days, I was convinced that the fate of the nation hinged on whether we defeated Michigan. I believed that my dad would suffer intensely, might have a stroke, if we lost. The other advantage is the inspiration of great coaches such as Dick Hanley, of Northwestern; Howard Jones, of Southern California; Bob Zuppke, of Illinois; or the late and beloved Knute Rockne.

But a fanatical desire to win and the inspiration of a coach won't take a halfback over, around or through a hard, fast line which averages 220 pounds from end to end. That's what you face when you line up against the Green Bay Packers, for example.

On a college eleven of championship caliber there are usually one or two outstanding linemen; if the line averages 185 to 190 pounds, it is considered exceptionally heavy. But on a winning professional team every position in the forward wall is filled by a man mountain who is as agile and heady as he is big and powerful. Nearly every pro team puts up a front wall which averages 210 to 215 pounds, or more. . . .

My first blunt lesson in the superiority of the pro defense was administered on Thanksgiving Day of 1925, when I played my initial game with the Chicago Bears against the Chicago Cardinals. A 25-yard return of a punt was my best effort in lugging the ball forward.

I was no "galloping ghost" in the eighteen games which we crowded into the next two and one-half months. I looked bad and disappointed the crowds. But they weren't half as disappointed as I was.

Part of my inability to gallop places was due to the wall-like defense the pros put up. Part of it was due to the fact that then, and during the following two seasons, I was compelled to play twenty-five minutes of each game, regardless of injuries, as per contract with our opponents. Once I went to the Polo Grounds on crutches, donned a uniform and played quarterback. I didn't carry the ball once. I couldn't. But to the crowd I was a "yellow bum." That hurt.

Those performances fired me with one resolve. I made up my mind that some day, somehow, I'd take another crack at the professional game, under better conditions, and show the sport world that I could still tote a football. Later I had that chance.

But I'm rambling away from my subject. It's hard not to do so, when I'm talking football. I've played it in organized form for fourteen years. It is still my biggest interest, the best part of my life.

The one chance a college team might have of scoring against a good pro team, in my judgment, would be by a forward pass; provided the passer could pick out his receiver and get the ball away before those big pro linemen broke through and smothered him; provided also the pass receiver could elude the secondary defense of the pros, made up of experienced men who are hard to suck out of position by decoys and fakes.

Forward passing of the college variety isn't feared by the professionals. Only one star who had a big reputation as a passer in college has continued to shine in that capacity in the pro league. I refer to Benny Friedman, formerly of Michigan, but last year with the New York Giants. Protected by his backs and his big linemen, Benny drops back and hits his mark more often than I like.

We played three games with the Giants during the past season. In the first game, which we won 7–0, Benny was coaching at Yale and didn't play. He played the second time we met, but we managed to keep him bottled up and won again, 12–6. But in our third game Benny was hot. He completed pass after pass and gained many yards by running. That game found us on the short end of a 25–6 score. Benny Friedman can, and does, take a terrific pounding without crying about it. That, by the way, is my conception of a man!

Aside from Benny, no highly touted college passer has immediately made good in professional football; many have tried.

Chris Cagle, of Army, who is now a New York Giant, carried a big passing threat in his college days, but that threat is a minor one to our Bear defense. Chris is a dangerous man, however, when he gets into the open. He is a bit light for crashing the line; hence the Giants endeavor to shake him loose with lateral passes and forward passes. When in the clear he is one of the hardest men in the league to bring down.

"How would running backs like Pug Rentner, of Northwestern; Marchmont Schwartz, of Notre Dame; or Jimmy Purvis, of Purdue, fare against pro tacklers?" fans often ask.

If I managed a pro team and had my choice of those three backs, I would choose Purvis, of Purdue, even though I consider Rentner the greatest college halfback I've ever seen and Schwartz one of the best of the past decade. My reason for choosing Purvis, however, is that he is the kind of rugged, durable back with powerful leg drive who clicks in the professional game. Russell Saunders, of Southern California, who made good in his first year in the league, is that kind of runner. So is Ken Strong, former New York University star.

Rentner and Schwartz depend more upon shiftiness than upon sheer driving power. Rentner, in particular, might find the going hard, at first, in pro football because the kinds of plays on which he often scores in college aren't successful against the professionals. Some football authorities have said his running style closely resembles my style in college. Rentner scored many times on spectacular runs, often on sweeps outside an end; I also scored frequently on runs of that type.

But those wide end sweeps won't work in pro football, as Rentner will discover if he ever tries his hand at it. Just as I found it out in my first game in 1925. Giant pro linemen break through to dump the interferers; the husky end, adept at using his hands to ward off the blockers, if any remain, gets the runner himself, or chases him out of bounds, or maneuvers him into a position where the defensive half can smear him at the line of scrimmage.

"That's the result of poor work on the part of the blockers," someone may contend. It is an easy answer, but hardly a true one. For not even Bronko Nagurski, of Minnesota, now Bear fullback, can knock the big pro ends in so that the half can run outside. With his 225 pounds of muscle and bone, Nagurski hits harder, the pros agree, than anyone in football.

The pros also agree that Nagurski and Herb Joesting both smack the line harder than Ernie Nevers, formerly of Stanford, later with the Chicago Cardinals. Nevers is generally conceded the edge in all-around ability — in passing, kicking, running, and tackling — over any other gridster, past and present. But many believe that Jim Thorpe, the famous Indian, was greater than Nevers as a football jack-of-all-trades. I played against Thorpe only once — in a pro game in Florida in 1926. By then, Jim was old, fat and slow, yet he could still hit hard. He smacked me once and I still remember it!

Of this year's crop of college linemen, Munn, of Minnesota, and Riley and Marvil, of Northwestern, constitute a trio who would probably make the grade in professional football, with further seasoning. I say "further seasoning" advisedly. Red Sleight, widely chosen as All-American tackle when he played with Purdue, furnishes a good case in point. Red was a fine college tackle, big and rugged. He entered pro football in 1930. During his first year he was a substitute and played only part of each game. Last year he played regularly. In 1930 and during the past season we designed special plays to take advantage of his weakness — that of playing wide. We shot plays inside of him successfully. To date I've played six games against him and in every game he has become tougher until right now he is one of the best. He has learned to vary his charge and mix his style. A man who performs his football chores according to fixed routine, who does the same job in the same way each time, as most college players do, is easy to fool.

"When you pro players are out there on the field," friends often say to me, "you don't have the snap that college kids have. You walk, rather than run, to the ball after each play. You look as though you're dead on your feet. Don't you keep in condition?"

That lack of bubbling enthusiasm on the part of the pros is good judgment, but bad showmanship; the fans like a display of fiery vigor. But running back to position, dashing up and down the line of scrimmage shouting encouragement to teammates, burn up energy. Soon after you enter the moneyed game you learn that energy is too precious to waste.

As to condition, the professional player must keep in good shape in self-defense. He is playing a game in which the purpose is for one man to run as far as he can before another knocks him down. A player who is out of condition is likely to clasp a lily in his folded hands. Furthermore, his livelihood depends on how well he plays. If he is not in condition to perform aggressively he soon staggers off the payroll.

The pros work out five days each week; they play on the sixth, and have their day off on Monday, instead of on Sunday, as is the case in college. The three hours of practice are largely devoted to football fundamentals, even though most of the men have played for years. Two or three times each week we hold a blackboard drill, in which our own plays and those of our opponents are outlined and discussed.

Mention of blackboard drills brings to my mind another difference between college and professional football. A college team plays its rivals only once during the season; the pros meet other teams twice, sometimes three times. So every player on the Chicago Bears is required to make a written report immediately after each game. He must write his observations of the opposing team, particularly in regard to his individual opponent. He describes his opponent's style, charts the positions he assumed on offense and defense, the plays which worked, or failed, against him, and records any weaknesses he may have revealed. These reports are filed and used for blackboard reference before the next game with the same team. Special plays are planned to take advantage of weaknesses disclosed in the preceding game.

My own case furnishes one instance of how the pros quickly spot any weakness in a new man. When I broke into the league I had the habit of shifting my weight, unconsciously, ever so slightly onto the foot nearest the point where the ensuing play was headed. That tipped off our opponents to the spot where I would try to break through and they could quickly adjust their defense to stop the play. The pros got wise to it in my first game and played accordingly. I was told about the fault several games later, and corrected it. I had been doing the same thing in college, but no opponent, so far as I have been able to learn, ever noted it. . . .

Most college teams do things according to Hoyle. But when you play against the Green Bay Packers, you don't know what to expect next. They are the Ty Cobbs of pro football when it comes to pulling the unexpected, and they have the speed, power and confidence to make what is supposed to be bad football look like a million dollars. I've seen them try a forward pass with the ball on their own one-yard line and complete it for a long gain. This ability to keep their opponents uneasy is one of the big reasons why they have been champions of the pro league for the past three seasons.

Punting is another department of football in which the professionals excel. The best efforts of college punters are usually mediocre in comparison with the distance which the average pro kicker gets. There are no collegians who can kick the ball like Lewellen, former Nebraska star. His high, lazy punts regularly travel sixty yards through the air. Along with some ten or twelve thousand spectators, I once saw the ball travel between seventy-five and eighty yards from his foot to the point where it struck the ground. Dick Nesbitt, former Drake star, now a pro, and Ken Strong, of New York University, both get almost as much distance as Lewellen. So does Joe Lintzenich, of the Chicago Bears, but in a different way. He places the ball to spots where it is almost impossible for the safety man to catch it, so that it usually rolls for many extra yards. He practices punting for hours at a time, and can kick within ten feet of any designated point. A good punter can do a great deal toward keeping his team out of trouble and the opponents in the hole. If a college team and a professional team should clash, I believe the great pro kickers would put the collegians in tough spots during most of the game.

Another difference between the professional and college players lies in attempts to block kicks. Most college linemen — not all — attempt to break through pell-mell and block every kick. The pros also frequently attempt to block punts, but when they do, instead of charging wildly in, they use devices which aim to draw the backs who are protecting the kicker out of position, thus clearing the way for a teammate to slice in and bat down the ball.

Often, however, when it is obvious that our opponents must kick, two words travel along the Bear line. The words are, "It's on!" That phrase means that the line is not to charge in and attempt to block the punt; instead, every man is to concentrate his efforts on knocking down his opponent, so that our safety man may return the ball for a substantial distance.

"Who pulls the most rough stuff against their opponents — the college teams or the pros?" That's something many people want to know, judging from the number of times I've been asked that question.

It's hard to give an unqualified answer. The most honest one is that today neither the pros nor the collegians resort to dirty tactics to any marked extent. Both have undergone the same thorough training in sportsmanship.

The most uncomfortable experience I've had, however, occurred in a college game, against a Big Ten team which shall go unnamed here. In that game, not one but several members of the opposing team, while screened by the pile-up of players, gnawed away at my hands, arms and bare legs. My legs and hands were dented with teeth marks when the ball game was over.

"You should have played on Friday," one wag said later when I related the experience. The ravenous team was not Notre Dame, I hasten to add; Notre Dame is not a member of the Big Ten, and, as I said before, this occurred in a Western Conference game.

But that experience isn't typical of college football. The men are drilled to play hard and clean.

The pros do not attempt to maim one another, but that does not restrain them from hard charging and smashing tackles. I can testify to that! After a game I'm a combination of all the races — red, black and yellow — with very little white.

When a pro player is hurt and his opponents know it, they carefully avoid aggravating his injury. This is not because the pros have an extra quota of the milk of human kindness. Their consideration is based on common sense. An injured man is comparatively easy to handle. Plays can be worked through him and he can't contribute his full share to the offense. If he received further injury which removed him from the game, he would be replaced by an able-bodied and much tougher substitute.

"Do you professional players miss the glamour, excitement, and organized cheering which accompany college football?" we're often asked.

We do, particularly for the first year or two out of college. When a college team loses, the student body is usually loyal; it is a tradition to stand by the team in defeat. When a pro team loses, its supporters have no hesitancy in giving the eleven a right royal razzberry.

But the pro players still get a big kick out of the game. Most of them are former college players and have been trained as competitors. They are out there to win. In the dressing room I've seen hulking pro gridsters shed childish tears after losing a bitterly fought game. I've shed a tear or three myself when the Bears have dropped a close one.

The pro players must like the game, for the pay isn't large and there are easier ways to make a living. The average pay for a professional squad is about $125 per player, per game; a team plays from fourteen to eighteen games each season. The highest salary any player in the league receives, I believe, is about $10,000 a season. Only highly publicized players, who draw fans to the box office, draw compensation which might be called substantial. The highest paid men in the league are Benny Friedman, Bronko Nagurski, and a fellow named Red Grange.

When a player is injured his hospital and doctor bills are paid by the club, and even though he may not return to the lineup, he draws his salary for the remainder of the season. The contracts between the clubs and the players are patterned closely after those governing the major baseball leagues. Players can be sold or traded.

The people who believe that college football in actual play is superior to the pro brand must, I believe, be largely those who have gained their impression from the earlier days of professional football. In those days fat, panting pro gridmen gave rather laughable exhibitions. But the league is now run on a businesslike basis. It is making rapid progress; in 1931 the professional season was the most successful, financially, in history, although college football receipts slumped. The material for the teams has improved in caliber. So many college athletes are now trying out for the pro teams that a newcomer is treated as a mere recruit, who may or may not make the grade, regardless of his college reputation.

The quality of the coaching has been stepped up greatly. In former days the pros had no coaches; it was assumed that the players were experienced enough to need no supervision. Today experienced football men direct the teams; such men as Ralph Jones, formerly coach at the University of Illinois; Potsy Clark, another famous Illini; and Curly Lambeau, formerly of Notre Dame.

The coaches maintain strict discipline. They are as absolute in authority as a major-league baseball manager. They do not give pep talks, exhorting the players to fight; they don't use psychology on the men. The squads are too adult to take seriously any of the old-time gags. The efforts of the pro coaches are devoted to strategy, conditioning, and discipline.

While I'm on the subject of coaches I want to say how I feel about Coach Zuppke, who directed me during my career at the University of Illinois. So far as I am concerned, Zuppke rates a place in the all-time top flight of college football coaches. He has had a couple of lean years and the wolves have already begun to howl for his job. But give him only average material and he will fashion a team that is far above average. You take Dick Hanley, or Pop Warner, or Howard Jones; I'll take Zuppke.

Suppose we get back to my opening contention. It's hard to see how any college eleven would have much chance against a leading pro team, when all the foregoing facts are added up. The best judges—the players who have had experience in both college and professional football—are unanimous in declaring the pro game much tougher and the players more proficient. They believe that there is almost as wide a gap between professional and college football as between major and minor league base-ball. When a charity game was proposed last fall between the Chicago Bears and some outstanding college team, the pro players were tremendously disappointed when the game fell through. Every man on the Bear squad would have donated his services for the chance to settle once and for all the question of superiority.

In conclusion, there is one thing in which I take plenty of pride. It is not in the fact that I gained more than two miles of ground in my twenty games at Illinois—thanks to superb blocking by the Illini, particularly by Earl Britton, Wally McIlwain, and Jim McMillen, a trio of the finest blockers who ever played football.

I do take pride in the fact that during 1931 I led the Chicago Bears, for the season, in average gain from scrimmage, carrying the ball 605 yards in 114 attempts, an average of 5.3 yards on each try. On many of those yards I carried a 225-pound lineman on my back for company. If ballcarrying in pro football gets any harder, I'll simply have to take up bridge.

Has there ever been a more exciting runner? You take Tony Dorsett, or George McAfee, or even Gale Sayers . . . I'll go with The King. If you never saw him play, statistics are scant measure of his eminence; but Mickey Herskowitz's vivid portrait, taken from his book *The Golden Age of Pro Football*, will do nicely.

MICKEY HERSKOWITZ

The King

"It's like when you walk down a dark alley. That's how I feel when I'm out in the open, all alone—as if I'm walking down a dark alley. And you see at the end of the alley a glimmer of light from the cross street—that's the goal line—and you're in a hurry to get there. But on the way, even though the alley is so dark you can't see a thing, you sense a telegraph pole to your right and you sheer away from it. A few steps farther, you know there's a doorway with a man in it, even though you can't see him. You just feel it. So you turn away from that, too. Haven't you had that experience many times? I have."

No, most of us never had that feeling, that free-as-the-wind feeling of slipping and weaving through a broken field, of dodging and ducking around people as though they were garbage cans. But we know what he means, we get the picture, from those twenty-year-old words.

Our man with the sixth sense, with the kind of wide-angle vision that told him at a glance where every tackler was staked out, was Hugh McElhenny. They called him "The King." He ran with the ball the way little boys do in their wildest dreams. He had speed and power and guts and the complete repertory of moves: the pivot, the sidestep, the change of pace, the sudden bursts, the spinning, the faking, and an uncanny gift for breaking a tackle. Perhaps more than any back who ever played the game he was blessed with instinct—the kind that tells you when a stranger is lurking in a doorway.

Those who were close to the San Francisco 49ers—including the bankers who held the team's notes—insist that Hugh McElhenny saved the franchise. He was never able to convert his immense talents into a title for San Francisco, not in nine seasons of trying, but he became the dominant running back of the 1950s. And the 49ers were fun to watch. It was an eternal contest to see if McElhenny, and Y. A. Tittle, could score touchdowns as fast as the 49ers defense gave them away.

People used to argue about his touchdown runs the way two guys on a beach argue about girls. The last one to pass by is always the prettiest. Descriptions of McElhenny runs were like passages out of children's fiction, liberally sprinkled with opposing players bouncing off each other, getting stiff-armed, and diving helplessly at his vanishing heels. It was pure Ripley. Things like that don't really happen, do they?

Against the Bears, in his rookie season of 1952, he fielded a punt at his own 6 and rocked on his feet for a split-second or two—a McElhenny habit that enabled him to see how the field was spread. Two Chicago ends thought they had him trapped. As they closed in, McElhenny zipped straight ahead and the two ends collided, bumping heads, a moment of fine burlesque. He changed pace and a tackler appeared on his right. In two steps he was in overdrive again. He swerved to his left and the leaping Bear landed two yards behind him. He straightened up and went through the rest of the Bears as though it were some kind of barn dance. The run covered 94 yards, not including the mileage he traveled sideways.

"That," said George Halas, never a man to mince words, "was the damndest run I've ever seen in football."

Later, McElhenny said, casually, "I thought I had caught the punt at about our twenty-six. If I had known it was the six-yard line, I would have let it go."

Of course, one never knew what McElhenny would do. He was impetuous and honest, qualities that tend to confuse people. Once, against the Giants his rookie year, he grew annoyed as Tittle mounted his racehorse offense, calling his plays quickly and getting back to the line, trying to stampede the Giants. "Dammit, Y. A.," McElhenny complained, as they broke a huddle, "give us time to get out there and see how the secondary is lining up, what they're trying to do."

Tittle was stunned. "If you don't like it," he snapped, "get the hell out of here and get somebody else in."

McElhenny shrugged. Without a word he turned and jogged off the field.

His attitude most of his career, most of his life, really, was a bit on the languid side. He would not have been bearable otherwise, with his raw talent and a temper that boiled suddenly.

Between Red Grange and Joe Namath, no college player arrived with more acclaim, for reasons that were not all flattering. "The King" was the most celebrated recruiting case of his day. His story, in fact, may have been the first to alert the public that college

"THE KING"—AS McELHENNY WAS CALLED — BROKE IN AS ROOKIE OF THE YEAR IN 1952, AFTER A SENSATIONAL COLLEGE CAREER AT WASHINGTON.

BIG ENOUGH TO GET THE TOUGH YARDS, HE WAS A SUPERB LONG DISTANCE THREAT, COMBINING SPEED AND ELUSIVENESS WITH A GREAT "NOSE" FOR THE END ZONE.

IN 13 NFL SEASONS, HE AMASSED 11,375 YARDS RUSHING, RECEIVING AND RETURNING KICKS.

Hugh McELHENNY

athletes were sometimes rewarded with more than locomotive yells, free laundry, and a wrist watch for playing in the Rose Bowl.

Some sixty-three colleges competed for the right to educate Hugh McElhenny, courting him by phone, mail, and limousine even as he was doing wonderful things for Compton Junior College. His decision to enroll at the University of Washington led to an investigation of the school's recruiting practices. The popular line was that he had found his way to Seattle by following a trail of twenty-dollar bills.

His 49ers' teammates never tired of boasting that he was the first player ever to take a cut in salary to play pro football (for $7,000 his rookie season). Financial inducements aside, the pros had to wonder about his reputation for being spoiled and unreliable. Certainly coaches do. As long as a team wins, a player with Bolshevik tendencies can be considered tolerable, if difficult. When you lose, they are merely difficult.

Hugh was indifferent to discipline, chronically late for practice. He drank, and drove away his wife. He was involved in a series of publicized fights, in one of which he knocked a cop over his motorcycle, something Emily Post has never recommended.

They couldn't tame him on the field, either. He broke every rushing record at Washington and his marks are still standing twenty-five years later.

Yet in the draft of 1952, seven players were picked ahead of him, half of the first round. Of course, they were not exactly tackling dummies: Ollie Matson, Babe Parilli, Ed Modzelewski, Les Richter, Larry Isbell, Jim Dooley, and Bill Wade.

Astonished to find him still at large, the 49ers claimed McElhenny as the eighth selection. If there had been any hesitation on the part of coach Buck Shaw, it was dispelled by a frantic, 2 A.M. phone call from quarterback Frankie Albert, in Honolulu, where he had watched McElhenny tear apart the Hula Bowl. In his enthusiastic haste, Albert assured his coach, "This is the greatest running back I've ever seen, Buck . . . don't let this guy get away," and promptly forgot to reverse the charges.

On his first play as a professional, "The King" ran 60 yards for a touchdown. As Albert crossed the sideline, he headed directly for Shaw. "Hey, the club owes me six and a half bucks," he reminded him, "for that long distance call from Honolulu." Albert collected. So did the 49ers.

You could never tell from his record that McElhenny played much of his career in pain. It was contrary to medical opinion that he played at all. At the age of eleven he stepped on a broken milk bottle, severing the tendons of his right foot. He missed a year of school, spent five months in bed and seven on crutches. His doctors doubted that he would walk normally again, which is why doctors make such lousy football coaches. In later years he would need a steel plate in his shoe, and pain-deadening shots in his foot. It was such a handicap he lasted only thirteen seasons, finally playing on a winner, with the Giants, in his next-to-last year.

In 1957, rookie quarterback John Brodie, who lived nearby, asked if he could ride to practice with him. When Brodie mused aloud one day that it was nice to have "The King" for a pal, McElhenny winced. "Listen, rook," he said, "I never want to get too friendly with anybody on this team. That's because the day will come when you have to say good-bye."

That day came in 1961 when Red Hickey, with whom he did not get along famously, dropped him into the expansion draft. The string took him to Minnesota, New York, and Detroit. At a retirement dinner, Frank Gifford, a friend and a foe since their college days, narrated a film of McElhenny highlights. One after another, long runs filled the screen: an 86-yard twister against the Packers, 81 versus the Bears, 71 through the Rams. "If there is a certain sameness to these pictures," observed Gifford, "well, there was a certain sameness to the way he ran."

How we love pro football's bad boys, the sauce and the spice: Johnny Blood, Bobby Layne, Hugh McElhenny, Joe Namath, Paul Hornung, and countless other loungers and lotharios. No malted-milk matinee idols for us; no sir, leave them to the college crowd. Here's a piece of pure fluff, lighter than air and utterly without redeeming social value. In fact, it's hard not to imagine Steve Martin lurking behind these words—a wild and *cuh-razy* guy! Obscured by the playboy image, however, was one hell of a football player. He made Vince Lombardi's power sweep the emblematic play of the 1960s, and the 176 points he scored in the twelve-game season of 1960 may be the game's most impregnable record.

PAUL HORNUNG
with Al Silverman

Football and the Single Man

Palm Beach . . . Hartford, Connecticut . . . Washington . . . Honolulu . . . Coral Gables . . . San Francisco . . . Escanaba, Michigan . . . Chicago . . . Nashville . . . Cleveland . . . Chicago . . . Paris, France . . . Chicago . . . East Point, Georgia . . . St. Louis . . . Dallas . . . Atlanta . . . Menasha, Wisconsin . . . Hollywood . . . Hollywood, California . . . Hollywood . . . Worcester, Massachusetts . . . Hollywood . . . Hollywood . . . Evanston . . . Toronto, Canada . . . New York . . . Indianapolis . . . Baton Rouge . . . New York City . . . Louisville . . . Nashville . . . Miami . . . Lexington . . . Cincinnati, Ohio . . . Louisville . . . Louisville . . . Chicago . . . Miami . . . Charlotte, North Carolina . . . Indianapolis . . . Miami . . . Dallas, Texas . . . New Orleans . . . Chicago . . . Burbank, California . . . Hollywood . . . Arlington, Virginia . . . Denver, Colorado . . . Columbus, Ohio . . . Hollywood.

The little black book for 1963.

I have one for every year. After you've been around the National Football League for three or four years, you naturally have your little book. When I was in college I had the greatest little black book in the world—alphabetical, by the numbers, rating system, the whole bit. And somebody stole the damn thing on me.

The little black book comes in handy when I haven't been in a city for a year or so.

I find myself forgetting names easily so I just get this little book out and look in and call the numbers and see if they're still there. Lots of them I keep in touch with, the ones I really dig.

And if I don't keep in touch with them, they usually keep in touch with me. Like in Green Bay during the season, I may get three or four calls a night from girls. Either they want to come up—and see me sometime, as Mae West would say—or they just want to talk, renew a friendship.

One night in the fall of 1964 when I was lying on the couch trying to rest the pinched nerve in my neck, I got this long-distance call from Richmond, Virginia. Here's a one-sided version of the conversation.

"Sure, I'm well. No, I'm not. I got a bad neck. . . . No, it's not real bad. . . .

"How long you going to be in Richmond? . . . Then you'll come and see me? . . . You like Richmond? A swinging town?

"You what? I love you, too. . . . Well, it's mutual. . . .

"I'm going to do a book and give you a whole chapter. Yeh. It'll be called, 'Marilyn Monroe II.' . . . Why? You lost weight? . . .

"Of course I want to see you. Whenever you get enough money to come and see me, I want you to come. . . . I can't afford to pay your way. If I paid your way, I'd feel kind of guilty about it, you know that. You what? Oh, well you want me to reimburse you? Hey, no chance, no chance. . . . Why don't you hop a plane and come up today?

"Oh, I was in love with you once. Yes, I was. No, there will always be something there between you and me, you know that. . . . Huh? I don't know. I haven't seen you. I don't get to see you that much any more.

"I'll be home in December, darling. About the sixteenth. Until Christmas. . . . Well, after that I'll be home all year. . . . You know, there's a couple of things I got to do. . . .

"Listen, give me your number where I can call you there. . . . What've you got, an apartment there?

"Sure, you can come and see me. Make it during the week, though. I'm booked up on the weekends (laughter). What? I got to work on the weekends. . . . Huh? I'm just kidding you, honey. I just want to see you. When would you like to come? Well, get yourself on the plane. Huh? All right. . . .

"Honey, we're going to Frisco this week. . . . Friday. You can come up Wednesday and Thursday. . . .

"All right, we'll go right after the season. We'll go to Jamaica. . . . Sure, I will.

"Of course I still love you. No, I'm just tired. You know I can never stay on the phone over three minutes. And this is five. I'll talk to you. . . . Get up here, you hear? . . . All right, honey, bye, bye."

Translated: I used to see this girl once in a while and she looks just like Marilyn Monroe and she called me with half a mind to come up and see me, but I wasn't about to encourage her, and I told her I'd see her after the season. Which I did. We didn't go to Jamaica together. We met in New York.

A fairly typical phone conversation. The big standing joke in Green Bay used to be—

Who's Hornung going to have in this week? I would import girls in every week, from Chicago, New York, etc. But in 1964, the year of my return to football, I didn't do it. I knew it would be a hectic year and I was more serious about things.

And that, I think, indicates something about me. Women have always been foremost in my thoughts—next to football. I'm a professional football player first, a bachelor second. And being a professional football player *and* single, there are never any problems about finding girls.

They call me on the phone like that fiancée from Richmond, and if they don't call, they write. Some of the letters I get are pretty preposterous. Like I got one from a boy who asked for an autographed picture and there was this "P.S." on it:

"I would like to have one, too. I am Jimmy's aunt. I just love big men. Why don't you just come with it."

And another one from a girl of sixteen:

"Dear Paul, I love you and the Packers very much. I love you and the boys more than the Beatles. I think they're fat. . . ."

A lot of times the girls write and enclose a picture. Usually, they try to be subtle, like this one:

"Dear Paul Hornung, my mother has been a fan of yours since your green Golden Boy days at Notre Dame. I'm going home at Thanksgiving and I would like to take her an autographed picture of you. Of course, I thought it only fair to send you my picture in return."

I never pay any attention to this type of letter, unless the picture is of an exceptionally good-looking girl. I never will forget a letter I got from a girl in Pennsylvania. She sent her picture along and I'll be damned if she wasn't Brigitte Bardot No. 2. She put in a couple of pictures, in fact, one in a low-cut dress, another in a bathing suit. She said, "You're real cute and I'm a pro-football fan and I'd like to meet you." I'm always a little bit leery of this kind of letter. Usually, I don't want to meet anybody who writes a letter like that. But this girl was an exception, she was just a flat knockout. So I jotted down her number in my book.

Then I was in Pennsylvania for a banquet and I called her. She drove up and it turned out it wasn't the same girl as the picture. She wasn't bad but I was expecting Brigitte Bardot, you know. She must have had a little intestinal fortitude just to show up. I asked her about the picture and she said, "Well, that was taken a couple of years ago when I was modeling real well." So we had coffee and I said sayonara.

Guys have come up to me and said, "What's the secret of your success?" And there isn't any secret. As I said, I'm a professional football player and I'm single. There are other guys in the league who are better-looking than me (though it hurts me to admit it). I remember the time I was introduced to Ben Agajanian. This was in 1961 when I went into the Army and Ben joined the team to help with the field-goal kicking. I was in the house combing my hair and staring into the mirror when Ben came in.

"This is Ben Agajanian," someone said.

I just kept on combing, kept on looking in the mirror, completely ignoring Ben. I looked at myself and said, "Gotta be the handsomest guy in the world." Ben broke up.

I've got this curly blond hair, which is mainly why they started calling me Golden Boy. And someone described me as having "clear blue eyes, dimpled chin, and sensuous lips." Which is all right, even if my eyes are green. I accept it. But what I think the girls really like about me is my *charm*. I drive a Cadillac, and that's part of the charm. I like to dress well, and that spells charm. (I have maybe twenty-five suits and a dozen sports jackets, more ensembles, someone said, than Perry Como. I only *wish!*) I like to take women to the nicest places, good entertainment, and have a nice dinner. I think this is all very attractive for a girl, naturally, to take them to the nicest places and all the night spots.

And you're in these spots with different girls and you start making the columns. Within one week, I was in Winchell's column as having fallen out of love with a girl in New York, and a few days later Ed Sullivan had me falling in love with someone else. And I think that's how the reputation spreads, and it is exaggerated.

But the image builds up. During my sabbatical there were rumors around that I was going to be traded to the New York Giants for Del Shofner. Just before the Giants' playoff game in '63 with the Chicago Bears, Giant coach Allie Sherman called a team meeting.

"You've all been hearing these rumors about me trading Shofner for Hornung," Sherman said. "Well, let me tell you, I wouldn't trade Del Shofner for Paul Hornung and *all* his girl friends."

With that, Mo Modzelewski jumped up and cried, "Wait a minute, Coach. Take a vote, take a vote!"

Dan Jenkins' novel *Semi-Tough* is set in the not too distant future; the excerpt below takes place on the Saturday before a Super Bowl showdown between the two New York teams. In the fashion of Jerry Kramer, Ron Mix, Dick Butkus, et al., the Giants' Billy Clyde Puckett has been keeping a diary, heretofore secret. While *Semi-Tough* may not be a true *roman à clef* (could there be a model for T. J. Lambert?), here's a *clef* to the identity of singer Elroy Blunt: like Jenkins he wrote for *Sports Illustrated*; he is represented in this volume; and he is in truth the composer of that deathless ditty *I'm Just a Bug on the Windshield of Life*.

DAN JENKINS

Rippin' and Roarin' and Ritin'

I may have to dough-pop Cissy Walford before I ever get around to the dog-ass Jets.

What she has done is semi-unforgivable and a rotten thing to do to somebody that she is supposed to be about half-crazy about, which is me.

I am hotter than a pot of butter beans right now, as you might guess. Shit, I'm hot.

What Cissy did was go squirt off her mouth to Boke Kellum, our friendly neighborhood fag Western hero, about this book I am writing.

And what Boke Kellum did was go squirt off his mouth to the newspapers about it, and here it all is, right here in my hand in the Saturday morning Los Angeles *Times*.

The dog-ass headline says:

PUCKETT TURNS AUTHOR FOR SUPER BOWL.

The story says:

All-Pro Running Back Billy Clyde Puckett, who may hold the key to the New York Giants' chances in tomorrow's Super Bowl, will be taking notes on the sidelines throughout the game.

The *Times* has learned that Puckett is keeping a diary of Super Bowl Week and will turn it into a hard-cover book for a major publishing house next fall.

Puckett's book will be most revealing, according to reliable sources.

It is understood that Puckett is delving into many personalities involved in the Super Bowl attraction, and will present some of the darker sides of the game of pro football itself.

Much of the book, the *Times* has learned, will be devoted by Puckett to describing exactly how the Giants prepared for the contest.

It is also believed that Puckett will describe how he developed his rip-roaring running style, a style which has made him the leading rusher in the NFL.

Parts of the book will also touch on some of Puckett's close friends, such as Boke Kellum, the handsome star of the hit TV series, *McGill of Santa Fe.*

There's some more but mainly it's quotes from some of the dog-ass Jets, like Dreamer Tatum, about me being so talented as to be able to prepare for a big game and write a book at the same time.

Boy, I am so hot right now that I could turn into some kind of T. J. Lambert.

If there was ever a bad time for something like this to come out, it is the day before the Super Bowl.

Cissy Walford has already cried a few times this morning and tried to make every-thing all right by grabbing me in the crotch but it hasn't helped.

I've told her that if I lay my eyes on Boke Kellum again I was gonna leave him every way but alone.

Man, I'm still hot. And all of this hit me more than an hour ago when I got up. I don't usually get hot like this for anything other than a football game. But I am hot.

Shake says that I shouldn't be so hot because a lot of other stud athletes have written books and everybody just figures that it's what a stud athlete does for money these days.

Barbara Jane said she didn't think it was anything to be bothered about.

"It's not as if we've just lost to Spring Branch." She smiled.

Barb said the best way to look at it was that the dog-ass Jets wouldn't know what to do, going up against a real live intellectual book writer.

I said what bothered me most was having to go to a squad meeting pretty soon and take a lot of shit from my pals.

But it's something I've got to do. And right away, in fact.

See you in a little while, gang. If there's anything left of me after T. J. Lambert gets through.

If not, I'd like my ashes pitched out of a taxi at the northeast corner of Fifty-fifth and Third.

That's where P. J. Clarke's is, of course.

It's probably asking too much of the owner, Danny Lavezzo, to hang my photo on the wall, back there in the back room where all the celebs hang out; back there with the checkered tablecloths and the Irish waiters.

There wouldn't be much status in having it hanging in the middle room, behind the front bar—the room where everybody stands in line, hoping and praying for a table in the back. There's nothing in the middle room but too much light, and some drunks standing around a garbage pail.

I guess I don't know of anybody who ever got his picture up on the wall in Clarke's, without dying. Not even a Greek ship owner or a columnist. If Frank Gifford or Charley Conerly or Kyle Rote couldn't do it from the old Giant glory days, I don't know how I could expect it.

Maybe my only chance is if T. J. Lambert turns me into a tragic legend.

"Oh, what could have been," they'll say in Clarke's.

And hang my picture.

Feelin' you is feelin' like a wound that's opened wide,
Feelin' you means troubles by my side.
Feelin' you ain't easy,
Don't know how much I can take.
Feelin' someone gone is feelin' nuthin' but an ache.

When you took my credit cards and headed north across the bay,
When you piled up all my clothes there in the hall,
When your anger made you laugh at all the bills I'd have to pay,
I could hear you laughin' louder while I kicked and beat the wall.

You ain't nuthin' but a servin' wench, it's true.
Serve it up and grab a tip or two.
Eggs fried greasy, coffee dark,
Donuts hard as sycamore bark,
But you'll trap another fool like you know who.

I just hope you'll keep on movin' down the road.
Movin' faster than I'm drivin' this old load.
Much more heartache I ain't needin',
Though your looks have got me bleedin',
I'm just about to get your memory throwed.

But feelin' you is feelin' like a wound that's opened wide,
Feelin' you means troubles by my side.
Feelin' you ain't easy,
Don't know how much I can take.
Feelin' someone gone is feelin' nuthin' but an ache.

Nothing helps trouble and woe, I think, like listening to music. I've been listening to some Elroy Blunt tunes here on the portable stereo we brought with us to our palatial suite.

One of my favorites among his new songs is "Feelin' You," which is those words I've just recited, in a semi-tuneful way.

It's late in the afternoon upon this Saturday in January. I've been back from the squad meeting for quite a while and had lunch up here in the suite.

Some of the Giant fans who have flown out for the game are having a party down around the cabanas by one of the swimming pools. That's where Barbara Jane and Cissy are. Shake Tiller and Hose Manning have gone over to the Beverly Wilshire to talk to some *Sports Illustrated* writers and editors and reporters and photographers.

We'll be heading out to Elroy Blunt's mansion for his party in a while. He drew up directions for our rented car on how to get there.

This hasn't been too good a day for the stud hoss, unfortunately.

All of my teammates had read that story in the Los Angeles *Times*, and of course they all clapped when I walked into the squad meeting.

I caught a whole bunch of heat.

Varnell Swist said, "Say, baby, you ain't gonna write anything about what a cat does on the road, are you?"

Puddin Patterson said, "Tell us about that rip-roarin' runnin' style. Do you just jive it on in there for six by your own self?"

Puddin said, "Er, uh, say, baby. Do you rip first, or do you roar first?"

There was lots of giggling among my pals.

Euger Franklin said, "If me and Puddin ain't blockin' nobody's ass, he just lay down, baby."

Varnell Swist said, "What you gonna say about the road, baby? Some wives is gonna read that mother you writin', you dig what I'm sayin'?"

Puddin Patterson said to the squad, "Lookie here, cats. Lookie here at the cat who holds the key to the whole jivin' tomorrow. Ain't he a dandy? He just gonna go out there tomorrow by his own self and win his self a Super Bowl."

I was trying to grin while I blushed.

Puddin said, "Cat gonna put that rip-roarin' jive on them other cats and they just gonna say, 'Oooo, he hit har-rud.' Cat just goes shuckin' and jivin' out there with nobody but his own self. Lookie here at this mean cat."

Jimmy Keith Joy said, "Say, baby. That *dark* side of pro football you gonna jive about. You ain't talkin' about brothers, are you?"

Euger Franklin said, "Show us that key you holdin' to the game, baby."

"It's them moves," said Puddin Patterson. "Say. Say, lookie here. The key is in them big old strong legs that lets this cat go rippin' and roarin'."

"Make my hat hum he hit so har-rud," said Euger Franklin.

Puddin said, "Everybody get down and cat say hup. Cat say hup-hup. Cat say hup-hup-hup. And old Billy Clyde go jivin' for six. Crowd say oooo-weee, he run so har-rud because he's a-rippin' and roarin'."

O.K., I said. Go ahead on.

Puddin said, "Everybody get down and cat say hup again. Cat say hup-hup. And Billy Clyde go hummin' for six. And crowd say oooo-weee, he run so har-rud and he writin' a book while he rip-roarin'."

T. J. Lambert hadn't spoke until he finished the sack of chili cheeseburgers he brought to the squad meeting.

He finally stood up and licked his fingers and bent over, with his butt toward me, and he cut one that must have been the color of a Christmas package.

"That's all I got for tootie fruities what write books," he groaned.

When Roger Kahn wrote this piece for *Time* in 1976, the Bucs had lost the first eight games of their existence; they were to lose eighteen more before victory came at last. Of the twenty-six consecutive losses, eleven were by shutout. This was slaughter of historic dimension. Yet amid the carnage John McKay was building a team, primarily through the draft, that would make the playoffs in 1979. No expansion team, not even the Dallas Cowboys, did so well so soon. And it was a black quarterback, that contradiction in terms in the minds of so many, who led the way.

ROGER KAHN

Aboard the *Lusitania* in Tampa Bay

The entry of John McKay into professional football, riding a swan boat across the glinting waters of Tampa Bay, was converted into a financial report by certain elements of the press. There is a lingering Neanderthal quality in some of our new sports journalism. If you can't find a sex angle, write money.

According to a glut of stories, McKay was leaving the University of Southern California—where he had won four national championships—for a salary of $175,000 a year, a $350,000 home, complete with furniture, maid, gardener and pool service, plus five new cars and a variety of land deals that could have seduced the Shah of Iran.

McKay's response was characteristic and brief. "Nonsense," he said. "The figures are wildly out of line. Actually, I'm going to Tampa for the cigars."

In becoming midwife to the Tampa Bay Buccaneers, currently staggering through their first season in the National Football League, John McKay won instant independence. At 53 he will not again have to worry about economic indicators. But by concentrating on the man's capital rather than his style, one misses the point. McKay was a great college coach who never publicly confused his success with the state of humanity. Football, he has suggested, is only a game. "You draw Xs and Os on a blackboard and that's not so difficult. I can even do it with my left hand."

Among the governors of the NFL, such talk is heresy. They insist that football is America, manliness, work ethic, integration, and Vince Lombardi saying for the thousandth time, "Winning isn't everything. It's the only thing." This, if it means anything at all, means that Lombardi saw a movie called *Trouble Along the Way* in 1953. Playing a football coach in that film, John Wayne mouthed the lines that everyone now attributes to Lombardi.

But like McKay, Lombardi had a style. It was ferocity. That, plus his victories at Green Bay, made him the focus for a generation of football writing. Presently, we heard from the right that Lombardi was the noblest Roman since Octavius. (Not Brutus. Brutus lost.) The left suggested that he would have made a perfect fascist. In the cacophony people forgot that Lombardi was only a football coach who put Xs and Os on a board— righthanded.

The Tampa Bay Buccaneers were formed from a pool of pro freshmen—"rooks" in the argot—and a group of veterans other teams considered expendable. Approaching Tampa, McKay said that it would take three years to assemble a competitive team. Meanwhile, he would do the best he could.

After three losses in exhibition games, the Buccaneers defeated the Atlanta Falcons, 17–3. "Ho-hum," McKay said, in controlled delight. "Another dynasty." Then came this championship season. Tampa lost consecutively to Houston, San Diego, Buffalo, Baltimore, Cincinnati, Seattle (another expansion team), Miami, and Kansas City. When I caught up with them in Denver their record was 0–8, but their spirits were stained with hope. The Denver Broncos had been playing poorly, and a Denver physician who played football told me, "We need a new quarterback and a new coach." That complaint classically signifies trouble, and trouble—somebody else's trouble— was what the Buccaneers needed most.

The afternoon offered a brilliant Colorado sky. Denver scored ten points in the first quarter and McKay lost Lee Roy Selmon, his best defensive lineman, with a knee injury. But the Buccaneers resisted collapse. Helped by three penalties, Steve Spurrier put together a reasonable touchdown drive in the second quarter. Later Dave Green kicked a field goal and tied the game.

After the half, Tampa, sensing the possibility of victory, drove to the Denver 9. They stalled. The Buccaneers drove again, reached the 18, and got a field goal. Two good drives. Ball possession for most of a quarter. And a total of only three points. Then that brilliant sky fell on McKay and his urchins.

The Broncos scored on a 71-yard pass play. Within a minute they intercepted and scored again. Soon the Broncos led by 48–13 and were trying for more.

Afterward McKay refused to congratulate his conqueror, coach John Ralston, who came to Denver out of Stanford. Instead, he called Ralston a ten-letter word, "for stacking on the points." When Ralston was mentioned in a press conference, McKay chomped a cigar. "He's a prick. He always was a prick. I hope he gets fired," said this devoutly civilized man. From another world Lombardi smiled ferociously.

In his office at Tampa the next afternoon, McKay had regained his poise. "I shouldn't have said those things. Bear Bryant, my best friend in coaching, says that after a bad loss you ought to stay in the closet for a week. I know Denver needed a win and maybe Ralston was saving his job by winning big."

Bob Moore, Tampa's starting tight end, played under Ralston at Stanford. "I'm not getting in between the two coaches," he said. "I'm used to winning. I won in college and I won with the Oakland Raiders and this is just awful for me. We lose every week and the group experience is negative. Sometimes I feel as though I were on the aft deck of the *Lusitania*."

Moore, who is black-haired and disciplined and handsome, shows how a pro can lose with the shadow of a smile. In three years I hope McKay shows the country how to win at professional football without presenting the game as a metaphor for life.

Winning is neither everything nor the only thing. It is simply better than losing on a Sunday under a high Denver sky. Then Monday comes and everybody, except the football players, has to go back to reality and work.

In 1958–59 Eugene "Big Daddy" Lipscomb, the six-foot-six, 290-pound behemoth of the champion Baltimore Colts, was the most feared tackle in the game. In 1960–61 Alex Karras, the younger and comparatively diminutive tackle of the Detroit Lions, took Big Daddy's place on the all-pro squad as Lipscomb moved on to Pittsburgh. So when fate brought these two defensive linemen face to face in 1962, as the Lions were whipping the Steelers 45–7, the fur was bound to fly. This scene is from Karras's memoir, *Even Big Guys Cry*.

ALEX KARRAS
and Herb Gluck

Big Daddy and Me

We're playing the Steelers in a home opener, and our offense had all its guns going early in the first quarter. I'm watching it all from the sideline, with particular emphasis on Big Daddy, who's showing me moves that I've never before seen by a defensive tackle. He probably woke up in a bad mood this morning, because the dirt is flying in his vicinity and our guards are coming out of it like drunks being tossed from a saloon. Anyway, we finally get into field-goal position. George Wilson sends in Wayne Walker to try one from 32 yards out. Then he decides to send me in to block on the line. This never happened before, so I run up to Wilson and say, "I'm *defense*, coach. You sure you want me out there?"

"On the double, Karras!"

I move to the guard position, which puts me directly in front of Big Daddy. Squatting down to face him, I see his lips fold back. Steam escapes from his mouth. "Ah'm gonna kill you," he says.

A few seconds later, Walker puts his toe into the ball. Big Daddy shoots up from the ground, deflects the kick, knocks me down, and grinds his foot into my ass three times. I get up and say, "Thank you, Big Daddy," and stagger off the field.

Next thing I know, our premier quarterback, Milt Plum, engineers a touchdown drive that brings forty-five thousand fans up off their seats. Once again Wilson sends me in, this time to block for the extra point. Sure enough, Big Daddy proceeds to beat the living shit out of me just like before, and I thank him kindly for doing such a swell job of it.

It goes on like this all afternoon. We keep on scoring touchdowns and I keep getting it from Big Daddy. On our fourth scoring play, Lipscomb gets so incensed he removes my helmet, hits me over the head with it, and almost buries me in the ground. Right then and there I make a vow that if this stupid quarterback of ours throws one more touchdown pass, I'll find a way to get thrown out of the game.

Wouldn't you know, Plum immediately gets back in the groove. He marches straight down the field on the strength of his arm for a fifth touchdown. And I go in again for the extra point. The count's set on four. I take off on two, punch Big Daddy on the mouth as hard as I can, and step back. He blinks, then snorts. The guy isn't human.

In desperation, I grab the referee and stick him between me and Big Daddy.

"Hey, ref, didn't you see what I just did? I not only jumped offside, I hit Lipscomb right in the face, which is a violation of rule number seven. You have to kick me out of the game. I want to leave right now!"

"I didn't see it," says the referee.

"Well, you better take my word for it. That's what I did. So kick me out of the fucking game."

Meanwhile, Big Daddy is kicking clumps of grass out of the turf like a crazed bull. This upsets the official, so he pipes up, "Okay, Karras, you're out of the game."

Feeling safe and home free, I beeline it to the sideline, but not before turning around to sing out, "Hey, Big Daddy, I don't know who you think you are, but I'm the toughest sonofabitch to ever come out of Gary, Indiana. If I ever catch you off the field, I'm gonna whip your ass!"

The man is three stories higher than me. As I look at him, his eyes are absolutely on fire.

About an hour later I'm back in my hotel. The phone rings; someone confirming a business appointment at a downtown restaurant. I get dressed up, then leave the room, whistling all the way to the elevator.

The numbers descend: 22, 21, 20, 19 . . . then stop. The doors open, and the wildest, meanest-looking guy I've ever seen in my entire life gets in. It's Big Daddy.

Immediately I remove my glasses, bow my head, and don't say a word. In total silence, we ride down to the lobby. Just as I'm getting out, feeling sure that Lipscomb hasn't recognized me, a huge paw clamps down on my shoulder.

"I know who the fuck you are, Karras."

Without missing a beat I say, "Big Daddy, have you read your NFL player's contract?"

"Naw . . ."

"Well, if you look at your contract, you'll see we have just added a clause that says we're all union brothers. And as union brothers we have to stick together, no matter what."

"Yeah?"

"That's right. By the way, do you know the union song?"

"Fuck no."

"Well, you better learn it."

I leave him there, scratching his head, and hope I never run into him again.

I never did.

The advent of the 4–3 defense created the position of middle linebacker; the man created to play the position was Dick Butkus. But by late 1972, when Murray Kempton wrote this item, Butkus was in physical and spiritual decline along with the Chicago franchise. Even George Halas, the ageless legend who had seen them all from Thorpe to Sayers and had weathered storms seemingly worse than this, despaired. The team famous for giving pro football the modern T formation was saddled with a stone-age offense led by a single-wing-type tailback. Ten years, three head coaches, and umpteen quarterbacks later, the Bears are still rebuilding.

MURRAY KEMPTON

Twilight of the Gods

The memoirs of Dick Butkus (*Stop-Action*, 1972), the Chicago Bears' middle line-backer, are as curiously and honestly affecting a document as the autobiography of King Kong might be. Think of what Kong, a beast of considerably more dignity and infi-nitely more sentiment than his proprietors, could have told us about the embarrassment of having to make faces for the sort of people who pay to see faces made. Think of what Kong would have said if he had stayed in his cage and endured seven years of that. He would have said what Dick Butkus says now:

"It seems they were just waiting for someone to fit the role. I came along and they hung that animal tag on me. Television shows, newspapers constantly build up this idea of how hard I play; that story about how I dream about knocking guys' heads off, knocking them right off . . . all that crap."

The years have left Dick Butkus barely able to endure the sight of man. We might take for granted a bill of exceptions for his teammates; yet, out of forty Chicago Bears, he seems to have genuine fraternal affection only for the other two linebackers. He has a co-belligerent's respect for three-fourths of the rush line; a baffled disgruntlement with most of the defensive secondary; a general irritation with the whole offensive platoon; a fierce disdain for the last of his head coaches; an amused disdain for his present one.

"It has got to the point," Dick Butkus says, "where I don't give a damn what the offense does. I just feel like playing, and, if I have to just play for myself, that's what I'm going to do."

Every one of the Chicago Bears seems to play for himself. There is, for example, Steve Wright, a tackle of inconspicuous achievement except for all those epic moments at Green Bay when his antic disregard for every canon of the church broke even the rock that was Vince Lombardi.

"Lombardi would fly into almost uncontrollable rages at the guy," Butkus reminds us. "One day he lost control completely and pounded Wright with his fists and screamed at him on the practice field. Steve just laughed at him."

You can measure the declining health of any organized religion from the smell of heresy on its underground saints. Wright was transferred to the New York Giants, where he was caught laughing at the game films, and then banished to the Bears where he yacked merrily on, no more bridled by exile than Trotsky in Mexico.

One day Wright said blithely to Butkus that, if the Bears didn't make him happy, he'd just go someplace else.

"That's a pretty good position you're in," Butkus replied. "Me, I can't do that. I'm locked up. I can say I'd like to go someplace else, but then somebody's going to say you can't, you're Chicago."

And how dreadful it is to have become Chicago. The Bears have lost one game, tied one, and are playing the Detroit Lions. There are less than two minutes left, and Detroit is a touchdown ahead with the ball on the Bear fifteen-yard line. It is one of those moments that legend certifies as the final test of the character of its heroes. Dick Butkus looks at the Lions' formation. He has the special pride in his finesse that consoles men universally exalted for their mere animal abilities. It is a notion that he can divine the quarterback's intention just by watching the set of his feet. Dick Butkus comes forward from his normal position and inserts himself in the front four. A five-man line glares at quarterback Greg Landry. There is the illusion that drums are beating somewhere and bugles blowing. And Greg Landry takes the ball; the Detroit center dexterously wedges out the fearsome monster whose doom it is to *be* Chicago, and Dick Butkus can only watch Greg Landry move across the goal line through the hole that might have been Dick Butkus.

The game that has so long obsessed us began in Chicago fifty-two years ago when George Halas brought his Decatur Staleys to town. There, in decent privacy, he commenced to play teams from Moline, Waukegan, and Hammond. In those days you could claim the championship of the universe if you could just beat Akron. But now, at Soldier Field, with Halas raging behind the glass of his cubicle in the press box, it could be sensed that the game had run its course.

It is never fair, of course, to legislate a universal disaffection from one's own withdrawal. Men are as various in what bores them as in what delights them; still, what is more tedious than halfbacks running at will with no one to stop them? Here was a game in which the Bears gained 253 yards rushing, the Lions 197. The Lions punted once, the Bears not at all. All day, forces hardly irresistible ran over objects anything but immovable.

The Bears indeed have arrived at the possession of an especially unique suspicion that the game's curve is descending. Their Bobby Douglass need only to maintain his early pace to be the first quarterback in the memory of the National Football League to play every game and to rush for a thousand yards in a single season — and pass for fewer.* He is a plow horse both earnest and honest; yet he has been four years in the league and no coach seems to have explained to him that there exists such a resource as an alternate receiver.

And yet, who does not remember the Bears of old? Once at Yankee Stadium, in 1965, when they were still being coached by Halas, the Bears were beating the Giants 28–7. Near the end, the Giants scored a touchdown with a pass in the end zone. As Chuck Mercein went up to catch it, Roosevelt Taylor, the Bears' cornerback, hit him with a tackle that would have left the Gordian knot a mess of broken threads. The Bears were not even in the Giants' division; according to the schedule, these teams would not meet again for three years, and Chuck Mercein did not have the likeliest prospects of being around when they did. Yet Roosevelt Taylor wanted Mercein to remember, wherever he went, what happens to anyone who makes the mistake of scoring in a zone assigned to the custody of a Chicago Bear. Such were the Chicago Bears, bound for Black Mountain with their razor and their gun, gonna cut you if you stand still, gonna shoot you if you run.

Nowadays there is universal agreement that the best — often the only — entertainment at a Bears game belongs to the journalist who draws the seat nearest George Halas's box. There he can listen to Halas curse. Halas curses, no doubt, with an imagination that would be taken as quite by-the-way in the East but that seems to make him a very Yeats of the obscene to provincials. Still it is hard to believe that he curses with conviction.

You are grateful to meet him; he has the almost twinkling charm that reminds the beholder that, in America, passion will assist a man to rise, but only passion combined with con can guarantee his rise all the way. Halas curses but he makes no effort to lift the curse; he may be ashamed of his team, but he is not embarrassed at the poverty of the spectacle it offers. He is immortal for a dozen reasons. The Bears have beaten the Green Bay Packers fifty-five times, a statistic as awesome in its way as the ninety-two novels of Balzac. A Halas team once beat the champions of the Eastern Division of the National Football League *seventy-three* to nothing. Only this season, under disputed circumstances, did someone finally break Halas's own forty-nine-year-old record for

*Close but no cigar. He rushed for 968 yards, a record, and passed for 1,246. — ED.

THE CHICAGO BEARS HAVE ALWAYS REFLECTED THE PUGNACIOUS PERSONALITY OF "PAPA BEAR," THEIR FOUNDER, OWNER, AND LONGTIME COACH —

George Halas.

LIKE HALAS, THE BEARS, AT THEIR BEST, WERE AGGRESSIVE, LOYAL, DURABLE, SKILLED, DEDICATED, AND TOUGH.

THROUGHOUT THEIR LONG HISTORY, THE BRUINS HAVE HAD MANY GREAT PLAYERS WHO EXEMPLIFIED THAT "BEAR SPIRIT," NONE MORE THAN

DICK BUTKUS

WHO DOMINATED RIVALS SO THOROUGHLY FROM MIDDLE LINEBACKER THAT HE WAS MORE THAN A STAR — RATHER A WHOLE CONSTELLATION — "URSA MAJOR."

running 98 yards with a recovered fumble. And when Halas did it, he was chased by Jim Thorpe. The Bears' owner is also immortal, as only a very few men are, for being possessed of one of those natures dried down to a bone-white simplicity. It can be described with an epithet: Mike Ditka, his great tight end, will someday be forgotten for everything except having described Halas as an owner who throws around nickels like they were manhole covers.

Yet Halas does not look like a miser; and we owe him the dignity of wondering whether he might not be something rather grander, let's say the Great Past enforcing its judgment on the Puny Present. After all, Halas can remember that Bronko Nagurski's is a name freighted with nostalgia for sentimentalists who never saw him, and that Bronko Nagurski's reward for helping the Bears win their first NFL championship playoff in 1933 was $210.43. (When the Bears won their last championship thirty years later, a back named Larry Glueck got $5,899 for his afternoon's work; Glueck's name was erased from anyone's memory well before that spring's thaw.)

The sense of historical injustice such reflections induce could explain, if it does not excuse, Halas's skimping. Any case he might offer for cheating his customers is much more forceful. When he brought his team to Chicago in 1921, Halas never carried with him any larger hope than that, on some balmy day, maybe 18,000 persons might turn out for a game. Now, as one of the few immutable statistics this civilization affords, he can be assured of 55,701 spectators every week. Those are all the seats he has to sell, and they are sold out before the season begins. Halas thus holds under key a set of prisoners of the sort that can never break their chains — addicts who are also such snobs that, if they ever withdrew from their addiction, they would be ashamed to admit it. There is nothing in George Halas's experience to suggest to him that such persons deserve honest goods for their money. For one thing, they are fans and he an old athlete; and, if one bond ties all athletes together, it is their hatred of fans. All of these people are strangers to Halas. And so we see him in his glass booth, as Henry Adams saw the Virgin enthroned in the window at Chartres, looking down from a deserted heaven, into an empty church, on a dead faith.

It is plain that Halas did make one great democratic leap in his choice of Abe Gibron as his present coach. Abe Gibron is the model of the man who kept thinking every year that he might manage to save enough money to buy a season ticket to the Bears and failed every year until it was terminally too late. Halas's leap then was not toward those who are exclusive but to those who are habitually excluded. Gibron was raised in Chicago and returned to the Bears as an assistant coach after service as an offensive guard for Paul Brown in Cleveland. Halas hired him because Halas cherishes Chicago football players — not because of civic pride, but because he thinks Chicago football players live with their mothers and thus will have no occasion to protest that their wages don't quite cover their rent. Gibron is a round little man, a Lebanese (in Chicago, ethnicity is not properly American unless it is unexpectedly exotic). After the Lions disaster, he appears to the press in the bowels of Soldier Field. He blames his defeat on the incompetence, if not the perfidy, of the officials. Thereafter, in the tone journalism appoints for asking the mother of Charles Manson whether she's heard from her son lately, a jackal in attendance wonders how Gibron now feels about his quarterback.

"Let 'em say what they're going to say anyway," Coach Gibron answers. "I say he's gonna make it. When this season's over, I'm gonna walk down Michigan Boulevard and I'm gonna take my pants down and there's one million guys that's gonna have to come over and kiss my ass."

And he capers off, King Lear stuck with playing Punchinello, and the Bears' dressing room is open for company. A huge and quite beautiful black man is asked a question. He leans down solicitously and says, "Pardon?" Resignation is depressing for the illusions but bracing for the manners. These graces embolden the journalists to dare Butkus himself. One of them timidly wonders whether the book had come up in the course of the conversations on the field. "The book didn't beat us," Dick Butkus says. "The Lions did. Why do you guys have to go starting something? I know you have to fill up your columns but. . . ." They had gone, poor gulls as they are paid to be, in search of the rage of Zeus and had found nothing grander than pique; the displeased god did not brood but only bitched. Most of them wander off to fry other fish. A few tarry to look at the back of Dick Butkus plunged upon the lacing of his shoes. It will never be a mean back, but somehow, in unknown places, it has ceased to be a transfiguring back. Men will die and worms will eat them, but no longer at the command of this back. Blotches have begun to work their way. There are enclaves of pallor inexplicable except by the surmise that, in some private place, the spring is losing its tension. This back may have begun to wonder, much as the memoir does, what in the name of the good Jesus it is doing here.

Dick Butkus has grown a moustache. It runs down below the corners of his mouth; the whole effect has become less of the cop on the beat than of the cop behind the desk. Butkus dresses, walks bruisedly to meet his wife. So long as wounded children scream in the night, there will always be sadder sights to see than the spectacle of a legend that has suddenly, almost pathetically, commenced to look like a myth. Still, the unimportant sadnesses do make their claim, and so do the unexpected sympathies. But after all we remember King Kong not because he was terrible but because he was badly used and a far, far better beast than his press clippings would ever commit the commercial blunder of suggesting.

Here are the game, the play, and the book which for the first time focused national attention on the offensive line — in particular, on Green Bay's right guard, Jerry Kramer. In the previous title game Dallas, trailing by a touchdown in the final minutes, drove to a first down at the Packer 2; in four tries they couldn't crack across the goal line. All year long they burned over that loss, waiting for this day of revenge, December 31, 1967. The Packers, for their part, were hoping to become the first team to win three consecutive championship games.

JERRY KRAMER
and Dick Schaap

Instant Replay

When I woke up this morning, after a good night's sleep, I knew it was cold. "It must be 10 below zero," I told Barbara. I thought I was kidding.

During breakfast, I found out the temperature was 16 degrees below zero, the coldest December 31st in Green Bay history, and I started to shiver. Still, I figured it would warm up a little by noon. It warmed all the way up to 13 below by game time.

[Don] Chandler and I bundled up driving over to the stadium and we didn't realize quite how bitter the cold was. As we ran into the dressing room we saw a helicopter hovering over the stadium, blowing snow off the seats.

When I got inside and began dressing, Gilly [Gale Gillingham] came over to me and said, "You gonna wear gloves?"

I hadn't thought of it. I'd never worn gloves before in a football game. I was about to say no, and then I thought, "Who the hell am I kidding? I don't use my hands out there."

"Hell, yeah," I told Gilly.

Maybe, if it were 5 above zero or 10 above, I would have passed up the gloves and tried to psych the Cowboys into thinking that the cold wasn't bothering me. But at 13 below I wasn't going to be psyching anyone. Everybody in the whole United States was going to know I was cold.

Gilly, Forrest [Forrest Gregg], Ski [Bob Skoronski], and I — the interior linemen — got gloves from Dad Braisher, the equipment manager. We're the only ones who don't have to use our hands in a game. We decided we'd wear the gloves outside to loosen up and see if we needed them for the game.

"With this cold," Ron Kostelnik mentioned to me, "it's gonna hamper us on defense. We won't be able to grab, to use our hands too well. You won't have to be afraid of popping people, Jerry. They won't be able to throw you with their hands." The thought warmed me up slightly.

We got dressed in our long stockings and our silk pants, and when we stepped out on the field — I was wearing my thermal underwear, but only knee-length and elbow-length, so that it wouldn't restrict my mobility — icy blasts just shot right up our skirts. It took Gilly and Forrest and Ski and me about three seconds to decide we'd keep on the gloves. "Hell, let's get another pair," I told Gilly.

I looked over at the Dallas Cowboys and I almost felt sorry for them. As bad as the cold was for us, it had to be worse for them. We were freezing, and they were dying. They were all hunched over, rubbing their hands, moving their legs up and down, trying to persuade themselves that they weren't insane to be playing football in this ridiculous weather.

We kicked off, and our defense held, and when I came out on the field for the first time we had the ball around our own 20-yard line. Bart [Starr] started right off with the 41-special, the new play we'd put in for the Cowboys. Gilly pulled out to his right, faking Lee Roy Jordan, the middle linebacker, into thinking the play was going that way, and Bob Hyland blocked on Gilly's man and I blocked on Jethro Pugh, and Chuck Mercein, at fullback, leading Donny Anderson into the line, blocked Lee Roy Jordan trying to recover. The play worked just the way we hoped it would. Donny picked up five yards before he got hit. He fumbled, which wasn't part of our plan, but Mercein recovered for us. With Bart calling that 41-special a couple of times, and with the aid of a few penalties, we marched all the way down the field for a touchdown. Bart passed to Dowler in the end zone, and, midway through the first period, we were leading 7–0.

The cold was incredible, cutting right through us, turning each slight collision into a major disaster, but, for me, the footing on the field wasn't too bad. The ground was hard, but by putting most of my weight on my toes, I could dig in and get a foothold. I handled Jethro pretty well, popping him more than I would under normal conditions, keeping his cold hands away from me, moving him on running plays and checking him on passing plays. We didn't say a word to each other; even if we'd had anything to say, it was too cold to talk.

The only conversation I had all day was with Lee Roy Jordan. When we tried a screen pass, Bob Lilly or one of their linemen read the play and grabbed the back, the intended receiver, by the jersey. Bart had no one to throw to. "Look, he's holding, he's holding," I screamed at the referee. But the referee didn't see the infraction, and Jordan smiled and said to me, "He wasn't holding, Jerry. Your guy just slipped and fell down, and we were just helping him up."

We had more conversation on our own bench, mostly over who'd get the good seats by the warmer. Hornung usually had one of them; the commissioner had said he could sit on our bench.* At one point, the warmer ran out of fuel and started to smoke, and we all jumped off the bench. Another time, Donny Anderson was sitting on the bench freezing, and he saw the CBS sidelines microphone, sponge-covered to kill the wind sound, dangling in front of him. He reached up and put his hands around the microphone, thinking it was some new kind of heater.

Early in the second quarter, when we had the ball on a third-and-one situation just past midfield, Bart crossed up the Dallas defense, faded back, and threw a long touchdown pass, again to [Boyd] Dowler. We were ahead 14–0, and I felt warmer. I was only worried about our tendency to let up when we get a few touchdowns ahead.

Less than a minute later, Herb Adderley intercepted one of Don Meredith's passes and returned the ball almost to the Cowboys' 30-yard line. If we can get this one now, I thought, we can forget it, the game's over, the whole thing's over. I had a beautiful feeling about the ball game—until we didn't score. Bart lost some yardage eating the ball when he couldn't find an open receiver, and we had to punt. I felt frustrated, terribly let down. I'd been so certain that we were going to get at least something, at least a field goal.

Then, late in the second period, deep in our own territory, again Bart faded to pass and again he couldn't get rid of the ball, and Willie Townes, their big defensive end, hit Bart and knocked the ball loose, and George Andrie, their other defensive end, swooped in and picked up the ball and charged to the end zone for a touchdown.

Forrest Gregg tackled Andrie just as he crossed the goal line, and I was only a step or two behind Forrest, and I suddenly felt the greatest desire to put both my cleats right on Andrie's spinal cord and break it. We had been victimized by these stupid plays—scooped-up fumbles, deflected passes, blocked kicks, high-school tricks—so many times during the season that I felt murderous. I'd never in my career deliberately stepped on a guy, but I was so tempted to destroy Andrie, to take everything out on him, that I almost did it. A bunch of thoughts raced through my mind—I'd met Andrie off the field a few times and I kind of liked him—and, at the last moment, I let up and stepped over him.

We couldn't do a thing when we got the ball—Jethro caught Bart for a loss one time, but I thought I'd checked him long enough; I thought Bart held the ball too long—and they took over again and added a field goal, and so, at the half, instead of leading 17–0 or 21–0 or something like that, we were barely in front, 14–10.

*Injuries had led to his retirement this year.—ED.

Ray Wietecha chewed us out pretty good between the halves. "One guy's giving the quarterback all the trouble," he told us. "One guy. C'mon. Don't let up out there. There's a lot of money riding. Get tough, dammit, get tough." Ray didn't mention any names, but we all knew that Ski was having a lot of trouble with Andrie, that Andrie was doing most of the damage.

We just couldn't get unwound in the third quarter. I still felt I had Jethro under control, but he caught Bart two more times, not back deep, but out of the pocket, after Bart had had enough time to throw if he could have found anyone open. The ends were having trouble cutting. On the first play of the last quarter, they used the half-back-option — an old favorite play of ours — and Dan Reeves passed 50 yards for a touchdown. We were losing, 17–14, and the wind was whipping us, too.

Five minutes later, my roommate was wide with an attempted field goal, and when the ball sailed by to the left I had a little sinking feeling, a little fear that the clock might run out on us. I thought maybe the time had come for us to lose. Dallas controlled the ball for about ten plays, staying on the ground as much as they could, eating up the clock, and all the time my frustration built up, my eagerness to get back on the field, to have another chance to score.

With five minutes to go, we got the ball on our own 32-yard line, and, right away, Bart threw a little pass out to Anderson and Andy picked up five, six yards. The linebackers were laying back; they were having trouble with their footing, trouble cutting. Chuck Mercein ran for the first down, and then Bart hit Dowler for another first down, and we were inside Dallas territory. I began to feel we were going to make it, we were going to go for a touchdown. At the worst, I figured we'd go down swinging.

On first down, Willie Townes got through and caught Andy for a big loss, and we had second and about twenty. But Bart capitalized on the Dallas linebackers' difficulties getting traction. Twice, with the ends still having problems with their footing, he threw safety-valve passes to Anderson and twice Andy went for about ten yards, and we had a first down on the Dallas 30, and I could feel the excitement building in the huddle. But we had only a minute and a half to play. Bart passed out to Mercein on the left and Chuck carried the ball down to the Dallas 11. I walked back to the huddle, wondering what Bart was going to call, and he called a give-65, and I thought, "What a perfect call. We haven't used it all day. What a smart call."

It's a potentially dangerous play, a give-65. We block as though we're going through the "five" hole, outside me. Gilly pulls and comes over my way, and everything depends on the tackle in front of him, Bob Lilly, taking the fake and moving to his left. The play can't work against a slow, dumb tackle; it can only work against a quick, intelligent tackle like Lilly. We figured Lilly would key on Gilly and follow his move, but we didn't know for sure. Everybody blocks my way on this play, Anderson coming for the hole as though he's carrying the ball, and nobody blocks the actual target area, Lilly's area. If Lilly doesn't take the fake, if he ignores Gilly pulling, he kills the actual ballcarrier, Mercein.

But Lilly followed Gillingham, and the hole opened up, and Chuck drove down to the 3-yard line. With less than a minute to play, Anderson plunged for a first down on the 1, and, with only two time-outs left, we huddled quickly. "Run over there," Gilly said, in the huddle. "Run that 55-special. They can't stop that."

Bart called the 55, and I thought to myself, "Well, this is it, toad. They're putting it directly on your back, yours and Forrest's." I didn't make a very good block, and the five hole didn't open up, and Andy got stopped at the line of scrimmage. We called a time-out with twenty seconds to play. Then Bart called the same play again, and this time Andy slipped coming toward the hole — I don't know whether he could have gotten through — and slid to about the one-foot line, and we called time out with sixteen seconds to play, our last time-out, and everybody in the place was screaming.

We could have gone for the field goal right then, for a tie, hoping that we'd win in overtime. We decided to go for the victory. In the huddle, Bart said, "Thirty-one wedge and I'll carry the ball." He was going to try a quarterback sneak. He wasn't going to take a chance on a handoff, or on anybody slipping. He was going to go for the hole just inside me, just off my left shoulder. Kenny Bowman, who had finally worked his way back to the lineup, and I were supposed to move big Jethro out of the way. It might be the last play of the game, our last chance.

The ground was giving me trouble, the footing was bad down near the goal line, but I dug my cleats in, got a firm hold with my right foot, and we got down in position, and Bart called the "hut" signal. Jethro was on my inside shoulder, my left shoulder. I came off the ball as fast as I ever have in my life. I came off the ball as fast as anyone could. In fact, I wouldn't swear that I didn't beat the center's snap by a fraction of a second. I wouldn't swear that I wasn't actually offside on the play.

I slammed into Jethro hard. All he had time to do was raise his left arm. He didn't even get it up all the way and I charged into him. His body was a little high, the way we'd noticed in the movies, and, with Bowman's help, I moved him outside. Willie Townes, next to Jethro, was down low, very low. He was supposed to come in low and close to the middle. He was low, but he didn't close. He might have filled the hole, but he didn't, and Bart churned into the opening and stretched and fell and landed over the goal line. It was the most beautiful sight in the world, seeing Bart lying next to me and seeing the referee in front of me, his arms over his head, signaling the touchdown. There were thirteen seconds to play.

The fans poured on the field, engulfing us, engulfing the Cowboys, pummeling all of us. Chuck Howley, the Dallas linebacker, got knocked down three or four times accidentally, and he was furious. I had to fight my way through the crowd to the sidelines; Bart came off the field looking like he was crying, and he probably was. The Cowboys still had time to get off two plays, two incomplete passes, and the game was over. I tried to get to the dressing room quickly, but I got caught around the 30-yard line, trapped in a mass of people beating me on the back, grabbing at my chin strap, grabbing at my gloves, trying to get anything for a souvenir. I had a sudden moment of panic, wondering whether I was ever going to get out of that mess alive.

Finally I reached the dressing room and I was immediately aware that the whole place was wired for sound. Cameramen and cameras were all around, and Coach Lombardi cussed the cameramen and ordered them, flatly, to get the hell out. When we were alone, just the team and the coaches, Vince told us how proud he was of us. "I can't talk anymore," he said. "I can't say anymore." He held the tears back and we all kneeled and said the Lord's Prayer, and then we exploded, with shouts of joy and excitement, the marks of battle, the cuts, the bruises, and the blood, all forgotten.

The TV people returned, and I was one of the first men led in front of the cameras. "There's a great deal of love for one another on this club," I said. "Perhaps we're living in Camelot." I was referring to the idea of one for all and all for one, the ideal of King Arthur's Round Table, and I meant it. And then I talked about Lombardi.

I'd been waiting for a chance to talk about Vince. A story had appeared in *Esquire* magazine a few weeks earlier making him look like a complete villain, like nothing but a cruel, vicious man. The story had hurt Vince; I had heard that his mother had cried when she read the story. I thought the story gave a distorted picture of the man; it showed only one of his many sides. "Many things have been said about Coach," I said on TV, "and he is not always understood by those who quote him. The players understand. This is one beautiful man."

I loved Vince. Sure, I had hated him at times during training camp and I had hated him at times during the season, but I knew how much he had done for us, and I knew how much he cared about us. He is a beautiful man, and the proof is that no one who ever played for him speaks of him afterward with anything but respect and admiration and affection. His whippings, his cussings, and his driving all fade; his good qualities endure.

Over and over and over, perhaps twenty times, the television cameras reran Bart's touchdown and my block on Jethro Pugh. Again and again, millions of people across the country saw the hole open up and saw Bart squeeze through. Millions of people who couldn't name a single offensive lineman if their lives depended on it heard my name repeated and repeated and repeated. All I could think was, "Thank God for instant replay."

In 1960, Robert Riger and Tex Maule combined their talents in an exceptional book entitled *The Pros*. They invited Tom Landry, then defensive coach of the Giants, to elucidate on the evolution of the game, which he did in brilliantly clear fashion. As the architect of the 4–3 defense Landry, once he became head coach of the Cowboys, contrived to destroy it through an abruptly shifting "multiple offense" of exotic formations. In the endless rhythm of attack and counterattack, defensive wizards of the ensuing decades came up with the zone, the stack, the flex, the 53 defense (which is not a 5–3 but a 3–4), and the nickel-back prevent. Complex? Yes, but as Red Grange and Vince Lombardi have said, all football theory comes down to blocking and tackling, and the team that does a better job of that will win.

TOM LANDRY

The Tactical Changes in the Game

After World War II, the 5–3 defense was the major defense used. This defense was carried over from prewar years. However, it became clear by 1948 that the linebackers were being forced to cover fast halfbacks off the T formation. (Diagram A)

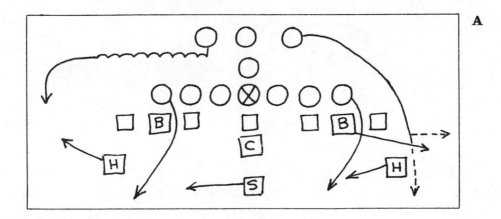

A

Greasy Neale, coach of the Philadelphia Eagles, came up with the idea of the "Eagle Defense," which utilized four defensive backs. With four defensive backs covering two fast halfbacks and two fast ends, the problem was solved. (Diagram B)

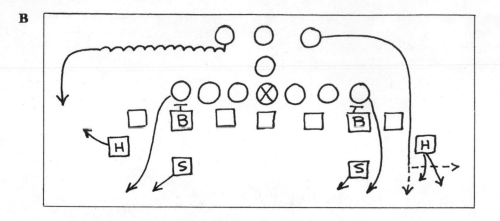

Two things happened offensively which eliminated the Eagle Defense as the best defense against the pro "T." First, the pass offense became very effective because of the lack of pass defensive strength over the middle. All an offensive coach would have to do to eliminate all linebackers would be to swing backs wide. (Diagram C)

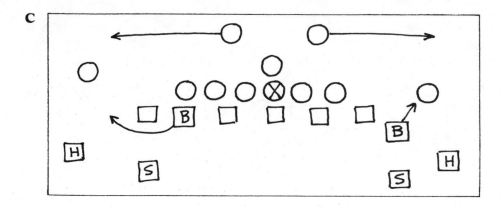

The result was that the defense lacked strength in the middle area. To alleviate this weakness coaches began to fill this area with another man. (Diagram D)

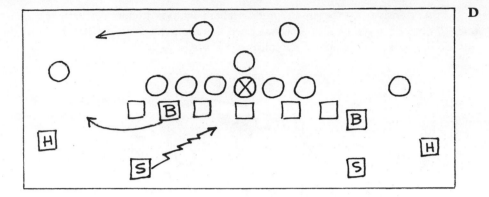

This formation, then, appeared to be the solution. However, the sweeping success of the "Split T" in college effected another major change in the early Fifties and led to the downfall of the Eagle Defense. With the introduction of the split line the middle guard found himself virtually isolated. (Diagrams E & F)

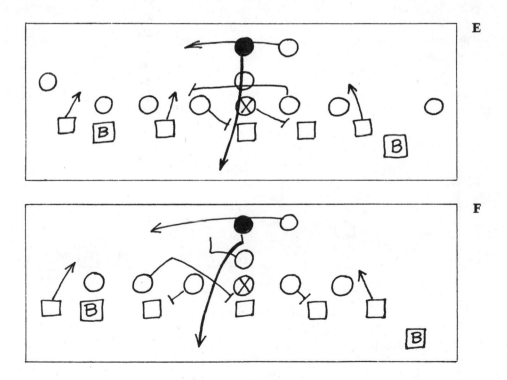

As the offensive play began the middle guard would "holler" for help. The only ones to help were the tackles, so they closed down on the offensive guards. Now the outside linebacker was isolated. A typical result is shown below.

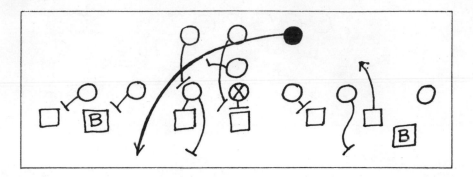

The Eagle Defense could not stop a running game with a split line. Now the defensive coaches had to turn to the only solution to their problem, a defense that would solve the two weaknesses of the Eagle Defense. The present 4–3 defense answered both needs.* Here was the blending of two defenses into one: the Eagle Defense of Greasy Neale's Philadelphia team and the 6–1 "Giants Umbrella" devised by Steve Owen. The following series of diagrams show step by step the evolution of the two defenses with the 4–3 defense resulting. This should be with us for some time — the linebackers are the key.

EVOLUTION OF THE EAGLE DEFENSE BY STEPS

1. *Original Eagle Defense*

*A defense is three lines deep but is named for the front two lines. Hence a 4–3 defense is a 4–3–4 alignment. — ED.

2. Countering the pass defense problem

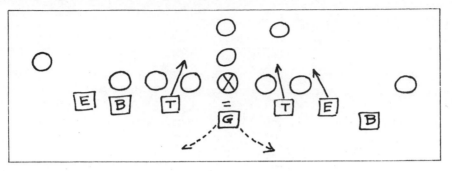

3. Tightening the tackles to help middle guard on split line

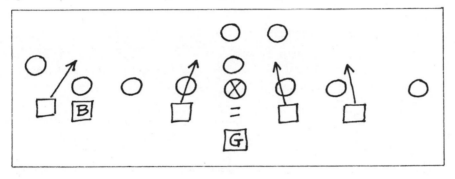

4. Putting ends inside linebackers to help them

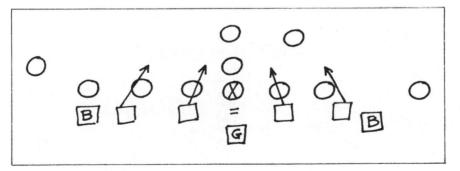

Giant coach Steve Owen picked up valuable personnel when the American Conference disbanded in 1950 and used these men to form his "Umbrella Defense," which was specifically designed to stop the new Cleveland Browns.

EVOLUTION OF THE 6-1 UMBRELLA

1. Original 6-1 umbrella defense

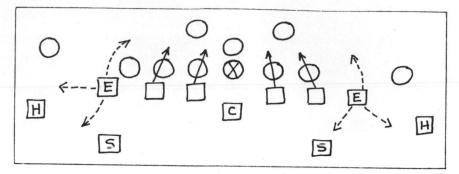

2. Switch from ends to linebackers

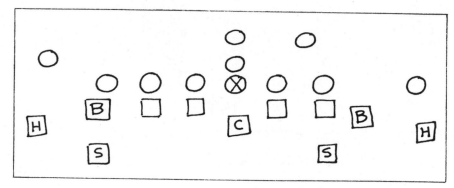

TODAY'S 4-3 DEFENSE

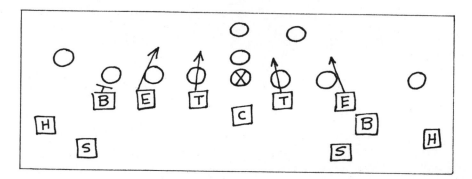

I don't believe that there is any question of the tremendous appeal of defensive football today. Back in 1950, when Owen's famed "Umbrella Defense" stopped the powerful Cleveland Browns, 6–0, the average fan could pass this feat off as "an off-day for the Browns." Today, you can think back over the last ten years to the one constant factor in championship teams—defense! The Philadelphia Eagles of the late Forties, the Cleveland Browns of the early Fifties, the Detroit Lions of the early Fifties and the Baltimore Colts and the New York Giants of the late Fifties were all defensive powers.

The tactical changes in the game are devised by the coaches—the ingenious generals of football—and are in most cases the result of the interactions in the offensive and defensive strategies of the various teams in the league. Below are diagrams of the three key offensive changes in the last decade.

1953: In 1953 teams began using more spread formations and the slot-back was introduced to combat the 6–1 umbrella defense. This loosened the 6–1 up and gave offenses greater passing areas.

Spread formation

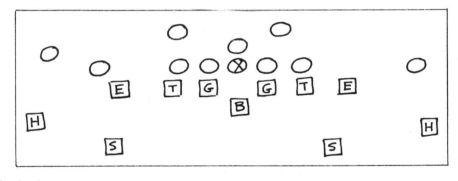

Slot back

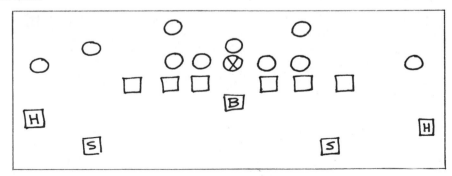

1956: Teams found, with the waning of the 6–1 and the more constant use of the 4–3, that they were now able to cover the spread and slot-back formations more adequately. Coaches felt, however, the offenses had to present a stronger blocking picture for the running game, and this resulted in the off-side end always spread and the end on flanker side closed for greater running strength.

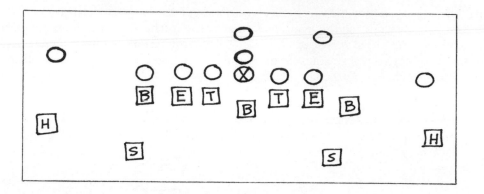

1959: Al Sherman and other offensive coaches were of the opinion that teams were beginning to leave the basic 4–3 a little and play defensive men in "gaps" — to destroy stronger blocking created by the closed end and add defensive strength closest to strength of play (strong side). Perhaps offensively now there will be another trend to try to combat these "gap" defenses. (Diagram below)

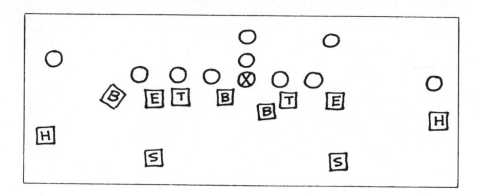

The AFL title match pitted the league's top offense, in the San Diego Chargers, against its top defense, in the Boston Patriots. In most such clashes the defense can be relied upon to prevail—the football version of the baseball adage that "good pitching stops good hitting." But on January 5, 1964, a balmy day in little Balboa Stadium, the Chargers proved the spectacular exception to the rule, winning 51–10. The game plan designed by coach Sid Gillman dissected the Boston defense to perfection, and Keith Lincoln put on the greatest one-man show in the history of postseason play.

WAYNE LOCKWOOD

The Anatomy of a Game Plan

It is one of those phrases that has passed from sports into the mainstream of society.

Game plan. Have an idea of where you are going and how you intend to get there. Evaluate the opposition. Study the problems. Allow for the unexpected. Everything is possible . . . if only you have a *game plan*.

Sid Gillman has had a game plan for as long as he can remember, and that's a long time. If there's a clipboard and a film projector handy—there always are when Sid's around—the seventy-year-old Gillman is at work on yet another scheme for success.

The endless permutations and combinations of X's and O's as they translate into the activity of large athletes have dominated this man's life for more than half a century. They fascinate him. They are an artist's tools, like musical notes on a page, waiting to be translated into something structured, yet unique.

"Game plans . . . " Gillman says. "If I had a dollar for every game plan I've drawn up . . . aw, hell, I'd probably still be doing what I'm doing anyway."

What he is doing, naturally, is drawing up a game plan.

Gillman has been at this sort of thing, man and boy, for parts of six decades. He began in the depths of the Great Depression and was still at it when the hostages returned from Iran.

The man has been a college assistant (Ohio State, Denison, Army, Miami of Ohio), a college head coach (Miami of Ohio, Cincinnati), a professional assistant (Chicago, Oakland, Philadelphia) and a professional head coach (Los Angeles, San Diego, Houston).

Gillman's career spans such distances that he played in the first College All-Star Game (1933) and coached in the last one (1976) as an assistant to Notre Dame's Ara Parseghian.

Those who worked with him worked with a master, and it shows. His former assistants include such people as Chuck Noll, Al Davis, Jack Faulkner, Don Klosterman, Bum Phillips, Ron Waller, and Ed Biles.

"Sid Gillman is a coach's coach," says Philadelphia's Dick Vermeil, latest in a long line of coaches with whom Gillman has been associated. "He can coach me. He can coach any coach."

"He's a genius," says Eagles quarterback Ron Jaworski. "He knows more about the passing game than any man alive. He's an offensive genius."

The genius is retired now, to his condominium just off the first hole of the golf course at La Costa, California. This retirement is at least as leisurely as his previous two retirements, one of which followed a six-way heart bypass operation in 1979 and lasted all of a few months.

Gillman is studying reels of every nickel defense faced by the Eagles in 1980, trying to devise a way for Vermeil's team to cope with those additional defensive backs in 1981.

This is Sid Gillman's game plan for retirement. On or off the field, motion is essential. "The first thing you have to know about all game plans is this," he says, settling to the task at hand. "They are really not that complicated, and they usually are overrated."

Sure. There are only three letters in $E = MC^2$, too.

The problem was the Boston Patriots, and no one had ever seen a problem quite like this one. The Patriots' defense, led by linebacker Nick Buoniconti and coached by Marion Campbell and Fred Bruney, blitzed from every angle and on almost every down.

The San Diego Chargers had scored a total of only 20 points against the Patriots in two previous meetings during the 1963 season, while scoring 379 points in twelve games against other opposition. The Chargers had rushed for a total of only 97 yards in those two previous games, despite the presence of two fine runners—Paul Lowe and Keith Lincoln—in their backfield.

This third meeting was for the 1963 American Football League championship. The Chargers already had suffered disappointing losses in two previous AFL title games.

"Campbell and Bruney devised the vast dogging [blitzing] system that teams like Atlanta use today," Gillman recalls. "The first time I ever saw anybody dog like that was Boston. It was feast or famine. They were going to come at you on every down."

In those days. Sid liked to name his game plans. The title of this one? "Feast Or Famine," of course.

"Basically, says Gillman, "there is no magic about a game plan. There is no way you can sit behind a projector for 185 hours or something, and, presto, come up with an idea that's going to make people disappear. You just do your homework, take your basic stuff and adapt it to what you think will be the best way to deal with what the opposition is doing.

"The big thing is to give it a different look. You may use different sets. You may use motion. But you won't add that many things. There just isn't time."

Just your basic stuff. A pile of uranium is pretty basic, too, until someone transforms it into an atomic bomb. But a little refinement is required.

In professional football, refinement begins with film study. And more film study. "You're not just looking to see where you want to throw the ball or run the ball," Gillman says. "What you're looking for is reaction and overreaction. We're always looking for overreaction on the part of the defense.

"The reason for that is, I want the big play. I don't want the little play, the average play. I want the *big* play. Hell, I'm not going to stay up all night trying to figure out how to gain three yards."

To Gillman, the big play means one thing: the pass. "There is no way . . . I'm not smart enough nor are there many other coaches who are smart enough to eliminate you defensively to the point where they can get a big play on the run, unless we're talking about the reverse," he says.

So the film study begins. Look for the big play.

When you play Boston, of course, the Patriots' defense is looking for the big play, too. The big loss. The sack. The turnover.

The Patriots are gambling that they can eliminate you with one swift stroke before you can drive the football the length of the field.

Movement and motion? It is present already. The Boston defense is doing it on every down. Overreaction? It is the Patriots' stock in trade.

The planning continues.

"Your game plan is well started out Monday night," Gillman says. "You hope by Tuesday night you have it pretty well formulated. Wednesday, it should be done. But, dang it, sometimes it's not done until Friday. You're making changes, adding, subtracting, changing formations. But you don't dare change your basic offense, like a lot of people *think* a coach does.

"They think it's all magic, all those brains working. 'What's he going to come up with now?' Well, coaches who do that sort of thing lose. That's what they come up with."

Gillman does not do that sort of thing. And he has been a winner everywhere he's coached. He tinkers, he adjusts, he fiddles. But all within a certain framework. "You get input from everyone on the game plan, from all your coaches," Gillman says. "That's what a good staff is for. Good assistants have good ideas.

"Chuck Noll [an assistant to Gillman with the Chargers in 1960], he was so bright. And what convictions! He'd fight you to the end for things he believed were right. He wasn't obstinate, you understand, but quite determined, very determined."

It requires determined people to do this sort of work. "You put in a lot of hours," Gillman concedes. "There's just no other way.

"There's one club I worked for that never worked at night. After practice, the day was done. But they started very early in the morning.

"I worked for another organization that felt they had to work most of the night. They both were successful."

Gillman is a graduate of the nocturnal school of thought. "I went into the night," he says. "I stayed at a motel across the street from the stadium. When we had our offices in a hotel, I had a room behind. I never went home during the week."

When the head coach was there, the assistants were expected to be there. But, ultimately, the decisions must be made by one man. "Somebody has to be in charge," Gillman says. "Somebody has to be the one to say, 'We're going to do this' or 'We're not going to do that.'" He was never bashful about being that man.

So there is input and there is argument. And the game plan begins to take shape.

"You build your offense from your basic running game, from what I like to call our 'Dirty Dozen,'" Gillman says. "It's as good a name as any for twelve plays we think are the best twelve plays our talent will let us run. We're going to maintain and keep polishing all these basic things because we know them well, and we're going to work like hell on execution. We're going to drill those plays and we're going to run them so well that on the other side it wouldn't make a hell of a lot of difference if Mohammed, Moses, and anybody else was over there. We're going to make it go."

The 1963 Chargers loved to run wide.

"Our basic play was the outside toss," Gillman recalls. "That was our key play, the one we dared you to stop. We had so much speed with Lincoln and Lowe. And we had [tackle] Ron Mix out in front. If you couldn't lead our toss, you couldn't play for us. Nobody could lead that play better than Mix."

The Chargers had experienced problems running wide against the Patriots, however, particularly during a 7-6 San Diego victory on a muddy field in Boston. Lowe had a net of no yards for four carries in that game.

"I think we've got Lowe's number," Buoniconti was quoted as saying. "Tell him we're going to be keying on him."

The basics are established. On to the modifications.

"Now we expand our selection to the 'Dirty Dozen Plus Four,'" Gillman instructs. "What's Plus Four? It's any special plays we think can be designed to beat the people we're playing. That's the maximum number you might add. It might be only Plus One or Plus Two. The more changes you make, the worse execution you're going to get. The result is you wind up getting your butt beat."

Boston used the mobility of linebackers such as Buoniconti to counter the Chargers' wide game. The Patriots could get to the corner almost as quickly as the San Diego backs.

It was time for some Plus Four remedies.

"We decided to use a lot of traps against them," Gillman says. "We would fake the toss and run the trap back inside. We even had some occasions where we would trap the linebacker when he dogged.

"One thing about the dog. If the linebacker doesn't make the tackle and you break it at the line of scrimmage, there's nobody there until you're well into the secondary."

We've established what we're hoping to do on the ground. The next decision is how to go about it.

"What formations do we want to run?" Gillman says. "We're going to run the Dirty Dozen Plus Four, but we're going to give you a different look. How much motion shall we put to those plays? What kind of motion? What kind of movement?"

The Chargers decided to counter the Patriots' blitzing with as much movement as possible. They frequently sent Lowe in motion, forcing Boston to send a linebacker with him.

"And," Gillman notes, "we shifted [tight end Dave] Kocourek into the backfield and motioned him to one side or the other. It changed the strongside-weakside alignments and really screwed up their dogs."

"The reason for movement is to create a soft spot some place," Gillman says. "We're looking for a soft spot — to get somebody to run with somebody. If it doesn't create soft spots for the pass or for the run, then there's no sense to it. Sometimes, in fact, movement hurts the passing game more than it helps it because you destroy the definition for the quarterback. But, more times than not, it might help the running game."

On to the passing game, Gillman's first love.

"Essentially, no matter who you're playing, you have a basic passing game just like your basic running game," the coach says. "You have so many passes to the tight end, so many passes to the strongside end, so many to the weakside end and running backs. It's all patterned.

"Again, we are going to decide, based on film study, what formations we want to run this out of. Do we want to use movement?"

The basic passing game of the 1963 Chargers, with ends such as Lance Alworth and Don Norton and quarterbacks such as Tobin Rote and John Hadl, was bombs away.

"Ups always have been a big part of our passing game," Gillman says. "We've always tried to go to our long game first, then to the medium and short. If you try to go long as a last resort, after other things haven't worked, you usually get in trouble.

"But if you go long right away, even if you don't hit it, you've put the fear of God *into them and probably opened up some other things. The threat of the long pass sets up your passing game.*

"We figured to throw a lot of 'in' patterns against Boston, but only after we'd thrown long a few times."

The basic passing game takes on an added dimension, a dimension of the running game, when play-action is added. A play begins as if it is a run, but the quarterback keeps the ball and throws it to an area where, it is hoped, a defender has reacted to the run fake a split-second too long.

"Play-action passes are the keys to the big play off the passing game," Gillman says. "Again, what you're looking for is overreaction. Frequently, that will happen on a pass off play action. That's where the big play comes in. And big plays are what win football games."

All right. We have the basic running game, plus refinements, and the basic passing game, plus embellishments. What now?

"Now we add what I call 'deceptions,'" says Gillman. "These would be the screens, at least three types, and the draws. They are the plays that keep people honest against your passing game, that prevent them from just teeing off on you.

"After the deceptions come the gadget plays—the reverses and bootlegs and things like that. You might run them only once a game, or maybe not at all. But you need the threat of them. The defense needs to know they are there."

These, then, are the basic elements of a game plan, omitting, of course, the kickoff, punt, and placement special teams and the deceptions (onside kick, fake kick, etc.) that must go with them.

Naturally, there also is the flip side—the defensive game plan that must be developed to counter all those schemes being developed by all the coaches on the other side as they squint through the night behind their projectors.

We have our offense. We know our plan of attack. We have some ideas we think will work. What now?

"Now," says Gillman, "you *really* begin to work. The hard part is ahead."

Oh.

"Now," he elaborates, "we come up against the biggest change in pro football. The biggest change in pro football these days is special situations—the special-situation offense and the special-situation defense.

"They used to say you couldn't tell the players without a program. That's *really* true now because they're running in and out all the time.

"Pro football has resolved itself into a special-situations game. You use your regular talent on first and ten, and maybe on second and five. But that's when your regular talent leaves the game. If it's third and seven-plus, you're probably going to meet a nickel [defense].

"You've got so many situations now. You've got short-yardage. You've got goal-line.

On the other side, the defensive coach has all his people around him and he's playing chess with you, moving people around. You're playing chess with him, moving people around. If it's third and eight and they've got their best people in there using nickel, then we'd better have our best people in there, too."

There was a time, perhaps, when most of the strategy was formulated before games. Now it evolves *during* them. "I have this big card I always use." Gillman says. "I get it from a computer. But we used to do it manually. On this card, it tells me what you do on first and ten. It tells me what you do on first and ten of a new series.

"I have to know your [defensive] fronts. I have to know your pass coverages. I have to know how many dogs you have and what the nature of your dogs are. What percentage of dogs do you use?"

This intelligence, mind you, covers only first down.

"Then," Gillman says, "we get to second down. We have second down broken down into second and one to three, second and six-minus, second and seven-to-ten, and second and eleven-plus.

"Now I have to know all the fronts, coverages, and percentage of dogs for these situations. The same thing is true for third down, of course."

There you have it, ladies and gentlemen. And the next time you wonder "What is that dummy thinking about on the sidelines," you will know. He is thinking about that card. And a few hundred other things.

"As the game goes on, you rely less on what's on the card," Gillman says. "There's not that much changing of a game plan as such during the game. The important thing is the proper selection of the things in your plan at the proper time.

"At halftime, you just try to pick out the things you have done that have been successful and you decide what you haven't done that might be successful. Then you go from there. Hell, there isn't that much time. You only have ten minutes."

Gillman has finished preparing his team for the Patriots. The card is ready.

"We will go with the same things we've been running all year," he tells members of the media, who may or may not be aware of the 'Dirty Dozen.'

"I feel we already do more things than most clubs. But there will be some adjustments. You can't play Boston like you do other people. You have to adapt."

Sid Gillman knows exactly what his adaptations will be. "Motion, movement, and lots of traps," he says. "That's what we figured could beat them. We also put in a little circle pattern to a back out of the backfield to take advantage of the area a linebacker would leave when he dogged."

Some days, you don't have to wait at all. On the first play from scrimmage, Rote faked a bomb and completed a screen pass to Lincoln for 12 yards. On the second play from scrimmage, Rote faked a quick toss to Lowe and handed back inside to Lincoln, who broke cleanly behind a trap block. He ran 56 yards to the Boston 4, where, slowing perceptibly, he was tackled, got up, stepped across the sideline, and threw up.

"I was too keyed up," he explained later. "I felt like I would have had trouble beating [300-pound] Ernie Ladd in a hundred-yard dash. I believe I would have done a lot better if I felt better."

No matter. The Chargers scored two plays later when Rote plunged over from the 2. Goal-line offense.

On San Diego's next series, Lincoln took a pitchout, broke a tackle, hurdled another would-be tackler, and ran 67 yards for a touchdown.

On the sideline, Gillman smiled: You've got to stop our toss first.

In quick succession, Lowe followed a 58-yard gain with an 18-yard touchdown run (Buoniconti being otherwise occupied), Norton scored on a 14-yard screen pass from Rote (the first screen pass thrown to him all season), Alworth caught a 48-yard touchdown pass from Rote off play action (the long pass is the key to our passing game), Lincoln caught a 25-yard touchdown pass from Hadl (on a circle route out of the backfield), and Hadl punched over from a yard out.

The Chargers had scored on their fourth play from scrimmage and on their sixth and their tenth. On his first two carries, Lincoln gained 123 yards.

San Diego won the AFL championship 51–10, establishing offensive records that still stand. The Chargers gained 610 yards and averaged a first down (10.2 yards) a play. Lincoln, the ailing Lincoln, accounted for 349 yards—206 rushing, 123 pass receiving, and 20 passing.

"Credit coach Gillman," Chargers' linebacker Emil Karras said. "He just did a fantastic job of getting us ready to play this game. It was brilliant to put a man in motion. It took a linebacker away from their red dog. It was something we hadn't done much this year and it really fouled up their defense."

Seldom had any game plan worked more successfully than this one. "Feast or Famine" turned out to be a piece of gluttony.

"No game plan works *that* well," Gillman says now. "I think it was just one of those days more than anything else. The big play was the fake toss and the trap to Lincoln. That's what sort of broke the whole thing open. You never expect a play to break as cleanly as that. After that, things just snowballed.

"You have to remember that Chargers team was a great team. . . . I honestly think one of the best all-time pro teams. It just had a hot day."

The best game plan in the world, Gillman insists, is no better than the people assigned to execute it. "We often make the error of thinking that we can accomplish something simply by drawing X's and O's," he says. "But those X's and O's don't mean a damn thing if you don't have the people to carry them out. One of the most important things is getting people ready to play. You're working on the mental aspect of the game as well as the physical. You can't emphasize one and forget the other."

Ironically, more than fifteen years after the Boston massacre, Gillman was on the same Philadelphia coaching staff with Marion Campbell and Fred Bruney in 1979 and 1980.

"It's kind of interesting," he says. "We've talked about the game several times. Funny, Marion's a fine coach but he's almost totally changed his thinking. Now he hardly dogs at all. He's very conservative."

It was a dog-day afternoon that warm January day in San Diego, a feast for one man and a famine for the other. Both still remember.

But they don't dwell on it much. There are, after all, new game plans to be drawn.

We tend to remember Vince Lombardi as the firesnorting, browbeating, yet in the end endearing leader who inspired men and molded great teams. Tackle Henry Jordan once was asked whether his martinet of a boss treated the Packers fairly. "He's fair," Jordan replied with genuine affection. "He treats us all the same—like dogs." So it is something of a surprise to read, from Lombardi's diary of a typical week in the 1962 season, that the hours before the big game are tranquil and that Lombardi is, too: no rabid pep talk, no whipped-up hysteria—just a businessman's attention to detail combined with a scoutmaster's concern for his "boys." For other views of the now legendary coach, see the pieces by Jerry Kramer and Steve Wright.

VINCE LOMBARDI
with W. C. Heinz

Sunday Morning

As I drive across the bridge at De Pere the first drops of rain hit the windshield. This is not going to help us a bit, but it's not going to help them, either. When I turn into the divided highway there is a bus ahead of me. In the back seat two small boys are wrestling and I see one head emerge and an arm encircle it and the head disappears. Then the other head comes up and another arm rises and curves around it and the second head disappears.

If we're going to take it right to them, I'm thinking, let's do it on the first play. The first time we get that ball let's go right to their strength, and if that's where we're going our Brown Right-73 might be the one to open with at that. I like it, come to think of it, because there's no doubt about that middle linebacker of theirs being a great one and the sooner we go to work on him the better. What I like about it now is that it will give us at least two people on the middle linebacker, and while I don't think we're going to discourage him we should, if Jim Ringo and Ron Kramer both get good shots at him, force him to be at least a little concerned about where those blockers are coming from. And that could be a help.

As I turn off Oneida Avenue and into the parking area one of the attendants in a yellow cap waves to me. Except for a half dozen cars parked up by the entrance to the dressing rooms the area is empty, and when I walk inside it is 10:25 and only Hank Jordan is there, getting out of his jacket in front of his dressing stall.

"Morning, coach," he says, smiling. "Nervous?"

"No," I say. "Are you?"

"Yes, sir," he says.

I'm telling the truth, and he is, too. The difference is that by now I have done all my planning and almost all my scheming, and he must still play his game. Also, over all the years that I have on him, I have learned to control it, and it won't hit me until that kickoff.

"How do you feel otherwise?" I say.

"Fine, thanks," he says.

I look around the room at the stalls, each with the name card and the pads above it, the gold pants hanging inside on the right, the green jerseys and blue warmup sweaters on hangers on the left, the floor of each stall covered with six or eight or ten pairs of football shoes at $23.50 a pair. I walk through the equipment room and Dad Braisher has his air hose out and is inflating the footballs to thirteen pounds. I open the door to the visitors' dressing room and wave to their equipment manager, who is the only one in there. Over these stalls the helmets are silver and, hanging within the stalls, the pants are silver and the jerseys white.

I walk outside. Two men are approaching the door, each carrying a sack of ice for the trainers. Then I walk to the ramp and look down at the field. The rain has stopped, at least momentarily, and Johnny Proski's grounds crew is rolling the tarpaulins off the field, green along the sides but brown in the middle from abuse.

"It looks like we may have a little mud battle," Phil Bengtson says, walking up to me.

"I'm afraid so," I say. And I'm thinking that after it is over, win or lose, somebody from the press will inevitably ask me whether I think it helped or hurt us.

"One thing we know," Phil says. "It evens up any game."

Then Phil goes into the dressing room and I walk under the stands. The refreshment people are setting up, and here and there fans, in rain gear, are coming through the turnstiles even at this early hour. Someone has put a polka on the p.a. system and this cavern is filled with it as I walk into the main ticket office to settle for the tickets I have sold.

"No, I'm sorry," one of our ticket men is saying to someone outside the wicket. "We've been sold out for months, and nobody has turned any in."

When I walk back the odor of boiling hot dogs and grilled hamburgers is in the air, complementing the noise of another polka. In our dressing room Earl Gros and Gary Barnes are undressing and in the trainer's room Ed Blaine and Ron Gassert, our two other first-year men, are standing on the tables and having their left knees taped by Bud Jorgensen and Dominic Gentile.

I pour some citrocarbonate into a paper cup and add water and drink it. Back in the dressing room the veterans are coming in now—Forrest Gregg and Dave Hanner and

Jim Ringo—and Hank Gremminger is getting out of his street clothes in front of his stall.

"You gonna grab about three today?" Henry Jordan is saying to him.

"I don't know," Gremminger, the worrier, says. "I've sweated through two T-shirts already."

"Is that a good sign?" Jordan says.

"Sure," Gremminger says. "I had breakfast and I was sweating so much I had to change, and now this one's soaked. That's the way I like to be, though."

"How about you?" Ringo says to Hanner. "You give the doctor another workout?"

"That's right," Hanner answers.

"What's the matter with you?" I ask Hanner.

"I felt hot and cold yesterday," he says.

"Did you go to the doctor?"

"Yes, sir. Then last night I went to bed at eight. I woke up at ten sweatin' like anything, but I feel better today."

I hope, I'm thinking. I hope you do, and I hope Jimmy Taylor walks in saying he feels better, too.

"How's Jim?" Ringo says. "Anybody know?"

"He says he had 101," Hanner says, "but he says he's gonna play."

Ron Kostelnik comes in, and he's wearing a new black fedora. Ringo has stripped by now and he takes the hat and puts it on.

"How do I look?" he asks.

"Like a hog head," Gregg says.

"I know why Jordan would buy one of these," Ringo says to Kostelnik. "He'd buy anything to cover that bald head, but I don't understand you."

"I'm gonna grow hair yet," Jordan says. "The next thing I'm gonna try is sheep dip."

Well, they're loose enough, I'm thinking, walking into the coaches' room. They've been too loose the last couple of days, but they'll be all right. It's much better than having them sitting around here like they're waiting for a time bomb to explode. They'll come up for this one.

Red Cochran is holding his dark blue Packer blazer in his left hand and, with his right hand wrapped in white tape, the adhesive side out, he is brushing lint off it. Phil is talking to Norb Hecker about yesterday's U.C.L.A. upset of Ohio State, and Bill Austin is on the phone checking with the airport about the weather.

"It could be off and on," he says when he hangs up. "Light rains all afternoon. The wind is East Northeast, 10 to 12 knots. That's about 12 to 15 miles an hour. That's surface winds, and they're different up higher."

"That's not the way the flags are blowing out there," Phil says.

"They're liable to be any way out there," Bill says.

I'm sitting at my desk and still thinking about our Brown Right-73 for our opening play, and I take a yellow lined pad and I diagram it:

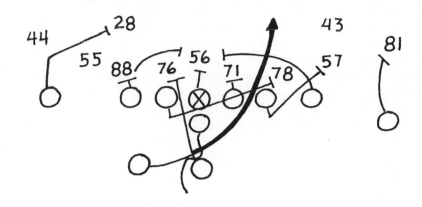

What I still like about that play, looking at it on paper now, is that it really goes to work on that middle linebacker. Jim Ringo sets him up with a drive block for Ron Kramer, who releases from his tight-end spot and comes across and bull-blocks him. Jimmy Taylor fakes up the middle and then takes that big 76 at right tackle. It's a tough block for Jerry Kramer on that 71 at left tackle, but if they give Hornung any daylight and his thigh is all right he should go. Another nice thing about it, too, is that it's a good influence play on their left end. Forrest Gregg pulls across his face, making him think the play is going outside, and when it goes inside you've got that trap on him.

"Bill?" I say.

"Yes?"

"Will you go over with your line our blocking on our 73? We're going to open with it."

"Right," he says.

I'm looking at our Ready List now, in its plastic envelope, the right formations on the one 8 x 11 card, the left formations on the card on the other side. The running plays are listed above the holes where they are designed to go, the passing plays are listed below, and I jot down a half dozen plays, any of which could be logical calls in our first sequence, depending on the result of our 73 and the reaction to it and to whatever we follow with it.

"Red?" I say.

"Here," Cochran answers.

"I want you people upstairs to keep your eyes open about how quick that safety man comes up on the strong side. I want to know if they're trying to keep Ron Kramer from releasing inside."

Red and Tom Fears will be up in the press box spotting for our offensive team and connected by phone with Johnny Roach on our sideline. Norb Hecker will be up there for the defensive team, phoning down to Howie Williams.

"But you won't get any pictures today in this weather," Red says.

"I know."

In good weather Red takes Polaroid shots of anything unusual, or otherwise trouble-some, that the opponent is doing defensively. We can then show these to our offensive team right on the sideline or during halftime.

"And Bill," I say, "let's not forget our 5–2 cards."

"Right," he says.

Each week, because you can't practice everything for every game, you take a number of calculated risks. This week we gambled that, although a couple of years ago the other people used a 5–2 defense against us, they would not use it today, so we spent no time devising and practicing an offense against it. We've seen it and drilled for it before, though, and so if we get it thrown at us today there should be no panic. We'll bring out those 5–2 cards on the sideline and show our offense the charts and the list of plays. In fact, a few years ago the Bears used to throw so many defenses at us that we couldn't possibly prepare fully for all of it and for every Bear game we were carrying to the sideline one of those big expansion envelopes filled with charts and play lists.

"How's Jimmy Taylor?" I say to Gene Brusky as I see him walk in.

"He had 101 last night," Gene says. "At midnight I took him off the medication. His temperature is normal this morning."

"Very good."

"I told him," Gene says, "that he's got to play a great game to make me look like a good doctor."

" — and I was thinking of it last night," Hank Gremminger, in his football pants and green jersey, is saying to Phil Bengtson.

"The goal line?" Phil says, and he goes to the blackboard. He draws one of the other people's pet goal-line pass plays. Gremminger looks at it, thanks him, and leaves.

"They know it just as well as we do," Phil says. "but they want to go over it and over it. They've got to have it letter-perfect, and confidence is the big thing."

Then I walk out to find Jimmy Taylor. It is quiet in the big room now. Most of them have finished dressing and are sitting in front of their stalls. If they are talking at all it is in low voices. Ron Kramer and Dan Currie are lying on their backs in front of their stalls, each with a towel under his head on the floor of his stall, legs up on a chair, eyes closed.

"Jim?" I say to Taylor. "How do you feel?"

He is pulling his jersey on over his head. When he turns I can see that his eyes are glossy and heavy, but whether that's from the fever or the medication I don't know.

"I'm all right now," he says.

"The fever gone?"

"Yeah," he says, "but I had 101."

"The doctor says you're going to be all right."

"I hope so," he says.

And I hope so, too. He is one of those performers who has to be emotionally up and I'm hoping not only that the fever hasn't drained him physically but also that it hasn't defeated him psychologically.

"I'm not even sure," Max McGee is saying, "that I should have gotten dressed. Does anybody know if the other people have shown up?"

"Jim? Bubba?" I say, and I get Ringo and Forester, our two captains, together. "If you win the toss, receive. If we have to kick off, take the north goal."

They both nod yes.

"And, Jim," I say, "if they're doing anything different out there today get a good look at it so we can discuss it when you come out."

"Yes, sir."

"Jesse," I say to Whittenton, walking by him. "How are you?"

"Fine, coach."

I don't have to remind him. He remembers as well as I do that broken-pattern play a year ago when he relaxed on that split end, that 89, and that 89 started up again and Jesse slipped and they hit right over him. I don't have to remind him, but it's in my mind.

"Willie," I say to Willie Davis, who is sitting there silent and, I know, worrying about his own performance, "you're going to have a great day."

"I hope so, coach," he says. "I'll try."

In the coaches' room Red Cochran is copying the Ready List into a pocket notebook. I change into slacks and pull on a pair of white woolen socks and the ripple-soled coaching shoes.

"All right," I say, "I want the quarterbacks in here."

"Bart! Johnny Roach!" Red Cochran calls as the others leave the room.

When Starr and Roach come in they sit down at the table, with Red Cochran standing behind them, and I sit down across from them. There are no notebooks now, because what they have in those notebooks and playbooks isn't going to help them, or us, if it isn't in their heads. By this time I have cut the number of our running plays down to a dozen and our passes to a half dozen, and I recite them.

"Generally," I say, "your sweeps should be to your left. As far as your pitchout is concerned, I'd use 48 to the left side. When you're going for short yardage you know you can expect the 6–1, so you use those short-yardage and goal line plays we've been working on.

"Versus the 6–1 these are all right formations," I say, and I enumerate several of them. "Now your 39-Toss can be run provided they don't bring that safety up outside. Against the Frisco your 34-X and 24 should be good. If they go to the Frisco Strong, just turn it around."

As I look at them they are intent and nodding. "Now for our first play let's try the

73. That's whether they're in the 6–1 or 4–3 or whatever they do. Okay?"

"Yes, sir," Starr says.

"On the goal line," Roach says, "had we better run 66 or 67?"

"Well," I say, "that 66, because it's to the left, would be the choice, except we run 67 better. Therefore I think that would depend upon what kind of success you're having. All right?"

"Yes, sir," Roach says.

"Yes, sir," Starr says.

As they get up and leave I look at my watch and it is 12:01 P.M. I follow them to the door of the dressing room.

"All right!" I shout. "Out in fifteen minutes! Let's start getting this dressing room cleared!"

"Players only!" Norb Hecker is shouting, as there are several members of the press and radio who have stopped in. "Players only!"

I sit down at my desk and make a few notes on a small pad. All week I have been talking to them about the importance of this game and so it is difficult on Sunday to think of still another way of saying it. After we come back from our warm-up, though, and it comes up at twelve-fifty-five, I have got to send them out with some kind of a blast-off.

"I just took a look out there," Tom Fears is saying, "and it's starting to rain again."

"It'll rain on them, too," Red Cochran says.

I look at my watch and it is twelve-thirteen and I put on my topcoat and transparent raincoat over it. I walk to the door of the dressing room and look at them, at the rectangle of them sitting in front of their dressing stalls. All of them are now in uniform and wearing olive-green rain jackets and dark blue knitted skullcaps. All of them are waiting.

"All right!" I say. "When we get out there let's have a good workout. You ends and backs, take a good look to see where it's soft. Are we all set?"

"Yes!" they holler, all standing up.

"Then let's go!"

"Let's go!" they shout, and they clap their hands in unison and start filing out. Their cleats make the sound of hailstones hitting the concrete and, as I follow them out and look up, the rain, still light and hesitant, hits my face.

"Hey, Paul! . . . Jimmy! . . . C'mon, Max!" the crowd, packed on either side of the walkway to the ramp, is shouting. "Jim Ringo!. . . Hey, Fuzzy! . . . Ray Nitschke! . . . Bart! Hey, Bart! . . . Good luck, Ron! . . . Willie! Good luck, Vince!"

With Phil and Bill and Dick Voris I follow them down the ramp and out onto the field. The stands are about two-thirds full and as we appear a roar floods down from them. We head for the far end zone and I stop and pick a couple of tufts of grass and stand there and throw one up and then the other. Right now the wind is happily not too strong and out of the northeast; so if we lose the toss and have to kick off we will stay with that choice of north goal.

In that far end zone Ringo and Forester are leading them in calisthenics. Behind me I again hear the roar from the stands and I turn and see the other team, in their silver and white uniforms, coming out, down the ramp and out onto the field.

We take the west half of the field now. Boyd Dowler and Max McGee are kicking to our punt-receivers and the coverage men are running down under the kicks. The receivers then throw to the offensive ends and backs, who run the balls back to the kickers.

"C'mon, Boyd," I'm shouting to Dowler. "Get your foot into it!"

Johnny Symank drops a kick. Jimmy Taylor drops a pass. What kind of a day is this going to be?

"C'mon! C'mon!" I say. "Let's catch that ball!"

At the 38-yard line, with Bart Starr holding, Paul Hornung and Jerry Kramer are practicing field goals. I stand behind them and watch for a while, then I turn and search the other side of the field until I find him, that other coach, my counterpart, and I walk over to him.

"How are you?" I say, and we shake hands.

"Fine," he says. "You?"

"All right," I say. "We drew a rotten day."

"We can't do anything about that."

"I'm sorry about the condition of the field, though," I say. "We've had rain most of the week, and they had a high school game here Friday night."

"I understand," he says.

"Well," I say, because he wants no more of this talk than I do. "Good luck, and I'll see you."

"Thanks," he says. "The same to you."

As I turn I see that the referee is bringing over No. 56, that great middle linebacker of theirs. All week, day and night, he had been invading my thoughts, and I have put in that opener just for his benefit. Now we shake hands. Ringo and Forester have joined us. Then I leave, and I'm aware that the light rain seems to have stopped.

On our side Starr and Johnny Roach are alternating, throwing to our pass-receivers and defensive backs. I watch for a while, then turn as Ringo and Forester come back.

"We won the toss," Ringo says. "We receive and they took the north goal."

"Good," I say. Now I'm hoping that we can make something of it. If we can go all the way from that first kickoff it could make the difference in a game like this one figures to be.

I walked down to where Bill Austin and Phil Bengtson have the offensive and defensive lines facing one another. They are reviewing assignments. It is now twelve-forty-five. We have been out a half hour, so I send them in, follow them up the ramp and into the dressing room.

They have tried the ground now and some of our backs and receivers are changing from the shorter to the longer cleats. Some of our defensive linemen resist the extra taping on their wrists. They hold off until the last minute, and they are having it done now. When they are all seated in front of their stalls, facing the center of the room, the other coaches and I leave them and go into our room and shut the door.

It is ten minutes to game time, and these three minutes that will follow, with just the squad members alone in the dressing room, is something I started when I first came here in 1959. I was reaching for anything then, any method or device, that would give them a feeling of oneness, of dependence upon one another and of strength to be derived from their unity, so I told the captains that before each game this period would belong solely to the players.

I do not know what is said in that room. I know that Ringo or Forester, or perhaps both, speak, and that if someone else wants to say something he does. I know that at the end — and this is completely their thought and desire — they all join in the Lord's Prayer. Then someone knocks on our door and the other coaches and I walk back into the room.

They are still sitting on those chairs. Some of them are relacing their shoes, some are readjusting their shoulder pads and here and there one is talking to another in a low voice. Now I have seven minutes and I walk among them.

"Willie," I say to Willie Wood, "let's see you grab a couple today."

"I'll be tryin'," Willie says.

"Paul," I say to Hornung, "it's going to take a top effort today."

"I know," he says.

"Bart, let's just relax and have a good ball game."

"Yes, sir," Starr says.

"And, Jerry," I say to Jerry Kramer, "remember to set to the inside, because your guy likes the inside rush."

"I know," he says. "I remember."

"And, Max," I say, "you've always had a good game against this club. You can do it again today."

"I'll try, coach."

"And remember," I say, "when you see that linebacker blitzing, cut off your route sooner."

"Right, coach."

I walk to the center of the room, and I'm running through my mind those notes I made on that small pad. I start out by going over, for the offense, the automatics we're going to use, the plays our quarterback will call on the line when he sees that the defensive alignment will negate what he called in the huddle, and I stress our 36 and 50.

"Now, we're going to receive," I say then, "and we've got the south goal. Remember that this club puts their speediest men as third men out from each side and they must be blocked, so let's take them out of there. Let's impress them, all of them, right on that kickoff.

"I don't have to tell you," I say, "about the importance of this ball game. You know as well as I do that you're meeting today the top contender, and that no one can win it now but you. For two years these people have been on our necks, but if you beat them today you'll be making your own job easier for the rest of this year. For you to do it, though, is going to require a top effort. You know the spirit with which this other club is coming in here. You know that they think they can beat you, that they've said they will. That's why I say it's going to take a top effort.

"And now," I say, "I want you, all of you, to know this. Regardless of what happens today this is a team of which I am proud. Regardless of the outcome today I'll still be proud of you. To win, though, you're going to have to run harder and tackle harder and block harder. It's going to take a great team effort, so let's have it! Let's go!"

"Let's go!" they shout, standing, and they bring their hands together in unison again. "Let's go! Go!"

There is the roar of the crowd again, the faces and bodies bordering the walkway. There is the jam-up going down the ramp, and we stand, waiting amid the shouts, for the p.a. announcer to introduce the offensive team.

"At center," he says, the sound of his voice filling the air, and Jim Ringo runs out onto the field through the V formed by the cheerleaders and the Green Bay Lumberjacks' band, "No. 51 — Jim Ringo! At right guard, No. 64 — Jerry Kramer! At left guard, No. 63 — Fuzzy Thurston! At right tackle . . ."

We follow the rest of the squad out, Bill Austin, Phil Bengtson, Dick Voris, and I. Now the names in the air are those of the other club's starting team, and then Ringo and Forester are walking out to the center of the field for the reenactment of the coin-tossing. When they come back the roar from the stands is beating down in waves around us and I am in the middle, crouching, with the squad pressing in around me.

"So we all know what this means," I am saying. "We all know what it means. We know we've got to go out there and hustle. We know we've got to go out there and hit. So let's do it. Let's take it to them. Let's go!"

They break then, with their exclamations, and our kickoff-receiving team runs out to my right. From the other sideline the other team is peeling out of its huddle. And now that nervousness which I have forestalled, which I have learned to control up to a point, starts to come. . . .

Paul Brown is said to have been the first to organize his special teams with care and give them their own practice sessions. Don Shula was the first to name a special-teams captain (Alex Hawkins), and George Allen the first to appoint an assistant exclusively for the "suicide squads." These coaches, winners all, recognized that the play of the special teams often makes the difference between victory and defeat. John Madden, a winner himself, tells you how.

JOHN MADDEN
with Steve Cassady

Practice Makes
Special Teams Special

Every team in the NFL competes along roughly the same lines. Every one has access to similar scouting information, and every one participates in the same draft. All teams adhere to the same rules of play, and they conduct the same length of training camp (there is a maximum but no minimum). They play the same number of preseason home and away games on approximately the same quality of field.

With such equal opportunities, the difference between winning and losing often is marginal. It's not always the result of some secret system, not the result of hiring this coach or signing that draft choice or this free agent. It's more often attention to little things—details such as those associated with special teams.

I remember the days when teams practiced all week, emphasizing only offense and defense. Then, on the day before the game, when everybody was running off the practice field, the coach would look at his watch and say, "Wait a minute. Come back, we've got to practice our special teams." There was no thought devoted to the kicking situations then, no practice time, and, in effect, no coaching.

As recently as the late 1960s, professional teams still were using their offenses on fourth down punt coverages, and their defenses on punt returns. For the most part, they were keeping the same eleven men on the field all four downs. Not surprisingly, examples abounded of teams playing well offensively and defensively, only to lose games on blocked punts and field goals, missed extra points, or long runbacks.

Nowadays, it's much more intricate. Most teams draft with special teams in mind. They trim their rosters with special teams in mind. An obvious example would be selecting a wide receiver for his ability to also return punts. A less obvious example would be drafting a linebacker who is adept at open-field blocking. He could play in the front line of the kickoff return unit. With the new rules prohibiting blocking below the waist, the positions in that four-man front are real specialties, which aren't always easy to fill. They require people who are big and tough, but also fast and agile.

Teams are devoting considerably more time to special-teams strategy these days. I helped broadcast a lot of the Philadelphia Eagles' games last year, and one thing that impressed me was the Eagles' attention to special teams. Just as for offense and defense, they have daily meetings for special teams, daily practice periods, separate scouting reports, and computer breakdowns.

In punting situations, special teams ensure field position, first by kicking the opposition into a hole without permitting a blocked punt, second by covering the punt without allowing a runback. It can work the other way. The offense can struggle like hell to reach its own 40, only to have the return unit come in and block the punt. It all goes hand in hand—offense, defense, and special teams helping each other, all equally important in winning and losing.

Consequently, planning for special teams can be as detailed as for offense and defense. It starts with a thorough scouting report. Take, for example, the information collected just for preparing the punt-return unit.

First comes field conditions. Assuming the upcoming game is scheduled for the opponent's home stadium, the scout charts the direction the wind blows. One way is to notice which end the home team chooses to defend if it loses the toss. Usually, it wants to start the game or the second half with the wind at its back.

Then he determines how far the punter kicks on the average. Then placement: if the ball is spotted on the left hashmark, does the kicker usually punt to the left? Aim it back toward the middle? Kick it across to the right? The scout would make the same notations for the right hash and the middle.

Next is hang time—how long the ball stays in the air after it leaves the kicker's foot. Then personnel. Punt coverage comes in waves. The first is the two end men, the ones who release with the snap and head in a vee toward the return man. The second is the front men, the center, two guards, two tackles, each sprinting upfield in lanes. The third is the two upbacks, who fan out and take the lanes between the front men and the end men, one up the right, the other up the left. And the fourth is the punter and fullback—the punter covering the left as one safety, the fullback the right as the other.

Who are each of these players by name and number? Which of them reaches the coverage area fastest? By what routes? Who makes most of the tackles?

Field position comes next. Some punters kick a certain way from their own end zone. They want it up and away quickly: in that situation, they don't worry about angling it one way or another. Inside the 50, they may do it differently, taking the time to kick it toward a corner, usually the same corner as the hashmark from which they're kicking.

Now, with all this information, it's possible to plan return strategies for the upcoming game. The first consideration against any punt is whether you want a return or a block. It's like defending against the pass. Either you cover it tight by dropping more people into the secondary, or you blitz by sending in extra rushers.

Say it's a return. You first position the safety at a depth equal to the kicker's average. If a stiff wind blows against you, you back up the safety another three or four yards; if it is with you, you move him up three or four.

There are a number of punt-return combinations. The basic one is a six-man front. The two outside men usually rush the kicker. At Oakland, we sometimes got the block when we were concentrating on a return. The reason? We had Lester Hayes and Ted Hendricks on the flanks. They are fast and rangy, good attributes for end men on the punt rush. They also knew how to pursue. You see, all punters line up 15 yards behind scrimmage, but no two hit the ball at exactly the same spot. You might face a two-step punter one week, a three-step the next. One might be a long-strider, the other a short-strider.

To figure it, we'd chart the precise point each kicker hit the ball, and that's the point at which we'd have our end men aim. It sounds obvious, but distinctions such as this often are lost. Little things such as rushing at the proper angle often are the difference between a block and no block, maybe even between winning and losing.

In setting up the return, the most important priority is fielding the ball. The two early coverage men must be detained, and the safety must catch the punt above all— it's the element that guarantees possession. Any yardage beyond the reception is a bonus provided by the blockers in the return scheme.

Basically, the four interior linemen try to hold up the coverage team's guards and tackles. Behind them, two linebackers divide the duties; one attempts to block the center, while the other blocks on the side of the return. The two halfbacks behind them are responsible for the end men. The safety tries to find open spaces in the direction designated in the huddle. Either it is a return right, to the left, or the middle.

Within the basic scheme, teams vary their approach, depending upon personnel. Maybe they want to double team a particularly effective end man and run away from the other. Maybe they want to switch the blocking assignment to find better matchups, the way you'd shift coverages in the defensive backfield. The idea is to find the combinations that prevent the coverage from mobilizing too quickly.

Most teams also factor in anticipated hang time. If a punter kicks with consistently long hang time, they might want to obstruct the coverage at the line of scrimmage, giving the safety a fraction more time before he is swarmed under. If he kicks with a lower hang time, they might want to immediately form a blocking wall for a more aggressive return.

Another consideration is eligible receivers. They all would have to be accounted for in the event of a fake punt, and by people with pass-defending skills.

At Oakland, we'd spend considerable time anticipating trick plays off punt formation. We would splice all available footage on the opponent's kicking game, and we would chart all the normal formations and alignments.

The fullback in punt formation often is an indicator, for instance. He is the punter's personal protector. He normally lines up on the side of the kicking foot, at a point he can most effectively take on the rush. He is pretty much committed to a predictable spot, so if he lines up differently — up or back, or on the other side of the punter — it usually signals a trick.

We'd mark other deviations as well, substitutions, upbacks cheating over, and so on.

All phases of special teams — kickoffs, kickoff coverage, punt coverage, punt returns, field goal, field-goal block, extra point, and extra-point block — follow this general pattern of planning. It's not like it was years ago, when the punter coming on meant it was time for television to take a station break and for the fans to head for the beer. Now, special teams are too important to be deemphasized or ignored.

So maybe it isn't the greatest game ever played, or even the most important. It is certainly the most famous. The sudden-death climax was a one-of-a-kind thrill, and it sparked America's love affair with pro football in the 1960s. It had much to do, as well, with the NFL's decision to expand and the AFL's decision to be. And it canonized Johnny Unitas and Raymond Berry; no subsequent heroics, and these were plentiful, could add to their luster. Unitas and Berry are in the Hall of Fame, of course, along with eleven others who were on the field that glorious day.

JACK MANN

Sudden Death in the Afternoon

Sports Illustrated, which caused it to be called "The Greatest Football Game Ever Played," didn't actually use the word "greatest." Tex Maule, the pro football curator, wanted to use the word. But his magazine had a rule against it. So they settled on the word "best," and people got the idea anyway. Maule also remembers *S.I.* merely giving the "Best Game" a two-page, one-picture spread. "Pro football just wasn't Madison Avenue in those days," he recalls.

"Those days" included the fourth-to-last day of 1958, when the Baltimore Colts needed eight minutes and fifteen seconds of history's first sudden-death overtime to complete a 23–17 conquest of the New York Giants for the championship of the National Football League, the only pro-football league there was in those days, when there was one basketball league and one hockey league.

These days Commissioner Pete Rozelle's television euphemizers would have called the extra period—over Commissioner Bert Bell's dead body—"Sudden Victory." Much more than that has changed, and much of the change began in the clammy gloaming of that December 28 in Yankee Stadium.

The game was heroically contested, a fierce confrontation between self-anointed underdogs. It was magnificently flawed: e.g., two fumbles, leading to a touchdown each, by Frank Gifford, the glamour-boy eminence, now a glamour-boy television sportscaster.

The game was exquisitely second-guessable from either side and came perilously close, several times, to being worth the routine treatment *Sports Illustrated* had planned for it. But withal, you can bet your genuine ceramic, Official, $6.95 Redskins ashtray, the very good game was the Greatest Thing that had ever happened to make pro football great: "Much above average," Webster defines the adjective, "in magnitude, intensity, etc."

Et cetera. While John F. Kennedy lived, a fad became a fixation and a coach a demigod; they played football games for money on the day a murdered president lay cold in the Capitol. Under Richard Nixon, a commercial entertainment became a public issue, and George Allen a knight of the realm.

The same wonderful people who had given us "I Love Lucy," the roller derby, and "The $64,000 Question" would have purveyed megalofootball in prime time and Living Color sooner or later. Sooner, perhaps, if the four previous NFL championship games hadn't ended up in unmerchandisable disarray: 59–14, 47–7, 38–14, and 56–10. Later, perhaps, if Baltimore fullback Alan Ameche had "thrown the goddamn ball," as teammate Gino Marchetti put it, when the '58 Colts had their sword poised at the Giants' throatlatch in the third quarter. They led, 14–3, and had a first down on the Giants' 3-yard line. If the Colts scored a touchdown, channel selectors would click from palm to pine. There would be no overtime, and probably no room for Ameche's bow on that evening's Ed Sullivan Show.

Alan was called "The Horse" because he could move forward in a very powerful manner, even dragging people. Little else was expected or asked of him normally, but the Giants had an abnormally obdurate defense, the one that gave identity and glamour to the DEE-fense business—being the first defensive unit to be introduced in the pregame rites. So the Colts' planners had "put in" a play to give Ameche another option, just in case of exactly what happened. Ameche gained two, Unitas nothing, Ameche nothing. Fourth-and-goal on the one-yard line.

Jim Mutscheller was the "inside" or tight end on the right. "I guess he was supposed to throw to me. Anyway, it was supposed to work because Alan hadn't thrown all year—couldn't pass at all. The play was Flow-28, a quick pitch to the halfback. With Lenny [Moore] out wide, Ameche was in the halfback spot."

"Ameche takes pitch, goes wide right," reads the mimeograph transcript. "Hit by Livingston on 5."

Possibly linebacker Cliff Livingston had taken the bait, made the rebuttable presumption that Ameche could not or would not pass, and diagnosed the run, leaving Mutscheller as free as the Colts' strategists had hoped. In any case, Ameche never got rid of the ball. The Giants' DEE-fense (it was chanted in Yankee Stadium first) had accomplished the implausible. "Reprieved," as in the final scene of *The Threepenny Opera*, would have been the appropriate chant for the OFF-fense, which five plays and an outrageous bit of luck later had New York back in the game, 14–10.

"It was slippery down there," Baltimore coach Weeb Ewbank remembered of the goal-line stand. Indeed, it seemed the leprechauns who often piloted the Giant-owning

Mara family among the shoals of fortune were having a good day, even if people named Gifford and Conerly were not. It was slippery down there, at the darkling home-plate end of the Stadium, because the day of the big game had dawned on Mara Weather: sunshine, not reasonably expected in a normally lousy New York winter.

The late Jack Mara and brother Wellington likely would have sold the 64,185 tickets that day if icebergs had been sighted in the Harlem River. They remembered those hard days when five-figure crowds had been a gleam in their father's eye. Right up to World War II it mattered to pro-football entrepreneurs whether it was sunny or cold; a heavy rain was a financial bath. In those days, or so it seemed to a lot of people, it hardly ever rained in New York on a Sunday when the Giants were playing at home. (Some Mara-watchers saw relevance in the family's connections as ranking Catholic laymen. Father Benedict Dudley is believed to be the first clergyman to go on the road as chaplain of a pro-football team, and after at least one game of that 1958 season there were seventeen priests in the Giants' dressing room, interviewing players.) So Mara Weather thawed the tundra enough that Alan The Horse, faltering like a thoroughbred on a winter track, never got footing to throw, if he planned to.

It was redemption time for the Giant offense, which was a sometime thing predicated on one of those decisions-not-to-decide that were the currency of leadership in Eisenhower's time-out decade. With incomplete faith in Charlie Conerly, because he was old, and in Don Heinrich, because he wasn't, the Giants would start Heinrich, who "probed" the enemy defense for a quarter or so until, by some inscrutable criterion, it was time for Charlie.

The Colts' bearing was jaunty, like the adhesive-tape spats that made Lenny Moore's feet a white blur as he sped down the sideline in a "fly" pattern before there was such a term. And it was daring, in the why-not approach of brash young quarterback Johnny Unitas, who in the sudden death would call a penultimate play so reckless as to make the winning touchdown anticlimactic.

There were other differences. The game was no morality play, but there were neo-Dickensian overtones. The Colts were clearly the have-nots of the piece, not only because the Giants had been champions before, but for instance: Cliff Livingston, rugged-handsome if you dug that new Richard Boone thing, but no Montgomery Clift, had a TV commercial in New York. There *weren't* such things in Baltimore. Stuff like that.

The sixth biggest city in the United States was on probation as a big-league town, having opened and closed in one NFL season after surviving the anschluss that closed out the All-America Conference.

The Orioles had been in town only five years, not long enough to fumigate their past as the St. Louis Browns. The Colts came back to Baltimore as a foundling of the NFL, which had unsuccessfully placed them in foster homes, first as the New York Yanks, then as the Dallas Texans.

The Texans were Gino Marchetti's first professional team (using the term promiscuously): "[Art] Donovan and I got tired of people settin' records against us. 'Hugh McElhenny [mimicking a public-address announcer] has just broken the Forty-Niners' record. . . .' In L.A. I scored my first touchdown and I felt pretty good. Then I heard the p.a. system say that made the score 46–6 — *at the half.*"

They still grumble in Baltimore that Commissioner Bell, a sedulous rail-splitter in the edification of the NFL, made the new owners sell 15,000 season tickets in front before they could have the Texas reject. They also griped that the 1950 owner, Abe Watner, who cried poormouth and tossed the franchise back to the league, could have made it. It's all part of being from "Ballamer," a factory city that would rather be known for white stoops and crabcakes, where that part of the populace that cares at all is aggressively defensive.

Awareness of this attitude may have moved Ballamer coach Ewbank to his finest hour, just before the kickoff. Not known before or since as a motivator of men, Ewbank came on in his pregame talk as a latter-day Marcus Antonius. Gino Marchetti, tough as his centurion's visage and blasé to the point of indelicacy on the subject of pep talks, is perhaps most objective of all the Colts who remember the speech, and they all do.

"In fourteen years," Marchetti said, "I heard 'em all. 'Win for Mother, Win for Father. . . . Don't disappoint all those people watching on TV.' Sometimes they just tell you how to act: 'Don't piss in the air with forty million people watching.'

"But Weeb really put it to us. He went down the roster, name by name: 'Donovan, they got rid of you — too fat and slow. . . . Ameche, Green Bay didn't want you.' Yeah, he named me, Unitas. . . . He didn't miss anybody."

Colts' personnel director Fred Schubach, as equipment manager, was privy to all the incitements to riot from the '53 reincarnation through the dark angers of Don Shula to Don McCafferty's easy ride to the Super Bowl. Weeb's is the exhortation he remembers. It left him feeling that "the only way we could get recognition would be to beat the Giants *in New York* — to show that New York press. . . . It would be the first big thing that ever happened to Baltimore."

Ewbank was taking a calculated risk. The massive Donovan, for example, was on the serious side of thirty, and his boyish figure was long gone, but reminding a four-time all-pro tackle that he once was somebody's wretched refuse can bring violent reaction. "I told them they were guys Paul Brown didn't want — nobody wanted," Weeb has since said. His credentials were in order. He had been an assistant in Cleveland in March, 1953, when Brown "backed up the moving van," to use Casey Stengel's phrase, and sent ten people to Baltimore for five. That gave the Browns Mike McCormack and three of the next four division championships. It gave the Colts Art Spinney, Carl Taseff, and Bert Rechichar, who was going out to kick off when Ewbank stopped talking.

"We started from scratch," Weeb recalled. "Trades, free agents, pickups. Bill Pellington [Colts' "meanest" linebacker for a decade] was cut from the Browns — as an offensive tackle. Gino was one, too, when I got him. Spinney and Alex Sandusky ['58 guards] were defensive ends. Nobody handed me a football team."

"He's right," Hall of Fame defensive end Marchetti said years later, from the nerve center of his hamburger chain. "Weeb was no great coach, but his great asset was a talent for recognizing ability."

They had worked too hard and sacrificed too much, Ewbank told his poor, huddled masses in conclusion, to be stopped now. Righteously indignant, they stormed out to meet the other underdogs.

To reach the title game, the Giants had had to "upset" the Cleveland Browns three times: 21–17 at Cleveland, 13–10 on Pat Summerall's 50½-yard field goal in a driving snow—when the 10–10 tie would have given the Browns the marbles—and 10–0 in a playoff. The last may have been the most persuasive beating a football team ever took by a score that low: Jim Brown, holder of the league record of 237 yards gained in one game, was held to eight. The Giants had beaten the Colts in New York, 24–21, but Unitas had watched lying in a hospital bed.

For the record, the "paper" odds on the championship game made Baltimore a 4½-point favorite. Nobody who was of betting age at the time seems to have met a man who got, or gave, more than three. By any account, the price was less than six points, which would become more important later, when it became apparent that the Colts were going to score either three or six points in sudden death.

After the goal-line stand and Ameche's nonpass, with the score still 14–3, thrusts by Gifford and Alex Webster got the Giants out to their 13, third and two. Conerly faked the short-yardage play (it was getting late for a team that grossed 86 yards in the first half and netted zero on five plays in the second) and lobbed the ball from his 5 to the Colts' 40, where Kyle Rote had a step on ankle-pained Milt Davis and made a good catch. Grabbed at the 30 by safety Andy Nelson, Rote dropped the ball on the 25. Along came Webster, scooped the bounce like Luis Aparicio and huffed to the one. Mel Triplett banged it over. The score was 14–10.

"Nobody thinks about overtime with a score like 14–3 or 14–10," said Mutscheller, who never thought about it at all until they were flipping the coin. Remarkably, the Notre Damer, later playing coach and now insurance broker, had never been informed that there was provision for sudden death.

"As far as I knew, a tie was a tie," he recalled recently.

Not so. The only reason there had never been sudden death was because there had never been a tie championship game.*

Tackle Dick Modzelewski ate up Unitas—Mo would sack him three times before the end, when John would make him pay—to get the ball back, and Conerly ate up 78 yards in three well-conceived passes, the last a 15-yard TD to Gifford, picking on Steve Myhra. The young placekicker was subbing for linebacker Leo Sanford, racked up in the game's second play. Gifford, no Nagurski, ran over a defender at the 5.

The Giants led, 17–14, and they were hitting, as coaches say. The Colts crossed mid-

*However, a tie championship game prior to 1947 would have remained a tie.—ED.

field on interference against Lenny Moore by anxious Lindon Crow; that fly pattern had burned Crow for 60 yards in the first quarter and a touchdown in the earlier game. The DEE-fense held, and Bert Rechichar, whose 56-yard field goal in 1953 would remain a record for seventeen years, was short from the 46.

Giant rookie back Phil King staged the next crisis, fumbling to the Colts on the Giants' 42. An imperative third-and-ten completion to the uncanny Raymond (nobody called him Ray) Berry put Baltimore on the 31, well within Rechichar's range and not far from Myhra's chip-shot territory. L.G. ("Long Gone" to the whimsical media, Louis George to his mother in Texas) Dupre got four yards, and then Andy Robustelli got in the game. The Giants' veteran end had the day's toughest job, trying to get past all-timer Jim Parker, against whom all offensive linemen must be compared if they pretend to greatness. This time Andy got by and sacked Unitas, 11 yards deep. Modzelewski then nailed him on the 47 and the Colts were out of field-goal range, or at least out of faith in Rechichar. Baltimore punted.

When the Giants made a first down on their 34, with little more than two minutes left, the press box was voting *Sport Magazine's* MVP Corvette to Conerly. (Five years later, Charlie's wife and Boswell, Perian, would lament in her memoir of Dorothy Unitas "driving gaily around Baltimore in 'my' Corvette.") One more first down . . .

Third-and-four on the 40, Conerly handed off to Gifford, sweeping right, Webster leading, both guards pulling. Webster blocked conerback Carl Taseff outside, and Gifford cut back in, but Bob Schnelker, the lanky end, was no match for the fierce Marchetti. Though the Giants' ultrapowerful Jack Stroud, an all-pro guard against the rest of the league, was switched to tackle against Marchetti, the play Conerly selected had Stroud keyed to linebacker Don Shinnick. "Gino grabbed Gifford first," recalled Colt center Dick Szymanski, "and then Shinnick stood him up." Tackle Gene (Big Daddy) Lipscomb, pursuing from the other side, finished off the play and Marchetti. Lipscomb's ponderous weight fell on Gino's right leg and snapped it above the ankle.

Referee Ron Gibbs called time to have Marchetti moved from the spot so the measurement could be made. "Charlie Berry [head linesman] didn't give us the benefit of the doubt," said Robustelli, now the Giants' general manager. Gibbs held his hands up, six or seven inches apart.

Roosevelt Brown, the Giants' John Henry of a tackle, always whipped his helmet off instantly at the end of a set of downs. This time he stood, helmet on, jabbing an index finger toward home plate. "I wanted to go for it too," Robustelli said more than fifteen years later. "Power play: Triplett into the line, Webster following. I wouldn't have given it to Frank the play before; he wasn't that kind of runner."

Some say the late Vince Lombardi, the offense lieutenant, wanted to go for the first down, too, and argued the point. "We have the league's best punter," head coach Howell explained in the autopsy, "or at least the second-best." The NFL's second-best punter (Don Chandler averaged 44.0 yards that year to Redskin Sam Baker's 45.4) got off a scenic spiral, 60 yards in the air to the Colts' 14, where Taseff let a fair catch be the better part of valor.

John Unitas, age twenty-five, three years removed from the quasi-pro Bloomfield Rams of the Pittsburgh suburbs, was incomplete with his first two passes. Now he had but to negotiate 86 yards in a minute and sixteen seconds against the most cunning DEE-fense yet conceived by man. Unitas managed 73 of them in five throws, the last three, totaling 62 yards, to the remarkable Berry. It was Howell's postfacto theory that mercurial Lenny Moore, "keeping us busy," set up Berry's record twelve catches that day. Moore had them bomb-shy, but Berry was just the best past catcher alive, a nebbishy-looking freak who could get free on a subway platform and catch buttered corn. When he button-hooked and ran — corseted back, short leg, contact lenses, and all — to the Giant 13, there were twenty seconds left. Though Ewbank remembers Myhra as "no sure thing," he didn't miss. There would be sudden death in our time.

The Giants' partisans roared presumptuously when referee Gibbs inspected the coin he had flipped and patted Kyle Rote on the helmet. The inequity in sudden-death play was, and is, the edge it gives the team that first gets the ball. The Giants gave it back in three plays. Third and six on his 24, Conerly couldn't throw and had to go. He gave it his best thirty-seven-year-old shot, making all but twenty-four inches of the needed six yards before Pellington and Shinnick knocked him sideways.

This time nobody argued about "going for it," and Chandler punted almost 70 yards. Unitas took over at his 20, with no time limit whatever. In a detailed analysis, when it figured out how important the game had been, *Sports Illustrated* called what ensued "The Thirteen Plays to Glory." There were five passes: first a 65-yard terror stroke to Moore, fingertipped away by the battle-fatigued Crow; then four complete, two to Berry.

The chopping-block rhythm of the drive was interrupted once, when Modzelewski crashed against and nailed Unitas for an eight-yard loss, leaving him a grim third-and-fifteen at his own 36. The game would have ended on the next play, had Berry contact lenses in the back of his head, or had he understood Unitas's frantic waving as Raymond buttonhooked. Cornerback Carl Karilivacz had slipped to his knees, and Berry had the field to himself. As it was, he made 21 yards. On the next play Unitas punished Modzelewski, who had been "blowing in too fast to suit me." Guard Alex Sandusky and center Buzz Nutter left the door open for "Little Mo" and Spinney crossed over to trap-block him as Ameche went past, up the middle for 23 yards. Sam Huff, who had been keyed on Ameche as he always was on Jim Brown, was "cheating" in Berry's direction by then, and tackle George Preas's diagonal block wiped him out.

Unitas's "plain ol' slant pass" to Berry gave the Colts a first down on the eight, and a lock. Myhra was swinging his leg on the sideline as Huff plugged the middle and held Ameche to a yard.

Then, groans were heard in the land, and in Ballamer screams, as the picture tube went blank. "Somebody kicked a cable," Ewbank recalls, "and the officials called time. John came over and asked, 'What do you think?'"

In 1956, after Pittsburgh cut him, Unitas was playing sandlot ball when a phone call from injury-plagued Baltimore put him back in the NFL. Two years later, he was the toast of the sports world when he led the Colts to a sudden-death overtime victory in the 1958 championship game.

From there — through countless last-ditch victories — until he retired after the 1973 season Johnny U. remained the most respected quarterback in football.

Johnny Unitas

What the coach thought, with second-and-goal on the seven, unlimited time, and the championship of everything at stake was: "Keep it on the ground. Alan's sure; he won't fumble. Worse comes to worst, we got the field goal." And a 20–17 victory — over everything but the point spread. "So what did that little son of a gun do?"

That little son of a gun went back and threw a pass in the flat to Mutscheller, who fell over the flag, on the 1-yard line. The drunks were on the field before The Horse cantered the last yard for the 6 points.

"No, I wasn't afraid," Ewbank said fifteen minutes after the game. "I'm used to John by now. He knows what he's doing out there."

"Sure he scared me a little," Ewbank said fifteen years after the game. "I was afraid it might go the other way."

What Ewbank means by "go the other way" was that any Giant who got to that ball before Mutscheller — linebacker Livingston, for example — would have had nothing in his way but winter-worn Merion Blue grass. "John had an answer, though," Ewbank remembered in his office as Jets' general manager. "He said that if there'd been anybody there he'd have thrown it out of bounds. But suppose somebody tipped his arm? I've seen things happen. . . ."

Mutscheller, now an insurance broker, took an actuarial view from hindsight. There was "not really that much danger," he said. "It was a diagonal-type pass, a 60-Diagonal Right, I think. I slant out at 45 degrees and John has to throw right away. If Crow doesn't follow Lenny, it's a touchdown to him."

Lodge brother Jim Lee Howell supported Ewbank's "no sweat" contention in the aftermath. "Great call," he said. "You have to do things like that in this game."

There was a lot of talk. Reports were circulated that Colts' owner Carroll Rosenbloom had been known to bet large sums on the outcome of sporting events. Not on his own team's games, Rosenbloom insisted.

"There's still a lot of controversy," Gino Marchetti said in the "San Francisco," his restaurant in Wayne, Pennsylvania. "People still ask my why we didn't kick a field goal. You don't kick a field goal on first or second down."

"A lot of people accused me of playing the point spread," Ewbank said. "I didn't even know what it was."

The visiting manager's dressing room in old Yankee Stadium was too small for all the reporters who wanted to ask questions after such a big event. When new waves of inquisitors kept asking about that next-to-last play, Ewbank became annoyed. "I told you," he snapped, "this is a game in which you have to gamble."

There was noise, some of it laughter.

"Coach, that's exactly what I was asking about," the reporter said. But nobody heard him.

Although Pudge Heffelfinger was, in 1892, the first man to have been paid in cash to play football (see Don Smith's story), ethically dubious payments "in kind" were common at least two years earlier. Dr. Harry A. March described the practice in his 1934 *Pro Football: Its "Ups" and "Downs,"* the first book ever devoted to the game. Proclaimed by Grantland Rice as "The Father of Professional Football," a hugely inflated sobriquet, March nevertheless had a uniquely broad range of experience in the game. He was a tramp college star of the 1890s, under assumed names "dying for dear old" Ohio State, Oberlin, Kenyon, and Mount Union. Then in 1895 he played fullback in what has been called the first professional game, between Latrobe and Jeannette of Pennsylvania. In the mid-1920s he was instrumental in bringing pro football to New York and became president of the Giants; in 1936 he organized the second American Football League.

HARRY A. MARCH

For Love or Money?

In the transitional period, during which it was nearly impossible to distinguish between professionals and amateurs, there are some interesting developments which it might be worthy of noting.

For example, in 1890–91, there were a number of athletic clubs in and about New York, composed of well-known college men who played on the various teams without a *thought* of monetary consideration. These teams included the Manhattan Athletic Club, the Orange Athletic Club in Jersey, the Crescent Club in Brooklyn, the Staten Island Athletic Club, and the Knickerbocker, which was a descendant of the Manhattan.

Snake Ames, Phil King, Parke Davis, until his death early in June, 1934, chief statistician for the Inter-collegiates (and our authority for this particular phase of the transition) and Furness—all of Princeton—played on these teams, as well as many Yale men, whom Mr. Davis courteously forgot. The boys played for only expenses and a "*trophy*"—all strictly amateur.

Now, here is the catch. The day after the amateur was presented with the "trophy," which was usually a pretty fine gold watch, one who cared to follow him would find him threading his circuitous way to some well-known pawnbroker where the watch was placed in "hock," the usual sum received thereby being a "*saw buck*"; in plainer words, twenty smackers. Then the player—still strictly amateur—somehow ran across the man who managed these amateur games and *sold* him the pawn ticket for another twenty dollars. By some special sense of divination, second sightedness, or mental telepathy, the promoter found himself urged towards the same pawn shop and under an irresistible impulse, retrieved the pawned watch, paying therefor a small interest and twenty dollars. Then, after the next game, the player received as his "trophy" the *same* gold watch, which went through the same identical loaning experience.

It is said some of these watches became so enamoured with the player owners that at last they refused to tick for anyone else, even the pawnbroker and the promoter. One player was so moved by the plight of the timepiece that he actually kept the watch and still has it though it has long been still. But *he* is still strictly a "simon pure" amateur.

The tale might have been penned by Kafka. Karl Sweetan, itinerant and, in the summer of 1972, unwanted quarterback, is desperate, but he has an idea. He purloins a playbook that, it develops, had no value to the Rams and sells it to the Saints, for whom, it develops, it also has no value. For thus trafficking in trash, the criminal mastermind is set up by the FBI and deposited in the slammer. To compound the absurdity, Sweetan was right in thinking that New Orleans coach J. D. Roberts would need help; the Saints finished that year at 2–11–1. However, Sweetan was wrong to think that help might come from the Rams; they finished just one notch above the Saints.

TEX MAULE

Would You Buy a Used Playbook from This Man?

In the ten years since he left the playing fields of Wake Forest, Karl Sweetan has worked as a quarterback—mostly intermittently and inauspiciously—for the Toronto Argonauts, the Pontiac (Mich.) Arrows, the Detroit Lions, the New Orleans Saints, and the Los Angeles Rams. A fortnight ago, having been released by the Rams and having failed to make it with the Edmonton Eskimos, he decided to change careers and try his hand at selling. He did not distinguish himself in that field, either.

Sweetan, along with a cousin, attempted to peddle a 1971 Ram playbook for $2,500 to J. D. Roberts, the head coach for the Saints. Roberts pretended to go along with the deal and informed the league; it called the FBI, which wired him up with a transmitter in one of football's more unusual plays. "All I did was ask questions," Roberts said after completing his agent's role. "The FBI did a helluva job." U.S. Attorney Gerald J. Gallinghouse said Roberts had, too, adding that the coach "executed each play the FBI called to perfection." Sweetan and his cousin were jailed, charged with interstate transportation of stolen property and fraud by wire and released on $5,000 bond each.

The case shocked pro football's coaches, largely because they could not see why a playbook could be thought to have such value. Dan Devine of the Green Bay Packers says he would not pay five dollars for one. Don Shula of the Miami Dolphins says, "What secrets are there, really? A book gives you a system, not a game plan."

What is a pro team's playbook, and could it have any value to a rival coach? Presumably, what Sweetan would have had to sell was an offensive playbook (pro teams have two—one for the offense, one for the defense). The books—usually loose-leaf notebooks—contain plays and variations, formations, audibles, nomenclature, house rules and, in some cases, exhortations to the players to give 110 percent.

The book Sweetan was accused of trying to sell was compiled by Tommy Prothro after he took over the Rams last year. Ironically, Prothro is not an advocate of playbooks. "I believe in them less than anybody," he said last week. "I really don't learn by reading things. I learn by seeing something and talking about it. Consequently, I've never believed in writing it all down. But all our other coaches believe in it, and if these young, smart guys believe in it, I'm all for having one."

Prothro said that the most valuable information to be gleaned from a rival's playbook is not what a team does, but what it doesn't do. "You never know when they are going to do something," he said, "but if you know something they won't do, then you don't have to protect against it."

Prothro admitted that he has trouble recalling the nomenclature in his own playbook. "I'll ask an assistant every once in a while, 'That pitch where the quarterback swings around end and we trap the first man from the tackle's nose outside, what the hell are we calling that now?' In the same way I don't remember what I had to eat tonight for dinner, but I know what happened on the second play of the third quarter of a football game in 1954."

Indeed, there is little variation in playbooks from team to team, except in nomenclature. With the wholesale exchange of game movies, teams are thoroughly conversant with the plays their adversaries run. In fact, they often know their opponents better than themselves and have to "scout" themselves every few weeks to make sure no predictable tendencies are showing.

Paul Brown, the part-owner and coach of the Cincinnati Bengals, does not place much value on an opponent's playbook as a secret weapon, either. "There is very little in a playbook that could help one team against another in a given game," he says. "Better you should have a quarterback who can throw the ball." The Rams, incidentally, probably have an old Brown playbook handy, in case Prothro should need it. "I often give a player—a *deserving* player—a playbook if he's ending his career and going into coaching," Brown says. "You can study a playbook in the off-season and pick up little ideas of nomenclature, little things you might like better than the way you're saying or doing something. But it's meaningless in preparing for another team. You can get everything you ever would want from a game film."

Hank Stram of the Kansas City Chiefs tells of a flight he once took from Dallas to Fort Lauderdale. "The plane stopped in New Orleans," he says, "and a bunch of youngsters got on board. They were members of an eighth-grade team going to a postseason game. While on the flight they took examinations on the plays they were to use in the game. I was surprised to hear that they were using our plays and terminology. Their coach had followed our team as a fan, liked our variety offense, and had been given a copy of our playbook by one of our former players."

Several years ago Paul Brown briefly experimented with shortwave transmissions from sideline to quarterback as an alternative to his system of messenger guards. The quarterback had a tiny transistorized speaker in his helmet so that Brown could talk to him in the huddle. According to a perhaps apocryphal story, the year Brown went electronic an assistant quit his club to work for the Giants, and during a New York-Cleveland game tuned in on Brown's frequency. Since he knew Brown's playbook, he shouted advice to the Giant defenders as soon as Brown called a play. The Giants won 21–9.

If true, this may have been the only instance in which a playbook helped an opposing team. In truth, scouting, movies, even tip-offs—inadvertent indications by a member of an offensive team that allow the defense to anticipate the type or direction of an upcoming play—have always been overrated.

In 1950 the Rams had a divisional championship team, but they could not seem to beat the Philadelphia Eagles, coached by Greasy Neale and quarterbacked by one-eyed Tommy Thompson. By assiduous study of Eagle movies, they discovered something about Thompson. If he was going to hand off for a run to the right, his right foot was in back of his left, and vice versa. If we was going to pass, his feet were parallel to one another. It was a perfect tip-off since it was visible to the defense well before the snap of the ball.

But at the half the Eagles led the Rams 28–0; at the end of the game it was 56–20. "We knew where they were going," said Ram linebacker Don Paul, "but they went there anyway." Which brings to mind something an NFL scout said after watching one of Vince Lombardi's Green Bay teams dismantle an opponent. When the game ended, he was asked what he had discovered. "Hell," he said, sadly, "how do you scout blocking and tackling?"

It is surprising that the Saints made a federal case out of the Sweetan matter. "This whole incident is sadly blown clear out of importance," says Paul Brown. "It's certainly not worth bringing in the FBI. I think those Saints were living up to their name. If Sweetan had approached me, I would have told him I wasn't interested in the book. I'd have also told him he was making a mixed-up mistake, and I would have tried to talk him out of it. Then I'd have called the Rams to let them know what was going on."

Norm Van Brocklin of the Falcons says he would have done the same thing, adding that his book is already being used around the league—the defensive volume by Minnesota and Philadelphia, the offensive by St. Louis.

Billy Wilson, once a star end for the San Francisco 49ers, has a garage full of playbooks. "I've got them from every year I played football," he says. "What's the going price? $2,500? I think I'll have a garage sale now. Two for $4,000."

Dick Nolan of the 49ers expresses the majority view of his fellow coaches. "Another team's playbook is not worth $2,500," he says. "My own playbook is beyond value, in a way, because a lot of hard work and thought went into it. What it really contains is one's own interpretation of the game. It is the philosophy, what I want from my players and what they are expected to give me in the way of effort. So that part of it is not of much value to the opposition. I mean, you learn that anyway—the other coach's philosophy—over the years. You see his films, you watch his games, you get your computer reports, and patterns begin to establish themselves.

"Sometimes you learn more from all the things put together than any playbook can ever divulge. And that's another thing. I don't have everything in our playbook. There are things we decide the week of a game, things we don't put down in writing."

Of the 300-odd plays in a playbook, most teams use from fifteen to thirty in a specific game, those being tailored for the clubs they are playing. Had Sweetan, on a Friday before a Sunday game against the Rams, sold the Ready List, it conceivably could have helped the Saints.

The audibles in the playbook would not. An audible signal allows the quarterback to change his huddle call to meet a different defense at the line of scrimmage. It is preceded by a live call in the huddle. The quarterback might mention the color orange as the live audible; if he wants to change the call at the line of scrimmage, he repeats "orange." Any other color—green, red—means the huddle call goes. The defense would have to know the live color and the meaning of the numbers called after it to know what the play would be.

The crux of the matter is that pro football is an incestuous business. Nolan, who was for years an assistant to Dallas's Tom Landry, has a playbook which varies little from the Cowboys'. There is a whole school of coaches in the league who received their early training from Paul Brown, including Weeb Ewbank of the Jets and Shula. All of them think alike, and when something new comes up, it appears on film and is immediately adopted by the rest.

Playbooks change with the game from season to season, probably about 20 percent a year. And very likely 80 percent of all playbooks are similar, with the exception of nomenclature. As Hank Stram points out, "It's a game of people, not notebooks. The Chiefs' playbook is a volume of communications so that the team can have a common language when we talk football both on and off the field. The only basic difference in plays used by pro teams is in terminology."

"The first thing in the playbook is a new language," says Prothro. "Nomenclature and semantics. There are so many things you want to talk about in football, both verbally on the field and in writing in a playbook, that we must have a form of shorthand. We must give things terms."

For instance, the Ram playbook uses "Switch" to indicate a linebacker dropping off in pass coverage opposite to his normal drop. "OX" means an end and a linebacker switching assignments. "Roger" is the right tackle looping to the outside, "Rinny" the right tackle looping to the inside.

Although Paul Brown is usually credited with creating the first playbook, it is more likely that Clark Shaughnessy, who coached the Rams in 1948 and 1949, originated the idea. Shaughnessy arrived in Los Angeles with trunks full of play diagrams that he had put into books. He had more than 300 plays in his collection and variations off each. "For a long time, the guards used to meet just behind the center on a running play," Norm Van Brocklin says of those Ram days. "They were pulling in opposite directions. I had to drop back in a hurry just to avoid being mashed."

Because of its complexity, the playbook can be a frightening thing for a rookie, so Prothro feeds the Ram newcomers theirs a page at a time. "If we gave a rookie a four-inch playbook when he hit camp, he would be overwhelmed, completely demoralized," says Prothro. "Our original playbook is almost just the binder. Then, as we put in plays and variations, we give them the pages on those. The book builds."

George Allen, Prothro's predecessor with the Rams and now head coach and general manager of the Washington Redskins, has no such tender feelings for rookies, but then he has never held them in much esteem. Under Allen, the Ram playbook was the handsomest in the league. It was bound in red and looked like an encyclopedia volume. It cost Allen a great deal of money to have his playbooks bound like library books, but he has never been one to scrimp.

Aside from the extraordinary amount of memory work a playbook demands of a rookie, it can be costly to him in other ways. Most clubs fine a player from $500 to $1,000 for losing a playbook. Explains Stram, whose rate is $500: "It's a part of the overall program of discipline. We give them the responsibility for the property and we expect them to take care of it, just like any other equipment we issue."

And when the Turk comes to call at training camp the playbook is the invariable symbol of dismissal. If an assistant tells a rookie — or a failing veteran — to see the head coach and adds, "And bring your playbook," that means the player is being cut.

Even Sweetan turned in his playbook when he was dismissed from the Rams. That was a Xeroxed copy he and his cousin were trying to peddle in New Orleans.

This game stands in the same relation to pro football as Game Six of the 1945 World Series to baseball: namely, the worst championship game in the sport's history, a game neither team deserved to win. Like the boy who delightedly offered his opinion of the emperor's new clothes, Larry Merchant looks through the gaudy raiments of the Super Bowl and sees—a football game. This essay is taken from his MCMLXXI book ... *And Every Day You Take Another Bite.*

LARRY MERCHANT

Super Bowl Five

The scenario of the 1971 Super Bowl was written with a pen dipped in slapstick irreverence. It was written by someone who thinks that football is a terrific game and a colorful spectacle and—you won't believe this, sports fans—no more, no less. Someone who sees the rest of the pro football mystique, from the cosmic musings of deep thinkers to the patriotic posturing of shallow thinkers to the huckstering Barnum of double thinkers, as a perfect spiral of lunacy.

The National Football League, according to this scenario, promoted the 1971 Super Bowl as SUPER BOWL V, so we could swoon at its self-image of epic grandeur. Presumably the Roman numeral was affixed to our gladiatorial circus to honor Proconsul Pete Rozelle and St. Vince Lombardi. Or to make certain we understood the gravity and significance of the event. Some of us had mistaken it for a mere game but Kenneth Clark surely would turn it into a chapter of *Civilisation,* his history of art. Unlike the World Series, which is simply the World Series, and the Kentucky Derby and the U.S. Open and the Indianapolis 500, this was SUPER BOWL V. A roll of drums and a flourish of trumpets, please.

The Baltimore Colts then beat the Dallas Cowboys XVI to XIII on a field goal with V seconds to play. But the game was something less than art or history. Many observers thought it was something less than football, at least as the professionals are supposed to play it. Whatever it was, it was entertaining, and instructive. It featured a total of XII fumbles and interceptions and XIV penalties (for CLXIV yards).

Depending on where you sat, or on whom you bet, this was either sacrilege or side-splitting comedy. One vote for comedy. It was a whipped-cream pie in the face of the pretentious boobs dedicated to making the NFL an eternal flame of truth, the quintessence of America. It was a banana peel under the anointed memory of Vince Lombardi, who was officially canonized for the occasion. It was a pair of baggy pants on television, which viewed the thing as though it were a solemn high mass.

The starting line-ups should have provided the first clue of what the day would bring:

BALTIMORE	Pos.	DALLAS
Groucho Marx	WR	Bert Lahr
Woody Allen	WR	Jerry Lewis
Danny Kaye	TE	W. C. Fields
Stan Laurel	RT	Bob Hope
Jackie Gleason	RG	Jack Benny
Emmett Kelly	C	Pigmeat Markham
Jack E. Leonard	LG	Don Rickles
Buddy Hackett	LT	Godfrey Cambridge
Harpo Marx	QB	Craig Morton
Flip Wilson	RB	Harry Ritz
Phil Foster	RB	Bill Cosby

This should have immediately brought into question some of the unquestioned premises of the game. Controlled violence, they call it. A microcosm of our society, with its machine precision and organization men and plastic armor and film studies and psychologic probing and computer planning and sophisticated specialization. "A Game for Our Times," with millions of man-hours invested in recruiting talent, talent brimming with character and courage and pride and high moral purpose. With coaches of such Himalayan intellect that only their love of the game keeps them from becoming captains of industry or statesmen.

But once the Cowboys and the Colts managed to tie their shoelaces, with some difficulty, they seemed stumped. So they played it for laughs. And they were super.

It is no more possible to detail every master stroke of buffoonery than it would be to eat all the pigskin in Iowa. A few highlights will do.

I—The Cowboys recovered a fumble on the Colt 9-yard line but had to settle for a field goal. II—After Craig Morton completed what would be his lone completion to an end, Bob Hayes, the Cowboys were on the Colt 6-yard line and had to settle for another field goal. III — The Colts tied the score when Johnny Unitas overthrew a receiver and wound up with a touchdown when another receiver, John Mackey, caught the ball after a Cowboy or two tipped it — followed by a missed extra point. IV — The Cowboys went ahead 13–6 after recovering another fumble and driving 28 yards — the longest successful drive of the game. V — The half ended with the Colts frustrated on the Cowboy 2-yard line after bypassing a field-goal attempt. Alex Karras, the clown prince of the Detroit Lions, was heard to speculate that the Colts just might decide to pass up a second extra point if they got a second touchdown.

Both teams put on their size-18 shoes and grease paint for the second act. VI and VII — The Colts fumbled the kickoff but the Cowboys fumbled back to them near the goal line. VIII — Earl Morrall, who had replaced the injured Unitas late in the second quarter, completed a substantial pass-run play to a back whom the Cowboys neglected to cover; but then on third down Morrall, under pressure, ballooned the ball into the end zone instead of grounding it to keep the Colts in field goal range, and it was intercepted. IX — Moments later the Colts struck hilariously again. On a play designed for the quarterback to hand off to a halfback who laterals back to the quarterback who throws downfield — the same razzmatazz that Morrall mucked up against the Jets in the 1969 Super Bowl when he didn't see a man all alone — the halfback had to throw instead because the Cowboys wrapped up the quarterback. Eddie Hinton caught the ball and zipped toward the end zone, only to fumble when he was hit two strides away, whereupon the Cowboys took one Ritz Brother pratfall after another chasing and squibbing the loose ball until it slid out of the end zone for a touchback.

By this time the bald-headed guys in the front rows were yelling "Bring on the girls." They got Morton, and he outdid himself. He threw three interceptions in eight minutes. X — One set up the tying score. XI — One set up the winning score after the Cowboys had possession in Colt territory with less than two minutes left. XII — The third was a last-play desperation heave, and it brought down the house.

Jim O'Brien, the rookie who missed the extra point, kicked the field goal from the 32, touching off wild celebrations across the land. Not only did it win the game but it ended it. For 80,000 people in the Orange Bowl in Miami and for 60 million in televisionland, all on the edge of their seats anxious to see who would trip over what yard line next, it was a sublime climax. The threat of a lingering sudden-death playoff was extinguished. The danger of milking the gag beyond endurance was averted.

Now it isn't unusual for a football to take funny bounces; it is deliberately shaped the way it is to confound and deflate us. It especially isn't unusual when defensive-oriented teams meet because it is their purpose in life to make offensive teams nervous wrecks as well as physical wrecks. The Colts and Cowboys simply brought this collision of resistible forces and immovable objects to its logical conclusion, and further, to caricature.

ITEM: It is a rule of thumb that when a team coughs up the ball four times in a game it must lose, unless the other team catches the cough. Midway through the fourth quarter the Colts led in turnovers seven to one but the Cowboys led by only one touchdown. You think that's easy, try it some day. Better still, have your local high school team try it. Without ten coaches who have access to banks of computers, it will take a lot of practice.

ITEM: It is an article of faith among the faithful that quarterbacking is the name of the game (when third down, defense, hitting, emotion, or something else isn't the name of the game). The quarterbacking in Super Bowl V was not even the middle initial. Except for his freak touchdown pass through what a clairvoyant sign labeled "The Friendly Skies of Unitas," Johnny Unitas, age thirty-seven, once great, was impotent. Earl Morrall, who had been exposed on the same field two years before, wasn't much better; he moved the Colts into scoring range three times and couldn't move them the rest of the way, which, after all, is the idea. It would be kicking a dead Cowboy to reflect on Craig Morton in gorier detail.

ITEM: The quarterbacks had gifted straight men. Other players with character, courage, pride, high moral purpose, et al., went to pieces in the big one. Bob Vogel, star offensive tackle for the Colts, admitted that he kept forgetting the snap count. Jocks are always blaming occult forces for variances in performance. What poor dumb vibration in the solar system got the blame this time?

ITEM: The coaches, as the earthly agents of God and the computers, had some curious moments too. Don McCafferty of the Colts made the XIIIth turnover when he decided to go for the touchdown instead of that field goal. Tom Landry, who called all the plays for Morton until the last two minutes, added to the merriment. Lulled by a precarious lead, he stuck to his game plan with the inflexibility of Buster Keaton's jaw despite the fact that it wasn't working. And he committed the last venal sin when he didn't use his time-outs as the Colts maneuvered into position for the winning field goal; he could have saved forty seconds for one final boffo fling.

But the game is far from the only thing on Super Sunday. This is pro football's showcase and they try to do it all. The showcase is a prism through which the holy and holier-than attitudes of the mystique, mixed in with the natural glories of football, are refracted in brilliant living color and deadly serious pretense.

The pregame and halftime shows were typical medleys of tooting and bonging and flagwaving. Before the game a formation of four jet fighter planes zoomed over the stadium, one of them peeling off, we were told, to symbolize the nation's concern for prisoners of war in North Vietnam. The planes arrived a couple minutes late but considering what went on in the game it was amazing that the symbolism didn't go down in flames. Similar flights of fantasy had taken place throughout the NFL for the last month of the season, following an attempt to rescue prisoners that its planners described as a heroic success although it failed in one minor detail: it rescued no prisoners. There was a much clearer relationship in that symbolism to the follies on the field.

At halftime a lady who fancies herself the Voice of America, Anita Bryant, sang "The Battle Hymn of the Republic," also contributing to the fun and gaiety of the spectacle. An appearance by the University of Chicago marching band — fifty students roaming chaotically and kazooing kazoos — would have been more in tune with the game.

Fulfilling its role as co-promoter with the NFL, television trained an unblinking but embarrassed battery of eyes on the show. The camera crews followed the bouncing ball faithfully, providing a continuous laugh-in of replays. But the announcers had difficulty with their focus. Not once did they indicate that something nutty was going on down there, that it wasn't classic playbook football but that it sure was an exciting mess, like a soufflé that blows up in Graham Kerr's face. They reacted as though they were watching a squadron of Communist pigeons defiling the Tomb of the Unknown Soldier. They daren't, or didn't have the wit, to put the show into the bemused perspective it needed. Merchandising right down to the solemn signoff, Curt Gowdy gave a soap-opera tribute to Earl Morrall for avenging 1969.

With its genius for stretching time, television created a five-hour spectacular of the three-hour game. An hour eulogy to Vince Lombardi, oddly, was not accompanied by organ music. In football's version of *Love Story*, an interesting man of many dimensions was reduced to a cardboard-thin myth. The next half hour juxtaposed Joe Namath, the *enfant* outrageous who had succeeded Lombardi as the dominant figure in the game even before his death. Namath, in previewing the Colts and Cowboys, omitted the crucial possibility that the Cowboy rush might discombobulate Unitas. And he made excuses for Morton's allegedly injured arm (Morton having passed for five touchdowns in the last game of the regular season when the opposition was weak Houston). But, in the manner of the child who adds incorrectly but instinctively or accidentally comes up with the right sum, Namath picked the Colts to win. That, as they say, can't be coached. You've got it or you don't.

The postgame show offered the standard package of unasked and unanswered questions, and a weepy presentation ceremony. Mrs. Marie Lombardi gave a trophy named for her late husband to Carroll Rosenbloom, owner of the Colts. Her tears undoubtedly were inspired by the certain knowledge that the great coach in the sky would be raging like Jehovah over the sloppy exhibition and demanding that both teams report to practice Monday. Rosenbloom, as is the custom with athletes who suggest that somebody up there likes them best, muttered that it couldn't have been done without divine assistance. Nobody had put Craig Morton in that league before.

What was America thinking about all this? A market-research team of one found that many fans, their brains washed and bleached by the NFL mystique, felt betrayed by the inelegant play. Some fans were amused, others confused, but most ultimately were swept up by the theatrics. All but 231 of the viewers were emotionally spent — the 231 who hadn't bet on the game. Having sweated out their bets until the end (the Colts beat the spread by a half point), the remaining millions empathized with Rosenbloom's ashen looks and choked-up speech.

The research team found something else. Within this vast constituency there was a relevant political cleavage, polarized by Vietnam and President Nixon's identification with football. For the hard-nosed hawks who saw football as the last frontier of discipline, the red-white-and-blue pageantry was offset by the disorder of the game. For the soft-nosed doves who equated football with violence and jingoism, the slapstick should have been consolation for any indignities of propaganda socked to them. Both parties would have been wise to remember that nearly 150 million Americans chose to ignore the whole thing.

Thus another Super Bowl with a moral. In Super Bowl I the Green Bay Packers beat the Kansas City Chiefs XXXV to X, preserving the known laws of the universe, i.e., the superiority of the establishment. In Super Bowl II the Packers beat the Oakland Raiders XXXIII to XIV, reaffirming the omnipotence of Vince Lombardi. In Super Bowl III Joe Namath and the New York Jets beat the Colts XVI to VII, upsetting the known laws of the universe with a victory for impetuous youth. In Super Bowl IV the Chiefs beat the Minnesota Vikings XXIII to VII, confirming the new order.

The 1971 Super Bowl reminded us that pro football is a terrific game, not an exercise in technology or any other ology. And that there are powerful opportunists getting in the way of the game, exploiting it with their political and moral righteousness.

In a postscript, the scenario also reminded us, with the private misery of public men, that football is played by a large but not larger-than-life breed of homo sap. Lance Rentzel of the Cowboys, arrested a month earlier on charges of indecent exposure (to which he later pleaded guilty), didn't play. Johnny Unitas, it was revealed two days after the game, had been sued for divorce on the grounds of adultery.

As the NFL is fond of saying, any of this could happen on any given Sunday.

"He was the greatest football player I ever saw," said Blanton Collier. "The man was a great, great linebacker. Believe me, he could do everything. He had no equal as a blocker; yes, he could do it all." Paul Brown said, "The greatest back I ever saw was Marion Motley. You know why? The only statistic he ever knew was whether we won or lost. The man was completely unselfish." And though he may not have cared about them, Motley had the statistics, too. In one game in 1950 he rushed for 188 yards in only eleven carries, an average of 17.1; for his career he averaged 5.7 yards per carry. Both are still all-time records.

MARION MOTLEY
with Myron Cope

The Color Line Is Broken

Hanging in clear view on a corridor wall in the Pro Football Hall of Fame at Canton, Ohio, is a squad photo of the 1921 Akron Steels of the American Professional Football Association, the forerunner of the NFL. Among the squad stand two black men. One was Paul Robeson, whose pro-football career came to be dwarfed by his career as a brilliant actor and great basso, as well as by his controversial role as a Marxist. . . . The other Negro in the photograph is Frederick (Fritz) Pollard, a beaming halfback sporting the sort of coiffure that almost fifty years later would come to be known as the natural Afro look. . . .

But pro football, having made a biracial beginning, gradually became lily-white. The handful of Negroes that had speckled the NFL in the 1920s vanished, and few others took their place. By the middle 1930s, the Negro had disappeared from pro ball; some say that a few clubs employed light-skinned mulattos, passing them off as Indians, but the notion is unverified. . . .

The year was 1946, and the nation was vigorously exercising her appetite for peace, having just come through another world war. A new league—the All-America Football Conference—was ready to challenge the NFL. In Cleveland, Paul Brown became head coach of the new AAC franchise to be known as the Browns. He quietly gave Bill

Willis a tryout and signed him. A week or so later, he tried out another Negro, fullback Marion Motley, and signed him. . . .

I visited Motley at his modest but comfortable home on the east side of Cleveland. A bulky, mustachioed man weighing in the neighborhood of 260 pounds, he wore a Browns sweatshirt and held a stout cigar in one hand and a glass of ale in the other. Physically he looked the part of a ward politician who has everything well in hand. A good host, he saw to it that I, too, had ale. But as he told his story, his mood occasionally darkened. . . .

In 1946, after the War ended, I was getting ready to go back to college, but in the meantime I had wrote Paul Brown and asked him about trying out for the Cleveland Browns. He wrote me back and told me that he had all the backs he needed. So I forgot about trying out for the pros. Matter of fact, my coach at the University of Nevada sent me a train ticket and I was all set to go back to school. But then one day I heard where Bill Willis had went to camp to try out for the Browns and was doing very well. And then one night I got a call from one of Paul Brown's assistants.

He asked me how would I like to come up and try out for the football team. Willis had made the ball club, see, and they had to have someone to go along with him. They wanted another colored fellow to room with him. I learned about this later. After my first season I got the word from a man who had heard it through the front office. I was only supposed to be a roommate for Willis.

In a way, Paul Brown and I went all the way back to high-school days together. I played three years for McKinley High in Canton, Ohio. We lost only one game each year I was there, and the one game we lost every year was to Massillon. Paul Brown was the Massillon coach. He was one of the great high-school coaches of the 1930s. In Canton we highly respected Paul.

The way I first came to play for Paul, and this was long before pro ball, was just one of those lucky things. I came here to Cleveland in 1945 to be inducted into the Service. I don't know how many guys were standing in line in front of me — must have been a hundred guys. The people in charge never asked 'em what branch they wanted. They'd just tell 'em. "Army! . . . Navy! . . . Army!" But when I got up there — and this shows you how fate worked things for me — they said, "What branch do you want?" I'd heard that in the Navy you'd get to see the world, plus I'd heard the Navy was much cleaner than the Army and had the best food. So I said, "Navy." If I'd said Army, I never would have played for Paul Brown and probably never would have played pro ball. This is why I say fate worked in a peculiar way there.

The navy sent me to the Great Lakes Training Center outside of Waukegan, and when I found out that Paul was coaching the football team there, I phoned him to see if I could get on the team. He said, "Yes, I remember you. Marion. Why don't you come over Monday and talk with me?" His main logic was to see if I had gotten real fat and out of shape. I was about twenty-four or twenty-five by then, but when he saw that I was down to about 220, he immediately said, "Well, yes, I'd like you to play for mc." So after I finished my twelve weeks of boot training they moved me into ship's company, which put me in safekeeping.

But one day in August, all of a sudden, I got orders to move out. I was going to be moved out right away with a unit going to Port Chicago, California. The trains came right up to Great Lakes to pick you up, and I was right there at the train when I phoned Paul and told him what was happening. He told me, "Don't you move. You stay right there at that phone."

Then he called the commandant and told him, "If you want me to coach this football team, you better stop that player and any other player that comes through there." Then Paul called me back and said, "You get your gear off that train and bring it back to the barracks."

I was elated to be playing under Paul, because I knew what a great coach he was. There was nothing complicated about his football, although he was a stickler for detail and a disciplinarian. Matter of fact, Paul was sitting on a train one Sunday afternoon at the same time that I and another player—a young kid—were sitting in another train on the next track. We were going out on liberty. This kid I was with didn't see Paul, but Paul saw *him* from the window of his train. The kid had a cigarette in his hand. On Monday morning Paul fired the kid. They sent him to Iwo Jima, I think.

You know, I'm probably the only player who ever knocked Paul down, or at least the only one who got away with it. Up at Great Lakes I had a toe that was real tender. I'd broken it badly in a game. Well, Paul had the team around him in a circle one day, and he was talking to the players, and while he was talking he backed up on my foot. Boy, I just hauled off and hit him with an elbow that sent him clean across that circle. He *flew* across that circle. He said, "What'd you do *that* for?"

I said, "You stepped on my foot. You stepped on my poor foot."

He just laughed and turned around, and after that he always told people, "Don't step on Marion's feet, 'cause he'll hit you."

Well, as I said, Paul later was coaching the Cleveland Browns in 1946, and I got invited to camp for a tryout. A cousin of mine drove me from Canton over to the camp in Bowling Green, Ohio, and I made it there in time to go straight out to the afternoon practice. That first day, we ran wind sprints and I was out in front of everybody. I beat all those guys—the fullbacks, anyway. So the next day Paul put me all the way up on the second team and I immediately saw resentment from the players.

As Bill Willis and I were going to our room after practice. I said, "Gee, I sure hate Paul putting me on that second team today, 'cause some of those backs was just acting awful snotty." They hadn't *said* anything, but I could feel the tenseness around me. I said to Bill, "I just wish Paul would put me back somewhere and let me *work* my way back up. Then I'll straighten some of them out up there."

I think Paul saw the resentment, because the next day he threw me back to the fourth team. But it didn't take me long to move back up. They had a scrimmage and I played mostly on defense, at linebacker, and I had 'em all standing on their ears. After the scrimmage was over, one of the guys asked Willis, "What the heck was eating Motley today? Was he trying to kill somebody?" Willis told him, "No, he's just trying to make the ball club." So from then on, there seemed to be a change of feeling toward me. I had the best times in the sprints, I ran the ball as well as any of the others, and after they saw that I had the ability, their attitude toward me changed.

Of course, Paul was very strong for fairness. In those early years that I was with the Browns, whenever any rookies from the South reported to camp they came right over to meet Willis and me. They'd come and find us and shake hands and make friends with us. Somewhere along the line they were told that when they got to camp they would have to do that or they couldn't play. I'm sure they were told, before they signed, that we were part of the ball club and that they were going to have to play *with* us. So best to make friends with us. But our opponents were something else.

In the very beginning, Paul warned Willis and me. He said, "Now you know that you're going to be in many scrapes. People are going to be calling you names. They're going to be nasty. But you're going to have to stick it out." It was rough, all right. If Willis and I had been anywhere near being hotheads, it would have been another ten years till black men got accepted in pro ball. We'd have set 'em back ten years.

I still got many a cleat mark on the backs of my hands from when I would be getting up after a play and a guy would just walk over and step on my hand. Look. You can see the scars. I couldn't do anything about it. I'd want to kill those guys, but Paul had warned us. The referees would stand right there and see those men stepping on us, and they would turn their backs.

The guy that finally broke it up was a referee out of Buffalo—one of the older referees. Oh, what the hell's his name? I shouldn't have forgotten it. Anyway, this is what he started doing. When he caught a guy stepping on us, he wouldn't tell him nothing. He'd just pick up the ball and start walking off fifteen yards. They'd ask him why, and then he'd say, "For stepping on that man." The other referees saw what this ref was doing, and they looked around and saw that we were bringing in the crowds as well as the white guys, so they started to protect us.

Of course, the opposing players called us nigger and all kind of names like that. This went on for about two or three years, until they found out that Willis and I was ballplayers. Then they stopped that shit. They found out that while they were calling us names, I was running by 'em and Willis was knocking the shit out of them. So they stopped calling us names and started trying to catch up with us.

We had a close-knit ball club, and I think this was why we won. Many times the guys wanted to fight for Willis and me. They'd want to take care of the guy who was playing us dirty. But I'd say, "What the hell, just let him go, because I'm going to run over him anyway." Actually, I loved the game.

Paul worked his psychology on everybody. The thing about him that used to irk me was that when I'd come out of the game for a rest—and maybe I'd been both playing offense and defense, working hard as I could, but maybe I hadn't done something I was s'posed to—when I came out of the game, Paul would walk up to me and in a low voice, almost like he was hissing at me, he'd say, "Do you know that you're *killing* our football team?"

Then he'd walk away from me, like nothing had happened. Boy, I could have walked up behind him and choked him. I'd go back out there, and the first jersey that got in front of me, I'd try to kill the guy wearing it.

(Although he never gained as much as a thousand yards in one season, there are some who say that Motley in his peak years was a more valuable fullback than Jim Brown, the man who signed with Cleveland two years after Motley's final retirement and came to be generally recognized as the greatest fullback in pro-football history. Motley lives but a few blocks from the small house in which Brown resided until his departure for Hollywood and an acting career; Motley knew him as a friend, and I recalled seeing Marion at the Brown home when in 1963 I had worked with Brown on a book. I wondered which of the two men was the better fullback in Marion's opinion.)

I can't answer that. The thing I probably would have had on Jim was the fact that I could block better. I had a knack for it. Blocking was no task for me. But I don't think Jim had anything on me as a runner, either. I was bigger than he was. I don't know who was faster, it's hard to say. I couldn't tell you. Of course, when I was a rookie I was twenty-six already, and when we went from the All-America Conference to the National Football League in 1950, I was an old pro by then. I was thirty. But the thing was, I didn't have the running plays Jim had. I had one wide play, the end run, and that was it. Just an ordinary ol' end run. See, I didn't have the flips. I often said to Paul, "Let me get them out there and scatter 'em. Let me take a few of 'em out there with me." But he'd say, "No, the flip wasn't designed for you." I had to make my yardage up the middle.

You know, during half of my eight years with the Browns—in fact, the whole four years I played with them in the National Football League—I had bad trouble with my knees. Geez, did I have trouble with them. And the way Paul handled the situation, he really shortened my career. In 1951 we were in training camp, getting ready to play the College All-Stars, and Paul was giving us fundamental drills in blocking and tackling. In one of these drills a player's knee hit my knee, and as soon as he hit me, well, I was *hurt*. By the time practice was over, my knee was like a balloon.

The trainer told Paul to give me a couple days off, but Paul said, "No. No, he can come out and run a little bit. If he can't run, he can hop around." So that's what I did. I ran on one leg. The ground at that particular time was like cement, and running on that one good leg, I wound up with *both* knees full of water.

Our team doctor was on vacation, so they sent me to see a doctor in Cleveland who's now one of the top surgeons in the country. A Dr. Lambright. He took two pans of water off my knees, and then he called the training camp and told our trainer that I shouldn't run for three or four days. So I went back to camp thinking I'm going to get a rest, but after I'd stayed off the field for one day, Paul Brown told me, "You get your suit on and be out here." I put on my equipment and stood around out there for a while, and then Paul said, "All right, Motley, get in here. I want you to run some." I tried to, but my knees locked up on me and swelled up on me big as a balloon. I had to have the water taken off again.

I went to Chicago and played in the All-Star game, and after the game I couldn't walk out of Soldier's Field. I had to lean against a wall while they brought my car to me. I couldn't move. I always had knee trouble after that, and football became a job.

The thing that burns me up is that the other ball clubs give their players a break when they're all through, but Cleveland didn't do anything for me. I didn't think Paul *owed* me anything, but I thought that I should have gotten a job or something. I felt I deserved a chance. Oh, I *asked*. I asked Paul for a scouting job, and then in 1964, when Blanton Collier was coach, I asked Collier and Art Modell, the owner, I told them, "I know that the white scouts are having trouble getting information from the Negro schools, and I think I'm well enough known that I could help you." This was a beautiful idea. Modell thought this was a beautiful idea. But I waited half the football season and never heard from them. Dante Lavelli was scouting for the Browns at that time, so I said to Lavelli, "What the hell's happening? Nobody's called me. If they don't call me soon and send me out to scout, I'm going to call the newspapers." I guess Lavelli told 'em right away, because that Friday they called me and told me they wanted me to go to Wilberforce.

But Wilberforce had nothing. Neither one of the teams in that game had anything. The Browns were just sending me there as an appeasement, to keep me from saying anything. I made two or three trips that year, but all this was appeasement. One day I caught Modell at the practice field. "Modell," I says, "what about the scouting thing that we talked about?" He's kneeling on one knee, looking at practice. He doesn't even look around. He looks out on the field and tells me, "Well, Motley, you know what? The only thing you can help us with is signing the ballplayers." I says, "Is that what you think?" He says yes, and I tell him, "Well, I thank you." And with that I walk off that field.

At the end of the season they hired a guy named Nussbaumer, who coached at Detroit, who hadn't ever given Cleveland a single day — they hired him as a coach and scout. So I blew my top. I wrote a statement. I blasted 'em. I don't know what all I said, but I really gave it to them. I had a newsman, a colored writer, put it on U.P., A.P., and all the rest of them. Later, I'm watching practice one day and Modell came over and said, "You did me an injustice." He said, "I'm not prejudiced. I always tried to help the Negro. I give to their community fund." I said, "I don't know nothin' 'bout that. It doesn't bother me what you give. But what you give *me* was nothin'."

I still wear my Cleveland Browns jacket. A lot of times somebody will mention it or make some kind of playful remark about it. Well, my answer is, "I earned it. I earned the right to wear this jacket."

Joe NAMATH

In 1965, the New York Jets signed Namath for $427,000, signifying that the upstart American Football League was playing for keeps. Yet almost no one took Namath seriously when he "guaranteed" an AFL victory in Super Bowl III. In one of pro football's biggest upsets, Broadway Joe led his Jets to a landmark 16-7 win.

In mid-December 1968, as his beloved Colts were marching toward the NFL title, Ogden Nash sang their praises in characteristic fashion, observing, for example, that the lot of center Dick Szymanski was "not all roses and romanski." By mid-January his heroes had been humbled by the lowly New York Jets, and Nash slunk off to his garret to compose the following.

OGDEN NASH

Prognostications Are for the Birds; Lay Off Me, Please, While I Eat My Words

The gods of sport outdid themselves
On that wildest of January Twelves.
So I weep with the army of loyal dolts
Who gave seventeen points and bet on the Colts.
As the ancient Greeks besieging Troy
Used words to bulldoze and pre-destroy
And boasted that their skill and bravery
Would doom the Trojans to death or slavery,
So Broadway Joe, like great Achilles,
Declared that the Colts were only fillies.

Less modest than Caesar in his claim,
He bragged of conquest *before* he came.
Some figured that he'd outgrown his pants
To count his chickens in advance.
Spectators came prepared to cackle
And hoot in glee at Joe's debacle.
Debacle indeed the record shows.
But whosever it was, it wasn't Joe's.
The Colts who clobbered the Rams and Browns,
Who gained the yardage on crucial downs,
Who gave defensive linemen conniptions
And ruined the offense with interceptions,
Those Colts, like Florida snow that melts,
Seemed to have trickled somewhere else.
They couldn't get anywhere in particular
As long as Joe remained perpendicular,
In which position he did remain,
Throwing strikes like Denny McLain.
Well, it might have been the finger of fate,
Or possibly something that they ate,
But I credit the arm and the tricky calls
Of the gay deceiver of Beaver Falls.
Oh, a cloud of Jets eclipsed the stars
And the only sound in Baltimore bars
Was the sickly hack of a Hong Kong cough
And the click of a TV set turned off.
The Super-Bowl Limited of the Colts
Was derailed with a grind of bumps and jolts
By the sabotage of the playboy whiz
Who is just as good as he says he is.
For the moment it's *Vale* Baltimoria,
And *Ave* Flushing, Queens, Astoria.
Sic transit gloria.

With football players from Red Grange to Lee Grosscup becoming authors, author George Plimpton decided turnabout was fair play. He had done this sort of thing before, impersonating a baseball pitcher before an all-star lineup at Yankee Stadium, where his performance did not compare unfavorably with that as quarterback of the Detroit Lions. After reading *Out of My League*, Plimpton's book based on his baseball "career," Ernest Hemingway remarked, "It is the dark side of the moon of Walter Mitty." So is *Paper Lion*.

GEORGE PLIMPTON

Paper Lion

Jack Benny used to say that when he stood on the stage in white tie and tails for his violin concerts and raised his bow to begin his routine — scraping through "Love in Bloom" — that he *felt* like a great violinist. He reasoned that, if he wasn't a great violinist, what was he doing dressed in tails, and about to play before a large audience?

At Pontiac I *felt* myself a football quarterback, not an interloper. My game plan was organized, and I knew what I was supposed to do. My nerves seemed steady, much steadier than they had been as I waited on the bench. I trotted along easily. I was keenly aware of what was going on around me.

I could hear Bud Erickson's voice over the loudspeaker system, a dim murmur, telling the crowd what was going on. He was telling them that number zero, coming out across the sidelines, was not actually a rookie, but an amateur, a writer, who had been training with the team for three weeks and had learned five plays, which he was now going to run against the first-string Detroit defense. It was like a nightmare come true, he told them, as if one of *them*, rocking a beer around in a paper cup, with a pretty girl leaning past him to ask the hot-dog vendor in the aisle for mustard, were suddenly carried down underneath the stands by a sinister clutch of ushers. He would protest, but he would be encased in the accoutrements, the silver helmet, with the two protruding bars of the cage, jammed down over his ears, and sent out to take over the team — that was the substance of Erickson's words, drifting across the field, swayed and shredded by the steady breeze coming up across the open end of Wisner Stadium from the vanished sunset. The crowd was interested, and I was conscious, just vaguely, of a steady roar of encouragement.

The team was waiting for me, grouped in the huddle watching me come. I went in among them. Their heads came down for the signal. I called out, "Twenty-Six!" forcefully, to inspire them, and a voice from one of the helmets said, "Down, down, the whole stadium can hear you."

"Twenty-six," I hissed at them. "Twenty-six near oh pinch; on three. *Break!*" Their hands cracked as one, and I wheeled and started for the line behind them.

My confidence was extreme. I ambled slowly behind [Bob] Whitlow, poised down over the ball, and I had sufficient presence to pause, resting a hand at the base of his spine, as if on a windowsill—a nonchalant gesture I had admired in certain quarterbacks—and I looked out over the length of his back to fix in my mind what I saw.

Everything fine about being a quarterback—the embodiment of his power—was encompassed in those dozen seconds or so: giving the instructions to ten attentive men, breaking out of the huddle, walking for the line, and then pausing behind the center, dawdling amidst men poised and waiting under the trigger of his voice, cataleptic, until the deliverance of himself and them to the future. The pleasure of sport was so often the chance to indulge the cessation of time itself—the pitcher dawdling on the mound, the skier poised at the top of a mountain trail, the basketball player with the rough skin of the ball against his palm preparing for a foul shot, the tennis player at set point over his opponent—all of them savoring a moment before committing themselves to action.

I had the sense of a portcullis down. On the other side of the imaginary bars the linemen were poised, the lights glistening off their helmets, and close in behind them were the linebackers, with Joe Schmidt just opposite me, the big number 56 shining on his white jersey, jumpjacking back and forth with quick choppy steps, his hands poised in front of him, and he was calling out defensive code words in a stream. I could sense the rage in his voice, and the tension in those rows of bodies waiting, as if coils had been wound overtight, which my voice, calling a signal, like a lever would trip to spring them all loose. "Blue! Blue! Blue" I heard Schmidt shout.

Within my helmet, the schoolmaster's voice murmured at me: "Son, nothing to it, nothing at all . . ."

I bent over the center. Quickly, I went over what was supposed to happen—I would receive the snap and take two steps straight back, and hand the ball to the number two back coming laterally across from right to left, who would then cut into the number six hole. That was what was designated by 26—the two back into the six hole. The mysterious code words "near oh pinch" referred to blocking assignments in the line, and I was never sure exactly what was meant by them. The important thing was to hang on to the ball, turn, and get the ball into the grasp of the back coming across laterally.

I cleared my throat. "Set!" I called out—my voice loud and astonishing to hear, as if it belonged to someone shouting into the earholes of my helmet. "Sixteen, sixty-five, forty-four, *hut* one, *hut* two, *hut* three," and at three the ball slapped back into my palm, and Whitlow's rump bucked up hard as he went for the defensemen opposite.

The lines cracked together with a yawp and smack of pads and gear. I had the sense of quick, heavy movement, and as I turned for the backfield, not a second having passed, I was hit hard from the side, and as I gasped the ball was jarred loose. It sailed away, and bounced once, and I stumbled after it, hauling it under me five yards back, hearing the rush of feet, and the heavy jarring and wheezing of the blockers fending off the defense, a great roar up from the crowd, and above it, a relief to hear, the shrilling of the referee's whistle. My first thought was that at the snap of the ball the right side of the line had collapsed just at the second of the handoff, and one of the tacklers, [Roger] Brown or Floyd Peters, had cracked through to make me fumble. Someone, I assumed, had messed up on the assignments designated by the mysterious code words "near oh pinch." In fact, as I discovered later, my *own man* bowled me over—John Gordy, whose assignment as offensive guard was to pull from his position and join the interference on the far side of the center. He was required to pull back and travel at a great clip parallel to the line of scrimmage to get out in front of the runner, his route theoretically passing between me and the center. But the extra second it took me to control the ball, and the creaking execution of my turn, put me in his path, a rare sight for Gordy to see, his own quarterback blocking the way, like coming around a corner in a high-speed car to find a moose ambling across the center line, and he caromed off me, jarring the ball loose.

It was not new for me to be hit down by my own people. At Cranbrook I was knocked down all the time by players on the offense—the play patterns run with such speed along routes so carefully defined that if everything wasn't done right and at the proper speed, the play would break down in its making. I was often reminded of film clips in which the process of a porcelain pitcher, say, being dropped by a butler and smashed, is shown in reverse, so that the pieces pick up off the floor and soar up to the butler's hand, each piece on a predestined route, sudden perfection out of chaos. Often, it did not take more than an inch or so off line to throw a play out of kilter. On one occasion at the training camp, practicing handoff plays to the fullback, I had my chin hanging out just a bit too far, something wrong with my posture, and [Nick] Pietrosante's shoulder pad caught it like a punch as he went by, and I spun slowly to the ground, grabbing at my jaw. [Carl] Brettschneider had said that afternoon: "The defense is going to rack you up one of these days, if your own team'd let you *stand* long enough for us defense guys to get *at* you. It's aggravating to bust through and find that you've already been laid flat by your own offense guys."

My confidence had not gone. I stood up. The referee took the ball from me. He had to tug to get it away, a faint look of surprise on his face. My inner voice was assuring me that the fault in the tumble had not been mine. "They let you down," it was saying.

"The blocking failed." But the main reason for my confidence was the next play on my list—the 93 pass, a play which I had worked successfully in the Cranbrook scrimmages. I walked into the huddle and I said with considerable enthusiasm, "All right! All *right!* Here we *go!*"

"Keep the voice down," said a voice. "You'll be tipping them the play."

I leaned in on them and said: "Green right" ("Green" designated a pass play, "right" put the flanker to the right side), "three right" (which put the three back to the right), "ninety-three" (indicating the two primary receivers; nine, the right end, and three the three back), "on *three . . . Break!*"—the clap of the hands again in unison, the team streamed past me up to the line, and I walked briskly up behind Whitlow.

Again, I knew exactly how the play was going to develop—back those seven yards into the defensive pocket for the three to four seconds it was supposed to hold, and Pietrosante, the three back, would go down in his pattern, ten yards straight, then cut over the middle, and I would hit him.

"Set! . . . sixteen! . . . eighty-eight . . . fifty-five . . . *hut* one . . . *hut* two . . . *hut* three . . ."

The ball slapped into my palm at "three." I turned and started back. I could feel my balance going, and two yards behind the line of scrimmage I *fell down*—absolutely flat, as if my feet had been pinned under a trip wire stretched across the field, not a hand laid on me. I heard a great roar go up from the crowd. Suffused as I had been with confidence, I could scarcely believe what had happened. Mud cleats catching in the grass? Slipped in the dew? I felt my jaw go ajar in my helmet. "Wha'? Wha'?"—the mortification beginning to come fast. I rose hurriedly to my knees at the referee's whistle, and I could see my teammates' big silver helmets with the blue Lion decals turn toward me, some of the players rising from blocks they'd thrown to protect me, their faces masked, automaton, prognathous with the helmet bars protruding toward me, characterless, yet the dismay was in the set of their bodies as they loped back for the huddle. The schoolmaster's voice flailed at me inside my helmet. "Ox!" it cried. "Clumsy oaf."

I joined the huddle. "Sorry, sorry," I said.

"Call the play, man," came a voice from one of the helmets.

"I don't know what happened," I said.

"Call it, man."

The third play on my list was the 42, another running play, one of the simplest in football, in which the quarterback receives the snap, makes a full spin, and shoves the ball into the four back's stomach—the fullback's. He has come straight forward from his position as if off starting blocks, his knees high, and he disappears with the ball into the number two hole just to the left of the center—a straight power play, and one which seen from the stands seems to offer no difficulty.

I got into an awful jam with it. Once again, the jackrabbit-speed of the professional backfield was too much for me. The fullback—Danny Lewis—was past me and into the line before I could complete my spin and set the ball in his belly. And so I did what was required: I tucked the ball into my own belly and followed Lewis into the line, hoping that he might have budged open a small hole.

I tried, grimacing, my eyes squinted almost shut, and waiting for the impact, which came before I'd taken two steps — I was grabbed up by Roger Brown.

He tackled me high, and straightened me with his power, so that I churned against his 300-pound girth like a comic bicyclist. He began to shake me. I remained upright to my surprise, flailed back and forth, and I realized that he was struggling for the ball. His arms were around it, trying to tug it free. The bars of our helmets were nearly locked, and I could look through and see him inside — the first helmeted face I recognized that evening — the small, brown eyes surprisingly peaceful, but he was grunting hard, the sweat shining, and I had time to think, "It's Brown, it's *Brown!*" before I lost the ball to him, and flung to one knee on the ground I watched him lumber ten yards into the end zone behind us for a touchdown.

The referee wouldn't allow it. He said he'd blown the ball dead while we were struggling for it. Brown was furious. "You taking that away from *me*," he said, his voice high and squeaky. "Man, I took that ball in there good."

The referee turned and put the ball on the ten yard line. I had lost twenty yards in three attempts, and I had yet, in fact, to run off a complete play.

The veterans walked back very slowly to the next huddle.

I stood off to one side, listening to Brown rail at the referee. "I never scored like that befo'. You takin' that away from me?" His voice was peeved. He looked off toward the stands, into the heavy tumult of sound, spreading the big palms of his hands in grief.

I watched him, detached, not even moved by his insistence that I suffer the humiliation of having the ball stolen for a touchdown. If the referee had allowed him his score, I would not have protested. The shock of having the three plays go as badly as they had left me dispirited and numb, the purpose of the exercise forgotten. Even the schoolmaster's voice seemed to have gone — a bleak despair having set in so that as I stood shifting uneasily, watching Brown jawing at the referee, I was perfectly willing to trot in to the bench at that point and be done with it.

Then, by chance, I happened to see Brettschneider standing at his corner linebacker position, watching me, and beyond the bars of his cage I could see a grin working. That set my energies ticking over once again — the notion that some small measure of recompense would be mine if I could complete a pass in the Badger's territory and embarrass him. I had such a play in my series — a slant pass to the strong-side end, Jim Gibbons.

I walked back to the huddle. It was slow in forming. I said, "The Badger's asleep. He's fat and he's asleep."

No one said anything. Everyone stared down. In the silence I became suddenly aware of the feet. There are twenty-two of them in the huddle, after all, most of them very large, in a small area, and while the quarterback ruminates and the others await his instruction, there's nothing else to catch the attention. The sight pricked at my mind, the oval of twenty-two football shoes, and it may have been responsible for my error in announcing the play. I forgot to give the signal on which the ball was to be snapped back by the center. I said: "Green right nine slant *break!*" One or two of the players clapped their hands, and as the huddle broke, some of them automatically heading for the line of scrimmage, someone hissed: "Well, the *signal*, what's the signal, for Chrissake."

I had forgotten to say "on two."

I should have kept my head and formed the huddle again. Instead, I called out "Two!" in a loud stage whisper, directing my call first to one side, then the other, *"two! two!"* as we walked up to the line. For those that might have been beyond earshot, who might have missed the signal, I held out two fingers spread like a V, which I showed around furtively, trying to hide it from the defense, and hoping that my people would see.

The pass was incomplete. I took two steps back (the play was a quick pass, thrown without a protective pocket) and I saw Gibbons break from his position, then stop, buttonhooking, his hand, which I used as a target, came up, but I threw the ball over him. A yell came up from the crowd seeing the ball in the air (it was the first play of the evening which hadn't been "blown"—to use the player's expression for a missed play), but then a groan went up when the ball was overshot and bounced across the sidelines.

"Last play," George Wilson was calling. He had walked over with a clipboard in his hand and was standing by the referee. "The ball's on the ten. Let's see you take it all the way," he called out cheerfully.

One of the players asked: "Which end zone is he talking about?"

The last play of the series was a pitchout—called a flip on some teams—a long lateral to the number four back running parallel to the line and cutting for the eight hole at left end. The lateral, though long, was easy for me to do. What I had to remember was to keep on running out after the flight of the ball. The hole behind me as I lateraled was left unguarded by an offensive lineman pulling out from his position and the defensive tackle could bull through and take me from behind in his rush, not knowing I'd got rid of the ball, if I didn't clear out of the area.

I was able to get the lateral off and avoid the tackler behind me, but unfortunately the defense was keyed for the play. They knew my repertoire, which was only five plays or so, and they doubted I'd call the same play twice. One of my linemen told me later that the defensive man opposite him in the line, Floyd Peters, had said, "Well, here comes the 48-pitchout," and it *had* come, and they were able to throw the number four back, Pietrosante, who had received the lateral, back on the 1 yard line—just a yard away from the mortification of having moved a team backward from the 30 yard line into one's own end zone for a safety.

As soon as I saw Pietrosante go down, I left for the bench on the sidelines at midfield, a long run from where I'd brought my team, and I felt utterly weary, shuffling along through the grass.

Applause began to sound from the stands, and I looked up, startled, and saw people standing, and the hands going. It made no sense at the time. It was not derisive; it seemed solid and respectful. "Wha'? Wha'?" I thought, and I wondered if the applause wasn't meant for someone else — if the mayor had come into the stadium behind me and was waving from an open-topped car. But as I came up to the bench I could see the people in the stands looking at me, and the hands going.

I thought about the applause afterward. Some of it was, perhaps, in appreciation of the lunacy of my participation, and for the fortitude it took to do it; but most of it, even if subconscious, I decided was in *relief* that I had done as badly as I had: it verified the assumption that the average fan would have about an amateur blundering into the brutal world of professional football. He would get slaughtered. If by some chance I had uncorked a touchdown pass, there would have been wild acknowledgment — because I heard the groans go up at each successive disaster — but afterward the spectators would have felt uncomfortable. Their concept of things would have been upset. The outsider did not belong, and there was comfort in that being proved.

Some of the applause, as it turned out, came from people who had enjoyed the comic aspects of my stint. More than a few thought that they were being entertained by a professional comic in the tradition of baseball's Al Schacht, or the Charlie Chaplins, the clowns, of the bullfights. Bud Erickson told me that a friend of his had come up to him later: "Bud, that's one of the funniest goddamn . . . I mean that guy's *got* it," this man said, barely able to control himself.

I did not take my helmet off when I reached the bench. It was tiring to do and there was security in having it on. I was conscious of the big zero on my back facing the crowd when I sat down. Some players came by and tapped me on the top of the helmet. Brettschneider leaned down and said, "Well, you stuck it . . . that's the big thing."

The scrimmage began. I watched it for a while, but my mind returned to my own performance. The pawky inner voice was at hand again. "You didn't stick it," it said testily. "You funked it."

At half time Wilson took the players down to the band shell at one end of the stadium. I stayed on the bench. He had his clipboards with him, and I could see him pointing and explaining, a big semicircle of players around him, sitting on the band chairs. Fireworks soared up into the sky from the other end of the field, the shells puffing out clusters of light that lit the upturned faces on the crowd in silver, then red, and then the reports would go off, reverberating sharply, and in the stands across the field I could see the children's hands flap up over their ears. Through the noise I heard someone yelling my name. I turned and saw a girl leaning over the rail of the grandstand behind me. I recognized her from the Gay Haven in Dearborn. She was wearing a mohair Italian sweater, the color of spun pink sugar, and tight pants, and she was holding a thick folding wallet in one hand along with a pair of dark glasses, and in the other a Lion banner, which she waved, her face alive with excitement, very pretty in a perishable, childlike way, and she was calling, "Beautiful; it was beautiful."

The fireworks lit her, and she looked up, her face chalk white in the swift aluminum glare.

I looked at her out of my helmet. Then I lifted a hand, just tentatively.

You can't tell the players without a scorecard, the vendors used to say. Nowadays it seems you can't tell what's happening without an advanced degree in nuclear physics. Mark Ribowsky's article on the deeper mysteries can be rough going in spots if you're not already an initiate. Stay with him, though, and you'll be rewarded with a fuller understanding of what it's really like down there on the field.

MARK RIBOWSKY

Reading Keys: What You Need to Know to Play in the NFL

The professional-football championship of the world in 1980 may well have been won because one player noticed something interesting about another player's rear end. It happened midway through the fourth quarter. The Pittsburgh Steelers were leading in the Super Bowl, 24–19. But the Los Angeles Rams had moved from their own 16-yard line to a first down on the Pittsburgh 32 on seven crisp plays. Lovely time for a surprise pass down the middle, the Rams decided. Throw in some play-action. Freeze the linebackers. Candy.

The Steelers have a middle linebacker who is hard to freeze. He moves with fluid grace, stands up nicely (a real talent when you're six-foot-four), and watches opponents before and at the precise moment of the snap for any hint about what play they're running. This is something all people in shoulder pads do, but when it comes to observing the anatomy, Jack Lambert may be the most perceptive. He's very good with rear ends.

"Just before the snap," Lambert recalled, "one of their offensive linemen had his can a little too high, because his weight was shifted back a bit on his heels, not the balls of his feet, where it should be if he's going to look the same every play. Guys lose concentration. They'll lean forward on their toes when they'll be firing out to run-block, and rock back on their heels if they're getting up to pass-block. This guy must've gotten a little anxious."

When Vince Ferragamo, the young Ram quarterback, faked a handoff and turned quickly to throw, Lambert, already in pass coverage, just kept right on moving back. "We practiced against that pattern — two wide receivers deep down the middle — the whole week before, because we saw it a lot in the films. They hadn't used it yet, but I figured they were setting us up. And as soon as Ferragamo looked middle and his arm came up right away — a sequence he hadn't shown before then — I thought, 'This is it,' and got a nice drop."

On defense, the Steelers had called their play: deep into the middle region of the strongside zone — which rotates to the strong, or tight end, side. Lambert, like any good middle linebacker, checked the weak side. He saw no backs coming out, but he did see Ron Smith looping across the field and paying no attention to the coverage. All this happened in about one second. "I got a good idea of his angle. He was coming right behind me." Ferragamo aimed for Smith at the 10. He didn't quite make it. Lambert intercepted the pass.

Ferragamo would say later that he didn't misread the zone. He just didn't imagine Lambert would be back that far, didn't even look for him. The NFL title had turned on a lineman's butt, a quarterback's slightly unusual motion, and the back of a receiver's head.

Sometimes, that's all it takes.

Have you ever wondered why a six-foot-eight, 275-pound lineman who can lift the front end of a Rolls-Royce doesn't survive in the NFL? And why a nearsighted free safety with gimpy knees does? The answer: one can read keys, the other can't. Someone leaning slightly. A three-inch difference in an opponent's longitude or latitude. A quick glance at the wrong time. Insignificant things that can add up to a big edge for a smart player. A certain kind of smart is what we're talking about here. Sometimes it comes with experience, sometimes it's just there, an ability to reduce all the possibilities of a play and make the right choice. In seconds. According to George Perles, assistant head coach of the Steelers, "All the height, strength, and speed in the world can be neutralized if the guy across from you gets a jump on the ball."

Correctly reading a key guarantees you nothing. A team with lousy talent doesn't beat a good team because somebody reads a key. The good team has the horsepower to bury the bad team from all sides. Everyone knew Vince Lombardi's Green Bay Packers would run their sweeps all day, but they still rolled over people like a herd of street thugs at a switchblade sale. "I always knew what O. J. Simpson was going to do," said Bob Matheson, a linebacker for thirteen years who was waived by Miami late in

August. "If he'd get a step deeper in the I [formation], I could start gearing for a sweep or pitch. But I still couldn't run him down too much. Sure, a lot of teams know they're giving you a key. But they won't change anything until you can stop them."

Nor are keys foolproof. A guy can be sure of a key but the other team may run a variation on the play. A linebacker, for example, may pick up a key to a run, then be attacked by a lineman he didn't key. Or he can fall for an intentionally false key.

"I'll take my chances, though," said Brad Van Pelt, the New York Giants' all-pro linebacker. "Because if you're reading one good key, you'll probably at least be in the right area and not have to look all over the place. Even if you read wrong, you're moving, not flat-footed. That's the whole point. Getting in position to play some football."

"It's more than a little guessing game you play at spare moments," said Perles. "It determines your decisiveness, anticipation, intuition. People are so big and fast today. They come at you out of crazy formations and on misdirection plays. If you're not ready, if you hesitate even for a split second, you're going to be on your can looking up." Perles can take a small bow for the advanced state of key-reading in pro football. His deceptive defensive sets have helped spur offenses to improve their key-reading. This, in turn, has brought about new keys for the defenses. And around and around. "Used to be," Perles says, "everyone could get away with maybe one key. Now you need a frigging checklist, and you got to go through it in a glance."

Definitely a long way from the prepubescent days when Peter Halas, a scout for uncle George's Chicago Bears, discovered how to read Greasy Neale's Philadelphia Eagle defense in the late 1940s. Seems Neale's middle linebacker, Alex Wojciechowicz, would use his fingers to signal the number of linemen. One hand across his chest meant a five-man line. Two hands meant a six-man line, the only other option. The game was innocent then. Real subtlety and deception were not introduced until the late 1950s. Every muscle twitch now has significance. You just have to know what to look for.

"My first couple of years at linebacker [after a trial at strong safety], I was absolutely lost," said Van Pelt. "I was always flat-footed, always getting knocked on my ass. At least at safety you had 15 yards to see the play developing. But then they put me in front of the tight end, and you never know what those guys will do. All the play fakes are aimed at the linebackers, and I went for evey one because I was just watching the play, not going on anything." The Giants tutored Van Pelt on keys after practice. "The offense hated me. They'd have to come out late and run every play in the book against one guy. But eventually, I learned to look in the right places for the right things."

Even now, Van Pelt doesn't know it all. Nor does Matheson. Both men estimate their reading percentage at about 80, "which may be a little higher than most, but not much," according to Matheson. "Hell, if you're wrong three plays out of ten up here, you're in the sewer."

A distinction must be made between two types of keys. The Alex Wojciechowicz type stems from carelessness, lack of talent, concentration lapses, or a player's mistaken confidence that no one will notice. The Ram lineman with his can up, for example, is a common tip-off to defensive linemen. "Those leans, they happen all the time," said Matheson. "Jim Braxton, when he played fullback for Buffalo, would lean forward when he was coming up the middle. Every time. A guy will try to make up for a lack of speed or quickness. He'll get low, get his weight forward, and his knuckles will turn white from the pressure on his hand."

Van Pelt's favorites include a back who jiggles his face mask before taking his stance if he's getting the ball and another who "looks me in the eye is he's coming out of the backfield, checking to see where I am. If he's not coming out, he looks at the ground." Perles talks lovingly about quarterbacks in the huddle who don't make sure their linemen screen them from the defense. "Their lips. You can read the snap count. Really. We've gotten it more than you'd think." One of Perles' own linemen took a lefthanded stance before an inside charge, a righthanded one before an outside charge. "I caught it in practice. Better then than on the game films."

Dave Logan, a wide receiver for the Cleveland Browns, was not so lucky. Logan was amazed one day in the film room last year when "I noticed that on pass situations I'd be facing in, and on a run I'd face straight ahead. I wanted to see the quarterback's lips if he audibled—your basic kindergarten-level mistake. I was doing it for two games before that, too. I'd missed it in the films and so did the coaches. But I bet a couple of defensive backs had a field day."

Players are elated over such tip-offs, but they don't spend much time looking for them. Usually, they're picked up by accident. What players *do* look for are positional keys, the placement of opponents and what moves they can make from those positions. This is the second type.

"Take the backs," said Matheson. "If the fullback is up a bit—maybe only a foot, so you really have to see the field in little sections—you know he's not going anywhere outside. Geometrically, he can't get the angle. He'd have to back up. And he can't get a block from the halfback. So it's probably a quick trap [a lineman won't block his man, who'll then be hit from the blind side by a pulling guard or a back], with him running or blocking the target lineman."

Van Pelt takes the theory one more step. "If he's wider and deeper, you know it's either a sweep or pitchout. But he has to get that position if he wants to get outside and turn the corner. So I'll start moving toward the sideline to cut off the angle at the snap or even before it, if I can time it right. If he's cheating in, I can ignore the possibility of an outside play. So my first step is straight ahead at about 100 miles an hour. If the strongside wide receiver, another of my keys, is also cheating in, I'll know he's coming back to block me. That first year at linebacker, I'd key just the tight end. He'd block down [inside], I'd follow, and the pulling guard would level me. Then when I'd wait, he'd push me down the field. That first step is everything."

For the offensive linemen, one tip-off that can't be disguised without sacrificing efficiency is the wide split where there is more space than usual between linemen. Said

Perles: "Say we get a split between a guard and tackle. That tells us they want to run in there, want a bigger hole. So our philosophy is to have our linemen shoot right through those gaps. Why not? If teams want to give us more room to get through, terrific." One reason it works for the Steelers is that Joe Greene, even now, is so quick penetrating from the inside that he messes up the timing of the blocks.

Even so, with their delirious rush, the Steeler front four would be vulnerable to false-key blocking — traps and suckers (where the lineman pulls and his man follows, often right out of the play) and variations — if it were not for their superb ability to read and react. "In our system, we can play with more abandon but that doesn't mean we're going the way the offensive line wants us to," said John Banaszak, the right end. "That's why we can read the trap as we go. For example, if I'm not blocked, if I see my tackle blocking down on the defensive tackle, I know it's coming. So I close like hell, at an angle, maybe 45 degrees. That way I can anticipate the near or far guard coming across to kick me out. I'll get low for leverage, and stuff him real good.

"Miami tries all kinds of crap like that: cross-blocking, delay blocking, the works. But we handled them pretty easily in the playoffs last year. Again, all I did was read those guards whenever my own man didn't come out to block me. But Joe's really vulnerable to traps. He's inside there with all those people, yet he's got to read the center and guard at the same time before he knows what's happening. I don't know how he does it."

"It's not that difficult, really," Greene said nonchalantly. "It's all in a team's tendencies. You see how they run those traps, and when. That's what key-reading is. It's knowing what to look for. It's a process of elimination. You know which plays a team can run on each formation and each down and distance."

He mentions a formation by way of example: backs split, tight end on his side. "I don't know why, but most teams run only two plays from that set into the No. 3 hole, which is mine. So I'd have only two keys to look for. And with a few teams, if the tight end is on the other side, I get *no* plays at all in No. 3, which means I can blow in harder, be more aggressive. An I formation? A little trickier, since the backs can go either way. But still, teams run almost totally to the weak side out of it. Except Houston. They go about 50–50." But the Steelers stopped the Oiler running game cold in the playoffs last year. "We got them out of the I. They went to a strange formation: the backs and tight end on the same side of center. They wanted us to think they could do a lot of things out of it. But we practice against every possible play run out of every possible formation, so we knew which ones they couldn't run and which keys to look for on the ones they could."

A number of defensive lines jump around up front, trying to confuse the offense. The Steelers do it on cue, in reaction to a good key. "Like with our Stunt 4–3," said Banaszak, referring to the set in which the tackles zero in on the center's head and run "stunts" or games. These are unusual, but predetermined, combinations of rushing routes by the defensive linemen. "Usually, we go to it in passing situations. But if one of us sees a trap key, we'll call a switch at the line. It's good against that kind of blocking, because traps are tightly coordinated, with specific targets."

Key-reading has come so far that it's possible to read *fake* keys before the snap. "Sure," Banaszak insisted. "You see the backs on the strong side and one of them is cheating up. So you know he's getting the ball on a quick pop into the line. But you also see a guard leaning, as if he is pulling. Now unless that back is giving a false key, which rarely happens because he wouldn't want to waste the step, the guard is doing it only to get you out of there with him."

Regardless of whether they can be read or not, teams don't usually rely on fake keys. Few football strategists consider trying to con somebody worth sacrificing vital positioning. "That's why you don't see linebackers trying to fake their blitzes too much," said Clark Gaines, a fullback for the New York Jets and a man who has to pick up those blitzers. "Sure, they'll jump around, give you a staggered start, but it's halfhearted. You know when they're coming. They get up on their toes instead of their heels, come up quickly at the snap. They don't care who knows it. They just want to get in. And that's how they *should* think."

Tom Landry, however, prefers finesse to brute force. "The Cowboys will give you fake keys 95 percent of the time, even with the backs. I think it's self-destructive," said Perles. "I mean, a running play is a well-timed thing. Why disrupt it to try to trick someone? In the Super Bowl two years ago, they gave us a trap fake, had Tony Dorsett up and in, then sent him on a sweep. Joe Greene ignored the key, which we always do with Dallas, and came in and hit him a lick. Hell, if they'd just had Dorsett go outside on a straight pitch, it wouldn't have happened."

"All those sets and shifts aren't kidding anyone," Van Pelt agreed. "You just identify and group things together, then say, 'This is the same as that,' and they're no different than anyone else. They want you to hesitate for a second, not identify a key because you're sorting out something else." Added Perles: "When you pull a lot of fake keys like that you just don't *feel* like a football team. You feel like a candy-ass team. And I've heard some Cowboys say that themselves."

Fakes *do* work when they happen unexpectedly, like Lawrence McCutcheon's option-pass touchdown in the Super Bowl last year. But even the suggestion of something different at the right time can work. "In the '68 NFL championship game with the Colts," said Matheson, who was with Cleveland then, "Don Shula stuck [tight end] John Mackey in the backfield with the two backs late in the first half. We hadn't seen anything like that since high school. It's all we talked about at halftime, but we didn't see it the rest of the game. And while we were looking for it, they ran all over us."

Gaines, who doesn't possess great speed but rushed for 905 yards last year on brains (he keys his own line for last-minute blocking changes), plays a little game of deception with defenses. "Linebackers key the backs very closely, and six inches can make the difference between one and ten yards or 80 yards. So I'll look to the right three times in a row when the play goes right, then look right when I'm going left, or vice versa. I'll get down and do the white-knuckles bit for a second, just to show it, then go wide.

And if I'm not in the play, I'll always give a misdirection move. It may not get me or the team a damn thing, but I'm not giving up a step or my normal positioning to do these things, so why not?"

"I never knew if Bob Trumpy [the former Bengal tight end] was doing that to me," said Matheson. "I was sure a couple of times I had a key on him, different hand down on outside and inside releases. But he'd break the sequence enough to throw me off. So if he was faking, it worked. He always gave us fits."

This kind of fake is dependent on a modicum of acting ability, however. "I mean, sometimes it gets ridiculous," said Banaszak. "You'll see a lineman leaning like the Tower of Pisa. Or shaking, you know, trying to make you think he's tense and making the big block. I just laugh."

Keys are not cut and dried. Often, they're in the eyes of the beholder. The Steelers said after the Super Bowl that John Stallworth's two stunning bomb-receptions (one a 73-yard touchdown, the other a 45-yarder) came on the same pattern. It was a hook-and-go, their normal hook-in but with a quick takeoff downfield, which was their response to keying the inside-outside coverage (defensive backs on both sides of the receiver) the Rams were giving them. "Everyone else plays over-under [defenders in front and in back of the receiver] on double coverage," said Terry Bradshaw, who threw the passes. "The receiver can't split the coverage, so you don't use that pattern."

But Rod Perry, the Ram cornerback, claims the 45-yarder was a fluke. "We gave them a fake blitz read before the snap and Stallworth took it. He just ran a slop route over the middle, but *Bradshaw* misread the key, too, and they got a break out of it. Because if it *was* a blitz, the middle would've been my coverage. I would've been right there." Bradshaw and Stallworth, of course, claim that version is fiction. "But that kind of thing has happened. You get a big one by accident, because the quarterback and receiver both read wrong," said Bradshaw. "But it's not a fluke because at least you and your receiver are on the same wavelength."

The good quarterbacks and receivers do that. Being able to read the same coverage keys at the same time is critical now that almost everyone plays zones. You don't know what kind of zone and rotation you'll be throwing into until the play has started. Not that a zone is so hard to read. Even the defensive backs will tell you they know they'll give up lots of yardage. What they play for is that one pass in ten when the quarterback doesn't hit the seam (the area between zones) or mistimes the pass in relation to the rotation. With man-to-man defenses not feasible anyway against speed-burners and rifle-armed quarterbacks, it's not a bad gamble, especially with a young quarterback who gets confused by different looks in the secondary. And wide receivers who don't know from keys.

Secondaries like Miami's in the mid-1970s and Pittsburgh's in the late 1970s can do enough to confuse experienced quarterbacks. "In the old days, you could read the zone by whether the strong safety got near the tight end. If he did, it was man; if he moved back, it was zone," said Bill Nelsen, the former Brown quarterback and now quarter-back coach for the Tampa Bay Buccaneers. "Now they line up all over the place. But still, you should be able to read it. A cornerback with one leg back and the other in a push-off position is going back into a deep zone. If he's loose, his feet parallel or his weight forward, he's coming up to jam the receiver, then to drop off and play a short zone or run with him in a man-to-man. And if a safety is slow, you can bet he's going to cheat backwards to get into those deep zones. If he's up, you know he's either blitz-ing, covering for a blitzing linebacker, or playing a short inside zone. Because he can't possibly get deep."

It's more likely the read will come when the deep defenders take their first steps after the snap. "Then, the keys get real easy," Logan said. "If the safety backs up and to the outside, I know he's got the outside third area and the cornerback will be inside. Even when the safety exchanges assignments with the cornerback, or with a line-backer, you can see who's going back, see the rotation. And every defensive back has his own personality. Somewhere along the line you can exploit it."

Paul Warfield, who was a master at reading those personalities, helped win a Super Bowl (Dolphins–Vikings) by picking on Minnesota cornerback Bobby Bryant, even when Bryant was in a zone. "Bryant was quick and smart, but I saw him peeking into the backfield if the quarterback took a short, three-step drop, like on third-and-five plays," Warfield, now the assistant director of pro personnel for the Browns, recalled. "He'd assume a quick-out pattern, then sit back there eight yards or so. Well, Bob Griese and I figured we'd give him all the information he wanted. Bob took a three-step drop and a look outside. I did a quick-out, saw Bryant come in, and went deep down the sideline. I had a bad leg that day, but I was all alone." For a 27-yarder.

Receivers have to be careful, though, because defensive backs can be devious. Some receivers pay little attention to being jammed in the five-yard zone off the line, but some of the jammers have a purpose other than slowing a receiver down and disrupting his timing.

"Receivers can be real wimps," said a well-known and very dangerous cornerback. "And because they are, you can make them fountains of information. That's why I try to belt a receiver every play. And you got to do it on the sly after five yards, but you can do it whether he's in the play or not. Because then he's going to do something when he's in the play to avoid me. He'll lean, make a move short, change his stance."

Van Pelt says the technique isn't bad with tight ends, either, especially the ones who don't go out for passes that much. "They're just not familiar with running routes and finessing by linebackers," he said. "There's this one guy who looks like one of those circus elephants on roller skates. I almost die laughing when he comes out. But, come to think of it, he's caught a few on me, too. You don't think he could be keying *me?* How I react to his act? Or my laugh? Hmmm . . ."

Postscript: Van Pelt was laughing when he said that.

Sort of.

When this article appeared in the Canadian journal *Macleans* in August 1975, the World Football League had regrouped from its debacle of 1974 and was facing the new season with optimism—an optimism that, it turned out, was unwarranted. The Chicago Fire failed in its effort to sign the fading Joe Namath, and the television contract that had been dangling under the league's nose suddenly vanished; with it went all hope of survival. On October 22, halfway into its 1975 campaign, the WFL at last gave up the ghost.

JOHN ROBERTSON

The WFL—
The League That Lost Its Shirt

When Johnny F. Bassett got into bed with the World Football League in the winter of 1974 and conceived the Toronto Northmen, he didn't figure on Minister of Health and Welfare Marc Lalonde—of all people—threatening to legally abort the new franchise in the House of Commons because the league's bloodlines weren't true-blue Canadian.

Johnny F. viewed it as a miscarriage of justice, but Lalonde insisted that the health and welfare of the paternal Canadian Football League was at stake and that if Bassett didn't go have his baby south of the border he would pass legislation making birth control retroactive for all existing WFL franchises in Canada.

Since Bassett had already spent 3 million dollars to lure Miami Dolphin superstars Larry Csonka, Jim Kiick, and Paul Warfield from the National Football League, not to mention another $500,000 for twenty lesser players, his labor pains were coming one payday apart. He had no choice but to flee to Tennessee and pick out a new name for the baby—the Memphis Southmen.

Lalonde's proposed legislation died on the Commons Order Paper when Prime Minister Trudeau called a July election. But Bassett feared Lalonde would ram the bill through the House as soon as parliament reconvened, so he left voluntarily rather than risk having his team turfed out of the country in midseason.

During his campaign to oust the Northmen from Toronto, Lalonde had referred to Bassett and his partners as "a few entrepreneurs out for a fast buck." But the Canadian Mint doesn't print them as fast as Bassett and Co. had to spend them just to keep afloat in the WFL's sea of red ink during the 1974 season.

With the 1975 season just beginning, I couldn't resist putting the question to him: "Do you have any messages you'd like me to forward to our esteemed Minister of Health?"

"Yeaah," snorted Bassett. "Tell him the Toronto Northmen are alive and well in Memphis, no thanks to him."

"How did it go?" I asked, knowing full well.

"Jeeeezzzzzzuzzzz," he moaned. "It was a disaster."

"Well, would it be safe to say you were the healthiest team in the League in 1974?"

"Keeeerist," he said. "Healthiest team? If it weren't for the Philadelphia Bell, we would have been an only child by the time the season ended. The other ten owners bailed out. We were averaging 24,000 fans a game until the damned league fell apart. Toward the end, I wouldn't have gone to the games myself if I hadn't owned the team. The last five games we played were against two teams that were bankrupt, one that didn't have any uniforms, one that said it was quitting before it took the field, and another that couldn't afford the plane fare to even come to Memphis."

"Now the big question," I said. "How much money did you lose?"

"I'll never tell," he said. "But to give you some small idea, it cost me $600,000 just to help bail other clubs in the league out of hock. The fact that the league is operating again is one of the great business miracles of all time. We have a new rule this year. To be an owner, you have to have some money. That's why we have ten new ones . . ."

How bad were the old owners?

The Detroit Wheel, who went flat midway through the 1974 season, three games to nine, left a sorry list of 122 creditors when the club went bankrupt.

The Jacksonville Sharks went belly-up, but not before owners Douglas and Fran Monaco borrowed $27,000 from their head coach and then fired him.

The Southern California Sun bankrupted their first owner and the man who bailed them out had to be bailed out himself when he pleaded guilty to making false statements in order to obtain bank financing.

The Florida Blazers, whose players performed for nothing in the last ten weeks of the season after the club ran out of funds, were in such dire straits that the coach had to dig into his own pocket to buy toilet paper for the dressing room. But the Blazers advanced to the World Football League's semifinals and came from behind a 16–0 halftime deficit to eliminate Bassett's Memphis Southmen 17–16.

"I've had to coach against some hungry football teams in my day," said Memphis

General Manager Leo Cahill. "But that was ridiculous."

You could always tell a WFL team when it gathered in a local diner for a pregame meal. The pep talk consisted of three words from the team general manager:

"Separate checks, please."

The Philadelphia Bell had announced crowds of 60,000 for each of their first two home games, but enterprising reporters discovered that 90 percent of the house had been papered. Presumably, the owner had let the fans in free — hoping they would pay to get out.

The Blazers were finally beaten in the World Bowl by the Birmingham Americans, coached by former Ottawa Rough Rider mentor Jack Gotta.

"I'll never forget that day," said Gotta. "We were in the dressing room afterward, quaffing some rented champagne, when some guy comes in with a court order to seize our uniforms because the team was bankrupt."

"What did the players think of that?" I asked.

"Well," chuckled Gotta, "they kind of suspected we were in a little financial difficulty when we couldn't pay them for the last few games."

Gotta and the Birmingham team are back in business again under new ownership, presumably with new uniforms.

The WFL claims to have guaranteed financial solvency for all eleven clubs in the 1975 season by forcing each owner to bank all players' salaries and all advance season-ticket money before the season began.

This means Bassett had to ante up a cool $700,000 to guarantee the salaries of Csonka, Kiick, and Warfield alone.

Some fast-buck entrepreneur, eh Mr. Lalonde?

In the Golden Age of Sports, with such heroes as Ruth, Tilden, Jones, and Dempsey, none occupied a loftier pedestal than Red Grange; for pure adulation, only Lindbergh was his equal. "The Galloping Ghost" (Warren Brown's coinage) was not simply a football player of extraordinary prowess, he was a social phenomenon and thus a money machine. There were Red Grange candy bars, Red Grange sweaters, Red Grange socks, Red Grange shoes, Red Grange fountain pens, Red Grange books, Red Grange films. All these deals were engineered by C. C. ("Cash and Carry") Pyle, Red's enterprising manager. Pyle's first move after Grange played in his final collegiate game was to sign him to the Chicago Bears, whom he then scheduled for ten games in eighteen days. New York was one of those stops, and Red's Gotham debut is recorded by a skeptical Damon Runyon in the *New York American*.

DAMON RUNYON

70,000 See Red; Record New York Gate: December 6, 1925

I here preach from the old familiar text:

It pays to advertise.

There gathered at the Polo Grounds in Harlem yesterday afternoon the largest crowd that ever witnessed a football game on the island of Manhattan, drawn by the publicity that has been given one individual — Red Grange, late of the University of Illinois.

Between sixty and seventy thousand men, women, and children were in the stands blocking the slides and the runways. Twenty thousand more were perched on Coogan's Bluff and the roofs of apartment houses overlooking the baseball home of McGraw's club, content with just an occasional glimpse of the whirling mass of players on the field far below and wondering which was Red Grange.

Twenty-two men, former stars of Yale, Dartmouth, Penn State, Notre Dame and other famous colleges of the land, were mixed up in the mud at the old P.G. at different times in the course of the game between the Chicago Bears and the New York Giants. But only one man mattered to the crowd. The other men and even the game itself, which was won by Chicago, 19–7, were merely incidental to the presentation of Red Grange, as a supporting cast and a play are largely incidental to an actor such as John Barrymore. If that comparison isn't too far-fetched.

Advertising did it, no doubt of that. No human being could possibly play football proportionately to the columns of newspaper space that Red Harold Grange has received. Great as he is in the field that he has chosen as a means of capitalizing his publicity, he is not that great.

It is said he took down in the neighborhood of $25,000 for his end yesterday, and the total gate must have gone well over $100,000. That is what the profession calls "heavyweight money."

Grange played through the first period and part of the second without performing any astonishing feats. Then he took a rest.

As the final period started Red was still absent; the huge crowd that had assembled on a peaceful Sunday to see him and no one else set up a concerted chant:

"We want Grange!"

As the roar passed around the packed stands, Grange came trotting out to take his place at left half in the lineup of the Chicago Bears. They gave him the ball at once, and he gained six yards. On the next play he lost two. The crowd applauded him whether he gained or lost, just as it applauds Babe Ruth hitting a home run or striking out.

He whipped an 18-yard forward pass to Joe Sternaman for a good gain, then Knop made four yards and first down on New York's 11-yard line.

They gave the ball to Grange again and he just failed of first down on New York's 1-yard line. The ball went to the big-town footballers, and they wiggled out of immediate danger, but a moment later McBride tried a forward pass to Bomar.

The muddy lean-flanked figure of Red Grange came from nowhere. He reached up, grabbed the ball in the air, whirled, and sprinted across the New York goal line for a touchdown. No New Yorker was close to him as he loped along, his knees lifting high with every stride and his hips swaying.

That satisfied the crowd. They could understand that play, though a lot of other very fancy stuff was lost on them.

Red Grange had made a touchdown! That was what they had paid to see.

Those plunges and tackles and whatnot were all right for the experts and those who understood the intricacies of the game, but the majority of those who paid all that money to see Red Grange found anything that did not include Red Grange quite mystifying.

They set up a regular college cheer as Red romped over for that score. Yet, outside of this one play, Red was not prodigious. He didn't do as much execution for his side as McBride, of New York, did for dear old Coogan's Bluff, for instance. He gained a total of 52 yards on plunging, but lost two, making his net gain 50.

BEFORE 1925, PRO FOOTBALL
WAS THE "POOR RELATION" OF
THE SPORTS WORLD —
UNPUBLICIZED AND
GENERALLY UNLOVED.

ALL THAT CHANGED ON
THANKSGIVING DAY WHEN
COLLEGE FOOTBALL'S
BIGGEST STAR,

Red
Grange

JOINED THE CHICAGO BEARS. HIS
CHARISMA DREW THE FIRST PRO
FOOTBALL SELLOUT TO WRIGLEY
FIELD AND TEN DAYS LATER
BROUGHT 70,000 TO NEW YORK'S
POLO GROUNDS. THEN GRANGE AND
THE BEARS TOURED THE COUNTRY,
WINNING THOUSANDS OF NEW FANS
FOR PRO FOOTBALL.

He wasn't much on defense. He never left his feet once to stop a man, and he was somewhat exclusive—almost snobbish, in fact—about mixing in on the plays.

Still he was playing his sixth game since Thanksgiving, and is booked on up to next Spring by his manager, the nimble C. C. Pyle, and has to conserve his energy. He was doing plenty of conserving yesterday until the crowd got to barking for him.

Sternaman and Walquist, both former Illinois men like Grange, were the stars of the Bears, if anyone wishes to hear any football in connection with a story about Red Grange, which seems improbable.

Moreover, it was a real good football game from start to finish, with none of the fumbling that characterizes college football. Only occasionally did the boys seem to get a little rough, and they played as hard as if their college letters depended on their efforts.

The result was something of an upset, as the New Yorkers were 6–5 favorites in quite a bit of betting.

The rain of the past week had softened up the green sward of Hennery Fabian's beloved field, and after the first few plays it was all tracked up like a marshy sheep meadow. Overhead the sun shone with pleasing warmth and the air was as soft and mild as a June day.

The management had provided as much atmosphere as possible in the form of decorations. They economically retained the red, white, and blue trimmings of the Army and Navy game, adding a few rosettes of orange and black, the colors of the Chicago Bears. Moreover, there was a band, which burst forth with "Boola Boola" and other college hymns at intervals.

The Chicago team wore helmets and jerseys of orange, thus preserving the color scheme with which Grange was familiar at college. Our hometown boys from Penn State and other points wore white helmets and red and blue jerseys.

The rush to the Polo Grounds began early and continued for fully an hour after the game began. Eighth Avenue and the Speedway were well picketed by police and they had their hands full. It was reminiscent of a World's Series crush.

You heard just one name uttered in public, and that name was Grange. It is safe to say that half the spectators present yesterday never saw a football game before and may never see another game again.

They had no interest in the contest and no sentiment for either team. They merely wanted to see Red Grange. Thousands were still dashing along the runways as the game started, and as they halted in their dash to peer at the field they were asking:

"Which one's Grange?"

"Where is he?"

There he was—a tall fellow in a flaming headpiece and jersey, looking no different from the other men around him, similarly garbed. His white stockings were muddy and after the first play Red's face was dirty.

He wore his old college number, 77, on his back. But he was not a particularly imposing figure. I think many of the spectators were sadly disappointed. They half expected to see a fellow with horns, snorting fire and flame through his nostrils.

Red carried the ball on the first two plays, gaining about nine yards. After that, Chicago seemed to rely more on Joe Sternaman. . . . With Joe lugging the ball most of the way, they started on their own 40-yard line and marched down the muddy yard 63 yards to a touchdown. They missed the goal from touchdown.

Thereafter Grange made about six yards through the line, and then three yards as the Bears began a second march. He whipped a forward pass of 14 yards to Walquist and Joe Sternaman swung around New York's right end for another touchdown.

Joe missed his show at goal from touchdown.

White, of Oklahoma, wearing a big round zero on his back, got into the game in the second period for New York and made a touchdown aided by two long forward passes. McBride kicked the goal.

During all this pulling and hauling, Grange had little opportunity to display his defensive ability. He had one tackle and knocked down a couple of forward passes, but in the main he seemed to hold himself aloof from the play. He is getting too much money to take undue chances and there was no occasion for him to die for the dear old Chicago Bears yesterday.

In the early stages of the game there was quite a vocal to-do from the crowd, which lent some real football atmosphere to the proceedings, but, of course, there was no organized cheering for either side.

Mr. Will Gibson, one of the owners of the New York team, thought some of going out in front of a section where a number of his fellow citizens of the Bronx were located, and trying to incite them to war whoops, but he abandoned the idea when someone told him he might be arrested for disturbing the peace.

At that, I was surprised at the volume of sound that arose from the spectators. They were positively excited at times. If ever Mr. Gibson and his associates can work up a tender hometown sentiment for their team, there may eventually be pop bottle hurlings at the P.G. and kindred scenes.

Late in the first half Grange made about 18 yards in a plunge off right tackle. Then he retired to the sidelines to take a rest. Presently Joe Sternaman called for recess while he changed his wet shoes for dry foot covering and tried for a 55-yard field goal. He missed it.

It seems that Joe cannot kick in wet shoes, so he always has a man posted on the sidelines with a pair of dry dog cases. He made a noble try and the crowd cheered the effort, also its failure.

Between the halves much silence prevailed. The band played a few popular airs and many citizens retired below decks to break the Volstead Act, but there was none of the atmosphere of a collegiate recess.

The boys in the center-field bleachers introduced an innovation to football by bombarding each other with newspapers. They were probably the old grads of the Hudson

Dusters and the Gophers, renewing their happy days on the campuses of their alma maters.

A number of young men appeared on the field wearing red and blue feathers on their hats, the colors of Mr. Gibson's territory of Coogan's Bluffs. They seemed greatly interested in Mr. Benny Friedman, the Michigan quarterback, who strolled about the field between the halves.

Big Bill Edwards, president of Mr. Enright's police college, was on hand with some of his undergraduates and many other famous ex-collegians were scattered about the premises.

Listening in on the various discussions of the experts, one gathered a consensus that the professionals presented a nice line of football.

The gridiron savants agreed that the boys were in there fighting hard and that they played as well as college teams, which is not surprising, in view of the fact that most of the players have been at it from six to nine years.

But, soft! What linebacker through yonder window breaks? It must be Dick Butkus, playing Montague to the newsman's Capulet. The misunderstood Bear has adopted Shakespeare as hopefully as others might Dale Carnegie. We are left to wonder what the Bard might have thought of Lite Beer (Shakespeare wasn't such a great speller, either). The item below comes from *Sports Illustrated.*

WILLIAM SHAKESPEARE

"He Jests at Scars"

Dick Butkus has become interested in the works of William Shakespeare. Don't bug him about it. "Some people think I have to get down on all fours to eat my couple of pounds of raw meat every day," he says, clearly exasperated, "but people who know me know that I can read. I move my lips a little but I can read things of a second-grade level—like newspapers—and I don't really need a rubber stamp to give my autograph." Butkus went on the Shakespeare kick when a friend suggested that readings from the Bard would improve Dick as a public speaker, and he found, as he explains, "that Shakespeare had a great understanding of the moods and language of men in action. His histories and tragedies are full of passages that are just as applicable to football players as to kings. There are some speeches in *Henry V* that would make great locker-room speeches—I can find things in just about all of the plays that can be applied to the game, the players, the coaches, and even the fans. Take this situation: one of our men is shaken up on a play and is slow getting up. The opposing blocker is standing over him, laughing. I walk over there and instead of swearing, maybe getting thrown out of the game, I just tell him, 'He jests at scars, that never felt a wound.' Now that is bound to set him thinking and teach him a little humility."

Or something.

In 1943, Sid Luckman of the Bears threw 28 touchdown passes, 45 Shapiro. What's a Shapiro? You'll soon find out, from this provocative essay that appeared in *The Coffin Corner*, the monthly publication of the Professional Football Researchers Association. What inflames the author and puzzles all who read him is why his solution to the problem of pro football statistics, at once ingenious and simple, was not adopted long ago.

DAVID SHAPIRO

Football Players Are Better Than Ever, Right?

It certainly sounds like it every Sunday afternoon and evening, every Monday night, and on occasional Thursday nights from July to January, as sportscasters, their color men, and their statisticians hype the big-money game with paeans about new records, near-records, threatened records, superstars, and superseasons.

Not only does it give the hard-pressed broadcast crew something to talk about during lulls in the game, which is at least two-thirds of the time, but it also makes the pro game sound bigger, better, more exciting, and more entertaining. That's a major factor when you consider that television time on pro games is among the most expensive advertising buys in the business and that time on the Super Bowl broadcast is *the* most expensive—$468,000 a minute this year on Super Bowl XIV.

One of their favorite ways to compare players is by season performances—the number of carries, yards gained, touchdowns scored, and so forth by a player (or team, for that matter) over an entire season.

To hear the TV jocks tell it, it seems like Jim Brown set season rushing records, then O. J. Simpson broke them, then Walter Payton came along to break *them*, and now

Earl Campbell sets new ones for Ottis Anderson to shoot at after Anderson's own record-breaking year, and so on.

Is there no end to this record-breaking?

No.

And there won't be any end to it because of the way season performance records are kept, published, and hyped by the NFL and its supporters in the media and in the advertising time-sales business. Because, either by design or by oversight, they are dealing from a stacked deck when they talk about season records.

The truth is that season records are incorrectly kept and that many great football players (and teams) have seen their names dropped from the record books unfairly for nearly forty years because of it. Since 1936, the first year in which all NFL teams played the same number of games per season, the season has varied in length from:

12 games in 1936 to
11 games in 1937 to
10 games in 1943 to
11 games in 1946 to
12 games in 1947 to
14 games in 1961 to
16 games in 1978.

But the NFL's official measurement of season performance has never been corrected for the different number of games in the seasons being compared. This is no different than keeping track records without regard to whether the distances run are measured in feet, yards, or meters.

Pro football records are officially compiled by the NFL Public Relations Department, meticulously kept on computers by Elias Sports Bureau, Inc. (this is the same kind of meticulousness as measuring for a first down to a fraction of an inch after the ball's forwardmost position is eyeballed by officials while the pigskin is being buried in a morass of ten to fifteen very large bodies), and published by NFL Properties, Inc. Everyone, even the prestigious Pro Football Hall of Fame in Canton, Ohio, buys them, reads them, believes them, and uses them. As a result, everyone using Elias/NFL seasonal statistics is using data that can best be described as "no-think."

When you deal from the Elias/NFL stacked deck and look at twenty-five major categories of season records (both individual and team), it appears that football players are indeed better than ever. Of these twenty-five standards, Elias/NFL would have you believe that:

2 were set in the '40s,
2 in the '50s,
14 in the '60s, and
7 in the '70s, 6 during the last three seasons.

But they're wrong and anyone with a $2.50 NFL Record Manual and a $4.98 pocket calculator can prove it.

To get the real season statistics, you must first correct for the number of games in the seasons you're looking at, compared to a sixteen-game season.

If it was a ten-game season, you have to add 60 percent to get a true comparison. If it was an eleven-game season, add 45.46 percent. If it was twelve, add 33.33 percent and for fourteen add 14.29 percent.

The results are startling and should be welcome to all those old pros who think they've been forgotten.

Applying these formulas to the same twenty-five season records, we find that, in reality:

9 were set in the '40s,

5 in the '50s,

9 in the '60s, and

only 2 in the '70s, 1 in '73 and 1 in '79!

At least in baseball, they have the class to insert a polite asterisk when they hit an anomaly like that, to wit:

*60 home runs, Babe Ruth, New York Yankees, 1927 (154-game season)

**61 home runs, Roger Maris, New York Yankees, 1961 (162-game season)

Baseball's record-keepers at least give you a chance to reflect on the fact that, given his pace of about one home run in every two and one-half games, Ruth would probably have hit 63 out of the park in a 162-game season. If he had had 246 games in which to bat — the same as going from ten games to sixteen games in football — it is reasonable to assume that the Babe would have produced 96 roundtrippers in a single season. Who says that the number of games you play in a season isn't important?

However, in pro football, you either use the Elias/NFL deck or you don't sit in.

Let's look at some of those new/old season records. For clarity, I have labeled the official records as " _ NFL." The figures corrected for the 16-game season, I have modestly labeled as " _ Shapiro." What the hell, Volta, Watt and all those guys named their units of measurement after themselves, didn't they? Why not Shapiro?

Individual records first.

Rushing Attempts
    Official record: Earl Campbell, 1979 Houston Oilers, 368 NFL
    Real record: Jim Brown, 1959 Cleveland Browns, 290 NFL (387 Shapiro)
    Walter Payton, 1977 Chicago Bears, 339 NFL (387 Shapiro)

Touchdowns Rushing
    Official record: Jim Taylor, 1962 Green Bay Packers, 19 NFL (22 Shapiro)
    Earl Campbell, 1979 Houston Oilers, 19 NFL
    Real Record: Steve Van Buren, 1945 Philadelphia Eagles, 15 NFL (24 Shapiro)

Passing Attempts
    Official record: Steve DeBerg, 1979 San Francisco 49ers, 577 NFL
    Real record: Sonny Jurgensen, 1967 Washington Redskins, 508 NFL (581 Shapiro)

Passing Yards
  Official record: Dan Fouts, 1979 San Diego Chargers, 4,082 NFL
  Real record: Joe Namath, 1967 New York Jets, 4,007 NFL (4,580 Shapiro)

Touchdown Passes
  Official record: George Blanda, 1961 Houston Oilers, 36 NFL (41 Shapiro)
  Y. A. Tittle, 1963 New York Giants 36 NFL (41 Shapiro)
  Real record: Sid Luckman, 1943 Chicago Bears, 28 NFL (45 Shapiro)

Total Touchdowns
  Official record: O. J. Simpson, 1975 Buffalo Bills, 23 NFL (26 Shapiro)
  Real record: Steve Van Buren, 1945 Philadelphia Eagles, 18 NFL (29 Shapiro)

Recasting team data is also most fruitful.

Rushing Attempts
  Official record: 1977 Oakland Raiders, 681 NFL (778 Shapiro)
  Real record: 1949 Philadelphia Eagles, 632 NFL (843 Shapiro)

Rushing Yardage
  Official record: 1978 New England Patriots, 3,165 NFL
  Real record: 1948 San Francisco 49ers, 3,663 AAC (4,186 Shapiro)
If the purists balk at this one because the 1948 49ers played in the AAC, no problem.
Just substitute any one of eleven other teams that had total rushing yardage in a single
season in excess of 3,165 Shapiro — say, the 1936 Detroit Lions with 3,844 Shapiro.

Touchdowns Rushing
  Official record: 1962 Green Bay Packers, 36 NFL (41 Shapiro)
  Real record: 1941 Chicago Bears, 30 NFL (44 Shapiro)

Total Touchdowns
  Official record: 1961 Houston Oilers, 66 NFL (75 Shapiro)
  Real record: 1950 Los Angeles Rams, 64 NFL (85 Shapiro)

Total Points
  Official record: 1961 Houston Oilers, 513 NFL (586 Shapiro)
  Real record: 1950 Los Angeles Rams, 466 NFL (621 Shapiro)

Pass Interceptions
  Official record: 1961 San Diego Chargers, 49 NFL (56 Shapiro)
  Real record: 1943 Green Bay Packers, 42 NFL (67 Shapiro)

There you are, twelve "new" NFL season records, courtesy of logic and a pocket
calculator, *and seven of them unbroken since the '40s*, buried all these years by the
strange statistical methods of Elias/NFL and perpetuated by a shallow sports philosophy

that doesn't bother to look beyond what it says in this year's Official Record Manual.

Even some of the existing record performances take on a new lustre when you convert them by the same formula.

Paul Hornung's 176-point record for the 12-game 1960 season becomes 235 points.

Dick "Night Train" Lane's 14 interceptions in the 12-game 1952 season becomes 19 interceptions.

Charlie Hennigan's 1,746 yards gained on pass receptions in the 14-game 1961 season goes up to nearly 2,000 yards. His 101 catches in 1964 become 115.

O. J. Simpson's 1973 standard of 2,003 yards gained rushing becomes 2,279 yards.

Don Hutson's 1942 mark of 17 pass-reception TD's becomes 25 TD's.

Some old familiar names deservedly come back out of the past when you look at their performances in terms of *true* comparisons.

And when you remember that the pre-1950 stars played on both offense and defense, their records become even more impressive.

Now what about the greatest season ever played by a professional footballer, setting aside for the moment the philosophical truth that there is never a greatest anything? Did it take place in the '70s now that the pro players are better than ever?

There have been many outstanding season-length performances in the past five decades or so, any one of which could justifiably be advanced as the greatest. Go over the last page or so and you'll find more than enough likely candidates.

But all things considered, I have to go back about thirty-five years and opt for Bill Dudley's all-around play in 1946 for the Pittsburgh Steelers as the most remarkable individual season-length performance ever in the NFL.

His stats for that year are stunning!

During the eleven scheduled games Bill Dudley had (converted to sixteen-game seasonal equivalents):

212 rushing attempts, first in the NFL
879 yards rushing, first in the NFL
47 pass completions in 131 attempts for 657 yards and 3 TD's
6 pass receptions for 159 yards and 1 TD
15 pass interceptions, first in the NFL
352 yards on pass interceptions, first in the NFL
39 punt returns, first in the NFL
560 yards gained on punt returns, first in the NFL
14.26 yard average on punt returns, first in the NFL
20 kickoff returns for 407 yards and an average of 20 yards per return
87 punts for a 40-yard average
17 extra points in 20 attempts
3 field goals in 10 attempts

Mr. Dudley did virtually all the Steelers' punting, punt returning, kickoff returning, extra-point and field-goal kicking, and pass intercepting as well as a preponderant majority of his team's rushing and passing, leading the league in seven categories while doing so.

One wonders where even the articulate Howard Cosell would find the superlatives necessary to describe such a season were Dudley playing today. After all, with "great," "remarkable," "extraordinary," "fantastic," "super," and so on used so loosely these days by our sports media brethren to cover just about anything that takes place on the gridiron, what's left to describe performances of Dudley's caliber?

One final note for those who are prone to accept the opinion that football players are better than ever today because they are bigger, faster, and stronger.

In 1946, Bill Dudley stood five-foot-ten tall and weighed 172 pounds.

Of course, if you consider that 1946 was an 11-game season and convert Dudley's measurements into Shapiros by adding 45.46 percent, he comes out to be eight-foot-six tall and weighing 250 pounds. I guess that proves that players *do* get better as they get bigger, right?

This was a fine story when Al Silverman wrote it for *Sport* in 1969, but it has become more resonant, more poignant with the passing years. We see Gale Sayers, Brian Piccolo, and Vince Lombardi in their prime, unaware that the Sword of Damocles was soon to fall. For Sayers, 1969 was a year of triumph as he returned from knee surgery to win the rushing title; however, in early 1970 he went down again with a wrecked knee, and this time he was through. Brian Piccolo didn't make it into the 1970 season, cut down cruelly by cancer in June. Nor did Vince Lombardi, who was also stricken with cancer and died in September.

AL SILVERMAN

Gale Sayers:
The Hard Road Back

Gale Sayers lay on his bed in a motel room in Washington, D.C., a day before the Chicago Bears' first exhibition game of the 1969 season. He was wearing white jockey undershorts and glistened like a bronze god. A friend, Henny Young, had come in the room and noted immediately that Sayers' skin was a deeper brown than usual. "You got a tan!" Young exclaimed. "Where'd you get that tan? You been sittin' in the sun?" Sayers laughed, a flashing, self-assured laugh, showing his white teeth and sharing his secret with no one.

The bronze body was hard and lean and the five-inch scar that ran along the inside of his right leg, thigh-bone to knee-bone, knee-bone to leg-bone, that jagged badge of fellowship among professional football players, was not noticeable. But it was there and it filled the room with its presence; unspoken questions, urgent questions, were in the air.

The knee had been cut into last November 10 and cartilage removed and ligaments sewn up and now the finest runner in professional football the last four years—until November 10, 1968—was about to play in his first game since the injury.

Finally, a question was asked, not to Sayers but, warming up, to Sayers' roommate, Brian Piccolo, who lay on his own bed, the whiteness of his skin a startling contrast to Gale's bronze look.

"There's one big difference in Gale now," Piccolo said. "He runs all right until the knee starts to wobble." He laughed and Gale laughed and the visitors in the room laughed and, suddenly, the air was lighter.

Piccolo played fullback at Wake Forest. He was born in Massachusetts but raised, he said, in Fort Lauderdale, Florida.

"By way of He-Hung-High, Mississippi." said Sayers.

Pick grinned. "Don't get me started. Massa Sayers," he said. But he was started. The two had become roommates two years ago in Birmingham, Alabama, before an exhibition game, when the Bears decided hastily to room men according to position.

"Of all the places to spring it on us," said Piccolo. "I came up to the room and saw Gale and said, 'What are you doing here?' But it's been okay. We talk about everything, whatever goes on."

"Mostly race relationships," said Sayers.

"We're okay," said Piccolo, ignoring Sayers, "as long as he doesn't use the bathroom."

Someone asked Sayers, "Who would you want as a roommate if you had a choice?" He replied, "If you're asking me, what white Italian fullback from Wake Forest, I'd say Pick."

Some people find it difficult to understand the black humor, the needling that goes on between Sayers and Piccolo. The two keep it up even on the field. When Ross Montgomery, a rookie running back from Texas Christian, first heard it, he was astonished. Sayers and Piccolo use it therapeutically, as a way of easing into each man's world, a world that has been vastly separate for so long. The needling helps take the strangeness from each man's world, and it lessens tensions.

Sayers said, "Pick, show him the letter you just got." The letter had come from Chicago, from a man who had actually signed his name. It began: "I read where you stay together with Sayers. I am a white man! Most of the people I know don't want anything to do with them. I just don't understand you. Most Italians I have met say that they stink and they really do."

Piccolo interrupted, "Well, of course that's true. You can't get away from that."

Sayers roared, shaking his head. "I don't like your racist attitude," he said.

The rest of the letter described how the Bears smelled, how they had no quarterback, no receivers, no offensive line. And, it ended: "Sayers will fold up like an accordion when he gets hit."

That was one question Sayers hoped to settle right away in the game with the Redskins. But he was disappointed to learn, earlier in the week, that he would not start, that he would be used only to run back kickoffs and punts.

Jim Dooley, a tall man with curly hair, who wears horn-rimmed glasses and looks more like a scoutmaster than the head coach of the Bears, explained why Sayers would

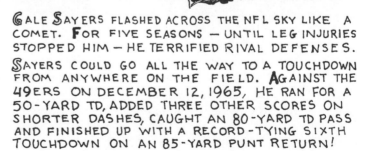

GALE SAYERS

GALE SAYERS FLASHED ACROSS THE NFL SKY LIKE A COMET. FOR FIVE SEASONS — UNTIL LEG INJURIES STOPPED HIM — HE TERRIFIED RIVAL DEFENSES.

SAYERS COULD GO ALL THE WAY TO A TOUCHDOWN FROM ANYWHERE ON THE FIELD. AGAINST THE 49ERS ON DECEMBER 12, 1965, HE RAN FOR A 50-YARD TD, ADDED THREE OTHER SCORES ON SHORTER DASHES, CAUGHT AN 80-YARD TD PASS AND FINISHED UP WITH A RECORD-TYING SIXTH TOUCHDOWN ON AN 85-YARD PUNT RETURN!

not be starting. "He's fine," Dooley said. "I know he wanted to start this game. I told him, 'Gale, look, we got an inexperienced line. Two of our regulars are out. They make a mistake — boom.' When he scrimmaged last week someone made a mistake and Butkus hit him. He understood afterwards."

Perhaps he understood, but he was not happy. "They're babying me," he said, "I know they are."

All along, Sayers had refused to baby himself. He would not use crutches when his leg was in a cast. Right after the cast was removed, he began to lift weights on the leg. He started jogging in early February. He was examined on February 27 and Dr. Theodore Fox, who had performed the operation told Sayers, "If there were a game this Sunday, you'd be able to play."

Dr. Fox believes in Sayers. He once defined the special quality that made Sayers the finest runner in football. "Factor X," he called it. "This stands for drive and motivation," he said. "Factor X elevates a player one plateau. It makes a star out of an average player and a superstar out of a star." Dr. Fox said that his operation on Sayers' knee would contribute 60 percent to Sayers' recovery and "Gale's strong desire to return — Factor X — will add the other 40 percent."

There could be no doubt about that desire. "I worked hard to get up there," Sayers had said midpoint in his recuperation period, "and I'm going to work twice as hard to stay up there." At that time, an article in a Chicago newspaper suggested that running backs with knee injuries rarely come back to top form and that Sayers might have to spend the rest of his career as a flanker or at some other position. The article infuriated Gale. "I saved it," he said, "because when I do come back as a runner, I'm gonna show it to him." And then, as if to underscore his determination, he drew out the words — "I . . . Will . . . Be . . . Back."

When rookie camp opened in Rensselaer, Indiana, in mid-July, Sayers was there. His first day in camp, he insisted on taking part in the scrimmage. On one play he started running to his right. Willie Holman, the Bears' huge and mean defensive left end, came across and blindsided Sayers, crashing him to the ground. Others piled on. Sayers got up by himself. He continued to play. Finally, the scrimmage was over. He had carried the ball a half-dozen times, gaining six yards through the middle once, five another time. But no one said a word to him. Sayers felt he was being ignored by the coach, the trainer, the Bears' doctor. But that was the game plan. Trainer Ed Rozy says, "The instructions on him were don't even mention it. Make him forget it."

In desperation Sayers went up to Ed McCaskey, who is the Bears' treasurer, a son-in-law of George Halas and a confidant of Sayers.

"How'd I look?" Sayers asked.

"You're all right," McCaskey said, and turned away.

When the veterans came in to camp, Gale was used sparingly. The younger backs, Mike Hull, Ralph Kurek, and [Ross] Montgomery, did most of the hitting. Dooley was going easy with Sayers, but also with veterans Piccolo and Ronnie Bull, who had a record of preseason injuries. But the lack of contact drills worried Gale because of his timing. "With Piccolo or Bull in there," he said, "the timing is different. The guards can be a little slower. But with me in there they've got to go full speed. I'm much quicker, so they have to set up their blocks fast. When I'm in there, I'm running up their backs."

But he did scrimmage a bit. In the Saturday scrimmage before the Redskins' game, he went up the middle. Someone grabbed him by the legs and Dick Butkus rammed him in the chest. Ed Stone, who covers the Bears for *Chicago Today*, was there and says that Sayers seemed to show his old moves. "I talked to Johnny Morris, who's on TV now," Stone says, "and he said that on a sweep it looked like Gale might have the slightest hitch. But," Stone said, "I can't see anything. It looks like it's all there."

On the morning of August 2, at breakfast, Sayers and Piccolo talked about Vince Lombardi and Washington and playing the first exhibition game of the season. Both men were dressed casually, in T-shirts and shorts. A waitress came over to Sayers, "Can I ask you your name?" she said to him. Pick mumbled loud enough for all to hear, "They all look alike."

Piccolo said he thought he would like to play a little bit for Lombardi before his career was over.

"I can arrange that," Sayers said.

"Would you? I'm tired of playing in your shadow. I want to be a legend in my own time."

The game was less than twelve hours away and they talked about what it meant to them. "You can't treat it as any game," said Sayers. "Do that and you have a short season. Every game is important, and you always like to start off with a win after all that training."

"But it's not like life or death," said Piccolo. "Lombardi and Washington is not the same as Lombardi and Green Bay. Certainly, you want to beat Vince, but it's not the same as beating him with a team that's in your division."

"I know Lombardi's going to be up," Sayers said. "The Redskins are going to be up." His thought suddenly became disconnected. "I hate to lose," he said. Then, as if the real meaning of the game had just come to him, he said, "I just want to show people I'm ready."

That was it — to show people that he was ready. It was a secret he had carried around for eight months, and even he did not know the answer. He had jogged, played handball, basketball, and touch football. He had run full speed, he had make his patented Sayers cuts, he had been hit in camp and, through it all, the knee had held up. Now there was one more test, contact in battle against another team. He was twenty-six years old with four glorious and rewarding years behind him and now he must know about the future.

While Sayers attended a midmorning team meeting, I talked with the Bears' trainer, Ed Rozy. He is a grizzled Walter Brennan type who has been with the Bears for twenty-two years. "I'd say Gale's 99 percent now," Rozy said. "The big thing to overcome is the mental attitude, the subconscious feeling—is it or isn't it? See, he's got to believe it, it's got to be proven to him. Better than that, he's got to prove it to himself. That's why he had to go right out that first day in camp and scrimmage and try to get it over with."

Rozy talked with admiration about Sayers' dedication. At Rensselaer, Sayers would come down to the basement at 8 A.M. each day. He would take a whirlpool bath for ten minutes to loosen up the knee, then go into the weight room and lift sixty pounds on the knee, lift those sixty pounds fifty times. Morning and night he would be down there lifting. "That's the mark of a champion," Rozy said. "The guy never quit on himself."

Rozy talked abstractedly about the injury. "It was a beautiful shot," he said of the film clip and still photo of the injury. "It shows Gale planting his foot with pressure applied to the outside of the leg. A beautiful shot," Rozy repeated, as if he were admiring a Picasso painting.

Sayers himself saw little beauty in the shot. One night last March he brought home the Bears' 1968 highlight film to show some friends, including his teammates George Seals and Frank Cornish. When the film came to the injury—the first time Sayers had seen it, Seals hollered in jest, "Get up! Get up!" And a chill, almost like an electric shock went through Sayers' body. After the guests had gone, he told his wife, Linda, "I'm never gonna look at that film again as long as I live." A couple of days later when he had to show the film to a group, he left the room just before the injury sequence. Eventually, he got over it, said to himself, the hell with it, and stayed and watched.

It was, no doubt, the most traumatic moment of his life. The Bears were at home and, in the second quarter, held a comfortable 24–6 lead over the 49ers in the ninth game of the season. Sayers had gained 32 yards in ten carries. That gave him 856 yards rushing for the season so far, well ahead of all the NFL runners; he seemed on his way to the best year of his career, perhaps a record-breaking year.

In the huddle, quarterback Virgil Carter called for a toss to Sayers. Gale broke left, hoping to go outside the defense behind the blocking of tackle Randy Jackson. The 49ers' right linebacker, Harold Hays, began to string along the line, keeping his hands on Jackson in order to control him and prevent Sayers from breaking to the outside. Right cornerback Kermit Alexander, who also had the responsibility of turning the play inside, was trying to strip his blocker. Hays was controlling Jackson and defensive tackle Kevin Hardy was barreling down the line toward Sayers. So Gale knew he couldn't go wide and he tried to slip inside the blocker, as he often does.

At the instant he planted his foot, Alexander hit him with a low, rolling block. The cleats of Sayers' right shoe were anchored in the turf, preventing give and the knee took the full shock of the blow.

Sayers knew immediately that the knee was gone. He thinks he turned to Alexander, who was standing over him, and said, "It's gone." He remembers motioning to the bench to come and get him and putting his arms around a couple of the Bear players. Then he passed out.

He came to as he reached the sidelines. Dr. Fox was there. "It's gone, Doc, " Sayers said.

Dr. Fox checked the knee, "It's okay," he said, and started to walk away.

"Come back here!" Sayers screamed. "Tell it to me straight."

Dr. Fox looked at Sayers for a moment, then said, "Yes, you have torn ligaments in your knee."

At that moment, Sayers felt an overwhelming sense of loss, also of self-pity. He asked himself, why me, why did it have to be me? And he began to cry.

He was operated on late that afternoon. The quicker the surgeon can get in there, the better job he can do. "You wait twenty-four hours after one of those things," Dr. Fox said, "and the injury is like a bag of mush. It really would be like trying to stitch together two bags of cornmeal mush."

In medical slang, Sayers' injury is called, "The Terrible Triad of O'Donoghue." This describes the tears of the three ligaments in the knee and is named after Dr. Don H. O'Donoghue of the University of Oklahoma, the dean of football physicians. It is a common operation now. The estimate is that there are fifty thousand football victims each year, fifty thousand who require knee surgery.

The operation took three hours and when Sayers came out of it he remembers the doctor saying, everything's okay, and Sayers not believing him. "You wouldn't lie to me? You wouldn't lie to me?" he kept repeating. Linda Sayers was there and she says that Gale actually got up and started screaming to Dr. Fox: "*You wouldn't lie to me?*"

He is much more emotional than has been generally understood. He is much deeper, too. In his first couple of years with the Bears he was very shy, a little frightened, unsure of himself off the field and wary, very wary, of strangers. He began to change about two years ago. Symbolically, he stopped cutting his hair short for football. He wears a natural now and someone wrote him a letter blaming his knee injury on his "long" hair. He became a stockbroker for Paine, Webber, Jackson, and Curtis in the Chicago office. He worked on his public speaking. He began to respond to people, and to the world around him. Recently, Ed McCaskey has helped make a reader of Sayers. McCaskey gave Sayers *The Autobiography of Malcolm X* and Sayers devoured it in three days. In quick succession he read a novel, *Siege*, Eldridge Cleaver's *Soul on Ice*, and the classic Ralph Ellison novel *Invisible Man*. All are on Negro themes and all seemed meaningful to Sayers. "Something," he says, "keeps you going into books and you don't want to put them down." He seemed to relate most to Malcolm X. "He was a drug addict for so many years and got out of it," Sayers said. "I believe he could do anything he wanted."

He admires people like that, people who can overcome. He is that way himself. In his rookie year, he would vomit before every game. Finally, he decided he had to stop, that he was using up too much nervous energy. "I would go out of the dressing room," he said, "tired, beat." So he started talking to other players, thinking of other things and he disciplined himself to stop vomiting.

Now the discipline, the fight, concerns the knee. He rested in his Washington motel room an hour before the team dinner, which would be followed by the ankle taping and then the bus ride to Robert F. Kennedy Stadium and a football game. The television set was on. The Baltimore Orioles were playing the Oakland Athletics and Sayers watched idly. And as he watched, the question was slipped to him:

"Do you think about the knee?"

"I think about it," he said. "I never stop thinking about it. When I'm in my room listening to records, I think about it. Every day a thought about it goes through my mind. I know it's fine, but I think about it."

He has considered seriously about going to a hypnotist. "I remember Don Newcombe went to one about his fear of flying. If I knew of a hypnotist in Chicago, I would probably go to one." But then he said he was not sure that he was the type to be hypnotized.

His mind was a jumble of emotion. He thought of an old teammate, Andy Livingston, who had hurt a knee against the Packers a couple of years ago, and was never the same again. But he also thought of the old Bear halfback, Willie Galimore, who had survived two knee operations and come back fine (only to die in an automobile crash); and of Tommy Mason, who has had six knee operations and still plays. Gale blamed the failures on human weaknesses. "They didn't work at it," he said. "I worked at it." He groped for words. Finally, words came. "I consider this my game. A damn injury like that is not going to keep me out of it."

Looking at Sayers in the Bear dressing room deep beneath RFK Stadium, the strong statement he had made a few hours earlier seemed remote and irrelevant. He sat slumped in front of his locker. It was five minutes to seven and he would have to go out on the field for pregame drill in fifteen minutes. He was wearing his cleats, his white game pants with the orange piping down the side, and a white T-shirt. He sat on a folding chair in front of his locker. He was bent over. His head was bowed, his eyes were closed. He was leaning on his elbows, holding his head in his hands, his two thumbs resting between his eyes. He sat there quiet as stone, as if in a trance. He was unapproachable.

George Seals, the 265-pound offensive guard, the man Sayers had ridden behind for so many of his long-gainers, was dressing in a corner. A close friend of Sayers, he was asked whether he felt any extra pressure to protect Sayers because of the knee. Seals shook his head. "To me," he said, "that would be conceding something. Football is a very emotional game. When you step out onto that field, you cannot concede a thing. Gale certainly wouldn't want it that way."

Seals, who had his own knee operation last March and was still far from being 100 percent, was with Sayers when the cast was removed from Sayers' leg. He was astonished to see that there was very little atrophy in the leg. "He's not human," Seals said. "After he got that cast off, he'd go out in the afternoon, morning, every night, doing things constantly. Many athletes come back from knee injuries lacking quite a bit. I feel if Sayers comes back, he'll be the one that comes back all the way."

And still Sayers sat there, bent over, trancelike, almost in the fetal position. Bennie McRae, the Bears' veteran defensive back, came over, leaned down, and whispered to Sayers: "Are you ready, man?" Sayers nodded. "You all right? You're gonna be all right," McRae said soothingly. "You're ready, I know you're ready." He put an arm on Sayers' shoulder. "Hang loose." Sayers nodded again. McRae drifted away and Sayers remained cast in stone.

I was thinking various things. I was thinking about the knee ... how it happened, could it happen again, how would it hold up ... hoping I could make it through the game. That's the mental torture of football and I think this is going to afflict me as long as I play this game.

Finally, it was 7:10 and the players started out. Backfield coach Ed Cody came close to Sayers and said, "About a minute, Gale."

Sayers shook himself, rose, slipped on his white jersey with the big navy-blue numerals, 40, picked up his helmet, and clattered out of the room.

As you come through the runway leading up to the field, a distorted sound hits you, an eerie sound, like a piece of heavy machinery sucking out air. It is only when you get through the runway and hit the dugout that you finally recognize the sound — it is the roar of the crowd.

It was a stifling night. The temperature was in the eighties, there was no breeze stirring and the humidity menaced the soul. The weather forecast was for scattered thundershowers, but the clouds in that Washington twilight looked benevolent.

Sayers was throwing left-handed with Ronnie Bull, he and Bull trotting up and down the field exchanging passes. Then the Washington Redskin players poured out of their dugout and milled around the entrance. Sam Huff was leading them. He stood there, waiting for them all to come out before leading the charge across the field. "Everyone up?" he asked. Vince Lombardi, wearing a shortsleeved shirt, black tie, black pants and the look of a bus driver, grew impatient with Huff. "Okay," Lombardi barked, "let's go, let's take 'em." There was joy and exhilaration in his voice as he ran out on the field with his men. Clearly, he was glad to be back in the game.

Sayers, taking part in a passing drill, caught a short pass and ran by Lombardi. The Redskin coach stopped him. They shook hands. "I'm very glad to see that you've overcome your injury," Lombardi said. Sayers mumbled his thanks.

Sayers remembered meeting Lombardi in Commissioner Pete Rozelle's office in New York last spring, the spring of his recuperation, the spring of his anxieties. Lombardi said to Sayers, "How do you feel, son? I hope to see you out there this fall." And Sayers said, "You'll see me August 2." And so he had.

Now it was 7:30 and two Bear players started the kicking drill. The punts came out of the sky like fireworks, except that the boom was heard first, then the ball was seen soaring in the air. Sayers caught the first punt and ran it back fifteen yards, crouched, darting, making the moves that had thrilled people for the last four years. He caught another punt, then a third, and a fourth. Then he was in another pass drill. He went down and out, toward the Redskin side of the field, taking a long pass over his shoulder. Two skinny Redskin kids, Number 5 and Number 3, the field-goal kickers, were together when he went by. They looked at Sayers, then turned to say something to each other, gossiping like a couple of old maids at a soda fountain.

Finally, the drill was over and the Bears returned to the dressing room to put on their shoulder pads and wait for the start.

It had been raining for five minutes when the teams lined up for the kickoff, a hard, slanting rain with thunder and lightning and a rising wind. The field, especially the skin part, the Washington Senators' infield, was already filling up with puddles.

The Bears were the receiving team. Gale Sayers was deep, at his 5-yard line, with Ross Montgomery stationed just in front of him. Just as the kicker moved forward, Sayers hollered to Montgomery to deploy right. Sayers, who captains the kick and punt return team, always tells the other deep back where to go. The idea is for Sayers to cover three-quarters of the field, to make sure that he gets the football.

He got the football. He took it easily on his 6-yard line and started straight up the middle. One man broke through the wedge and came on to challenge Sayers. "I feel I can always beat any man one-on-one," Sayers has said, "and two-on-one I can beat 75 percent of the time." Sayers gave the one man his inside move, a head and shoulder fake, and the man was out of it and Sayers was flashing to the right, toward the sidelines.

"The thing that makes Gale different," Brian Piccolo had said earlier, "is the way he's able to put a move on somebody and not lose a step. He gives a guy a little fake and he's full speed. I give a guy a move like that and it takes me fifteen yards to get in stride."

Sayers was in full stride now, streaking down the sidelines. Two Washington defensive backs angled in on him around the Redskin 40. One lunged at him and Sayers just pushed him away with his left arm. The other threw himself at Sayers, jostling him momentarily. But Sayers kept his feet, regained control and sped triumphantly into the end zone. There was a purity, a shining purity to that run, that contrasted in a strange and rather beautiful way with the indecent weather and the spongy field. The first time he had carried the ball in combat since his knee injury, which was the worst kind of a knee injury you can have, he had broken one. It was as if all the questions had been answered, all the doubts resolved about the condition of Gale Sayers. It was an illusion, of course; it was much too early to form a judgment on Sayers' recovery. But the illusion was heightened by the clap of thunder that accompanied Sayers' last step into the end zone.

One illusion was, however, quickly dispelled. It was not a touchdown after all. The referee ruled that Sayers had stepped out of bounds on the Redskin 25. Sayers said later that he could not see the sideline markers because they had been obscured by the rain. But it was still a 69-yard run and surely it held some meaning for Gale Sayers, for the Chicago Bears—and maybe for those fifty thousand players who fall victim to a knee injury every year.

And that was all there was to the game, really. Later, the Bear coaches had to throw out the films of the game because nothing could be seen. After the Sayers run the rain intensified and the entire first half was played in a blinding cloudburst that ruined the field and left the players dispirited. The Redskins won 13–7. Sayers came out on the field twelve times, but carried the ball only once more. Dick Butkus took a short kickoff and lateraled to Sayers who piled 17 yards up the middle before he was pulled down in the glop.

The next morning Sayers was eating breakfast at 7:15. He had hardly slept that night. He says it usually takes him a day and a half to unwind after a game. He ordered ham and eggs but ate sparingly.

He listened while a friend read accounts of the game from the Washington morning newspapers. Sayers, it seemed, had almost gotten equal play with the Redskins. One story began this way: "It took the sellout crowd of 45,988 at RFK Stadium last night only a matter of seconds to see for themselves that Gale Sayers is as good as ever. . . ."

He grinned when he heard that. He thought it was true and now he felt more assured because he had passed the first test. After months of hard work, months filled with doubt and pain and the mental torture that only a knee victim can understand, he had passed his first test. He knew it was only a beginning, but it was a good beginning.

As Don Smith acknowledges in this article, the basis for dethroning John Brallier as the first pro football player is a research paper on the origins of the game by one "Nelson Ross": the quotation marks surround that name because nobody really knows who he was. One day in the early 1960s a man walked into the office of Pittsburgh Steeler executive Dan Rooney clutching a package. He hastily introduced himself, plunked down his forty-nine-page manuscript, then walked out. Rooney, distracted at the time, didn't realize until later what a bombshell he had been handed; by then he could only remember that the man's name was "Nelson Ross, or Ross Nelson, or something like that." The manuscript has gone on to the Hall of Fame but "Nelson Ross" has not been heard from since.

DONALD R. SMITH

The First Pro

Check out almost any history on professional football and, nine times out of ten, you will find John Brallier listed as the world's first professional football player.

Back in 1895, sixteen-year-old John Brallier was induced to quarterback the Latrobe, Pa., YMCA team against nearby Jeannette, Pa. For agreeing to play, the erstwhile signal-caller of the Washington and Jefferson College team was to receive the princely sum of ten dollars and "cakes"—in modern jargon, expenses.

Some say the game was played on September 3, 1895—most report it was on August 31. Some write that Latrobe won, 6–0—others say the score was 12–0. But on Brallier's financial involvement, all historians agree.

Ever since the Pleistocene Age of professional football, this has been the "establishment" version of how it all began. Even the Professional Football Hall of Fame in Canton, Ohio, devotes a large space in its exhibition rotunda to commemorate that historic "first."

Now wipe the slate clean and start anew.

Based on more recent material gathered, ironically, by the Pro Football Hall of Fame and its first director, the late Dick McCann, it now is certain that Brallier, instead of being No. 1, was actually No. 7 or even lower on the list of those who first "tainted" themselves by accepting cash for playing football.

1890's Football

EMPHASIZED KICKING, MASS PLAYS, AND BRUTALITY.

A FIELD GOAL COUNTED FIVE POINTS WHILE TOUCHDOWNS WERE WORTH ONLY FOUR DURING MOST OF THE PERIOD.

THE FORWARD PASS WAS ILLEGAL. THE BIGGEST OFFENSIVE INNOVATION WAS THE "FLYING WEDGE."

SLUGGING WAS COMMON, BUT MOST INJURIES OCCURRED WHEN PLAYERS WERE TRAMPLED BY THE HERD.

THE FOOTBALL — REALLY A RUGBY BALL — LOOKED LIKE A LEATHER WATERMELON. THOUGH HARD TO HOLD ON TO, IT WAS PERFECT FOR KICKING.

THE MOST POPULAR "HELMET" WAS LONG HAIR. "PADS" DEPENDED ON HOW WELL A PLAYER HAD BEEN EATING.

As accurately as can be determined, the list of *known* pro pioneers should read like this:

1. Willaim (Pudge) Heffelfinger, Allegheny Athletic Association of Pittsburgh, Pa., $500 for one game, November 12, 1892.

2. Ben (Sport) Donnelly, Allegheny Athletic Association, $250 for one game, November 19, 1892.

3-4-5. Wright, Van Cleve, and Rafferty (first names not available), Allegheny Athletic Association, $50 per game (under contract) for the entire 1893 season.

6. Lawson Fiscus, Greensburg, Pa., $20 per game and expenses for the entire 1894 season.

7. John Brallier, Latrobe, Pa., YMCA, $10 and expenses for one game, August 31, 1895.

As a youthful member of the Brallier clan said recently on a visit to the Pro Football Hall of Fame when informed that his famous forefather really wasn't No. 1: "You'll have to prove it to me!"

For openers, let's start with a meticulous forty-nine-page paper written by researcher Nelson Ross, who describes in detail the events leading up to the confrontation of the Allegheny Athletic Association (AAA) and the Pittsburgh Athletic Club (PAC) football teams in November, 1892.

The AAA team, formed in 1890, and the PAC, started in 1891, were already heated rivals when they struggled to a 6–6 deadlock early in the 1892 season. Adding fuel to the fire was the AAA claim that the PAC's top player and coach, William Kirschner, was a professional because, as a paid instructor for the PAC, his salary went up and his class load down during football season. With controversy raging and interest mounting, both sides began to explore methods of beefing up their squads for the return match.

To fully describe the situation, the story must now shift elsewhere. "Back East" the practice of the time was for many leading AAU grid clubs to reward their stars with expensive trophies (which they could sell) or with expense money (usually far in excess of actual expenses). The trophy arrangement had been tabooed by the AAU, but the expense money policy was allowed to continue.

"Out West," the Chicago Athletic Association team formed in 1892 adopted the "usual double expense money" practice and as a result, had trouble scheduling games in the "Windy City" with college or "pure amateur" clubs.

One of the Chicago stars was Heffelfinger, who had been an All-America guard at Yale in 1889, 1890, and 1891. He was America's biggest football name at the beginning of the Gay Nineties. In 1892, he was a low-salaried railroad office employee in Omaha, Nebraska, but he was granted a leave of absence so that he could join the Chicago team on a six-game tour of the east. According to Chicago newspaper reports, the only consideration to Heffelfinger would be "the usual expenses arrangement."

Meanwhile back in Pittsburgh, Kirschner had been sidelined with an injury and the PAC manager, George Barbour, decided to scout the Chicago team in Cleveland in the opening game of its eastern tour. Chicago defeated the Cleveland Athletic Association, 29–0, and Heffelfinger had a great game. Barbour was convinced that Pudge would make an ideal replacement for Kirschner.

The Pittsburgh Press on October 30, 1892, reported: *A very improbable sort of a story is being circulated at present about the PAC offering Heffelfinger and Ames of the Chicago football team $250 to play with the East End team on Saturday, November 12, against the AAA."*

Thus alerted, the AAA did a little missionary work on its own. On contacting Chicago players in New York after the final game of their tour, AAA representatives found (1) that Ames had decided against risking his amateur status, (2) that Donnelly and another player named Malley would be willing to play for the usual double expense money and (3) that Heffelfinger had decided not to risk his amateur standing for a mere $250.

Thus, in effect, pro football had its first "holdout" even before it had its first pro. For it developed that, for $500, Heffelfinger would play. AAA representatives, eager to outdo their PAC rivals, agreed.

Was it worth it to the AAA? Victory was the goal, so the answer must be "yes." Heffelfinger, who played left guard, scored the game's only touchdown on a 25-yard fumble return following one of his patented bone-jarring tackles. Touchdowns were worth four points in 1892 so the AAA won, 4–0. Financially, the AAA netted $621.00 on the game, in spite of the "bonus" payoff to Heffelfinger, and expense payments of $25.00 each to Heffelfinger, Donnelly, and Malley.

The Ross paper goes on to report that Donnelly was paid $250 to play the following week and that the AAA had at least three players under regular contract in 1893. Although it names no names, the report says the PAC did the same thing in 1893.

McCann as early as 1963 sought to confirm the findings in Ross's "white paper." Confirmation came in the form of a yellowed and parched expense sheet of the Allegheny Athletic Association, signed by manager O. D. Thompson and detailing expenses of several AAA games in 1892 and 1893. Every detail checks out exactly with the Ross report.

As for Fiscus, the "History of Greensburg, Pa.," published in 1949, recalls the great town teams of 1892, 1893, and 1894 and innocently states: "Except for one or two players, these organizations were strictly amateur." Fiscus himself admitted that he played for expenses only in 1893 and then for $20 and expenses each game in 1894.

So now we are back to Latrobe and August 31, 1895. There are those who will insist that this was the first pro *game*, implying that everyone was paid to play. Even the National Football League guide, in its official chronology, makes this notation.

Logic seems to refute this theory. For under those circumstances, there would have been no reason to make such a fuss over Brallier, if he were merely one of thirty or so players in the game who were paid.

The noted football historian, Vernon C. Berry of Latrobe, says his town's first all-pro team came in 1897. He should know for his brother, newspaper publisher David J. Berry, organized the original Latrobe team.

Undoubtedly there were more early-day "pros" whose names may never be known. It also might be argued that those earlier AAU players who received trophies and/or expenses were in reality the first professionals.

But on the basis of what is now known, Heffelfinger must rank as the first person to openly accept payment for playing. And in this first pro venture, he still received his heavy expense allowance.

As for Brallier, it might be said in jest that, through all these years, he simply had a better publicity man. His "publicity" was so good, in fact, that in 1946 the NFL, on the assumption that Latrobe was the true "birthplace of professional football," actually gave preliminary approval to that city as the site for a future Pro Football Hall of Fame.

Now the evidence contradicts all the earlier theories.

And it also looks as though the Pro Football Hall of Fame will have to make a few alterations in its "First Game" display!

Here's a tale of three kickers whose best of times came in the Southwest Conference, their worst of times in the NFL. Although a few field-goal specialists have had phenomenally durable careers, for most the stay is that of a mayfly: the leg long retains its power but pressure soon shrivels the nerve. This sobering story of how Tony Franklin, Russell Erxleben, and Steve Little dealt with that pressure may give us pause before next we are inclined to boo.

GARY SMITH

The Snapping Point

"There are twenty-two guys locked in a feud. Sometimes they can't settle it. So they call on the hit man. He fires that one shot nobody else will. He makes it, or misses and takes the blame from everybody else.

"You can tell a hit man just by looking at him. His walk is a hard strut. His posture is that of a man who knows he will do it. And his eyes are Roberto Duran eyes. Charles Manson eyes. Very few men were born to be hit men."

— BENNY RICARDO, Saints' kicker

"We found kickers to be completely unique from other NFL players. Incredibly exhibitionistic, much more independent, and having a strong need for external rewards. A quarterback can complete 55 percent and get accolades. But 70,000 people expect perfection on demand from the kicker. Often the torment of their teammates hurts them more than the fans' torment. As slight men in a world of giants, they are treated as childlike. They get put down with negative nicknames.

"Many overreact to failure and rejection. They seek some form of temporary relief: drugs, booze, ladies. The judgment on them is always immediate: heel or hero. How many human beings can handle that kind of pressure?"

— BRUCE OGILVIE, sports psychologist

AUTUMN, 1977, A SATURDAY.

Stab a map, just north of Dallas, with a pencil compass and sweep the lead in a 500-mile circle. You have just surrounded the three most acclaimed college kickers of all time.

More than just a quirk of geography and time has called them to the same circle. The Southwest Conference has always been a kickers' hive, for the air here is warm, the ball alive, and little boys who grow up in Texas learn to do everything with a football except put it away for summer.

Gametime: 1 P.M. Showtime: noon. At three different stadiums the scene is the same. The same people who stare through airport windows have come early, just to stare at Steve Little, Russell Erxleben, and Tony Franklin.

Little, the handsome kid from the University of Arkansas, digs his size-7 shoe into a 40-yard field goal and the ball climbs over the goalposts, over the net . . . and over the three-story Frank Broyles Complex at the end of the stadium. The ball does a jig on the roof and the awe ruptures in ooohs. "I used to love the ooohs," says Little.

Due southwest, Russell Erxleben of the University of Texas has just finished swatting 50-yard field goals and a series of long, arching punts that cut the sky like a bird with its wings tucked. "I even used to tell my holder what side of the uprights I was going to put it through," says Erxleben.

At Texas A&M, Tony Franklin has just scuttled to the 40-yard line and turned to face the end of the field where the other team warms up, mischief curled all over his mouth. They hear the whump of bare foot ripping into leather, look overhead, and cringe.

Then they turn and scowl at the little man. "I never even had what you'd call a slump," says Franklin.

Life is grand, a leg snap and a fist in the air. The three of them coax the best from each other. They flash 65- and 67-yard messages to one another on Saturday afternoons and drink beer with pretty women on Saturday nights.

Within two years the NFL drafts them as high as or higher than kickers have ever been drafted. The pros put cash on every snap of their leg. They take away their tees that made it easy to get under the ball and drive it into the sky. They take away the week-old practice balls Erxleben and Little sometimes used in games. They slash the target area from 23⅓ feet wide to 18½ feet. They ask them to do it in ice and wind and raw cold, against special teams that spend hours practicing to snuff them.

The position they knew becomes a mystery and the storylines shift. For nothing stabs so straight at what is weak in a man, and bleeds it so pale, as kicking in the NFL.

I. TONY FRANKLIN

"Tony Franklin has an ungodly leg, the best in the league. I hope he doesn't ruin it with his attitude. I tried to like him—I couldn't. I put up a case of beer every time we

play the Eagles, for anybody who puts him out of the game. Not hurt him—just put
him out."

— RUSSELL ERXLEBEN

"I hate Tony Franklin. He had to go barefoot just to get recognition. He thought he
was hot stuff."

— STEVE LITTLE

The speedometer said 75 and the driver said *sheeeeyeet*. A white Toyota was using
Tony Franklin's personal lane, the farthest one left on Interstate 95.

The Toyota didn't surrender. Franklin cut to the center lane and passed, but you
could see that compromise hurt. Vet Stadium went by the window and Franklin looked
twice. "We *did* have off today, didn't we? I *think* Dick said we did."

Dick had, and the streak continued. The 1981 season was almost half over and Vermeil and Franklin hadn't scraped fenders yet.

An impish grin spread over Tony Franklin's cousin's face. David Wood was remembering the time he and Tony noticed a hitchhiker and slowed in the right lane. Tony
stuck his head out the window and hollered, "Need a lift?" "Yeah," said the hitchhiker.
"Then stick a jack up your ass," hollered Tony, as they peeled away.

A knowing grin spread over Tony Franklin's professor's face. "If you don't really
know Tony Franklin," said Jerry Elledge, a close friend of Franklin's at Texas A&M,
"he'll piss you off just like that. You'll say, 'I'm going to knock that little turd's butt
off.' He's actually a hell of a nice guy. He's got a hell of a mouth, but the strange thing
is, he can back most of it up. As long as he does, he's fine. The moment he can't. . . .' "

A man who grew up on a farm watched Franklin function in the Eagle locker room
for fifteen minutes Tony's rookie year and knew where he'd seen it all before. A bantam rooster on a recruiting mission, he called him. It's in the way Franklin walks, talks,
drives, the way he wears no shirt under a denim jacket in late November, the way he
bounces from player to ballboy to trainer in practice, telling off-color jokes, blowing
bubbles, knocking hats off people and stepping on them. He does not mean harm, but
five-foot-eight Texans are expected to remember there are six-foot-four Texans.

The Eagles could live with a bantam rooster under their feet as long as he could steer
a football through two sticks from 50 yards away. The boys did decorate his locker with
hot-dog wrappers, a blowup Oscar Mayer doll that had Franklin's No. 1 on the back
and a huge plastic bottle of French's mustard, and blasted the locker-room stereo system
with "I wish I were an Oscar Mayer weiner"—a blues version, jazz version, country
version, even Spanish and French versions. "Just a subtle hint, nothing too strong," said
Ron Jaworski.

Franklin ripped down the decorations and stomped away. A mistake. "On this team,"
said special-teams coach Lynn Stiles, "if you can't take a joke, you *become* one."

He was homesick and single and in a large northern city for the first time. There was too much nervous energy ripping through him to stay home, and he'd never asked for any help or any water with his Jack Daniel's. He snapped on his hat, veered to the left lane, and he and his black Corvette became part of the night.

The reports came in, sometimes just a few hours later than Tony. The Eagle coaching staff got calls from a man who threatened to take care of Franklin if the team didn't keep him away from the man's wife. Tony couldn't win. "He politely refused a woman once," a friend said, "and she felt so scorned that she told her husband Franklin was coming on to her, and the husband got all hot."

He made 23 of 31 field-goal tries that 1979 rookie year, including a 59-yarder against Dallas that was the second-longest in league history, and Vermeil held his terrible swift tongue. Then, in the playoff finale against Tampa Bay, Franklin tried an onside kick when Vermeil had called for a deep kickoff and The Little Dictator took his teeth out of the way of his tongue.

Franklin's intentions were good—he'd seen a seam in the Tampa Bay kick-return deployment—but the relationship with his coach was doomed anyway. Vermeil once ran sixteen miles to raise money for a charity. Franklin once ran sixty feet through a Pizza Hut wearing nothing but a ski mask. Vermeil fined him $1,600 for the kickoff. "It's tax deductible anyway," touchéd Tony.

Next season came the moment Tony Franklin's professor worried about. *The moment he can't.* . . . Franklin missed three field goals in San Diego and the Eagles lost by a point. "He came in sick, but that's no damn excuse," Vermeil fumed. He missed two short ones against St. Louis but the Eagles won anyway. He missed three against Dallas and they lost by eight. "I hope he grew up today," Vermeil stewed, "but if he didn't, he won't be kicking in this league anymore." He had three field goals blocked in the playoffs, with some help from blocking breakdowns. He crashed from fifth to twenty-sixth in an NFL kicking rating, missing 15 of 31, and at the depth of his confusion he even missed the warmup net from a few feet away on the sideline. Instead of just his right foot, all of Tony Franklin felt naked.

"I dreaded going on the field," said Franklin. "I knew if I missed I'd get ripped. I had rabbit ears, I let the jeers and boos get to me. I lost my confidence. I'd never been through a real slump before. Missing three against Dallas was the low point. My last kick, Vermeil said, 'Just relax, you can't kick any worse.'"

Franklin lay down in the backseat of a friend's car that night and didn't speak for hours. Nobody wanted to hear about the limited practice time he was getting because of a foot injury from the final exhibition game, or the emotional upheaval over his brother's successful battle with cancer of the bone marrow. Except for family and a few close friends the fight was Franklin's alone.

"He'd drive from the locker room to the practice field alone, and be the first guy out of the locker room after practice," said Jaworski. "One day it was 10° and we're out there practicing, freezing our butts off, and Tony shows up late and stands on the sideline drinking coffee, talking with an owner of Bookbinders' restaurant. I can't tell you all the stories of players who tried to take him aside to cool his act. In Oakland, maybe he'd have been perfect, but on this team — no way."

"Bloodshot eyes? Are you kidding?" said Lynn Stiles. "We had several incidents that made it look like Tony Franklin was about to self-destruct. On game days, he thought he'd perform; the rest of the week he'd just tolerate. He missed meetings and got fined. Nobody on this team was bowing down to him and he didn't understand it."

There were four phases to Vermeil's offseason strategy. First he tried to trade Franklin. "If I'd have been offered a fourth-rounder," said Vermeil, "he'd have gone." He blistered Franklin's ears in a personal conference, openly criticized his maturity in the press, and drafted a kicker on the seventh round.

Now the whole tone of the conflict had changed. Vermeil could chew Franklin or his paycheck in private and the bantam rooster could still continue about his mission. But machismo is more appearance than substance, and that's where Vermeil had aimed his desperation blow.

"Vermeil had Tony believing he wasn't any good," said Jerry Elledge, "and I didn't think *anybody* could do that."

Deep inside, rejection stung Tony Franklin more than he had ever let the world guess. A neighbor's child once refused to let him join his club. Franklin: "I set fire to his clubhouse, burnt that mother down."

He staked out his space in junior high with his fists. He widened it in high school with his foot. He was one of the least affluent members of his suburban Fort Worth school and spent hour after hour smiting footballs so no one would have an excuse to turn a nose up at him. Franklin: "Now a lot of those rich kids are driving trucks and I'm making pretty good money, and I'm laughing my ass off at them."

Physically, he matured earlier than most of his peers, and then in junior high they all grew by him. The bigger they got, the bigger he carried himself.

"Deep-seated, a lot of that macho stuff is to make up for size," said high-school friend Don Grantham. "He was always the smallest in any group he ever hung out with. Tony was so busy keeping his front up, he made people mad at him without meaning to. He's just a nice, normal guy when you get him one-on-one."

A hot temper was waiting for him when he was born; both parents had red hair. "I always told him he was No. 1," his mother Joyce said. Speck, who worked at a water-treatment plant, whistled to Tony when he wanted him to throw a curveball, and became his son's only kicking coach. Tony was the oldest child in a tough three-boy family that could turn a game of Crazy Eights into a civil war, but God have mercy on the first outsider who kibitzed.

He went barefoot everywhere; it would have been unnatural to kick in shoes. David Wood and he would kick over the swing set in his cousin's backyard, using a shoe for a tee and crying out "Stenerud style!" when they tried it soccer-style. Franklin kicked with a sock all through high school and then, during a practice in a downpour his freshman year at A&M, wearied of wringing it out and left the foot naked. *I'll be damned:* The ball went even farther.

"But I think A&M hurt him in some ways," said Merlin Priddy, his high school coach. "Hell, he all but had his own valet there. They let him be separate from the team. He came on the field separate before the game, then he had his own separate writeup every game.

"Right off he was a sensation, and he never recognized he wasn't something A&M wouldn't live and die with. If Vermeil had known what had happened to him in college, I don't know if they'd have even drafted him. Tony *needed* to go to the well a few times and come up with a dry bucket."

Franklin kicked a 64- and a 65-yarder the same day, torched eighteen NCAA records and began noticing that when people met him they looked at his foot before they looked at him. Was it any surprise, when the first dry bucket came up in 1980, that Franklin's self-image was shattered? "I always thought he had plenty of confidence," his father said. "But maybe underneath it all, he's just a scared little boy."

"The writers up here are a bunch of nerds."

The voice came from somewhere around a corner and behind a bathroom door. Sally is small, good-looking, and feisty; in short, a perfect addition to the Franklin clan. They married last offseason. She is Dick Vermeil's secret weapon in his crusade to salvage Tony Franklin, the force he counts on to keep the ungodly leg stretched in front of a TV set at night and 65 percent accurate by day.

They met in Human Diseases class his senior year. "She walked in in tight jeans and I said, 'Holy Mackeroooola,'" said Franklin. He offered her a ride home one day, refused to let her out of the car, detoured her to the bank and chiropractor, accompanied her to class and sat through the film of a natural childbirth when what he really wanted to do was be sick. Sally was impressed. He took her to one of his favorite dives that night, nearly got in a fight with a six-foot-six drunk who didn't believe he was Tony Franklin and told Sally to hide behind the bar until he was through with him. Sally was *real* impressed. "I realized," she said, "he was misunderstood."

She realizes she is one of the few who gets a glimpse of the good-hearted person her husband basically is. "He did drink a lot," she admitted, "but I put a stop to it."

"I drank Jack Daniel's like it was ice water," Franklin said. "It became a weight problem."

"The press here made Tony out to be a hot dog, out on the town all night chasing women. I know he went to bars, but so what? Tony bowls until 1 A.M. and I fall asleep watching him, that's what a swinger Tony Franklin is."

"They could write what they wanted about me, but when it made my wife cry, that's when I got pissed," Franklin said. "I wish I had half the time to do what they said I did at night. But if you worried about what people said about you, you'd go stark-raving mad."

Tony went stark-raving mad. He reported to camp in 1981 bent on shutting mouths, and if it took shutting his own, so be it. He blew away the opposition, nodded to all the coaches, mingled more with his teammates and drilled 18 of his first 20 field-goal tries in exhibitions and the first part of the season.

"I learned how to handle myself as a professional," he said. "I may have taken my ability for granted last year. I came to camp in good shape and didn't let the press or coaches get to me. I decided to abide by the rules laid down. I just stay as far away from Vermeil as I can, and he hasn't messed with me this year. I'm still bitter about the things that were said. But last year is dead. Bury that sonofabitch.

"Marriage has helped a lot. There was a helluva void, but now there's somebody to come home to and bounce things off . . . instead of my fist. She's a strong woman, and it's nice to have somebody to draw strength from."

"He's much more mature this year," said Jaworski. "Now Tony Franklin has a lot of friends on this team."

The first test came November 1 against Dallas, when Franklin hooked a 34-yarder with 1:51 left and the Eagles lost by three. "I was scared that night, he was so depressed," said Sally. "He was saying he just doesn't have it anymore."

He slouched into Dick Vermeil's clubhouse the next day and teammates and coaches told him to forget it. He did not burn that mother down. By afternoon he had self-destruction on hold again and was singing with the radio.

"Maybe I'm naive, maybe it's put on," said Lynn Stiles, "but I like what I'm seeing. Maybe Satan isn't going to have his way with Tony Franklin."

II. RUSSELL ERXLEBEN

"I always liked Russell. He missed some field goals and lost confidence and then he'd go out there thinking more about the ones he missed than the one he was taking. The last time I saw him he seemed a lot like me—more reserved."

—TONY FRANKLIN

"Hell yes, I like Russell. Me and him could always agree on one one thing. He couldn't stand Tony Franklin either."

—STEVE LITTLE

A week in the life of a twenty-three-year-old kicker. . . .

Four seconds left in the 1980 season opener, the Saints trail the 49ers 26–23. Russell Erxleben's 34-yard field-goal try goes wide. Ballgame. As he watches it, agony makes him a child again. He goes belly-down to the floor, buries his face in the artificial grass and flogs it with his fist. The boos come down the aisles and press like a boulder on the small of his back.

He staggers to his locker and breaks down in tears. In a roomful of twenty-inch biceps and forty-nine-inch chests, it is not the wise thing to do. "I'd have rather seen him kick a few benches or pound a few lockers," grumbles a teammate.

He gathers himself and goes out to meet his new bride, who has just seen him play for the first time. Never a football fan, she is bewildered by the hatred in the seats and the red rims around her husband's eyes. "It was scary," Kari said. "He went home and tortured himself with the TV set."

When the news comes on, he clicks from channel to channel to sample the miss and the criticism on all three stations. "When I woke up the next morning," said Kari, "he was listening to some idiotic disc jockey that would ask, 'What do you think of Russell Erxleben's kicking?' and then squeeze one of those laughing bags."

He tells his wife he is going to quit, goes to practice and advises special-teams coach Whitey Campbell to consider finding another kicker. He places the ball on the same spot in practice and makes 20 straight. Then his leg tires and he misses five of the last six. That's all the radio reporter shows up in time to see, and all Russell hears on his ride home.

He stops at a convenience store to buy orange juice. At the counter, he hears a voice behind his neck. "Don't take his money, lady, he hasn't earned it. Let me pay my money. *I earn it.*" Erxleben glares but doesn't respond. The man follows him to his truck. "Fella, I've never been in a fight in my life," Erxleben tells him, "but you might be my first."

He shoves the man down and gets on top of him with a raised fist. The man apologizes, so does Erxleben. "I worried for two weeks about a lawsuit," he said.

A few days later, Russell's sister, Cathy, makes a surprise visit from Texas and finds him asleep. She shakes him again and again, but he doesn't awaken. Then he begins to splutter in his sleep, "Go ahead, boo me, boo me, I don't care."

A few weeks and misses later, he goes to a hypnotist, to a psychiatrist, and to coach Dick Nolan. "I told him, 'Bring someone else in or I'm leaving. I ain't going to take this anymore.' That one kick had ruined me for the rest of the season. My confidence was shattered in everything. Golf, checkers, jacks — anything I touched I felt I'd lose.

"I wished I'd never become a kicker. I didn't feel I was a good person."

The long, thick leg lashed and the foot was suddenly up near Russell Erxleben's blond mustache. One after another the punts left like they were hit by a baseball bat and came down still warm from the Superdome lights. "I don't believe I've ever seen a man kick like that," said Bum Phillips the morning after the October practice.

"I'm the best practice kicker in the world," agreed Erxleben.

He handled just kickoffs and punts in 1981, averaging 40.8 yards through fourteen games, and he was like a man who'd had the noose removed at the last minute but couldn't get the smell of hemp from his nostrils. Call it haunted relief.

"I don't even practice field goals anymore," he confided. "I don't want anything to do with them."

Sandwiched around his punting and kickoff workout each day, he plays four other positions in practice: wide receiver, halfback, quarterback, and center. Let other kickers sip coffee, this is Erxleben's cry for acceptance.

"I would walk in the locker room my rookie year," he said, "and my teammates would just laugh at me."

Chosen eleventh in the 1979 first round, Russell Erxleben was paid highest and drafted second highest of any kicker in NFL history, by a pockmarked franchise with more pressing craters to fill. ("A mistake," Erxleben calls the selection now.) The fan and media greeting was split between suspicion and delirium. One local TV station zoomed in on his foot and proclaimed, "This is the foot that will put the Saints in the Super Bowl."

The expectations combined with the transition were suffocating. People stared holes in his back with every shank. He was quoted in camp as saying he had a ruptured disc. A hasty press conference was called to deny it and a few weeks later the pain in his back was gone. He was quoted as saying he missed his holder and snapper from college — he says he meant he missed them as friends. "I don't even feel like snapping for you anymore," Saint center John Hill snapped at Erxleben.

An illustration appeared in the New Orleans *Times-Picayune* of Erxleben wearing a diaper and sucking his thumb while Dick Nolan held his pacifier and coloring book.

He squibbed a 19-yard punt and botched 32- and 35-yard field goals in his first NFL exhibition. He admitted he was awestruck. "For the first time ever, I felt like I was not allowed to miss a field goal," Erxleben said.

He sent the 1979 season opener into overtime with a last-minute field goal, and then retrieved a bad snap in overtime, heaved it as he was hit in his own end zone and watched the pass become a game-ending TD interception. His nickname was altered from Thunderfoot to Blunderfoot.

A quadricep injury from college recurred in practice before his second game. Just as that healed, the blood vessels in his leg swelled, finishing his season. Doctors called it pseudo-gout and said it might have been from nerves.

Meanwhile, his marriage to Ava Elsik, the girl he had dated since junior high, was unraveling. "I'd married her right before training camp. I didn't want to go off by myself. Two weeks later I knew it was all wrong. We weren't friends. She'd get upset if she just saw me talking to a girl outside the locker room. She loved the glamour and I didn't give a damn for it."

Friends say the most crucial thing Ava didn't give Russell was encouragement. By the time his rookie season was gone, Ava was, too.

Blond, tall, thick, good-looking, instantly likable, a hero in Texas — it took Russell Erxleben only a month after he met Kari Hoff to marshal the nerve to ask her for a date. "You better believe he has a fear of rejection," said Kari.

They met after his divorce in June 1980 and he left for camp in July. He told the press he had found religion over the offseason. The season grew closer, the phone bills higher, the need for a pillar stronger. He flew Kari to camp and they were engaged to be married in January. She went home and Russell called her. How about Christmas?

Okay. He called back the same night. How about Thanksgiving? Okay. He called back the next day. How about next month, just before the season opener? Okay, Russell, okay.

"To be really honest," he mused thirteen months later, "I don't know that much about her."

The relationship, nevertheless, seems to be working. Punters make better husbands than placekickers do, and Kari's apathy toward football helps keep her husband's life balanced. She also has replaced Russell's sister Cathy as night watchman for his flickering ego.

"We were so close, I used to take him on my dates to the drive-in," said Cathy. "I'd call him every other night when he was in college. I talked him out of quitting once [just before his junior year, when Erxleben says he became tired of the routine of football]. He's so sensitive to criticism, I'd have to go to him whenever he got down just to tell him how good he is. When he missed three field goals at Boston College [his sophomore year], I knew what he'd be like. I jumped in the car and was there to meet him when the team got back at 4 A.M. There were tears in his eyes — he felt he couldn't do it anymore."

From first grade through high school graduation, his sister's straight-A record was smudged by just one B. Russell, two years younger and the only other child of a kindly small-town Texas postmaster, felt that against such brilliance football was the only way he could stay in the sunshine of his parents' smiles. Football excused his B's and C's. It became the mirror he looked into.

He ran away from home once and made it as far as the corner. When he returned, his parents looked in the suitcase he had packed. They didn't find clothes. They found his football trophies.

The mirror never cracked, because six-foot-four, 219-pound Russell Erxleben overpowered the competition in high school and college. He averaged 44.2 yards punting at Texas and made 49 of 78 field goals, including the record 67-yarder. There were warning signals, though. He once drowned an entire set of golf clubs in the Guadalupe River after a bad round of golf, and he cried when he didn't get the starting quarterback job at the beginning of his junior year in high school. But the failures were always too brief to condition him for the monster that is NFL kicking. His high school coach, Jerry Hopkins, noticed early how criticism affected Russell. "I told all my assistants to leave the boy alone," he said. "I made a point of not yelling at him."

Erxleben considers the years and shakes his head. "I guess everything went too perfect. I thought everything was supposed to be that way. I remember going on the field for field goals in college and we'd actually be laughing. But that got lost somewhere. I think I've ruined it for kickers ever being drafted in the first round.

"If Bum Phillips hadn't come this year, I don't think I'd have played at New Orleans. I just wouldn't have come back. Sometimes I think I'm in a syndrome where I'll never be good here. The people think I'm an ass because of what's been written here. I just wish they could cut me open and see what's inside."

The missed field goals have already performed the incision, but most were too busy with rage to see. The second season still haunts. Erxleben can remember going home to Austin after it ended, to heal, and getting the New Orleans newspapers mailed to him. The compulsion to know what they were saying about him had always been too powerful to ignore. And when what they were saying was bad, he would crumple the sports section and run out the door and not slow for a mile, maybe two, and Kari would go after him on her bicycle to calm him.

And when the self-destructive scream in him stopped and he got back to the house, he would go to his backyard to let the sweat cool him, to the artificial grass he had laid out to simulate the Superdome's where he buried his face. He would stare up at the two goal posts he had planted there, two cold skeptical arms standing there waiting for the day Russell Erxleben wishes he was a placekicker again.

III. STEVE LITTLE

"I think about him all the time—there's hardly a day he doesn't flash through my mind. Our situations were so similar. He had it all together his whole life . . . and then boom. I'd like to have some kind of benefit golf tournament for him."

— RUSSELL ERXLEBEN

"We never got along in college. He told me I'd never be in the same class as a kicker. But you wouldn't wish this on your worst enemy. I'd like to get together a benefit golf tournament for him."

— TONY FRANKLIN

He awakes most days when the daylight is dying. The drapes are drawn and all that comes through is a sickly pale gray that dulls the soul in places only shut-ins and night-shift workers can know. In the dusk of the walls, when his eyes adjust, he can just make out the two Razorback quilts, the plaques from college, the montage of his thrashing footballs at Arkansas. There is nothing on the bedroom walls that says he was ever a St. Louis Cardinal.

In the corner sits a motorized wheelchair that he can't use just now, because there are sores on his buttocks from spending too many hours in it. Moderation was never one of his vices.

As much as possible, the old life-style has been dragged across the void to the new. On the headboard there is a monster of a music box that keeps murmuring music without anyone listening. Near it is an empty glass from yesterday's Jack Daniel's and two empty Miller bottles, one with a terribly long straw sticking out the mouth.

The bed is a water bed, king-size, and on it floats a man who can't move from the top of the chest down.

"'Nother beer, Rip," Steve Little hoots. His attendant at his Little Rock home, George Green, brings back a cold one, sends the straw down its throat and holds it just close enough for Steve to catch it with his mouth. He sucks a third of it away.

"Whoooooooeeeee," he says. "It doesn't take much to get drunk through a straw. I don't know if it's psychological or if it's just that you don't take in as much air that way.

"How 'bout a smoke, Rip."

Rip lights a Marlboro and lays it on Little's lips. "It's weird," says Steve, "but when I smoke one of these, I can feel a tingle in my feet."

"You want something to eat?" asks Rip.

"Nah." Then, to his visitor: "You know, I can't even tell when I'm hungry now. I'd make a great hunger-striker."

On TV, the Rams are playing the Falcons. The camera catches two cheerleaders and then moves away. "Hey, go back to those two babes on the sidelines, goddammit!"

He is asked about the wheelchair, which has a tote bag hanging from the back with "The Kid" stenciled on it. He calls it his Rolls-Royce. "That thing cost $6,000. It *costs* you to get screwed up, man. I'm okay financially [he gets a $2,000-a-month disability pension from the NFL] unless something catastrophic happens—like I break my neck again."

The flip humor comes again and again, because if you feel bad then he'll feel bad and then you'll leave and there'll be nothing but the sickly pale gray and then that will leave, too, and there will be nothing but the night.

"Sunday afternoons," he sighs. "Nothing like it. Drinking beer, watching TV, laying in bed. . . ."

Three days after the car accident, Steve Little woke up in traction. Soon he would have four screws in his head, with a halo brace to coax his crushed spine back into alignment. A tracheotomy would be necessary to clear the congestion from his lungs and he would have to breathe and speak from his diaphragm because the nerve that controlled his chest-wall muscles was dead. Doctors would also have to chip a piece of bone from his hip and fuse that and wire into his neck to support his vertebrae. If the spinal contusion had occurred one-sixteenth of an inch higher, his brother says, Steve Little would have been dead.

Many who knew him considered that the more logical alternative. His entire life had hinged on physical activity—camping, skiing, speed-skating, golfing, kicking, and partying with a ferocity that sometimes frightened his friends. Ten percent of quadriplegics commit suicide.

"About a month after the accident, I thought about suicide," he admitted. "I could go to heaven and walk again. I'd get depressed at night, when I was by myself. I felt so distant, torn apart from the world. When everybody would leave, I'd try to move and couldn't. It's a weird feeling. I could feel myself moving, but I couldn't see anything move. Then I just tried to accept it. God must have some reasons for it. There's always someone who has it worse."

These feelings were rarely — if ever — freed during his ten months in the hospital. Jay Shaw, a unit clerk at Central Baptist Hospital in Little Rock, said Little was the only paralysis victim he'd ever dealt with who never once let out his grief or terror. "Sooner or later they all crack," he said. "With Steve, it was like he was silently gritting his teeth. He'd always be joking."

A difference of opinion exists over how Little has adjusted to a life with just limited movement in his right arm and neck. Some are amazed he is still winging one-liners and partying his way through the night — hey, all right, the same old Steve. And some say the 4 P.M. wakeups and empty Millers are just escapes, that it might have been healthier to hear the wail in the night and then a serious discussion of what he faces.

"Once," he said to me, 'I wish I could hold my head in my hands,'" said Betty Brinkley, a nurse at the hospital. "But most of the time, when someone tried to talk to him about serious things, his goals, he'd turn it into a comic scene. His Cardinal teammates came here and stared at him for what seemed like days. They didn't know what to say until he made the first crack. It became a kind of mechanism. Steve's a jewel, a delightful person. But he still hasn't accepted it. He isn't ready yet to go out into a new crowd. I suggested he organize a kicking clinic and he nixed it right away. People stare. With a celebrity, they stare twice.

"He likes to be No. 1, surrounded by his friends. If he comes into a room and can't establish himself as the center, he'll turn around and leave. He needs to get up in the morning and go to work. He was doing some public-relations work for the Rolling Razorbacks, a wheelchair basketball team, until he got this problem with sores. He's got to take advantage of his great name in this state within the next few years, or people will say, 'Steve Who?'"

Little: "At nights, my eyes close but sometimes my mind won't stop. The beer takes your mind off thinking about it. It's nothing you'd want to get hooked on. It's just something to relax, let my mind take a break.

"Do you feel sad now? You mean, good grief, Charlie Brown? Nah. Crying makes my nose clog."

They hopped in her mother's Mercedes-Benz and pointed the nose at Colorado. When they reached Aspen, a thought struck Cindy Sagely.

"My daddy's going to hang me for running off with you like this," she said.

"He'll get over it," shrugged Steve.

"He'll think you carried me off. He'll tear into you, too. Maybe we should get married."

"Okay," shrugged Steve. At least that's how Steve remembers it happening. And if he had to think an idea over twice, it usually wasn't of much use to Steve Little.

He and Cindy drove into the mountains, looking for a proper place for a wedding. They found a boulder near a waterfall at a spot named Independence Pass, then fetched a minister. And in the summer before his senior year of college, in blue jeans, flannel shirt, and hiking boots, in air on which he could watch the breath of his vows, Steve Little married a pompom girl from the University of Arkansas.

A week before, said his brother, Gene, they weren't seeing each other.

Almost before the vapor of their vows disappeared, there was trouble. "I thought marriage would settle me down," said Little. "Obviously, it didn't." He was a thoroughbred on a football field and a bronco off it, and nobody was going to break Steve Little. He was too good and too good-looking to sign any compromises. Life was like all the mountains he had skied down as a kid when his father was transferred to Norway. Lean your face into it and let 'er ride.

He led his Norwegian Little League team to the European finals. He became an All-American quarterback, defensive back and kicker on a Shawnee Mission South high-school team just outside Kansas City that went 11–0 his senior year and which some rated the best scholastic team in the country. Arkansas coaches camped on his doorstep every Sunday that he returned from visiting another school, to let him know they still loved him, too.

His failures were all trivial; his shock that they could happen to Steve Little was not. He struck out once in a Little League game and fired his bat over the backstop. He quit his high-school basketball team because he wanted to fastbreak and the coach didn't. "A hellacious temper," said Gene. "We'd play fast-pitch baseball in the cellar, and when he'd strike out he'd let the bat fly. It didn't hit me *often*.

"But he'd never really had the heat on him. He could walk through the john and come out smelling like a rose. He was the darling of Arkansas, he never heard a single boo."

Only nine of his seventy-two kickoffs were returned his senior year, his 67-yard field goal tied Erxleben's NCAA record, and his punting average was 44.3. Then the Cardinals drafted him on the first round in 1978 and the world U-turned.

He struggled for trajectory without the use of a tee. Sometimes a whisper would run down the trenches in practice and all the linemen would collapse just as he began to kick. "Want us to get a little lower?" they'd taunt. Sometimes Little would answer with a bullet at one of their faces.

Including exhibition games, the Cardinals lost ten of the first twelve of his pro career. After Shawnee Mission South and Arkansas, it came as culture shock. "Something about me couldn't accept losing," he said. "I couldn't concentrate."

He lost the placekicking job to Jim Bakken his first year and averaged 38 yards punting. His second year he made 10 of 19 field goals, missed 8 PATs and averaged 38.2 a punt. St. Louis was outraged. "He punted once from midfield," said his father, Ron, a fleet sales manager for Caterpillar, "and as soon as the ball started turning end over end in the air, the boos started. It went out of bounds on the 3-yard line."

More and more, the kicker went out and numbed his mind to it. "By then," he said,

"I didn't give a crap about football." Just before his third season, Cardinal coach Jim Hanifan summoned Little to cool the night life he thought was deadening his kicker's skills. They talked and Hanifan asked him to return the next morning at ten. When Little strolled through the office doors at noon, Hanifan realized it might be hopeless. "I'll throw your frigging No. 1 ass out this door!" he screamed into Little's face.

"I was just being me," Steve said. "I wouldn't do anything different. The [Cardinal] coaches can all screw themselves. After the accident Hanifan came to the hospital and said, 'Cindy, I'm sorry, but life must go on.' [Hanifan says he meant no harm, he was just groping for encouraging words under difficult circumstances.] If Cindy'd had a gun, she might have shot him. When he gets fired, I'll send him a letter. 'You're on the streets, Jim, but life goes on.'

"They messed up my mind from the day I got there. First they said I was the punter, then the placekicker, then both. One game, I hadn't practiced placekicking for a couple of weeks and they stuck me in in the middle of the game, then took me out when I missed two extra points."

Instead of throwing tantrums, he would shrug and laugh. The laugh was hollow; the pain inside was eating with the steady hatred of an acid. But nobody was going to break Steve Little. His teammates interpreted it as a depraved nonchalance. The ones that talked to him called him Orbit.

"Guys just turned their backs on him," said Dave Stief, a close friend and road roommate. "I'd draw the line at 1 or 2 A.M., but for Steve it was 5 A.M. He'd sleep right through the morning meeting sometimes; they'd have to wake him up and almost baby-sit him. When we were on the road, he'd come in the room for bedcheck and then leave. He stayed out all night one Saturday night before our game at Washington. All kinds of girls, girls I didn't think were nearly as nice as Cindy.

"I'd say, 'Steve, you just can't keep screwing up your talent like this,' and he'd joke it off. Don't let anything from the outside world mess with Steve Little's world."

The hurt for a friend was all up in Dave Stief's eyes, the hopelessness for a stranger all down in his voice. "He'll joke it all off," he said, "until the day he dies."

October 15, 1980 came to St. Louis damp and chilled. When practice ended in the late-afternoon gloom of Busch Stadium, Jim Hanifan ordered his players not to leave. Two men, getting sixteen bullets each to put one another away, at least deserved an audience.

It could never happen at any other position. But then, man has never understood placekicking, and universal mysteries often push him to aberration. Jim Hanifan had scheduled a duel, sixteen shots from 32 to 42 yards away for the right to kick for the St. Louis Cardinals. Steve Little, three for eight with two PATs blocked after six games, vs. free agent Neil O'Donoghue.

The two tried hard not to find each other's eyes. Then there came a silence, broken only by the holder's terse signal and the thump.

The Cardinals said Little made 9 of 16, O'Donoghue 14. Little, for some reason, remembers he'd won.

The next morning he was cut. His eyes were red and moist when the reporters found him. He put on sunglasses. "I'm elated," he said. "I feel great because now I can go out and start all over."

First things first. "I'm going to go sit down," he said, "and drink a few cold ones right now."

He telephoned Cindy, who was living in Little Rock at the time, and told her to drive his Blazer land rover to St. Louis so they could pack. He left a rose and a note on his apartment kitchen counter. "Cindy—We'll start all over again. I'll be home soon. Love, Steve."

He was not home soon. He went to two bars, Fourth and Pine, and the Oz. Customers at one bar insulted him. He told them to shove it. He does not remember how many beers. Only that the number took more than two hands. "He was laughing and joking," said teammate Larry Swider, who was with him at Fourth and Pine.

Near 2:30 A.M., he walked to his Mazda sports coupe and began the twenty-eight-mile drive to his suburban apartment. The damp chill had become a slanting rain.

A few miles from home, on Interstate 270, he looked into his rear-view mirror and saw the approaching yellow eyes of a truck convoy. He cut to the right lane to let them spray by, hit a pocket of water and went into a spin. An exit sign stopped the spin.

They found him on the passenger's side, his head where your feet go, his feet where your head goes. The only damage showing was a trivial gash on the head.

Cindy said it was now her mission to take care of Steve. After 10 months of stress, she filed for divorce. Friends say it was bound to happen, even without the accident. "She kept telling me, 'You can do this, you can do that,'" said Steve. "I'd say, 'You're not sitting in this chair.' She could have left before the accident—I thought it was an odd time to do it."

On their last day together, the anger crested and Little searched his entire body for a muscle to move against her. "There was nothing I could do," he said, "so I spit at her."

He lies on the water bed, four days away from the one-year anniversary of the wreck. "I think I'll have a wreck party," he said. "Only, everyone's got to come in taxis and stay here when they get wrecked."

The subject changes to the second year after the wreck. "I don't know what my purpose is yet," he said. "But when it comes, I'll be ready for it. Maybe I'll do a movie before the people forget me. I'm sure I'm still here for something. Maybe God kept me alive to teach somebody something."

Maybe to teach the two men he dueled with in college, who still may have time to learn. Maybe to teach all the kickers who never come prepared to bleed.

These three men were arguably the best ever to play their positions, and in 1973 they entered pro football's Valhalla together. All three were fierce competitors, but their hallmark was the intelligence with which they went about their business. Every slow but crafty receiver who came after him is compared to Berry; every prowling, keen-eyed middle linebacker, to Schmidt; every offensive lineman who emphasizes technique over power, to Parker. And every ink-stained wretch who ever stumbled upon an elegant phrasing hopes to be compared to Red Smith, who entered the Valhalla reserved for writers just as this book was completed.

RED SMITH

Three for the Ages

Raymond Berry, Jim Parker, and Joe Schmidt were tapped for the Professional Football Hall of Fame the other day, proving that the ingredients of immortality are manifold. In a single election, the panel of sportswriters that enthrones deities for veneration in Canton, Ohio, chose a genius, a giant, and a dragon.

If, as Carlyle said, genius is an infinite capacity for taking pains, then Berry's qualifications are of the highest order. A rather bony individual out of Southern Methodist with 185 pounds on a chassis measuring six feet two inches, he regarded improvisation as a mortal sin. "No," he would say flatly if somebody tried to make up a play in the huddle. "I haven't practiced it. I'm not prepared."

He was John Unitas's favorite target on passes because he ran his patterns with scrupulous precision and the quarterback always knew where he would be on a given play. He had no great speed, and his patterns were designed like a Swiss watch, the product of endless hours of studying films.

"Can Sally cook?" Billy Pricer, the fullback from Oklahoma, asked Berry shortly before his marriage.

"I don't rightly know," Raymond said, "but she runs the projector." He thought that over for a moment. "I guess we'll eat a lot of sandwiches," he said.

One of his legs was shorter than the other, or he thought it was, so he wore regular cleats on one shoe and long mud cleats on the other. He had a gimpy back, or thought he did, and always wore a leather girdle. He laundered his own football pants so they would feel exactly right, not too stiff, not too tight. His name is Raymond and he hates to be called Ray.

Jim Parker played tackle and guard on the Baltimore offensive line. He weighed 275 pounds, was approximately as fast, as light, and at least as smart as any of his professors at Ohio State.

"I worked two years on a single move against Parker," Henry Jordan of the Green Bay Packers said one night, "and it fooled him just once."

Jordan weighed 250 and thought of himself as small, at least when he was talking about Parker or the six-foot-eight Doug Atkins of the Chicago Bears.

"I'm nowhere near big enough to handle Parker," Henry said, "so I decided I'd try to use his weight against him, like judo. I would come up out of my crouch, and as he fired off the ball I would stick my face up in front of him like this, so he'd have to take a swing at me. Then I'd grab his wrist and jerk.

"As I say, there was no way a guy my size could handle him, but we have a film showing me throwing him through the air, over my head. It worked just once, and I never could trap him on it again."

Competitive fire rather than size distinguished Joe Schmidt when he was middle linebacker and unquestioned leader of the Detroit Lions. He was a 220-pound six-footer, but he said he had stood six-foot-three when he played fullback for the University of Pittsburgh. With his pale Teutonic face straight as a string, he would explain that a dozen years of diving headlong into the interference had driven his neck down between his shoulders like a stake.

When George Plimpton was working out as the last-string quarterback of the Lions, he was fascinated by Schmidt, and the linebacker appears prominently in Plimpton's *Paper Lion*. One story concerns the Pitt-Notre Dame game of 1952 when Red Dawson, the coach, asked Schmidt to give the pep talk in the dressing room. "You guys whip Notre Dame," the captain told his playmates, "or so help me, I'll whip you." Pitt won, 22–19. "We were more scared of Joe Schmidt than Notre Dame," one of the players said.

Then there was the 1962 game that is the climax of *Run to Daylight!* the book W. C. Heinz did with Vince Lombardi. Detroit was leading Green Bay, 7–6, and with less than four minutes left Paul Hornung missed a field goal that would have put the Packers in front, 9–7. Coming off the field as the offensive unit took over, Schmidt told Milt Plum to call running plays to eat up time. He was confident that if Detroit had to kick, the defense could contain the Packers on their side of midfield.

Instead, Plum mixed passes in with the running plays. Two were completed for first downs, on the Detroit 34-yard line and on the 47. On third and eight with a minute and forty-six seconds to play, Plum tried another pass, Herb Adderley intercepted and ran the ball back into field-goal range. This time Hornung's kick won the game.

"It took Joe Schmidt a long time to get over it," Plimpton wrote, "and perhaps he never did. For many games thereafter, when Plum and Schmidt passed each other on the field as the defensive unit came off and the offensive players were taking over, Schmidt would say disdainfully: 'Pass, Milt, three times and then punt.'"

Plimpton protested that this sort of talk from the captain couldn't have done much for Plum's morale, or the team's.

"The quality that makes Schmidt a leader," Bob Scholtz, the center said, "is his absolute honesty. The guy never said anything, ever, he didn't believe in. Schmidt took that for a dumb call in that Packer game, and there's no way in his book it can be rubbed out."

That Jack Tatum was an effective safety is impossible to deny: four times he was named an AFC all-pro. That he played within the letter of the NFL law is likewise beyond dispute. The controversy surrounding Tatum concerns his avowed intent to separate players from their senses as well as the ball. The book from which the words below are excerpted caused a flurry of outrage upon its publication (which hindered sales not in the least) for Tatum had come to be best known, regrettably, as the man whose tackle of New England's Darryl Stingley left the receiver paralyzed. These are hard words to read, but the direction of professional football is bound up in our reaction to them.

JACK TATUM
and Bill Kushner

They Call Me Assassin

In my first collegiate game I won no All-American honors, but I did make the other teams on our schedule wary of me. I was only a sophomore, but I had earned a starting assignment as a linebacker. We were playing Southern Methodist, a school known for putting the ball in the air. That meant people would be running pass patterns in my area looking for the ball instead of the linebackers. Believe me, when you catch someone with a good shot who isn't expecting it, you're going to hurt him.

Early in the first quarter I spotted a wide receiver running a quick slant over the middle. The receiver was concentrating on making the catch and never saw me coming. He was my first collegiate knockout victim.

Later in the same period, I saw a running back slip over the middle and look back for the pass. He became my second knockout. The 85,000 fans watching the game were delighted. The action was gruesome, but that's what the fans love, violent contact. The Ohio State fans loved the action I had provided and so did my coaches. Once again I was a hero.

By the time my college career ended, I had more knockouts than Joe Louis and Muhammad Ali combined. I won every defensive award the Big Ten had to offer and more. Three times I was among the top vote getters for the Heisman Trophy, and twice I was voted the nation's best defensive player. I was certain that my next adventure would be professional football.

I have mentioned a word that is synonymous with boxing: knockout. Actually, though, knockouts do occur in many of the nonpassive sports. It's just that the very purpose of a boxing match is built around one's ability to knock his opponent into a senseless mass of blood and flesh. Football and the other contact sports do have a different purpose. In football there are various degrees of violence and contact, but the two basic objectives of the game are to score points and prevent points from being scored, and not to knock people out cold. However, when you put an offensive team on the field for the purpose of advancing the ball forward, and the defensive team has quite the opposite purpose, it all becomes a war, and I am simply a warrior in a very physical way. As a warrior I must discourage running backs and receivers whenever they attempt to gain yardage against the defense. It is a physical and a violent job, and quite often the end results are knockouts or serious injuries to my opponent. But it is just part of a very risky business.

The first round of the college draft went as I expected, and I became the property of the Oakland Raiders. After eight years of hard work in high school and college, I was at last part of the NFL.

Several weeks after the draft, I flew out to Oakland for contract talks with Al Davis, a partner and general manager of the Raiders. Al Davis talked my language. I asked, "How much?" and he answered with a $50,000 bonus check and a three-year, no-cut contract worth six attractive figures. I signed the contract.

When the paperwork was finished, there was a statement in the press to the effect the Raiders had just hired the Assassin that no winning team could be without . . . and his name was Jack Tatum.

"Assassin?" I thought. "That makes me sound like a gangster." But, actually, I was a "hit man." I didn't rush out and buy a dark suit or fedora, but I did think about my career. The Raiders had invested in me and I had to produce. Professional football is vicious and brutal; there's not much time for sentiment. I was being paid well for a service, and if I didn't deliver, they'd go and find someone else who would.

I was committed to play my first professional game with the College All-Stars against the World Champion Baltimore Colts. The game was an annual charity affair held each year in Chicago, but it was also much more.

As All-Americans we wanted to prove to the Colts that we belonged in the NFL. We weren't concerned with showing off or pretending that we were already professional superstars. We just wanted to go out, play a good game, and earn the respect of the best team in professional football. But for some reason the old pros turned nasty and tried to beat our heads in. Every time they got off a good play, they would smart-mouth us or cuss. I thought it was very unfair of them to treat us as if we didn't belong in the same stadium. We had only played together for ten days, and the Colts had years behind them. I don't think that any of the All-Stars seriously believed that we could win the game, but still, we didn't expect to be disgraced.

Before very long, the Colts had a seven-point lead but were acting as though they had a seventy-point lead. On a third down and eight play, I started thinking that maybe Earl Morrall would look for his tight end, John Mackey. Earlier in the game Morrall tried a quick pass to the tight end, and it had worked for good yardage. That first time, as I went after Mackey, someone had partially blocked me and I hadn't made good contact. Mackey got up, shrugged his shoulders, and walked back to the huddle laughing and hollering in my direction, "Hard-hitting rookie . . . what a joke."

Morrall took the snap and dropped straight back looking for the tight end. I carefully avoided the blind side blocks and drew a bead on Mackey's rib cage. Morrall hadn't thrown one of his better passes, and I could have easily intercepted, but I had other plans. I wondered if John Mackey would still think I was a joke after he was really hit. As Mackey reached back for the ball, I drove my helmet into his ribs and knocked him to the ground. It was a good hit. Mackey was on the ground flopping around like a wounded duck and gasping for air. Standing over him, I glared down and asked, "How funny was that joke?" Of course, I admit I cussed at him, too.

John Mackey wasn't the only Colt I ran into on that particular night. Later in the game I found another tight end, Tom Mitchell, roaming in my area trying to catch one of Morrall's terribly wobbly passes. I introduced myself to Tom, but I don't think he heard the name. Tom was my second professional knockout.

Immediately, sportswriters started comparing me with Dick Butkus, a linebacker for the Chicago Bears. Butkus was supposedly the meanest, dirtiest, hardest-hitting football player to ever put on a pair of cleats and walk out onto the field. I resented the comparison because I had seen Butkus play. I admit that Butkus was mean and there was strong evidence he played dirty (teeth marks on running backs' ankles), but for anyone to think he was a hitter was absurd. Butkus even admitted that he couldn't hit. When he traveled across the country doing TV shows, he said, "Whenever I get a clear shot at the ball carrier, I don't want him turning around to see who did the hitting. I want him to know without looking that it was Dick Butkus."

Any fool knows that when you hit someone with your best shot and he is still able to think, then you're not a hitter. My idea of a good hit is when the victim wakes up on the sidelines with train whistles blowing in his head and wondering who he is and what ran over him. I'm not saying that Butkus wasn't a fair linebacker, because after all, he was an All-Pro. But in my estimation Butkus was most definitely not a hitter.

As a defensive player I had resigned myself to the fact that I would never rush for 1,000 yards during a season and I would never score many touchdowns. But at the same time I vowed to earn my reputation in professional football with aggressive tackling. I knew that in professional football or even high school football, the team that can dominate physically will usually win. Punishment is demoralizing, and few teams can withstand a painful beating without it warping their will to win. I never make a tackle just to bring someone down. I want to punish the man I'm going after and I want him to know that it's going to hurt every time he comes my way.

Violent play can make a defensive team much sharper, but there is a limit. I believe that running backs and receivers are fair game once they step onto the field. If they want to run out of bounds to avoid the tackle, then fine, let them run away from the action. But anyone that comes near me is going to get hit. I like to believe that my best hits border on felonious assault, but at the same time everything I do is by the rule book. I don't want to be the heir to Butkus's title, because his career had shadows. Some people say that Butkus bit, while others say he didn't. My style of play is mean and nasty and I am going to beat people physically and mentally, but in no way am I going down in the record book as a cheap-shot artist.

After the All-Star game I joined the Raider training camp at Santa Rosa, California. I guess it was surprising that my helmet still fit over my head. I was starting to believe everything the press wrote about me, and I'm afraid I became overconfident. After all, I was considered a superstar in high school and I was a collegiate All-American two times. Then came the All-Star game and my two professional knockouts. It was a lot for a twenty-one-year-old man to grasp and still keep both feet on the ground. The Oakland Raiders had a man named Fred Biletnikoff, now retired, who put things in proper perspective for me, however.

Fred Biletnikoff was a balding but hippy-looking wide receiver for the Oakland Raiders. When I was instructed by my coaches to cover Fred one-on-one during a pass defense drill, I laughed to myself. Fred Biletnikoff had a great pair of hands and could catch anything near him, but he was slow by NFL standards. I've played against big receivers, small receivers, and fast receivers, and they couldn't burn me. Now, for my first test in an Oakland Raider camp, they put me against a slow receiver.

Fred ran his first pattern and I showed him why I was all All-American. Covering him like a blanket, I nearly intercepted the ball, and after the play I told Fred, "You're lucky that we aren't hitting."

On the next play Fred drove off the line hard and made a good move to the outside. I was too quick for him though and reacted like an All-Pro. But then he broke back across the middle and left me tripping over my own feet. Needless to say, the quarterback laid a perfect pass into Fred's hands, and he scored. On the way back to the huddle, Fred showed me the football and asked, "Were you looking for this, Rookie?"

That got me upset and I started cussing. I told him, "Try me again and see what happens, Chump!"

Fred came at me again with about five different fakes and just as I went left, he went right and scored again. Fred Biletnikoff started running patterns that quickly deflated my ego and taught me humiliation. He burned me time and time again so bad that I went back to the locker room feeling very uncertain as to whether or not I had what it takes to make it in professional football. Deep down inside my pride was scorched.

Later that same evening I bumped into Fred and we started talking about practice.

Fred turned out to be a pretty good guy. After a few minutes we were talking like old friends. Fred told me that he grew up in Erie, Pennsylvania, and it didn't sound like paradise. While he was talking about the mills and factories of Erie, I was picturing the filth and dirt of my hometown, Passaic, New Jersey. After a great high-school career in Erie, Fred accepted a scholarship to attend Florida State University, and there earned All-American honors. The more we talked, the better I liked the man.

"A man has to adjust," Fred was saying about the NFL, "and if he doesn't, he's gone. The difference today was that I knew you could knock me out if you hit me with a good shot but you didn't know that I could burn you. Now it comes down to respecting each other and adjusting."

I listened to everything Fred told me, because he had the experience and wanted to help my career. He told me that receivers are the biggest bunch of cons going. Fred warned, "Some receivers will fake with their hips, feet, head, shoulders, eyes, or anything to gain a liberated step. Don't be sucked in by a fake; go after what's real. Remember, Jack, all the quarterbacks in this league can hit the one-on-one pass. If some receiver gives you a fake and you trip over your own feet going after nothing, then it's just God and green grass between that man and six points."

Fred started working with me and taught me how to think like a receiver. By the time the exhibition season opened up, I didn't have all the answers, but I gave my best. Maybe if Fred hadn't given me some of his time, my stay in the NFL would have been a short one.

I got burned a few times, but luck was with me. It seemed that if a receiver caught a pass over me, I was able to stick the next attempt in his rib cage. Still, though, I was undisciplined enough to be hazardous. Aggressiveness is as common to football as helmets and shoulder pads, but I had yet to learn how to channel my aggressive style of play into aspects of the game where it would do the team the most good.

In one game we were holding a 21–14 lead over the New Orleans Saints. Late in the fourth period the Saints quarterback threw over the middle for his wide receiver, Danny Abramowicz, who was well covered by our strong safety, George Atkinson. In my eagerness to assist, I blasted in from the weak side and creamed everyone. It was a double knockout. I got Abramowicz, but I got George too.

After that my play became sloppy. I'd go after the ball and slam into anyone that got in my way. It was early in the season and I had already knocked out seven men. That would have been a good start, except that four of those knockouts were Oakland Raiders. I knocked out our Captain, Willie Brown, got Nemiah Wilson and cut his eye pretty bad, too, and then there was George Atkinson. I knocked out George twice. It got to the point where our defensive people were starting to worry more about me than the real enemy.

After George recovered from his second knockout, he took me aside and said, "Damn, Tate, are you colorblind or something? I wear the same color jersey as you do. I'm on your side and the deal is gettin' the other team."

After he felt that I was sure which team I played for, George started teaching me some of his techniques. I learned how to anticipate the offensive man. For example, if a running back went wide on a play and there was good outside pursuit, then I'd position myself inside and hope the back would cut against the flow. That way I'd be waiting, and from there it was a matter of building up my speed and hitting the enemy. On passing situations I talked with other defensive backs and asked how they were going to play a particular receiver. That way I sort of knew where my people were going to be and how they were going to play the situation. For example, if Willie Brown said he was going to play his man loose and go for the ball, then I went for the receiver. It started working so well that most of the time I let the other backs go for the interception and I'd punish the receiver.

George Atkinson started teaching me a few more of his other tricks. George said, "I was going to teach you the 'Hook' when you first came into the league but you were having identification problems. Now that you seem to know who's who, let me show you the best intimidator in the business, the Hook." Of course, the rules governing the Hook have changed recently, but back then it wasn't just legal but an important weapon in a good hitter's arsenal.

The Hook is simply flexing your biceps and trying to catch the receiver's head in the joint between the forearm and upper arm. It's like hitting with the biceps by using a headlock type of action. The purpose of the Hook was to strip the receiver of the ball, his helmet, his head, and his courage. Of course, you only use the Hook in full-speed contact, and usually from the blind side. Using the Hook effectively was not as easy as it may sound. Very few defensive backs used the Hook because if you were a little high with your shot, the receiver would slip under and get away. Also, if you weren't careful and you hit with the forearm, it became an illegal tactic.

Another trick that George taught me was the "Groundhog." The Groundhog is a perfectly timed hit to the ankles just as the receiver is leaping high to catch a pass. The Groundhog isn't as devastating as it looks on TV but it does have a tendency to keep the receiver closer to the ground on high passes.

As the free safety for the Raiders, I never have a specific responsibility. I am given the freedom to help out wherever we feel the offense is going to concentrate its attack. If a team is running good against us, then I move closer to the line of scrimmage and try to get a good hit on a running back. Most of the time one good hit will slow down any running back and wake up the defense. That's what I meant about punishment demoralizing and warping a team's will to win.

I started feeling comfortable about halfway into the season. It seemed as though everything was falling into place rather nicely, and best of all, I hadn't knocked out any of my teammates for three games. I worked hard at practice, studied game films of coming opponents, and showed improvement weekly. My career was getting off to a solid start, and I felt good about the overall development I had shown. I was doing my job, getting well-paid, and no one had any complaints. At least no one on the Oakland Raiders had any complaints.

If ever a man did have a reason to complain about my style of play, it had to be Riley Odoms, a tight end with the Denver Broncos. During a game at Denver's Mile High Stadium, I leveled the best shot of my career against Riley. It was a clean hit, not a cheap shot, but I was upset because I really thought I had killed the man.

Late in the game we had built a 27–16 lead, but Denver's offense was getting fancy. They singled out Nemiah Wilson, our left cornerback, as the man in the secondary to exploit. Nemo was small, only about 170 pounds, and he was playing with an injured leg. This seemed to be an invitation for Charley Johnson, Denver's quarterback, to do his passing around Nemo. Denver positioned both of their wide receivers on opposite sides of the field, away from Nemo, and put him one-on-one with Riley Odoms. Riley is one of the best tight ends in professional football. He's big, standing six-foot-four and weighing 235 pounds; he would be a lot of man for Nemo on this particular Sunday, or any day of the week, for that matter.

Since I had the option of roaming around and policing the secondary, I decided to help Nemo. When the play started to develop, I dropped back a few steps to give Riley the impression I had deep coverage. Riley saw me dropping off and made a quick move over the middle. It was a great move because Riley had Nemo off balance and he broke open by five yards. Quarterbacks love to see that type of situation, and Charley Johnson wasted little time releasing the ball toward Riley. I just timed my hit. When I felt I could zero in on Riley's head at the same time the ball arrived in his hands, I moved. It was a perfectly timed hit, and I used my Hook on his head. Because of the momentum built up by the angles and speed of both Riley and myself, it was the best hit of my career. I heard Riley scream on impact and felt his body go limp. He landed flat on his back, and the ball came to rest on his chest for a completion, but Riley's eyes rolled back in his head and he wasn't breathing. I had another knockout, and maybe this time, I had even killed a man. God knew that I didn't want something like that to happen.

I've used the word "kill," and when I'm hitting someone I really am trying to kill, but not like forever. I mean I'm trying to kill the play or the pass, but not the man. Football is a violent game, and people are seriously injured; sometimes they are killed. But any man that puts on a uniform and doesn't play hard is cheating. The players of the NFL are paid good money and risk serious injuries because the structure of football is based on punishing your opponent. There is nothing humorous or even vaguely cheerful about playing in the NFL. It is a high risk but high-salaried job.

Riley was scraped off the field and carried to the sidelines. He was shaken and hurt, but thank God he was still alive. After the game I went over to the Denver locker room and talked with Riley. He said, "Damn, Tate, don't ever hit me like that again. You nearly killed me." Then he laughed and I slapped him on the back and smiled with relief. Very few people understand the camaraderie and mutual respect professional athletes feel for each other. We admire each other's abilities and appreciate the man who has the guts to do his job well. My coaches, sportswriters, and even football fans talked about how hard I hit Riley. People called that hit everything from vicious to brutal but I never heard anyone say it was a cheap shot.

During the years that have followed I have continued my style of play and have registered many more knockouts. I remember one game, again it was against Denver, when the Broncos' best running back, Floyd Little, took a handoff and swept around left end with a herd of blockers leading the way. As he turned the corner, the reds and blues of Denver had gone south and I was coming up fast. Floyd didn't see me coming and there was a collision at mid-field near the sidelines, right in front of the Denver bench. I whipped my Hook up under Floyd's face mask and landed a solid shot flush on his jaw. Floyd looked like a magician practicing levitation just before all the lights went out. His head snapped back, his feet straightened out, and the ball and one of his shoes shot into the stands. I was coming so hard that my momentum carried both of us into the Denver bench.

The play had started close to the sidelines and I could have pushed Floyd out of bounds, but instead, I hit him with everything I had to offer because if you just push a guy like Floyd Little out of bounds, then he'll start getting some bad ideas about you. Floyd would probably start thinking that I was soft, and that would lead to him wanting to take advantage of me. Before long every team in the NFL would be gunning their game plans at me, and when that happened the Raiders would get someone else, someone that would beat a running back out of bounds rather than give him a sissy push.

Some of the players moaned when I hit Floyd and a few of them even cussed at me, but once again no one even suggested that I hit Floyd with a cheap shot.

My ferocity seemed to influence the entire Raider defense. Everyone started talking about getting a "knockout." Guys who used to tackle just to bring someone down started to punish people, and that made the defense much sharper. If a running back got off a good play and picked up, say, 15 yards but got his head rattled so badly that he had to leave the game, it was worth the 15 yards. I started taking shots at everyone wearing a different colored uniform. I'd take shots at every receiver and running back. They didn't like it, and sometimes they'd send a lineman after me, but I didn't care; I'd take a shot at him, too. . . .

During my second year George Atkinson suggested that he and I start a contest for who would get the most knockouts over the course of the season. It sounded like a good idea, and we agreed on a set of rules. First of all, neither of us wanted to get penalties called against us so we agreed that our hits must be clean shots and legal. Next, the man you hit would have to be down for an official injury time-out and he had to be helped off the field. That would be considered a "knockout" and it was worth two points. Sometimes, one of us would hit a man and he'd take the injury time-out but would limp off the field under his own power. We called that a "limp-off" and it was worth one point. When the season started, so did we. Actually, it was all part of our job, but we made a game out of it. Guess who won?

The seasons had a way of piling up, and before I knew it, I was a veteran of seven years. When I stopped to look back and see what had happened over the course of my career, I was shocked. I came into the NFL wanting to be the most intimidating hitter in the history of the game. At this stage of my career, people were scared of me because they knew I was accomplishing my objective. But something else was also happening and I resented it. Some people considered me a dirty player and a cheap-shot artist. I can live with rumors, but when I see my name published in the San Diego *Union* along with football's top ten dirty players, I get upset. When my attorney calls me from Pittsburgh and tells me that Sam Nover of Channel 2 and Myron Cope of Channel 4 are doing specials on my dirty tactics, I become angry. After a few questionable incidents, everything has mushroomed into a problem serious enough for Howard Cosell to dedicate one of his halftime shows on "Monday Night Football" to George Atkinson and me and our "cheap shots." Even NBC Sports used prime time for a special, "Violence in Sports."

It started with a normal football game, a few good hits, a knockout, and a certain coach's "criminal element" speech. From there it was picked up by the press and traveled into the office of the Commissioner of the NFL. From there some fines were issued, which then I refused to pay, and now every official in the NFL is throwing quick flags in my general direction. However, I doubt that I'm going to change how I live my life or how I play the game because, as I told the Commissioner, "I plead guilty, but only to aggressive play."

"When the going gets weird, the weird turn pro," quoth Dr. Thompson. So having bid *bon voyage* to Richard Nixon and his merry pranksters, the scourge of Washington joined the pros in the media circus that was Super Bowl VIII. By game day in Houston fatigue as well as fear and loathing had infected the ranks: nothing is more enervating than writing about nothing.

HUNTER S. THOMPSON

Fear and Loathing at the Super Bowl

The floor of the Hyatt Regency men's room was always covered, about three-inches deep, with discarded newspapers — all apparently complete and unread, except on closer examination you realized that every one of them was missing its sports section. This bathroom was right next to the hotel newsstand and just across the mezzanine from the crowded NFL "press lounge," a big room full of telephones and free booze, where most of the 1600 or so sportswriters assigned to cover The Big Game seemed to spend about sixteen hours of each day, during Super Week.

After the first day or so, when it became balefully clear that there was no point in anybody except the local reporters going out on the press-bus each day for the carefully staged "player interviews" that Dolphin tackle Manny Fernandez described as "like going to the dentist every day to have the same tooth filled," the out-of-town writers began using the local types as a sort of involuntary "pool" . . . which was more like an old British Navy press gang, in fact, because the locals had no choice. They would go out, each morning, to the Miami and Minnesota team hotels, and dutifully conduct the daily interviews . . . and about two hours later this mass of useless gibberish would appear, word for word, in the early editions of either the Post or the Chronicle.

You could see the front door of the hotel from the balcony of the press lounge, and whenever the newsboy came in with his stack of fresh papers, the national writers would make the long forty-eight-yard walk across to the newsstand and cough up fifteen cents each for their copies. Then, on the way back to the press lounge, they would stop for a piss and dump the whole paper — except for the crucial sports section — on the floor of the men's room. The place was so deep, all week, in fresh newsprint, that it was sometimes hard to push the door open.

Forty yards away, on comfortable couches surrounding the free bar, the national gents would spend about two hours each day scanning the local sports section — along with a never-ending mass of almost psychotically detailed information churned out by the NFL publicity office — on the dim chance of finding something worth writing about that day.

There never was, of course. But nobody seemed really disturbed about it. The only thing most of the sportswriters in Houston seemed to care about was having *something* to write about . . . anything at all, boss: a peg, an angle, a quote, even a goddamn rumor.

I remember being shocked at the sloth and moral degeneracy of the Nixon press corps during the 1972 presidential campaign — but they were like a pack of wolverines on speed compared to the relatively elite sportswriters who showed up in Houston to cover the Super Bowl.

On the other hand, there really *was no story*. As the week wore on, it became increasingly obvious that we were all "just working here." Nobody knew who to blame for it, and although at least a third of the sportswriters who showed up for that super-expensive shuck knew exactly what was happening, I doubt if more than five or six of them ever actually wrote the cynical and contemptuous appraisals of Super Bowl VIII that dominated about half the conversations around the bar in the press lounge.

Whatever was happening in Houston that week had little or nothing to do with the hundreds of stories that were sent out on the news-wires each day. Most of the stories, in fact, were unabashed rewrites of the dozens of official NFL press releases churned out each day by the league publicity office. Most of the stories about "fantastic parties" given by Chrysler, American Express, and Jimmy the Greek were taken from press releases and rewritten by people who had spent the previous evening at least five miles from the scenes described in their stories.

The NFL's official Super Bowl party — the "incredible Texas Hoe-Down" on Friday night in the Astrodome — was as wild, glamourous, and exciting as an Elks Club picnic on Tuesday in Salina, Kansas. The official NFL press release on the Hoe-Down said it was an unprecedented extravaganza that cost the league more than $100,000 and attracted people like Gene McCarthy and Ethel Kennedy. . . . Which might have been true, but I spent about five hours skulking around in that grim concrete barn and the only people I recognized were a dozen or so sportswriters from the press lounge.

Anybody with access to a mimeograph machine and a little imagination could have generated at least a thousand articles on "an orgy of indescribable proportions" at John Connally's house, with Allen Ginsberg as the guest of honor and thirteen thoroughbred horses slaughtered by drug-crazed guests with magnesium butcher knives. Most of the press people would have simply picked the story off the big table in the "work-room," rewritten it just enough to make it sound genuine, and sent it off on the wire without a second thought.

The bus-ride to the stadium for the game on Sunday took more than an hour, due to heavy traffic. I had made the same six-mile drive the night before in just under five minutes . . . but that was under very different circumstances; Rice Stadium is on South Main Street, along the same route that led from the Hyatt Regency to the Dolphin headquarters at the Marriott, and also to the Blue Fox.

There was not much to do on the bus except drink, smoke, and maintain a keen ear on the babble of conversations behind me for any talk that might signal the presence of some late-blooming Viking fan with money to waste. It is hard to stay calm and casual in a crowd of potential bettors when you feel absolutely certain of winning any bet you can make. At that point, anybody with even a hint of partisan enthusiasm in his voice becomes a possible mark — a doomed and ignorant creature to be lured, as carefully as possible, into some disastrous last-minute wager that could cost him every dollar he owns.

There is no room for mercy or the milk of human kindness in football betting — at least not when you're prepared to get up on the edge with every dollar *you* own. One-on-one betting is a lot more interesting than dealing with bookies, because it involves strong elements of personality and psychic leverage. Betting against the point spread is a relatively mechanical trip, but betting against another individual can be very complex, if you're serious about it — because you want to know, for starters, whether you're betting against a fool or a wizard, or maybe against somebody who's just *playing* the fool.

Making a large bet on a bus full of sportswriters on the way to the Super Bowl, for instance, can be a very dangerous thing; because you might be dealing with somebody who was in the same fraternity at Penn State with one of the team doctors, and who learned the night before — while drinking heavily with his old buddy — that the quarterback you're basing your bet on has four cracked ribs and can barely raise his passing arm to shoulder level.

Situations like these are not common. Unreported injuries can lead to heavy fines against any team that fails to report one — especially in a Super Bowl — but what is a $10,000 fine, compared to the amount of money that kind of crucial knowledge is worth against a big-time bookie?

The other side of that coin is a situation where a shrewd coach turns the league's "report all injuries" rule into a psychological advantage for his own team — and coincidentally for any bettor who knows what's happening — by scrupulously reporting an injury to a star player just before a big game, then calling a press conference to explain that the just-reported injury is of such a nature — a pulled muscle, for instance — that it might or might not heal entirely by game time.

This was what happened in Houston with the Dolphins' Paul Warfield, widely regarded as "the most dangerous pass receiver in pro football." Warfield is a game-breaker, a man who commands double-coverage at all times because of his antelope running style, twin magnets for hands, and a weird kind of adrenaline instinct that feeds on tension and high pressure. There is no more beautiful sight in football than watching Paul Warfield float out of the backfield on a sort of angle-streak pattern right into the heart of a "perfect" zone defense and take a softly thrown pass on his hip, without even seeming to notice the arrival of the ball, and then float another 60 yards into the end zone, with none of the frustrated defensive backs ever touching him.

There is an eerie kind of *certainty* about Warfield's style that is far more demoralizing than just another 6 points on the scoreboard. About half the time he looks bored and lazy — but even the best pass defenders in the league *know*, in some nervous corner of their hearts, that when the deal goes down Warfield is capable of streaking right past them like they didn't exist. . . .

Unless he's hurt: playing with some kind of injury that might or might not be serious enough to either slow him down or gimp the fiendish concentration that makes him so dangerous . . . and this was the possibility that Dolphin coach Don Shula raised on Wednesday when he announced that Warfield had pulled a leg muscle in practice that afternoon and *might* not play on Sunday.

This news caused instant action in gambling circles. Even big-time bookies, whose underground information on these things is usually as good as Pete Rozelle's, took Shula's announcement seriously enough to cut the spread down from seven to six — a decision worth many millions of betting dollars if the game turned out to be close.

Even the *rumor* of an injury to Warfield was worth one point (and even two, with some bookies I was never able to locate) . . . and if Shula had announced on Saturday that Paul was definitely not going to play, the spread would probably have dropped to four, or even three. . . . Because the guaranteed absence of Warfield would have taken a great psychological load off the minds of Minnesota's defensive backs.

Without the ever-present likelihood of a game-breaking "bomb" at any moment, they could focus down much tighter on stopping Miami's brutal running game — which eventually destroyed them, just as it had destroyed Oakland's nut-cutting defense two weeks earlier, and one of the main reasons why the Vikings failed to stop the Dolphins on the ground was the constant presence of Paul Warfield in his customary wide-receiver's spot.

He played almost the whole game, never showing any sign of injury; and although he caught only one pass, he neutralized two Minnesota defensive backs on every play . . . and two extra tacklers on the line of scrimmage might have made a hell of a difference in that embarrassingly decisive first quarter when Miami twice drove what might as well have been the whole length of the field to score 14 quick points and crack the Vikings' confidence just as harshly as they had cracked the Redskins' out in Los Angeles a year earlier.

It is hard to say, even now, exactly why I was so certain of an easy Dolphin victory. The only reason I didn't get extremely rich on the game was my inability to overcome the logistical problems of betting heavily, on credit, by means of frantic long-distance phone calls from a hotel room in Houston. None of the people I met in that violent, water-logged town were inclined to introduce me to a reliable bookmaker—and the people I called on both coasts, several hours before the game on Sunday morning, seemed unnaturally nervous when I asked them to use their own credit to guarantee my bets with their local bookies.

Looking back on it now, after talking with some of these people and cursing them savagely, I see that the problem had something to do with my frenzied speech-pattern that morning. I was still in the grip of whatever fiery syndrome had caused me to deliver that sermon off the balcony a few hours earlier—and the hint of mad tremor in my voice, despite my attempts to disguise it, was apparently communicated very clearly to all those I spoke with on the long-distance telephone.

How long. O lord, how long? This is the second year in a row that I have gone to the Super Bowl and been absolutely certain—at least forty-eight hours before game-time—of the outcome. It is also the second year in a row that I have failed to capitalize, financially, on this certainty. Last year, betting mainly with wealthy cocaine addicts, I switched all my bets from Washington to Miami on Friday night—and in the resulting confusion my net winnings were almost entirely canceled by widespread rancor and personal bitterness.

This year, in order to side-step that problem, I waited until the last moment to make my bets—despite the fact that I knew the Vikings were doomed after watching them perform for the press at their star-crossed practice field on Monday afternoon before the game. It was clear, even then, that they were spooked and very uncertain about what they were getting into—but it was not until I drove about twenty miles around the beltway to the other side of town for a look at the Dolphins that I knew, for sure, how to bet.

There are a lot of factors intrinsic to the nature of the Super Bowl that make it far more predictable than regular season games, or even playoffs—but they are not the kind of factors that can be sensed or understood at a distance of 2000 or even 20 miles, on the basis of any wisdom or information that filters out from the site through the rose-colored, booze-bent media-filter that passes for "world-wide coverage" at these spectacles.

There is a progression of understanding vis-à-vis pro football that varies drastically with the factor of *distance*—physical, emotional, intellectual, and every other way.... Which is exactly the way it should be, in the eyes of the amazingly small number of people who own and control the game, because it is this finely managed distance factor that accounts for the high-profit *mystique* that blew the sacred institution of baseball off its "national pastime" pedestal in less than fifteen years.

There were other reasons for baseball's precipitous loss of popularity among everybody except old men and middle-aged sportswriters between 1959 and now—just as there will be a variety of reasons to explain the certain decline of pro football between now and 1984—but if sporting historians ever look back on all this and try to explain it, there will be no avoiding the argument that pro football's meteoric success in the 1960s was directly attributable to its early marriage with network TV and a huge, coast-to-coast audience of armchair fans who "grew up"—in terms of their personal relationships to The Game—with the idea that pro football was something that happened every Sunday on the tube. The notion of driving eight miles along a crowded freeway and then paying three dollars to park the car in order to pay another ten dollars to watch the game from the vantage point of a damp redwood bench fifty-five rows above the 19-yard line in a crowd of noisy drunks was entirely repugnant to them.

And they were absolutely right. After ten years of trying it both ways—and especially after watching this last wretched Super Bowl game from a choice seat in the "press section" very high above the 50-yard line—I hope to christ I never again succumb to whatever kind of weakness or madness it is that causes a person to endure the incoherent hell that comes with going out to a cold and rainy stadium for three hours on a Sunday afternoon and trying to get involved with whatever seems to be happening down there on that far-below field.

At the Super Bowl I had the benefit of my usual game-day aids: powerful binoculars, a tiny portable radio for the blizzard of audio-details that nobody ever thinks to mention on TV, and a seat on the good left arm of my friend, Mr. Natural. . . . But even with all these aids and a seat on the 50-yard line, I would rather have stayed in my hotel room and watched the goddamn thing on TV. . . .

Nineteen thirty-two had been a year of struggle for the NFL, its existence threatened by the Depression and a stultifying string of low-scoring standoffs. The Bears and the Spartans deadlocked for the championship, the Spartans having played four ties and the Bears *six*; the title was resolved in a famous indoor playoff. The following year brought innovations born of desperation: the goal posts were moved up from the rear of the end zone to encourage field goals; forward passes were permitted from any point behind the line of scrimmage (formerly a pass had to be released at least five yards back of the line); and the league was divided into two conferences, creating the first scheduled championship game on December 17, 1933. Return with me now to those thrilling days of yesteryear—the leather helmets and the watermelon ball, a cloud of dust and a hearty "Hi-ho Bronko!"—the game is played again.

JOHN THORN

The First NFL Championship Game

A raw, wet wind blows in from the east, and mist and fog hang over Wrigley Field. Kickoff for this first NFL championship is at 1:45, only a few minutes away.

As we take our seats on the 50-yard line, the eighteen men of each team race onto the field to a roar of anticipation. The match figures to be a beaut, for both the Giants and Bears coasted to their divisional titles and split two hard-fought regular-season meetings. New York's single-wing offense, led by the passing of tailback Harry Newman and the running of fullback Ken Strong, is the sensation of the league, having piled up a record number of points. The Bears, on the other hand, boast the NFL's second-stingiest defense along with a T-formation attack in which fullback Bronko Nagurski supplies the power and everyone is a threat to pass. The football will be flying today, I assure you, in a razzle-dazzle display rarely if ever equaled since.

In the week before the championship, Giants' coach Steve Owen readied his troops for every known variation in the Bears' whirling T. He still burns over the midseason loss in which Chicago end Bill Hewitt threw a pass off an end-around for the winning score. And in the "skull drill" meeting last night Ray Flaherty, who is the team's right end, captain, and assistant coach, drew particular attention to the fake-plunge and jump-pass with which Nagurski won last year's title.

Now the teams line up for the kickoff, the Giants to receive. The ball sails into the arms of Newman, who returns to the 30. The dark-jerseyed, leather-helmeted Giants line up in the single wing, the form of attack employed by every NFL club this year except the Bears. An unbalanced formation — with both guards on the same side of the center — it is founded on power blocking rather than on the deception of the T. The single wing is designed to pit two blockers against each key defender on football's basic play, the off-tackle run to the strong side.

Essential to the success of the single wing is a tailback who is a triple threat. Harry Newman, a rookie All-American from Michigan, is that and more: he is the league's top passer; leads his team in rushing; returns kickoffs and punts; plays defensive halfback; and chips in with an occasional field goal, extra point, or quick kick. Joining Harry in the backfield are fullback Ken Strong, who joined the Giants this year when the Staten Island Stapletons folded; wingback Dale Burnett, the club's speed merchant and best receiver; and blocking back Bo Molenda, a bruiser who weighs nearly as much as the interior linemen. At the ends are two-time all-pros Red Badgro and Ray Flaherty. And in the trenches, where football's most important players toil in obscurity, are tackles Len Grant and Bill Owen (the coach's brother), guards Potsy Jones and Butch Gibson (faster than many backs), and center Mel Hein (simply the best there is).

Now for some high-powered offense, right? Hardly. The Giants run three times and punt. The Bears do the same. Another cautious possession follows for each team — not a pass thrown, not a first down gained. This is caveman football. When will we see the promised fireworks, you ask?

Soon, soon. For the time being, coaches Halas and Owen are content to feel each other out. Like two boxers in the early rounds of a long fight, neither wants to create the first opening with a mistake. Despite this year's liberalized passing rule, pro football is still learning how to put the ball in the air; interceptions are frequent. It still borders on heresy to throw the ball inside your own 40-yard line. So teams will run and punt, run and punt — often kicking away on early downs — until a break comes along.

At last it does. Keith Molesworth, the Bears' diminutive halfback, lofts a punt to Newman, who finds a crack straight up the center and scoots some 20 yards to midfield. On first down Strong sweeps left for six before being run out of bounds. Now Newman fields the snap and readies to arch his first pass, to Burnett over the middle — but the ball is batted away at the line of scrimmage. (Harry stands only five-foot-eight, not an ideal height for a passer.) Third down, four yards to go, with the ball still at the left hashmark.

The Giants line up unbalanced to the right, with left tackle Grant standing to the right of center Hein. Now comes a surprise the Giants have cooked up especially for this game: in a simultaneous shift, left end Badgro pulls back from the line, wingback Burnett steps up alongside Flaherty, and Newman moves in behind center, just as a T quarterback would. Thus Burnett has become the right end, Flaherty is no longer an eligible receiver, Badgro is a back, and the left end is . . . Hein! Mel snaps to Newman, who drops the ball back into Mel's hands before spinning and "tripping." George Musso, the Bears' behemoth tackle, pounces on the fallen tailback and actually shakes

BRONKO NAGURSKI

SYMBOLIZED GREAT LINE-PLUNGING TO FANS IN THE 1930's. THE RUGGED CHICAGO BEAR FULLBACK "RAN HIS OWN INTERFERENCE" AND SMASHED RIVAL DEFENSES INTO TINDER.

him, looking for the ball. Meanwhile, Hein fakes a block and strolls downfield, concealing the ball and waiting for his interference to form. But after walking 10 yards unnoticed, Mel becomes excited and hightails it up the sideline. All that stands between him and end-zone glory is Molesworth, the last man back in the Bears' 6–2–2–1 defense, who is about to be cleared out by Badgro and Burnett. But Hein's haste arouses Moley's suspicions; the safety dashes off in pursuit before the Giant blockers can converge on him. Having the angle on Hein, he fences him in at the 15-yard line.

This center-eligible play, coined the Hein Special, has given the Giants the game's first scoring threat, but they do not capitalize. On fourth down they scorn the easy field goal and are stopped at the 7. The Bears take over, but Owen doesn't mind too much; indeed, his game plan is to keep the Bears bottled in their own territory, where their laterals and reverses and halfback options are taboo.

But Chicago plays hot-potato with the ball immediately. On first down quarterback Carl Brumbaugh flips back to Molesworth, who quick-kicks over the head of safety Newman, who had been playing only 20 yards off the line. The pigskin hits at the Chicago 45, then takes a huge Bear bounce. Ken Strong races back into Giant territory to retrieve the ball, but is dragged down at his own 42.

On first down, Newman tries to keep up the pressure. He passes over the middle for Flaherty, but the throw is behind him. Linebacker Nagurski plucks it out of the air easily and charges to the New York 26, where he is finally hauled down by five Giants. Now the Bears can play all of their cards.

The backfield consists of: Brumbaugh, the team's quarterback since 1930, when the Bears added the man-in-motion to football's oldest formation; Molesworth, the left halfback who generally throws more often than Brumbaugh; right halfback Gene Ronzani, a quarterback in college who also wings the ball quite a bit but is prized for his blocking; and the incomparable Nagurski, a 238-pound fullback who tramples would-be tacklers with his head down, his torso nearly horizontal to the ground, and his knees pumping. Before today's game, coach Owen assigned two men to cover this human locomotive on every play and instructed the Giants to throw themselves at his legs in hopes of tripping him, rather than risk life and limb by tackling him head-on. At the ends are Bill Karr, a rookie from West Virginia who became a starter in midseason when Luke Johnsos broke an ankle, and Bill Hewitt, an all-pro from Michigan (where his quarterback was Newman) who can be spotted easily because he wears no helmet. At the tackles are George "Moose" Musso, a 270-pound freshman, and Link Lyman, a thirty-five-year-old veteran who revolutionized defensive line play in the 1920s by shifting position before the snap. The guards are Zuck Carlson and Joe Kopcha, each an all-pro, and the center is Ookie Miller, who plays linebacker along with Nagurski.

On first down Brumbaugh hands to Ronzani, who busts off right tackle for 11. But the next three plays yield only eight yards, and on fourth and two Halas brings in "Automatic Jack" Manders to attempt a field goal. He splits the uprights and the Bears lead 3–0. Where Owen had opted for defensive field position, Halas went for the points. They will matter.

Following the kickoff, the Giants are stymied inside their 25. On third down reserve halfback Kink Richards, in for Strong, attempts a quick kick. Bill Hewitt rushes in to block it, but fortunately for New York, Burnett recovers. Now, on fourth down, Richard drops back and gets the boot away. The veteran Red Grange, in the game for Brumbaugh, takes the line-drive kick at his own 30 and navigates skillfully to the New York 46. Since Grange wrecked his knee in 1927, he has been "just another straight runner," he acknowledges, "and the woods are filled with straight runners." But Number 77 is still a threat on offense, and one of his generation's great defensive backs.

The first quarter ends on that punt return, and the Bears open the second with Molesworth at quarterback, Grange and Ronzani at the halves, and Manders at fullback. On first down Ronzani takes the handoff from Molesworth, then flips the ball over the line to him. Moley makes a marvelous grab and carries down to the 29. Repeating the play but this time keeping the ball, Ronzani picks up two; but then a couple of incomplete passes and an offside penalty move the Bears back to the 32. Halas calls for a field-goal attempt from the 40, a prodigious blast in these days, and Manders complies, knocking it over the crossbar with several yards to spare.

The score is only 6–0. Still, you can't help feeling that the game is slowly slipping away from the Giants. Their running game has gone nowhere, and their only pass completion has been the trick play, in which the ball traveled perhaps six inches in the air. After Flaherty returns Manders' squib kickoff to the 38, the Giants continue in their inept ways, to the delight of the crowd. Newman overthrows Flaherty on first down, and his next toss is batted down by Lyman. Luckily, an overzealous Musso anticipated the snap and charged offside. With a second and five, Newman can call for a run or a pass; he slips the ball to Kink Richards on a counter play off left tackle. Richards, an unheralded swifty from little Simpson College, weaves his way through the Bears' secondary for a 28-yard gain.

Heartened by this first productive conventional play, Newman goes back to the air. He spots Red Badgro 10 yards downfield, with a full stride on the defender. Badgro catches the ball in motion and gallops to the end zone untouched. Strong adds the point, and suddenly the Giants lead 7–6.

What a turnabout! The stadium is still; the Bears scarcely know what hit them. They run through their plays in a daze, and for the next few series the game reverts to a punting duel. In the final minutes of the half, however, Nagurski and Ronzani pound the Giant line for several solid gains which produce three first downs. With the ball on the Giant 26 and seconds to play, Grange sweeps left end for 17 yards but does not manage to get out of bounds. Chicago has consumed all of its time-outs, and as the crowd buzzes nervously, the Bears hurriedly assemble in field-goal formation. Manders gets the kick off as time runs out — but his sharply angled 17-yard attempt sails wide to the right.

The first half has been tense and well played, but certainly no barn-burner. The Bears outgained the Giants by a wide margin, especially on the ground, yet walked off the field on the short end of the score. At intermission, coach Halas will labor mightily to combat his team's sense of frustration. It is critical that the Bears, with the opening possession of the second half, retake control of the game.

George Corbett, a chunky little back from Millikin University, brings the second-half kickoff back to the 24. Nagurski rips off runs of 14 and 7 yards, knocking defenders down like bowling pins. After an incomplete pass, Ronzani bursts through the Giant line, suddenly made of cheesecloth, for 15. Now Brumbaugh takes the snap and hands to Corbett, who circles left while the quarterback slips over the line. Corbett pulls up and lobs a little pass to Brummy, who makes it all the way down to the 13. The Bears have moved upfield almost at will; but here, in the shadow of their own goal posts, the Giants stiffen their resolve. The next three plays net only three yards, and the Bears must settle for Manders' third field goal of the day. (During the entire regular season he knocked home five — and that led the league.)

Fielding the kickoff on the 5, Newman returns to the 27. With the Bears' linebackers positioned tightly behind the line in expectation of a run, Newman rolls to the right and fires to Burnett for 23 yards. The play worked so well that Harry calls it again, and this time it clicks for 13. Now comes a bullet over the middle to Richards, good for 15. The Bears' backs are like ducks in a shooting gallery, being picked off no matter which way they turn. With the ball on the Chicago 22, Newman rolls left behind Grant and Gibson but stops just short of the scrimmage line. He shovels a pass to Badgro, who takes it upfield to the 9. An illegal-motion penalty and an incompletion stall the Giants momentarily; but from the 14 Newman connects with reserve blocking back Max Krause on a sideline pass down to the 1. Richards' thrust up the middle is stopped for no gain, then Krause burrows under his blockers for the score. Strong tacks on the point and the Giants are back on top, 14–9. We have seen five scoring plays already, more than most entire games provided this year.

Strong kicks off to Corbett, who only gets as far as the 23. The Bears try to better their field position on the ground, but Corbett is stopped for no gain and Nagurski picks up a mere two. Rather than chance an interception on third and long, Molesworth drops back in punt formation. But instead of punting, he shot-puts the ball to midfield, where Corbett runs under it. Twisting and dodging, breaking tackle after tackle, little George weaves his way downfield — then laterals to Bill Karr, who goes all the way to the New York 8, a gain of 67 yards!

Two rushes by Molesworth bring the ball to the 6 as the Giants once again try to bend without breaking. On third and goal, Nagurski drives toward the center of the line, then stops, jumps, and fires to Bill Karr for the touchdown. Despite Flaherty's warnings last night, no Giant is within five yards of Karr. Manders' point-after puts Chicago back on top for the third time, 16–14.

Strong lugs the kickoff back to the 24, and Newman picks up where he left off. Throwing caution to the winds, he hits Flaherty for 11, Burnett for 18, and Badgro for

11. With the Bears back on their heels, trying to figure out where the next dart will land, Newman sends Strong up the middle for 14. From the Chicago 22, he again finds Burnett at the right sideline, and Dale spins upfield to the 8 as the gun sounds ending the third quarter. In this period alone, Newman has completed 9 of 10 passes for 131 yards. To appreciate the magnitude of this aerial display, consider that for the entire season, fourteen games, Newman passed for only 69 yards per contest—and established a new pro record at that!

On the first play of the final period, with the ball spotted at the right hashmark, the Giants line up unbalanced to the right, a formation which seems to indicate either a pass or an inside run. Yet, at the snap, Strong loops behind Newman, takes a short pitch, and motors toward the left end. The play is slow to develop, however, and the right side of the Bear line closes off the outside. About to swallow a loss, Strong heaves an overhand lateral back across the field. The ball flutters over to Newman like a dying quail, for Strong can scarcely close his hand on the football to throw it: a few years back, he injured his right wrist playing baseball and the doctor who operated on him removed the wrong bone, thus ending his prospective career with the Detroit Tigers.

Newman juggles the ball, then scrambles right, dodging tacklers while giving up ground to the 15. As the entire team focuses its energies on corralling Newman, Strong drifts unaccompanied into the left portion of the end zone and waves for the ball. Newman heaves it nearly 50 yards across the field. Strong runs to the corner, snares the pass, then stumbles out of bounds. This sandlot hocus-pocus is pure inspiration, though in later years it will find its way into the Giants' playbook (it will never work again). Strong provides the extra point, and the Giants go ahead 21–16. The fans can scarcely believe what they are seeing.

In the first half we wondered when we would see some offense; now the question is when we will see some defense. Will the last team to have the ball be the winner?

After the kickoff, the Bears move briskly from the 28 to their 45, all but three of the yards provided by Nagurski thrusts. Then on three disastrous wide runs by Molesworth, Corbett, and Ronzani, the Bears lose a whopping 25 yards and are forced to punt.

Now, with most of the final period left to play, the Giants turn conservative in an effort to protect their lead. They rush the ball routinely three times and punt, then their defense holds the Bears to a lone first down. Once again, the Giants eat up the clock with three rushes, but this time Strong's kick is low—Molesworth grabs it on the run and scoots to the New York 48. This looks to be a great opportunity, but on third down and one, Ronzani's surprise pass is picked off by linebacker Max Krause and returned to the Giant 34.

Owen isn't going to let Newman throw the ball this late in the game, so the Bears brace for the run. Three ground plays net a mere four yards, and once again Strong drops into deep punt formation. In the face of a mighty rush from ends Hewitt and Karr, Ken shanks the kick out of bounds at his own 46—a mere eight yards from scrimmage. Can New York's defense hold again?

Brumbaugh returns to the game in place of Corbett, and on first down takes a pass from Molesworth for nine. On second down Nagurski bulls his way up the middle for four, putting the ball on the 33. Less than two minutes remain to be played. Grange, a superior blocker, comes in for Molesworth. Brumbaugh lines up not under the center, Ookie Miller, but behind right guard Zuck Carlson. He takes the snap, fakes a handoff to Red, then slaps the ball into Nagurski's belly. Bronko lowers his head, aiming for the middle again, but instead of proceeding through the hole, he straightens up, leaps, and lobs the ball to Hewitt some 10 yards downfield. Hewitt takes two steps, with Burnett on his heels. But before Hewitt can be thrown down he laterals to Karr, who races toward the right corner chased by Strong and Newman. One or the other should nail him at about the 8—but out of nowhere comes Ronzani to throw himself in front of the two Giants and knock them both "right on their cans," as he will say after the game. Karr trots into the end zone as the fans yell themselves silly. The Bears lead 22–21. Halas lets Ronzani try the meaningless PAT. Gene boots it through, and the Bears prepare to defend their lead for the final minute.

The Giants have made a classic mistake, one that will be repeated as long as football is played—they packed up their offense before the final minutes. Trying to sit on a scant lead, they thought time was their ally; now it is certainly their foe.

They get an unforeseen break: Strong returns the kickoff straight up the middle to the 40, nearly breaking away for the distance. Now the Giants need only 25 yards to move within the range of Strong's powerful right leg. They must rev up their passing game once more, if they haven't forgotten how.

Less than a minute remains to be played. Everyone in the park is on his feet. Newman lines his men up, then calls for a shift to the center-eligible play which bedeviled the Bears in the first period. He takes the snap, whirls—but this time he does not return the ball to Hein, instead pitching back to Burnett, who has the strongest arm on the field. Once the ball is pitched out where all can see it, Hein, incredibly enough, is allowed to drift downfield to the Chicago 30. Burnett rears back to fire the long pass across the field but is hit just at the moment of release. The pass wobbles toward Hein, seeming to take forever to reach him. Brumbaugh, nowhere near Hein as Burnett cocked his arm, has time to race over from his safety position and tip the pass away.

Time now for just one more desperation play. Returning to the single wing, Newman fakes to Strong while Badgro and Flaherty run patterns to the left side of the field. Then he flips a little pass off to the right to Burnett, who runs straight at Grange, playing some 20 yards off the line of scrimmage in a 1930s version of the "prevent" defense.* Jogging undefended alongside Burnett is Hein, ready to receive a lateral the moment Grange makes a move for Burnett. But Red looks in Burnett's eyes, senses his own dilemma and, with the instincts of a truly exceptional player, makes what George Halas in years to come will describe as "the greatest defensive play I ever saw": He tackles

*Red Badgro insists that he and not Burnett received this pass; Steve Owen agreed. George Halas, Mel Hein, and Red Grange recall the receiver as Burnett. There is no official play-by-play, no game film. Researchers, man your stations!

Burnett around the chest, pinning his arms so he cannot flip the ball to Hein. Grange doesn't even try to bring Burnett down; he is content to lock him in a bearhug as Hein pleads for the ball and time runs out.

The conclusion leaves us gasping. This game has had it all — laterals, reverses, flea-flickers, fake punts; bull's-eye passing, power running, deadly kicking; stratagem and counterstratagem. The Bears have won the first NFL championship game, but the real victor is the league itself, which has shown the nation the brand of ball the pros can play. The college coaches will call it basketball, but soon they will imitate it. The future of football has been glimpsed today.

How many wrongs make a Wright? Six NFL coaches got tired of counting, but they add up to a great deal of fun in the lineman's book *I'd Rather Be Wright: Memoirs of an Itinerant Tackle*, from which comes the item below. Although Steve Wright played tackle for nine years in the NFL, he will be best remembered as the inspired tormentor of Vince Lombardi.

STEVE WRIGHT
with Bill Gildea and Ken Turan

My Years with Lombardi

I may have loved Lombardi, but I sure had a knack for getting him pissed off. And I mean pissed. He'd scream at me in the team meetings, I was one of his favorites. Invariably he had the evidence against me, right there on film. We used to joke about it afterward, on the way to the field for practice. Forrest Gregg would look at me and say, "Well, you got the Oscar again today, didn't you?"

One time they filmed a scrimmage and Willie Davis just ate me alive. I didn't know which end was up. Vince would keep running the film over and over and getting madder and madder and I'm just sitting there smiling, unconsciously, really, and he'd yell, "Goddamn it, Wright, wipe that silly smirk off your face." Like I couldn't do anything right.

Just once I got lucky. We had played Baltimore, it was 1965, and it was Hornung's last big game. He scored five touchdowns. And he did it all with no help from me, that's for sure. I was awful. My knees were killing me that day, tendonitis or something. I mean I was in pain, I was dying every time I was in there. But it was foggy, so foggy you couldn't see from one end of the field to the other. It was so foggy the films didn't turn out. Vince couldn't see a thing.

Usually, though, I would be right up there on the screen in black and white, and

Vince would go berserk. Three times that year, for some reason I pulled the wrong way on the famous Green Bay sweep. Knocked down two guards, a center, and a tackle. Boy, were they surprised to see me coming at them. Kenny Bowman nicknamed me Bullwinkle for that, for Bullwinkle Moose of the TV show, "Rocky and His Friends." If you've heard the line by Bullwinkle you'll know why. "Go, go, go, but watch where you're going."

The first time it happened Vince just accepted it, but the second time he went crazy, and the third time he was just livid, unbelievable. He stopped the projector, stood up, turned the lights on, and started chewing me out.

"What's the matter with you, Wright, can't you hear? The play's thirty-eight, not thirty-nine. Eight and nine, they don't even sound alike.

"Bart, say eight." So Bart says, "Eight." Then Vince says, "Now say nine." Bart says "Nine."

"Now they don't sound alike, do they, Wright?"

"No, Coach."

"Well, why'd you do it?"

"I don't know why, Coach."

He had the projector stopped and was screaming at me for three or four minutes, which is a hell of a long time.

But the worst temper tantrum he ever had was out on the field at practice, and naturally it happened because of me. It turned out that he was bothered by it more than I was. I didn't realize the effect it had until he wrote about it in an article for *Look* magazine (September 5, 1967).

This is what he wrote:

> We were all out on that field across Oneida Street from Lambeau Field, and suddenly I was rushing at one of my players and flailing away at him with my fists. I am fifty-four years old now, and he is eight inches taller than I am and outweighs me by fifty pounds. If he had brought both of his hands down on me, he probably could have driven me into the ground, but he just stood there, warding off my blows because he understands me. Fortunately, all of the Packers understand me.
>
> What was I doing? Did I hate him, or even dislike him? No, not for a moment. I'm fond of him. He's one of the most likable men on our squad. That's his problem. He has all the size and ability he needs to be a great one, but he loves everybody. In a game, they beat on him. Everybody whacks him, and he laughs. When you criticize him, he laughs, so what was I doing? I guess I was trying to reach him in the only way left. I guess I was trying to get him to hate me enough to take it out on the opposition, because to play the game, you must have fire in you, and there is nothing that stokes that fire like hate.
>
> I'm sorry, but that is the truth.

To put it in perspective, Vince wasn't in a good mood to start with. Two or three days earlier we had had a bad practice and I had busted a play and, to Vince, busting a play in practice was the same as busting a play in a game. You just don't do it. I'm looking at him out of the corner of my eye and I can see he's looking right at me and he's saying. "Don't you smile, Wright, don't let me see you smile, I'll run you off this field right now if I see you smile."

So I suppose I was fresh in his mind a couple of days later when we had another bad practice. We were standing in the huddle when he came charging up and just started ranting and raving, and all of a sudden he turned and looked right at me. It was one of those things. I just happened to be in the wrong place at the wrong time and I was looking at him and our eyes met and I had a kind of blank expression on my face. I think that made him even madder.

He was saying something and he just broke off the sentence and directed all his wrath at me: "You, you, who do you think you are? You could be the greatest tackle in the world but you don't care, do you?"

And there he was beating on my chest. And I'm looking down at him like, What're you doing? Go away. I actually laughed and tried to push him away. I got to laughing and I couldn't stop and this made him even madder.

Three times he started pounding on me and three times I pushed him back. He'd hit me and I'd push him away, he'd hit me and I'd push him away.

None of the other guys said anything. Just silence. But you could tell from their faces what they were thinking. It was like, Well, you did it again, didn't you, Wright? I don't have to go looking for trouble. It's easy to find.

Like this other time before a game. About forty minutes before the kickoff most of us would go out to warm up, then come back in, do whatever we had to do, and get our pads on. That day it was just one of those times when I had to go to the bathroom.

So I was sitting in there reading the newspaper and doing my thing, making it an enjoyable experience, and when I was done I walked out into the locker room with my pants still down around my knees. As soon as I got there I knew something was wrong. All of the players were at one end of the room and Vince was right in the middle of them.

He turned around and saw me and right then I knew I should never have come out. I guess I had flushed the toilet right at the dramatic high point of his spiel and he just started yelling at me. "What are we running here, a goddamn nursery? Can't you do anything right, Wright?"

I guess the answer to that is no.

Football does not propagate figure filberts to the same extent as baseball does. In baseball virtually all the action is individual, pitting one man against nine; in football every snap propels twenty-two men into action, with the critical encounters taking place among those who do not have the ball. Nonetheless, football statistics have their fascination, as Paul Zimmerman illustrates in this chapter from his erudite book, *A Thinking Man's Guide to Football*.

PAUL ZIMMERMAN

Statistics Are for Losers —and Sportswriters

I can prove anything by statistics except the truth.

—George Canning, 1826

There are three kinds of lies; lies, damned lies and statistics.

—Benjamin Disraeli

Every time I hear a ballplayer tell me, "Statistics are for losers," or the other maxim: "The only statistic that matters is win or lose," I wonder why everyone crowds around the bulletin board when the league stats are posted. The punt-return men look and see if they've gone up a couple of spots or slipped a few. So do the kickoff returners.

The stars, like Joe Namath or Lance Alworth, pretend they don't care, but they'll sneak looks when they think nobody's watching. And after a game, the stat sheets are the first things grabbed up, especially if "tackles" and "assists" and "pass-defense plays" are noted. Then the defense suddenly becomes statistic minded.

Everyone tells you that statistics don't matter, but those stats have a strange way of making an appearance during contract talks—on both sides of the table.

The basic things you have to remember about the statistics you read in the paper every week are (1) they're not accurate . . . almost but not quite, and (2) they are not as meaningful as they could be.

Statistics are not accurate because there is a human element involved. During a game the yardage is entered on a master sheet, or a work sheet, by the two men the home club hires to handle its stats. At the end of the game, it's tallied up and phoned in to Seymour Siwoff and the Elias Sports Bureau, Inc., in New York, a baseball statistics bureau that Pete Rozelle hired in 1960 to make some order out of the statistical chaos.

Seymour and his sixteen-man staff used to have fifteen hours to get everything added up and prepared for release, so the papers and the clubs can get it for the Tuesday editions. (Monday night football has made that impossible, though, so Wednesday's paper is the new target date.) But often those two men in the press box are in a hurry to go to dinner that Sunday night, so they don't recheck their stats with the official play-by-play sheets, and an error in addition remains an error—forever, or until the Elias Bureau has enough breathing time to spot it and fix it. It doesn't always happen.

Plays often are forgotten in the excitement of the game. The most common error involves two running backs or two receivers with similar-looking numbers, i.e., 35 and 36, and 87 and 89. Number 35 might get No. 36's 10-yard gain, and 87 might get credit for the pass that poor No. 89 caught. These errors are never apprehended, and they happen in *every* game, including the big ones at the end of the season. The Kansas City Chiefs, for instance, got robbed of a rightfully acquired first down in the 1970 Super Bowl. Leroy Kelly never got credit for one hard-earned five-yard gain in the 1969 NFL Championship game. It happens everywhere. Players seldom notice the mistakes, and even if they do, they rarely do anything about it. But there are exceptions.

Late in the 1966 season, the Jets' George Sauer was battling San Diego's Lance Alworth for the AFL pass-catching lead. In one game the Jets' statisticians credited Sauer with a catch that tight end Pete Lammons had made. Sauer brought the play-by-play sheets to the team's PR man and showed him the error—which was corrected. Sauer finished second to Alworth that year—but by more than one catch.

Exhibition-game statistics are scanned, noted, and then thrown away. They are completely unreliable. The statisticians are often hometown collegians, and many times they don't even know the professional scoring rules. So they'll credit a quarterback's dumps to "yards lost rushing," as it's done in the colleges.

"Meaningful statistics" are anything that can give you an insight into a player's contribution in the game, or his worth at his position. For instance, if you read that Leroy Kelly gained 82 yards on 23 carries for a 3.6 average, you know nothing. Ten other backs in the league might have done the same thing that Sunday. But if you are told that he carried the ball eight times on third-down, short-yardage situations and got the first down on seven of those eight tries, you've learned something about the kind of a day Kelly had.

Two punters might have the same average—say 40 yards per kick—but one might have had his punts returned for two yards all day, and the other for 150 yards, and you'll never know it by checking the punter's record in the papers. A passer's stats don't tell you what he did in the last two minutes of each half, or what the score was when he got the bulk of his yardage. And a 50-yard passing play is still 50 yards on the books, whether the quarterback laid a perfect 50-yarder into someone's hands, or whether he threw a little safety-valve pass and the receiver shook off three tacklers and gained the 50 on his own.

The Xerox Company began to recognize the need for more incisive statistics toward the end of the 1969 season, so they handed out little analysis sheets in the press boxes, showing a runner's performance on each of the four downs, a passer's breakdown according to downs, his performance in the last two minutes, etc. They never got much notice in the papers because everyone was too busy with other things to try and dissect a bunch of new, albeit meaningful, statistics. The only stories I saw that mentioned them at all were offbeat features about how nutty Xerox was, how they'd dream up anything for a little publicity. Next season, Xerox gave up.

I have developed my own set of statistical rules in an attempt to separate general statistics from "meaningful statistics." I try to keep track of the passing game with a chart of my own that I found out is called a "field chart" (ex-Boston coach Clive Rush once explained to me what I was trying to do).

The purpose of this intricate bit of mumbo jumbo is to show not only passes and completions, but to give a history of each receiver and each pass defender. Every pass thrown to a man, whether it results in a completion, an incomplete or an interference penalty, is noted in the offense section (for the receiver) and the defense section (for the pass defender). I try to use symbols for such things as the types of pattern, whether or not the defender made a good play, or if the pass was poorly thrown (on an incomplete)—also, what kind of a misfire it was: overthrow, wide, etc., or whether it was just a deliberate throwaway.

The tally I can get at the end of the day tells me (1) how many times each receiver was thrown to, (2) whether the offense was picking on a certain defender, and (3) if the passer was having a bad day, what particular type of misfortune he was having.

On running plays I try to note the blocks by the linemen, if the play picks up anything worthwhile . . . usually four yards or more, depending on the situation. I write the number of the players making those blocks under the gain itself (which I have recorded in my chart book). If the defense comes up with a good play . . . holds the runner to three yards or less, or keeps him from a first down on a short-yardage situation, worries the passer into a bad throw, covers the receiver well, etc. . . . I put the number of the defensive man (in different-colored pencil) underneath the play.

All this tells me how a blocker did during the day (blocking stats are never given out). It also tells me how many "meaningful" defensive plays a man made. A mere record of tackles will tell you something, but there is a difference between a lineman making a tackle after he's been driven eight yards downfield, and a defensive man tackling a runner for a loss. And when a man rushes the passer and chases him into the arms of someone else, only the tackler will get mentioned on the official sheet, but actually it was the rusher who did the work. So I give them both a call.

A meaningful punting statistic to me is the one that tells you about the runbacks. Never mind the average yardage of the punts themselves, unless it's something phenomenal. At the end of the season most punters end up within a few yards of each other anyway. They pay off on runbacks — and on how many punts are returned and how many are fair-caught.

All this dedication requires a very busy pencil during the game, and there are limits to how much you can write down in the break between plays. Just as an experiment, I pushed myself to the limit during the 1970 Super Bowl. I tried to get the lineup of players on kicking and punting teams, and I tried to diagram the defenses both teams used, but I had stepped over the line. It was too much. I started missing plays, and finally I snapped and regressed completely, sitting there stunned for a whole series while someone else filled in my chart book for me.

It taught me one thing, though; how far I could go with this stuff.

Statistics are like love; you're either hooked or you're not. I happen to be a statistics nut, and I wouldn't wish it on other people, and I try to keep my game stories relatively uncluttered with numbers, although if I come up with some *particularly* meaningful stats, I'll drop them in . . . quietly.

Most successful statisticians are in love with their work. A statistic isn't just a cold number, it's a little story. And a good statistician can usually smell out something that doesn't sound right.

"When I redid all the old books," says Siwoff, the most dedicated statistician of them all, "I had to throw out a lot of old stuff and just start in all over again. A stalwart . . . like Jimmy Brown and Joe Namath . . . will get personalized treatment. I'll go through every game of their career and make sure their lifetime totals are correct. Don't forget, the AFL didn't hire our service until 1967, and the stats before that were a mess.

"For instance, nowhere in the AFL prior to 1966 is there a record of just who played in which game. When I asked them about it they said, 'What do you need that stuff for?' And six years before that, when I first started with the NFL stats, I found some weird things. For one thing, there was no record of trades. Merle Hapes and Frank Filchock, the two Giant players who got in trouble for failing to report a bribe, had been wiped out of the books. But I went and researched them. You don't pass moral judgments with statistics."

Siwoff pointed to a jumbled pile of papers in a corner. "See that pile," he said. "The league records were worse. I had to rummage through all of them to try and get lifetime records. I lost a couple of years on Bronko Nagurski. It was frustrating as hell. Don't forget that statistics never even got into the papers until Bert Bell begged them in in the 1940s. And they were only publicity gimmicks in those days.

"I can look through the books and smell a phony statistic. Beattie Feathers, the old Bear halfback, gained 1,004 yards rushing in 1934. No one had ever gone over 1,000 before, and no one did it again for thirteen years. You see a statistic like that and it shakes you. It's like a bolt of lightning. I'm not saying anything, but I have a feeling some punt and kickoff returns were added into that rushing total."

Siwoff admits that things are far from perfect. Some modifications and amendments will have to be made. He would like a passer's totals to show the yardage of the pass and the yardage gained after the catch, so people can get a true reading on the actual passing efficiency, but that would put greater strain on the stat men in the press boxes. He's still looking for the perfect formula to rate the passing leaders at the end of the season. . . .

From 1931 to 1945 the leaders were ranked according to completion percentage, although you find mysterious inconsistencies when you look through those old books. From 1946 to '49 they were ranked according to how they rated in the league in six separate categories—completions, percentage, yards gained, touchdowns, fewest interceptions, and lowest interception percentage. By 1949 the category of interceptions was dropped. The system was junked in 1950, and for the next 10 years passers were rated by only one criterion, average yards gained for each pass they threw.

In 1960 the six-category grading system was restored, only this time average-yards-per-pass became one of the six categories. The NFL dropped two categories in 1962 (total yards gained and total completions) and installed the rating system that is used today. The AFL did the same thing five years later when Siwoff took over.

The system works like this: Say a passer finishes first in the league in pass-completion percentage. He'll get a grade of "one" in that category. If he's second in TD passes, he'll get a two; first in lowest interception percentage (total passes attempted divided into interceptions) and he gets a one; and, say, fourth in average yards per attempt, he'll get a four. The grades are added, and his total comes out to eight. Another man, say with grades of three, four, four, and one, will end up with a total twelve, so he'll be behind the passer with eight. It goes down the list, with any passer who has thrown 140 passes or more (10 a game) eligible to be graded. Lowest grade wins.

"One category still bugs me," Siwoff says. "Touchdown passes. It's an absolute total. Every other category is on a percentage basis. I'm trying to figure out a way of making touchdown-passing efficiency become a percentage category, too."

People are always willing to help. The best system I've seen was suggested by an ex-Columbia tackle named Alfred L. Ginepra from Santa Monica, California. His idea is to grade touchdown passing by dividing the TD passes into the total completions, and you come up with a figure representing touchdown efficiency. If you would have applied that formula to the 1969 and '70 passing totals, most of the winning quarterbacks would have moved up a notch or two.

Some statistics that are mindlessly repeated as gospel don't make any sense. People will tell you that a quarterback's record of how many third downs he cashes into first downs is the real tip-off on his ability. They say that 50 percent is the desired figure. Right, and $100,000 a year is the desired income, too, but few of us reach it. No quarterback has a 50-percent third-down record for a season. Some passers kill you on first and second down, and they could run up a 28–0 count without cashing a single third down. Third-down efficiency is a nice little statistic to play around with, but it's not the whole answer.

During the year the Jets won the Super Bowl, for instance, Joe Namath had a 29-percent efficiency rating on third-down- and fourth-down-short-yardage (when the team went for it) situations. But the Jet defense allowed rivals only 27 percent. Next season, Namath was up to 33 percent, but so was the Jet defense, so the team slipped.

Namath is an avowed scoffer at statistics. Sauer liked to look at them, but he had reservations.

"Going into the last game in 1968 I was leading the league in pass catching," Sauer said, "but our last game was an easy win over Miami, and I came out early and I only caught two passes that day. Alworth caught me for the title. But suppose I'd have caught a lot of passes and taken some unnecessary chances and gotten hurt? I'm out of the championship game. The thought of it would have haunted me for the rest of my life."

Jimmy Brown used to say that every time he broke another record he turned into more and more of a statistic, instead of a person. But sometimes the have-nots show an uncommon interest in numbers. Philadelphia fullback Tom Woodeshick, for instance, has a lifelong goal of reaching 1,000 yards rushing for a season.

"The men who get 1,000 yards are the elite," he said toward the end of the 1968 season, when he was within smelling distance of the magic number. "Very few have done it. I want to be one of them. I want the prominence and standing that go with it. And if I don't get it because of those three quarters I missed in one game, or the 60-yard run I got called back against the Bears, if I fall a few yards short, I'm going to be very disturbed. Right now I'd have to say my chances are getting slimmer — just like me." (He never made it.)

The *Dallas Times-Herald*'s Steve Perkins tells about the time he helped Bob Hayes win a championship — the 1968 punt-return title. The Cowboys were beating Pittsburgh pretty easily in the next to last game of the season. Hayes had just returned a punt 90 yards for a touchdown, and he was well in front of the rest of the NFL's punt returners. But he was still one return short of the minimum 14 needed to qualify. Perkins told him about that on the sidelines during the Pittsburgh game.

"Suppose they don't kick to you in New York next week, or you have to fair-catch them all?"

"OK," Hayes said, and he handed Perkins his cape, ran a punt back three yards, and ran out again. "Does that do it?"

Against the Giants the following week, Hayes returned a punt 63 yards for a touchdown. "I have just figured it up," Perkins wrote, "and if I hadn't talked Hayes into running back that three-yard punt against Pittsburgh, which dragged his average down, he would have broken Jack Christiansen's NFL punt-return record by a full yard."

And that's why they build a press box for writers — and statistics nuts — and keep them off the field.